A
PRIVATE
PRACTICE

A PRIVATE PRACTICE

Patrick Reilly, M.D.

MACMILLAN PUBLISHING COMPANY · New York

This book is dedicated to:

Agnes Sullivan and Mary Ann, to Mike and Carol and Whiskey, to Bill and John Patrick. And to Diane, who puts up with me . . .

I love you

And to the memories of Francis Matthew and Frankie and George Zehe . . .

I miss you.

Copyright © 1984 by Patrick Reilly, M.D.

Macmillan Publishing Company
866 Third Avenue, New York, N.Y. 10022
Collier Macmillan Canada, Inc.

Library of Congress Cataloging in Publication Data
Reilly, Patrick, M.D.
A private practice.
1. Reilly, Patrick, M.D.   2. Drug abuse—Patients—
Biography.   3. Depression, Mental—Patients—Biography.
I. Title.
RC464.R45R37   1984   362.2'93'0924 [B]   83-26780
ISBN 0-02-604410-2

10 9 8 7 6 5 4 3 2 1

Designed by Jack Meserole

Printed in the United States of America

B & J
4/8/4
15.95

Much of what is written in this book really happened. Names of individuals and places have been changed and certain details altered so that no individual or institution is exposed.

ACKNOWLEDGMENTS

My sincere gratitude to the following people who came into my life and, each in his or her own way, made a difference:

Joe MacMillan, M.D.	Jay Thompson, M.D.
Mike McKee, Ph.D.	Bill Keck, M.D.
Father Jim O'Brien	Joe Doody
Barbara Girion	John-Henry Pfifferling, Ph.D.
Paxton Davis	Elizabeth Morse-Cluley
Kathleen Barber	Jane Jordan, R.N.

And a special thanks to:

Walter James Miller, poet, author, and Professor of English at New York University for being a constant source of encouragement, support, and much-needed criticism

and

John A. Ware, literary agent, New York City for his friendship, his confidence in me and his enthusiasm for this book.

To Dr. Bob, Bill Wilson and the recovering alcoholics and drug addicts of northeast Ohio, thank you for helping me to maintain my sobriety and some semblance of sanity.

Thank you, Kathy Kline, for your contribution.
Thank you, Denise Horning, for typing the original manuscript.
Thank you, Betty Ford, for your example.

1

THEIR EYES were getting wider as they stared at me. It was happening again.

My jaw muscles were tightening and I had to start speaking unnaturally slowly and deliberately. The medical students shared their uncertainty with each other through furtive glances, and then their eyes would rest back on me. I was losing my concentration.

We were in the main clinical teaching auditorium. Also known as the pit. It was an old, narrow room with a high ceiling. One hundred and fifty seats were arranged in semicircular rows that ascended steeply away from the small podium. It was designed so that the audience remained, almost literally, on top of the speaker.

The pit would be the ideal place for a stoning.

I was beginning to tremble. I had to think of a way to quickly end my lecture. I rested both elbows on the podium and began to massage my jaw muscles. I was desperate. I had never felt such embarrassment.

"Is there anything wrong, Dr. Reilly?" asked one of the students sitting in the front. He was the one who, when walking, appeared as if he were falling backward.

"Something wrong with my parotid glands," I lied as I continued to massage in front of my ears.

"Mumps?"

"Yes, I think that might be it. Mumps."

He beamed.

"Have you ever had mumps before?" asked one of the others. "You can't have mumps more than once."

"You can have inflamed parotids many times," snapped an asthenic young woman, the only black female medical student in the group.

I held up my hand to stop the discussion. I knew I had only about fifteen seconds' worth of intelligible speech left.

"Let's finish this tomorrow when I feel better," I said. I did not add that I would be better fortified with Valium.

By the time I got to my office my jaws were closed tight. I could open my mouth, but it took conscious effort. I wrote a note to Diane, my nurse and self-appointed office manager, saying that I was sick and had to go home. She assured me that she would reschedule all my appointments.

Diane was almost five feet tall, beautiful, trim, and had fantastic legs. The kids in my practice loved her. And so did their parents. She would tell every parent that theirs was "a beautiful child" and "you certainly do a wonderful job raising your children."

After my last patient every Saturday afternoon, she would come into my office and tell me how many patients I had seen whose parents would be unable to pay their bill. It was usually eight or ten. Then she would raise up to her full height and say: "You've got to stop giving yourself away, Dr. Reilly. I want to run this office like a business. I'm going to give these overdue accounts to a collection agency next week."

She never did.

Diane gave me a look that was filled with both concern and disappointment. This was the third time in two weeks that I had had to go home "sick." She knew something was wrong.

"I did schedule one sick child, Susan Nicks, to see you this afternoon," Diane said. "Her mother called a little while ago and said Susan started to have a fever and a runny nose this morning and was sleeping a lot. What should I do?"

I quickly walked into my private office, locked the door, and sat at my desk. I unlocked the bottom right-hand drawer and took out one of the bottles of Valium. God, it was comforting to hold those pills in my hand. I took three ten-milligram Valiums. In about twenty minutes I would be able to talk, and my trembling would stop. But I would still be a seething cauldron inside, and ineffective. I needed to go home and sleep.

I took a pen and steadied my right wrist with my left hand so I could write legibly.

Call Mrs. Nicks and tell her to bring Susan in first thing in the morning. Thanks.

With some difficulty I locked my pill drawer and left my office. I handed the note to Diane as I left and waved to her.

"Get well, Dr. Reilly," she called to me. "Please."

As I drove home, it became clear to me that I couldn't continue to do this. I could not keep going home and drugging myself to sleep in order to interrupt these anxiety attacks. I had to do something.

I looked at the list of pharmacies that I kept in my car. I didn't like to go to the same pharmacy more than once every two or three months. It didn't look good. I put a date after each pharmacy to make sure I didn't go to the same one too often.

I had not been to O'Donnell's on Fairmont since December sixth. It would be safe to go there. The Valium I had taken at my office would have taken effect by the time I got there. So I headed for O'Donnell's.

"Doc Reilly, how are ya?"

"Pretty good, Sam. How's business?"

"Good . . . real good. You and me, Doc, we're necessary evils, you know? People will always get sick. They'll always need us. You write the prescriptions," he laughed, "and I'll fill 'em. Yeah . . . necessary evils."

Sam had one of the few neighborhood pharmacies left. And he wasn't doing very well. The chains were selling their medicines at a cheaper price. It was only a matter of time until he would be out of business and retire.

"What can I do for you, Doc?"

"I need some injectable Valium, Sam. I decided I ought to keep some around the office . . . just in case a kid seizures. I'd better get some syringes, too. And a tourniquet."

"O.K., Doc. It'll be a couple of minutes." He walked slowly, stoop-shouldered, back into the aisles of drugs. "How long has your dad been gone now?" he called out.

"About five or six years, Sam. I didn't know you knew my father."

"Oh . . . a long time ago." Sam had emerged from the aisles and was busily doing something on the counter behind the glass partition. "We were good friends in the forties. He was such a carefree, happy guy. We drank together. Had some good times. Boy, would we get drunk on Saint Patty's Day. Go see the parade . . . go to the flats. What a time."

Sam looked at me. He shook his head.

"I lost him somewhere in the late fifties. He just got so angry and unhappy. I could never understand that. He alienated himself with his temper. I thought I had him back when Kennedy got elected. But then . . . November Twenty-second happened."

Sam looked up and held out a paper bag with the medicine.

"Here it is," he said.

I walked to him and reached for the bag. Sam's expression became serious.

"I was at your father's wake and you and I talked. And I've talked to you about your father before. Don't you remember?"

"Yeah, Sam . . . sure . . . I remember. . . . I've just been preoccupied a lot lately . . . Sorry. . . . I'll see ya."

"Are you sure you're all right, Patrick? You look kinda nervous."

"I'm all right. . . . Thanks . . . bye."

When I got in my car, I crossed O'Donnell's off my list. I would never go there again.

I pulled out one of the small containers. Valium for Injection Only. I had my answer for the panic attacks.

When I got home, I swallowed two ten-milligram Valiums. I then took two Dalmane capsules, broke them open and poured the powder on my tongue and washed it down with a glass of wine. Alcohol gave me a certain predictable jolt when mixed with sedative drugs. Sleep was the only thing that interrupted these extreme anxiety attacks. And I wanted to get to sleep before Irene came home.

I woke an hour later to see Irene, obviously alarmed, looking down at me. I am not normally home sleeping at three o'clock in the afternoon.

"Another panic attack, Pat?"

I nodded.

Irene sat on the bed and reached for my hand. She was becoming increasingly upset with me and these anxiety attacks, which were affecting both our lives. She had tried everything. Remonstrances. Sarcasm. Ridicule. Affection. Tears. Nothing worked. I was impervious to all of them.

I knew she would be upset with me for several hours, but by bedtime, I'd be able to manipulate her into being affectionate again.

Irene wasn't very talkative all evening. Even when she answered my questions about her weaving, she spoke in monotones and short sentences.

As we climbed the stairs on our way to bed, I stopped her and put my arm around her. She stiffened in an impersonal gesture. That had never happened before.

"What's the matter, Babes?"

She looked at me.

"I wish I were strong enough to leave you," she said. "You're destroying me." Her voice dripped with a coldness and an indifference I had not heard in ten years of marriage. I was stunned.

The phone rang, and I ran to my study. I got it on the third ring. It was Eddy. He and I had been classmates in high school, college, and medical school.

"Where were you at noon, Pat?" he asked angrily. "We were supposed to play racketball."

"What are you talking about? I don't remember having a court at noon. We weren't supposed to play today."

"The court was reserved in your name, man. You made the reservation."

"I'm sorry. I guess I forgot."

"Sounds like you had a blackout, Pat. Better stay off the sauce." I couldn't tell if he was serious.

"C'mon, Eddy," I said indignantly. "When have you ever seen me take more than one drink?"

"Pat, you and I used to have a really close friendship. You were my best friend. What's happened? Why have you isolated yourself so much the last two years? If there's something wrong, I'd like to help you."

"I'll reserve a court for tomorrow at noon, Eddy. See you then. Bye."

Irene was in bed reading the latest Ludlum. I lay down next to her and stared at the ceiling.

"Who called?"

"It was Eddy. He was angry because he said I was supposed to meet him at noon for racketball. He's crazy. I never . . ."

"Pat! You really have been forgetful lately. Two weeks ago we went to see Breaker Morant. You didn't remember seeing it two months ago. What's the matter? I'm worried about you. Could you have a brain tumor, or something?"

"No. I doubt it. I am forgetting a lot of things, though. I don't know why."

"Pat, will you see Scott tomorrow?"

"Yes. I'll call him in the morning. If a clinical psychologist can't help . . ."

I looked at Irene and was tremendously relieved when I saw her look of concern. I didn't deserve this lady.

It was almost eleven o'clock, and it was time to go to my study and start choosing the combination of sedative drugs that would get me to sleep. Although I kept small stashes of tranquilizers in the bedroom, in my car, and in my office, I kept my main supply of drugs locked in a closet in my study.

I poured myself a glass of wine, unlocked the closet, and stared at my boxes of drugs. I enjoyed choosing my pills every night. It was my last conscious decision of the evening. And the wine added ceremony to the occasion.

I knew I could take as many as twelve pills and still function the next day. I finished the wine and chose two Valiums, two Libriums, one Miltown, one Dalmane, one Placidyl, and two Doridens. I stayed away from narcotics because they produce euphoria and are addictive. I didn't want artificial ecstasy. I wanted anesthesia.

I noted I was running low on some of the drugs. I'd have to call the local pharmaceutical representatives in the morning. They always responded quickly and with enthusiasm when I needed more drugs.

I looked at the nine pills in my hand and said quietly: "God, please don't let these kill me." I then swallowed them. No need for water with only nine pills.

I went to the bedroom and Irene was lying on her side, her eyes closed. She becomes totally silent when she sleeps. I could never even hear her breathe. I turned out the light and got quietly into bed and lay facing her. I put my hand gently through her hair. It had been a long time since we had made love. I wished I could have her now.

I closed my eyes and tried to remember the last time we had made love. It was after the last time we had taken a shower together . . . at least six months.

"Pat," Irene whispered ". . . please."

Her hand was slowly moving inside my shorts. She moved closer.

"Please . . . honey . . . it's been so long. . . . I love you."

I rolled over, turning away from her.

Impotence is profoundly emasculating.

"C'MON, PAT, it's after six o'clock. You have to get to the hospital."

Getting out of bed in the morning took a long time.

"God, I wish I could sleep as soundly as you."

"You could," I said in a whisper I hoped she hadn't heard.

Thank God. She still didn't know.

Irene was walking out of the bedroom but stopped and faced me.

"Aren't you ever going to make love to me again?" There was hurt and anger in her inflection. "If you're having a problem, for God's sake see somebody. Or are you just trying to punish me?" She turned and headed for the door. "We can't go on like this."

"I'll be back at one, Diane. I'm going to the Y and play racketball with Dr. Willis. I'll keep my beeper with me."

The office phone rang as I walked out the door.

I was near the elevator when I heard Diane's excited voice.

"Dr. Reilly . . . Dr. Reilly—"

"Diane, can't you take a message?"

"It's the emergency room. You'd better take it."

I hurried back into my office and picked up the receiver.

"This is Dr. Reilly."

"Sir, this is Debbie Andrews, admitting resident. We have a patient of yours, Susan Nicks, a three-year-old white female who was brought in here one hour ago convulsing. She had a petechial rash and a temperature of one hundred and four.

"We stopped her seizures with rectal paraldehyde and I.V. Valium. Then we did a spinal tap. Her spinal fluid was loaded with white cells and organisms that appear to be meningococci on gram stain.

"We've given her a loading dose of penicillin and her vital signs are stable. We're going to put her in the intensive care unit."

"Good work," I said. "Sounds like you may have saved her life. I'll be over to see her later, Debbie. Tell the parents. And by the way, admit her to Dr. Fagan's service."

"Dr. Fagan? You don't want her under your care? Well . . . all right. Dr. Reilly, the child's mother said they saw you this morning at eight o'clock." Debbie's voice was hesitant but had an accusatory tone. "She said the child had a rash then and a fever."

I didn't remember seeing the child.

"That's not possible," I snapped. "I'm sure the child did not have the rash or a stiff neck. I always check for a stiff neck on kids with a fever this time of year. I'm not going to miss a meningococcal meningitis. Do you think I would?"

"No . . . of course not. But the mother said—"

"I'll check my records, Debbie. Thanks."

March 4 8:00
Susan Nicks. 3 yr. old.

· 7 ·

Runny nose, fever, sleeping a lot x 1 day.

No diarrhea.

Temp. 102°. Ears normal. Throat normal.

Chest and heart normal. Abdomen soft.

Petechial rash. Child somnolent.

Probably viral syndrome with rash.

No meds.

Call me in two days if child not better.

My hand trembled as I held the match and burned the record.

"That's your last patient today, Dr. Reilly. Your three-thirty canceled."

"Thanks, Diane. I want to run over to the hospital and see the Nicks child. Then I have an appointment at five. Who's taking my calls tonight?"

"Dr. Andrews . . . Debbie Andrews. She called a little while ago and said she'd be over to pick up your beeper."

I went into my office and locked the door. Seeing Susan Nicks's parents was not something I was looking forward to. As I sat at my desk, I could feel my jaw muscles begin to tighten.

Not again. Please, God, not again. Why was I so vulnerable to anxiety? Why do I fall apart so easily? Why can't somebody help me deal with stress? Maybe I'm in the wrong specialty. Too much pressure. Maybe I should be in public health. Or research. No life and death stuff there. I'll have to look into that. But now . . .

Larry and Michelle Nicks . . . I need to look strong . . . and confident.

I unlocked the bottom right-hand drawer and took out the injectable Valium and the tourniquet. And the syringe.

"Susan seems to be fairly stable, Larry. Hopefully she'll continue to do well."

It was difficult for me to look at Michelle.

"Hopefully?" Larry mimicked my inflection.

"Meningococcal meningitis is a very serious disease." I sat down with Michelle and Larry at the small table in the waiting room of the intensive care unit. "There's no evidence at this time that the organisms got into her blood. That's a strong point in her favor." They looked at each other, shared a small, hopeful smile, and touched hands. "Susan is getting the best care possible. I want you to know that."

Larry took two Marlboros from the pack on the table, gave one to Michelle, and lit both cigarettes with a long, thin green lighter that had the inscription Easy Does It. That was one of the slogans of Alcoholics Anonymous. I hoped this wouldn't start the poor guy drinking again.

"Larry, you and Michelle are going to have to take some medicine now because you've been exposed to this disease. Do you have any other kids?"

"Our five-year-old, Willie," Michelle said with a trace of surprise in her voice. "I bring him to see you. Don't you remember? You always joke with him. You tell him he's got a great name for a second baseman."

"Sure . . . sure. I remember Willie. How is he?"

Michelle nodded her head and then looked at Larry.

"Dr. Reilly," Larry put the cigarette to his lips, bent forward, and rested his arms on the table. "Why is Susan under Dr. Fagan's care?"

"Well . . . ah . . . I think Dr. Fagan is better than I am at treating this disease. He'll take good care of her. I promise you."

"You missed it, didn't you?" There was a piercing quality to Michelle's voice.

I took a deep breath.

"When I see a child with a runny nose and a fever, meningococcal meningitis is not the first thing I think of. It could—"

"She had a rash, too."

"Yeah, Dr. Reilly." Larry took the cigarette from his mouth. "What about the rash?"

"A rash can be caused by a lot of things. Everything Susan had was consistent with a viral illness. And that's what I thought she had. I see a lot of kids . . ." I sat back in the chair and looked at Michelle. "Yes. I missed it." I stood slowly and looked down at them. "I'm sorry. I'm very sorry."

Because of my schedule I could never see Scott Walsh before five P.M. By that time he had usually taken off his white coat, had his sleeves rolled up, and his tie was loose at the neck. He looked tired but always interested.

Although he had several degrees, including a doctorate in clinical psychology, he had no diplomas on his walls. Rather, some interesting Chinese prints hung where diplomas normally would. He never sat behind his desk when we talked. We would sit across from each other near a window in plain but comfortable chairs.

He slouched in his chair as we made small talk for a few minutes. He then told me that Irene had called.

"She told me how you used to be. She talked about how self-assured you once were and how you used to be interested in so many things. She liked your honesty and gentleness and your ability and willingness to show affection.

"She describes you now as a helpless, reclusive, anxiety-ridden man who is becoming less able to deal with even a minimum of stress. She still loves you, Pat, but for what you once were. Not for what you are now."

"Well," I said, trying to appear unmoved, "she hasn't said anything new then."

"And you know she wants to adopt a child. But she won't because of the way you are."

Scott slouched further into his chair and rested his head on the back. His upper eyelids closed halfway so I could see only the whites of his eyes. His face took on an ethereal quality. He appeared as if he would levitate momentarily. He always assumed this position when searching for a metaphor.

After about a minute and a half he moved his feet and opened his eyes. He began pushing himself up to a sitting position. He was becoming less casual and his expression was unusually intense.

"Pat, let me create a situation for you. Say there are two people in the water, and one of them is drowning, and he's flailing away and screaming for help. In other words, he is doing a lot of gesturing but nothing substantial.

"The other person is a marginal swimmer at best. She's frightened and getting very tired. What would you tell her to do?"

"I'd tell her to save herself. I'd tell her to swim away. Did you tell Irene to leave me, Scott?"

"No. That's a choice she would have to make. But if she left, I would support her."

"I don't want to lose her, Scott. But . . . maybe . . . maybe she should leave. I must not be very attractive these days. Panic attacks. Forgetful. Afraid of everything. Impotent. And I don't know what to do."

"I'm finding it difficult to help you, Pat. Nothing seems to work for you. You're virtually refractory to biofeedback. Your response to stress is pathologically severe. The constant anxiety you're experiencing is exhausting whatever emotional reserves you had.

"And I'm frustrated as hell. I'm not helping you. I've been seeing you for fourteen months, and if anything, you're worse. I hope this doesn't smack of abandonment, but I may have to refer you to someone else. You're very puzzling. Unless . . . sometimes I feel there's something you're not telling me. Have you been completely honest with me?"

"No."

I stood and walked to some shelves of books that went from floor to ceiling. The way Scott stacked his books was a good indication that neatness was not among his priorities.

I kept my back to him.

"This is very difficult, Scott." My voice was cracking. "I take a lot of drugs. Sleeping pills and tranquilizers. I'm having memory lapses. My medical judgment is impaired. I missed a meningitis this morning." I slowly rolled up my left sleeve and turned. There was a spot of dried blood where I had injected myself. "I did this today. Valium. I've never injected myself before. I don't want to do it again. I'm terrified. Please help me."

"Sedativism!" He slapped his knee. "Goddamnit. I should have known. You're crippling yourself, Pat. You're an emotional basket case. You've got to stop."

"I've tried to stop so many times. I can't. I don't think I'll ever be able to get off these drugs. What do I do?"

"You'll need help."

He went to his desk and paged rapidly through a notebook. He then wrote something on a small piece of paper and handed it to me. His handwriting was unbelievably bad.

"I can't read this. You write like a neurosurgeon."

"The Hogarth Hospital. It's in Toronto. You can read the telephone number, can't you?"

"Yes. I'll think about this for a few days and let you know, Scott."

"No. You'll call them from my office now. I'll wait outside."

I dialed the number.

I sat trembling, holding the receiver to my ear with both hands as the phone rang for the eighth time. Apparently no one was going to answer. I felt somewhat relieved and was about to hang up.

But then there was a small, distant voice.

"Good afternoon. The Hogarth Hospital and Research Institute."

"Could you please tell me something about your admission policy?" I asked.

"One moment, please. I'll transfer."

Another voice. "Admitting."

I repeated the question.

"Is the problem with drugs or alcohol?"

"Drugs," I answered.

"Are you a physician or are you the person with the problem?"

"Both."

"Oh. OH! Just a moment, please."

There was a click and silence. I felt betrayed. I had just admitted to a voice that I was a doctor and that I was a drug addict. Maybe this call was being traced. I started to hang up.

"This is Dr. Randolph. Can I help you?"

I repeated the basic information. But I adroitly avoided giving my name.

"What's your name?" he asked.

"Cleveland, Ohio."

I heard him chuckle. I was not going to surrender my name that easily.

"What drugs are you addicted to, Cleveland?"

"How much time do you have?"

"Well," he said, "give me some idea of what you're taking."

"Valium, Miltown, Placidyl, Doriden, Quaalude. The list goes on."

"Any alcohol?" he asked.

"A little."

"Well, we have a waiting list of about three months. But we try to get physicians in as soon as possible. Could you be here on March nineteenth?"

"That's only two weeks away." I paused and tried to think of reasons why I couldn't go that soon. None came.

"All right, I'll be there on the nineteenth," I said with some resignation.

"Do you want to give me your name?"

"Patrick Reilly."

"O.K., Patrick. I'll see you in two weeks. Between now and then I'd like you to get yourself admitted to a hospital—a psychiatric ward, if necessary—so that you can be kept away from drugs. Will you do that?"

"No. Absolutely not."

"Well . . . let's see. Will you call Alcoholics Anonymous today and tell them what you told me?"

"A.A.?" I laughed. "That's absurd. I won't do that."

"I'm trying to keep you from dying," he snapped. "You're going to be particularly nervous in the next two weeks. I don't want you to accidentally overdose and kill yourself. How about Antabuse? Will you at least take Antabuse every day until you get here?"

"Yes. I'll do that."

"Good. You sound like you're going to be a somewhat reluctant patient. As a rule physicians are our most challenging patients. Prepare yourself for an interesting experience, Patrick, an experience that will change your life."

It was unusually warm for early March. I sat on the hood of my Citation staring at the baseball diamond where I had played when I was young, content, and self-absorbed. During the summer months my whole world had centered around this diamond.

I played shortstop then, and I was good. Very good. Always the all-star shortstop. But I remembered precious little about those days. The game-winning hits. The throws from deep short. The double plays. The drugs I had taken in the past fourteen years had robbed me of the details of my life. Memories were gone forever. Experiences never happened.

I had to face Irene. Now she would know the reason for the decay. She would now know the reason for my wetting the bed ("Gee, my bladder's getting weaker"), the reason I paid pediatric residents from the hospital to take my night calls ("A good night's sleep is one luxury I will allow myself"), the reason she couldn't arouse me after I went to sleep ("My father slept this soundly, too"), the reason I was sterile ("I guess the X rays have done this to me").

All lies. All bullshit.

I couldn't face Irene and tell her these things. Not now. I couldn't face anybody. I couldn't move.

There was a light, barely perceptible mist, and things were becoming vague, blurring into the darkness of early evening.

There was some movement near the third base dugout. Something was moving slowly in the direction of home plate. I focused on it, and the outlines became precise. It was a boy wearing a baseball cap, riding in a motor-driven wheelchair. He had a baseball bat on his lap. I got off the car and walked closer to the diamond.

He stopped when he got to home plate and took the bat off his lap, grasped it near the handle, and started taking some slow swings as if warming up. He would stop near the end of his swing and point the bat toward the pitcher's mound.

He was now ready. He held the bat cocked near his right shoulder, waiting for the pitch. His upper body lurched forward, but he wasn't swinging. He snapped his head toward the right. He had a look of incredulity and anger. He started shaking his head slowly.

He tapped the plate with the bat again, regained his composure. Practice swings, each one ending with the bat pointing toward the pitcher's mound. He cocked the bat again, waiting. He swung the bat mightily, and he almost fell from the chair. He sat erect quickly and dropped the bat. He looked toward left field, and a smile of accomplishment came to his face.

He started wheeling toward first base, stopped after a few feet, looked to left field, and then raised his arms above his head exultantly. He continued on to first base, rounded the bag as best he could, and moved on toward second, near the edge of the outfield. As he got to second, he raised his left arm high in the air, fist clenched. He crossed second base, and the left side of the wheelchair bounced and tipped him to the right.

I felt a burst of panic and I started toward him but stopped when the chair righted itself and he continued on toward third.

I walked toward home plate.

As he rounded third, he took off his hat and waved it as he looked toward the empty seats. He saw me when he was halfway to home plate, and his grin disappeared. He became uncertain. His chair slowed.

I kicked the bat out of the third-base line so he could continue to home. The chair speeded up slightly, and I held out both my hands, palms up. He smiled, and as he crossed home plate, we slapped hands.

The chair stopped, and he began turning around.

"Thanks, mister. I forgot about the bat."

"You live around here?" I picked up the bat and handed it to him.

"Yeah. Over there. About half a block. Mom knows I'm here. I like to come over here and pretend. I can do Reggie Jackson. Mike Schmidt. But my favorite is Carlton Fisk. Remember that time in the world series? Remember him pushing that ball fair? Gee . . ."

"Who did you just do?"

"That was me. That's the way I'd do it. Wanna see Yaz?"

"I can't son. There's something I have to do. But I'd like to see you do all of these guys some time."

I waved and started to go. When I got a few feet I stopped and turned back to him:

"Hey, son, I like your style."

4

I HAD no choice but to face Irene and tell her. My mother, Sarah, lived in North Carolina now, and I felt no urgent need that she know. My sister, Gabe, lived only a few miles away in Cleveland Heights. We had been so close once. I would have to tell her something.

I'm glad Logan was dead. He wouldn't have been able to handle knowing that his son, his only son, was a drug addict. He would have got mad, I'm sure. He was like a shark. He responded to every uncertain, frustrating, or threatening situation with rage. Logan was never physically violent with Gabe, me, or my mother, but there was always the threat of it.

He never cared if he were loved or respected by his family. He wanted—and got—submission.

When I was young, Logan would take me to see the Indians ball games, and we would buy popcorn and Cokes and holler a lot and have a good time. I enjoyed that so much because it was the closest we ever got.

The man was incapable of intimacy.

Logan was a pharmacist but had started out in medical school. After his first year he married Sarah. Gabe thinks they got married because Sarah was pregnant with her. Sarah became ill during the pregnancy. She developed high blood pressure and edema and had to spend the last six months of her pregnancy in bed. Logan dropped out of school and worked. He never went back to medical school.

Whenever Sarah and Logan argued, he would always say, "If it hadn't been for you, I'd have been a doctor. I'd have been somebody."

Sarah would respond, "*You* got me pregnant."

"Yeah," Logan would holler and point at her, "but you knew what you were doing."

A glaze seemed to come over Logan's eyes at about this time, and he would be trembling. Sarah would retreat then, terrified.

Logan later got a degree in pharmacy by going to school part-time for eight years.

"Don't be a pharmacist," Logan once told me. "I hate it. Packing pills . . . making sodas . . . shit. Make something of yourself. Be a doctor or a priest. Nothing else is worthwhile."

I didn't love or respect Logan, but I believed him.

He made every decision for me. When I was in Little League, he told me to play shortstop, not third base, which is what I wanted to play.

"If you play third," he said, "they'll expect you to hit home runs like Al Rosen. You're more like Harvey Kuenn. Hit for average. Think singles and doubles."

I did what he said and hit four hundred. I made the all-star team at short.

In high school I wanted to play guard on the football team. "There's no glory on the interior line," Logan said. "Play end." So I played end and was an all-city end in my senior year.

Since I could not have his love or his affection, I would do anything for his approval. I wanted desperately for him to put his arm around me and congratulate me for doing something well.

The day it was announced in the *Cleveland Press* that I was second team all-city at end, I ran to his store and into his office. "See," he said. "You wanted to play guard." That's all he said.

I was seriously considering the priesthood when I was a junior in high school. I told Logan that one morning at breakfast. He never looked up from his newspaper. "Forget it," he said. "You don't have enough humility. Be a doctor."

From day one in college I took courses that would best prepare me for medical school. This was the way Logan wanted it. In my junior year I signed up for an elective in English, and he got incredibly angry. "Don't putz around with that junk."

So I dropped it and took an elective in advanced calculus.

I graduated from college with a 3.8 average. Logan told me I could have had a 4 point "if you only applied yourself."

Six months before I was going to leave for medical school, I realized that I had never made a decision that I wanted to be a doctor. And four years of medical school were staring me in the face. I had prepared myself for nothing else. What if I failed? What would I do? I didn't want to disappoint Logan.

Anxiety struck like a thunderbolt. And struck repeatedly. Daily. Hourly. Depression settled in, suffocating me. I lost my appetite, my enthusiasm. I couldn't sleep. Insomnia panicked me. How could I perform in medical school if I couldn't sleep?

I was afraid that I would live.

Dr. Dennis Duncan was the psychiatrist I saw, and he put me on Valium. All the symptoms of unhappiness and pessimism left me.

"This Valium is magic," I told him.

"It's only made your unhappiness more tolerable," he said. "It hasn't solved any of your problems." He told me later, "I don't want you to consider medical school for at least one year."

I told Logan this.

"I thought you were tougher than this," he said. "What a disappointment you are. It's up to you now. Do what you want."

I never really considered not going to medical school. I just wished that I had made the decision to be a doctor. Dr. Duncan said I had to resolve some things with myself before I began medical school.

"You don't have the emotional reserves for medical school right now," he told me. "You shouldn't go."

I went, of course. Logan kept me well supplied with Valium, which I took five or six times daily. I wasn't a very good student, although I got good grades. I lived from one test to the next. When I got above an 85 on an exam, I would send it home to Logan. And I started to receive glimpses of approval.

He started to say things:

"You're doing well," or, "I liked the grade you got on your last Anatomy test." And he flaunted me when I came home. He wanted me to stay at his store, and he would tell everybody whom he could engage in conversation:

"That's my boy. He's in medical school."

During Christmas vacation of my senior year, he brought me into the kitchen.

"What are you going to specialize in?" he asked. "I'd like to see you in neurosurgery or maybe plastic surgery."

"I'm thinking more in terms of internal medicine," I said. "Or pediatrics."

He laughed derisively and shook his head.

"No," he said. "No. I don't like that. No glory. No money. Start out in general surgery and then get into a surgical subspeciality."

It was after midnight and we were in the operating room amputating a leg. I was accomplished, I thought, at appearing interested while in surgery. There was little for me to do with this particular operation since the other medical student was suctioning and tying off the bleeders.

The chief surgical resident was talking about a "piece a ass" he had gotten the day before.

"It was fantastic," he said. "Fan-fucking-tastic."

I yawned audibly.

"Reilly," he snapped and handed me the saw. "Get in here and get yourself a piece a this operation."

"I don't want any of it."

"Then get out. Get the fuck out."

I got a D in Surgery. I should have failed.

"You can acquire the dexterity if you want to," Logan said. "And don't feed me any bullshit about that personality stuff."

"I'm not planning on taking any surgery during my internship," I said with, I hoped, definiteness.

I shrank as his anger grew volcanic. But I stood my ground.

"And what about that Irene you've been seeing? I hope you're not being taken by a pretty face and a nice ass."

I couldn't respond to that. I left the house.

Logan began to realize he was no longer in control of me. In the years before he died, we spoke less, and his anger became more severe and unfocused. Just being around him was penance.

He died in 1975. In the summer, I think.

Soon after Logan died, Sarah began using her maiden name, Carlyle.

Sarah was sixty-four now and tall, thin, dark, athletic, and beautiful.

She still taught modern dance, which, I'm sure, was her only real passion in life.

She realized Logan's emotional inadequacy and his inability to be close to his children. She tried to compensate by showering Gabe and me with affection that was sometimes not genuine.

Logan did not approve of Sarah's dancing in public. So she confined her dancing to her classes. Except once. She substituted for someone who became ill and danced in *Appalachian Spring* at Cleveland's Music Hall. I was seventeen then, and her dancing was the most beautiful thing I had ever seen. I remember having an erection as I watched her and feeling jealous of my father.

Sarah was often preoccupied with something. Something that would make her serious and quiet for minutes. Her lips would move slightly, as if she were holding a conversation with someone. This would annoy Gabe.

"Mom, what are you doing? Who are you talking to?"

Sarah would be embarrassed.

"I'm sorry, kids, I'm trying to work through something."

On Saturday afternoons when the other kids would be off at matinees, Sarah kept Gabe and me home with her and we would take turns reading to each other: *Alice's Adventures in Wonderland* . . . *Charlotte's Web* . . . *Peter Rabbit* . . . *The Wind in the Willows* . . . *Wizard of Oz.*

Gabe and I liked Lewis Carroll best. We had great fun speaking as if we were walruses and oysters and lobsters. Sometimes when we went to the Cleveland Zoo, we would have pretend conversations with the animals. One time Gabe and I were holding a four-way conversation with two gorillas when the gorillas started having sex.

We didn't know what they were doing so the conversation stopped. But Gabe started making grunting noises in a husky gorilla voice, and I did the same. Some adults who were around us started laughing at us, so Gabe and I grunted louder. Until Sarah saw what was going on and whisked us away.

"They love each other," Sarah said in response to our questions.

"Is that what love looks like?" Gabe asked Sarah.

"Yes," Sarah snapped, "for gorillas . . . and some men."

She would talk to us and listen. Really listen. I was important. My opinion mattered. Logan was disregarding and disdainful of our thoughts and our opinions.

When Sarah, Gabe, and I were alone, there would be loving, touching, and laughing. But when Logan came home, all touching stopped. His very presence made it seem wrong, sinful. We would become uncomfortable, impersonal. We would not look at each other when we talked. And only Logan had the freedom of expression, of stating opinions.

Logan was resolutely and passionately an Irish Catholic and a liberal Democrat. In that order. Fortunately he was often making novenas to various saints and that kept him out of the house some evenings. I used to think that he really believed in novenas. He probably did. But I think it was also important to him that he be a visible Catholic. We never talked about God at home. Talking about God requires a certain amount of intimate self-disclosure.

When John Kennedy was elected president, Logan changed for a while. He celebrated at the Hibernian Club for two weeks. And when he was home, he actually exhibited some warmth. It was the only time I ever saw him touch Sarah.

When Kennedy was killed, Logan became worse than he had ever been. His anger was more violent, and he became increasingly remote. And he added pointedly cruel sarcasm to his repertoire of distancing devices.

Sarah began staying away from the house on the evenings when Logan was home. He must have trusted her implicitly. Or else he didn't care.

Sarah had converted to Catholicism when she married Logan, but they only went to church together with Gabe and me on Christmas and Easter. Those were social occasions, really, not religious ones.

Sarah would go to early Mass three or four times a week. I used to go with her and enjoyed being with Sarah in church. She would become so quiet, so oblivious. I sensed a certain closeness, a communication, a commitment that Sarah had with God that I envied.

When I was twelve or thirteen, Sarah began going to confession often, sometimes every other day, and taking Communion less. After about a year she stopped going to confession and stopped taking Communion.

When Logan died, Sarah was like someone who had just had major surgery for cancer. There was a lot of pain but also relief knowing that the tumor was gone. Living and thriving was again possible.

Six months after Logan died, Sarah married a sculptor who lived in Cleveland Heights. He had never been married, and there had been a tacit understanding that he was a homosexual. Sarah was fifty-nine. Vic was about ten years younger.

Sarah took Communion at her wedding.

For a wedding present Gabe gave Sarah a decoupaged plaque with a quotation from Shakespeare:

When you do dance
I wish you
A wave of the sea
that you might ever do
Nothing but that.

Sarah and Vic moved to Asheville, North Carolina soon after their wedding. He began teaching in a crafts school, and Sarah opened her own school of modern dance.

"One of my fourteen-year-old students taught me clogging," Sarah wrote me. "It is a totally exhilarating experience. Vic and I go into town on Saturday nights and clog until we can no longer stand.

"This is an area protected by God. People sustain themselves on some very basic pleasures."

I look forward to Sarah's letters. She writes and reveals things about herself that she never did when Logan was alive.

"I didn't know I was capable of this much happiness," she wrote. "I wish so that I had Gabe and you now to share this with me.

"I have the mountains, of course, and I have my work. (Dare I call it work?) And I have Vic. This man adores me, Pat. He simply adores me. Can you imagine that? I can be spontaneous with him. What a luxury! And he is teaching me intimacy. What a gift! It is so incredibly wonderful being with this man.

"Never, Patrick, never for a moment doubt the existence of God."

She is now Sarah Carlyle-Drew.

Gabe . . . She told me the facts of life when I was about twelve. It was unimaginable to me that Logan and Sarah could have ever been physically that close.

"Do you really think Logan and Mom ever did that?" I asked her.

"Well," she said, "at least twice."

Gabe and I spent a lot of time together as we grew up. That made Logan uncomfortable and, of course, angry.

"You're going to be a sissy if you keep hanging around with your sister," he told me. "I don't want you being with her so much."

That was one thing Logan wanted me to do that I disobeyed.

Although most people considered Gabe shy and weak, she was neither of those things. She was, rather, quiet and thoughtful and had clearly defined goals. She wanted a Ph.D. in English, she wanted to teach and to write. She wanted marriage, too, but she would "hold out for someone like Updike."

She started showing me her poetry when she was a freshman in college. Her poetry annoyed me because I was never sure what she was saying.

> The restless repetition of imprecise feelings,
> The cruel mastery of the thrusting male reality.
> These things being a dimness, a cargo of uncertainty.
> And I lie here struggling for my pride
> As it slips away.

Gabe was much like Sarah—tall, thin, dark, attractive, sensitive—but she rarely dated. And the men she did go out with were not her equals. They were unattractive, generally, or not very smart.

When she was a junior in college, she did get involved in a relationship with a man I finally approved of. Kenneth was fifteen years older than Gabe and a professor of English. She openly lavished her affection on him, something I had not seen her do before. I was happy for her.

> Quiet.
> Laughing . . . giggling . . . sighing . . .
> Moaning . . . crying . . . screaming . . .
> Quiet.
> A silent time of throbbing anticipation.
> Of exhaustion and sadness.
> Guilt is unimaginable.
> Anguishing.
> Wanting.
> Having.
> Never ambiguous.
> Never peaceful.

I found out later Kenneth was married.

Gabe was one year away from her Ph.D. when she announced she was getting married. His name was Roger Gross, and he was a senior medical student. Roger's eyes were large and far apart, and he never blinked. He rarely smiled. (Sarah said that looking at Roger was "like having a guilty conscience staring at you.") Roger could drone on for hours assuming that he was interesting, about his ham radio activities.

"Roger," I once said to him, "I'd like to be able to join you in a conversation. I know nothing about ham radio. I like sports, movies, plays . . . good restaurants."

"Those are frivolous things," he said, "for the shallow-witted."

Logan gloried in the fact that his son-in-law was going to be a doctor. As he came down the aisle of Saint Timothy's with Gabe, Logan had an exaggerated, foolish grin. Sarah cried at the ceremony. Everyone but me thought she cried out of happiness. Roger wanted me to be his best man, but I refused. I would witness the ceremony, damnit, but I wouldn't be a part of it.

I was angry when I saw Gabe come down the aisle. My beautiful, intelligent sister was marrying a creep, a fucking dud, someone I couldn't imagine with an erection.

Sarah and I thought it appropriate when Roger announced he was going to be a proctologist. Gabe never got her Ph.D. She taught school while Roger went through his internship and four years of residency. Then he divorced her.

Gabe would never tell me what happened, but I think Roger finally realized he was overmatched.

Gabe continued teaching high school until she married another loser. Martin was a lawyer, a churlish asshole who was divorced twice, drank heavily, and was abusive to her, sometimes in public. The bastard was also a Pittsburgh Steelers fan. Gabe and Martin separated about once a year, every time he got involved with another woman.

She had her first and only child, Adrian, in 1972. He is the closest thing to a son that I will ever have.

I had acted out my disapproval of Gabe and her choice of men by being aloof from her. But because of Adrian we have established ourselves once again as brother and sister.

During the football season Gabe lets me have Adrian on Sundays. She knows I will not allow my nephew to be a Pittsburgh Steelers fan. She allows me to "purloin," as she puts it, her son on Sundays and take him to the Browns games. Logan got season tickets to the Browns home games in 1954, and he left them to me. Great seats on the forty, upstairs near the rail.

Adrian has become a Browns fan, to his father's consternation. Two years ago after a game against Seattle, Adrian met Ozzie Newsome, the Browns' tight end, in a restaurant. Newsome had seen Adrian staring at him, and he came over to our table, got down on one knee next to Adrian, and said to him: "Hey, my man." They slapped hands.

Adrian has a singular devotion to Ozzie Newsome now. He prefers to be called Ozzie and during the football season will not respond to anything else. He has six Cleveland Browns jerseys all with number 82. He tries to walk like Newsome and spices his conversation with "you know . . . you know." Once he told me he wished he was black.

"Ozzie is not an appropriate name for a white kid from Cleveland Heights," Gabe says. She and Martin refuse to call him Ozzie. The four of us have negotiated a settlement that only Adrian is happy with. We call him Eighty-two.

Gabe told me that Adrian/Ozzie/Eighty-two occasionally in his sleep still says: "Hey, my man."

5

MACBETH wagged his tail furiously as I walked in the door. He was a small hyperactive terrier of uncertain parentage. Lucifer, mostly Labrador, just rolled over on his back, hoping I would scratch his stomach. They were both approaching their third birthday.

Sometime in June almost three years ago, I was passing by the dog pound and stopped in. Our first dog, Puddles, had died about a week earlier. As I walked into the building, a morbidly obese man with short hair and a big cigar walked gruffly past me carrying two puppies. I asked him what he was going to do with the dogs.

"Gonna gas 'em," he said.

I brought home the puppies and their intestines full of worms. Irene loved the puppies but decompensated when she saw the worms.

Gabe once said that Lucifer was becoming like me. Irene and I had some good laughs about that. Lucifer farted all the time, was not yet housebroken, sniffed everybody's ass, got an erection when his belly was scratched, and urinated when he got excited. What Gabe meant was that Lucifer was passive, friendly, and slept a lot.

Macbeth was more Irene's dog than mine. He would sit near her loom for hours and watch her weave. He is an alert dog who has to find the source of every noise and comment on it with an appropriate bark.

Lucifer, we think, is a virgin and shows no interest in the opposite sex. Macbeth has his "lady" down the block.

It was my week to see that dinner was ready at six-thirty, so I had picked up some Chinese food on the way home. Irene loves sweet and sour pork. I brought home an extra serving for Irene's middle-of-the-night snack. "Snack" is her word.

"I can't get back to sleep unless I have a snack at about three o'clock, when I wake up," she has told me.

Usually in the morning there are used pots, pans, plates, and glasses sitting in the sink that weren't there when we went to bed. I would love to witness one of these snacks. But at three A.M. I am unarousable.

Irene weighed one hundred eighteen pounds when we got married. After ten years she is only two pounds heavier, and at five feet six she wears one hundred twenty pounds quite well.

She wears T-shirts and faded blue jeans most of the time. On the backside of one pair of jeans she has screen printed the head of a camel. And she drinks Vernors Ginger Ale. She is never without a can of cold Vernors. And Moon Pies. She is always eating Moon Pies. I tasted one once. It was a disastrous combination of marshmallow, chocolate, and graham cracker. It was awful. And about five hundred calories per bite. I once saw her eat three Moon Pies at one sitting. I offered her an injection of insulin.

"I lecture to medical students on nutrition," I told her. "And the main staple of my wife's diet is Vernors Ginger Ale and Moon Pies. Where have I failed?"

But Irene can be formal when necessary. Whenever there are functions at the medical society or the hospital, she will dress appropriately and look terrific. I keep glancing at her, however, to reassure myself that she is not sitting on the floor.

On Irene's birthday in 1977 or 78, she came home with her hair in what she called a curly perm. She had destroyed her long, beautiful auburn hair, I thought. It changed her appearance drastically. It made her look frenzied and . . . well, corruptible.

But within a few days I found myself liking it. She looked good. I could never imagine her with any other hairstyle. And I loved touching her head full of soft curls. Especially when we made love. I still found myself feeling a twinge of sexual excitement any time I saw a woman with auburn hair and a curly perm.

And the only pictures of Irene that I carried and had on my desk were those of her with her curls.

I not only love Irene, I am proud of her. She spends a lot of time weaving and produces some beautiful pieces. She has exhibited in New York, Toronto, and Chicago. She spends one month every two years in Mexico learning new techniques.

And she laughs at my jokes. Most of the time. Once she was waiting for me in the hospital lobby. We were going to have lunch, and the lobby was more crowded than usual. She was sitting when she saw me coming. I motioned for her in a stiff, clinical way. When she was about five feet from me, I said, in a loud voice:

"Miss, the V.D. Clinic is one floor up."

She got me back for that, as she always does, about two months later.

She was exhibiting in a private gallery in Detroit, and I came to see the exhibit three days after it started. She was in the curator's office when I arrived.

I went to a secretary and asked for Irene Reilly. The secretary pressed the intercom:

"Mr. McMichael, Ms. Reilly's husband is here."

Irene's voice came back.

"Husband? What husband?"

"But he says..."

"Wait a minute." Irene's voice. "Is he about six feet two, light brown hair?"

"Yes. Yes."

"That guy's been following me around for months. Get rid of him, will you?"

I had never wanted to get married. I thought myself too much like Logan. I was not going to inflict myself on a woman and produce children who would be unhappy because of me. I avoided any sustained close relationships with women. I would be like Larry Darrell in *The Razor's Edge*. Strong, alone, aloof, enigmatic, searching, passionate.

I met Irene in 1968. She was pretty and genial and refreshingly lacking in cynicism. She assumed everyone was honest. And she still believed everything that was in the Baltimore Catechism. She had four older sisters.

"They were all virgins on their wedding night," Irene told me proudly. And she had no intention of breaking with tradition. I respected that. For a while.

We had a good time together. We laughed and talked and shared ideas. At a dinner party once soon after we met, a question was asked of the guests:

"If you could have dinner with any three people who lived in the twentieth century, who would you choose?"

A lot of names were bandied about. John Kennedy . . . H. L. Mencken . . . Pearl Buck . . . Chaplin . . . Dylan Thomas . . . Joan Baez . . . Harry Truman . . . Tennessee Williams . . . Hemingway . . . Bob Dylan . . . Brando . . . Claire Boothe Luce . . . Elia Kazan . . . Churchill . . . Eldridge Cleaver.

Irene's answer: "Bobby Kennedy . . . Martin Luther King . . . Anne Morrow Lindbergh." I was going to name Kennedy, King, and Pete Seeger.

She made me feel good about myself.

"You're such a gentle person," she told me. "And you have a tremendous capacity for loving. Don't be afraid to show you care."

Touching was important to Irene. At first I was uncomfortable *always* holding hands. Or having her arm locked in mine in public. But as we got closer, I found I liked it. Soon it felt natural.

Irene told me she loved me on our fourth date. And repeated it often. It took me three months to tell her that I loved her. I had only said those words to Gabe and Sarah, never to anyone else. It was on Saint Patrick's Day, and we were drinking green beer at Pat Joyce's Tavern. I had to yell it. On the way home I repeated it twice, rather stiffly. I did mean it but didn't think I was convincing. I had several motives.

I had decided that my exclaiming that I loved her meant we would be going to bed. I was wrong.

Irene and I had some monumental battles over sex. Or the lack of it in our relationship. Her resolve to remain a virgin was firm. I would plot and scheme and calculate how I would get her into bed. I even plied her with alcohol. Nothing worked. I would be so angry with her that I wouldn't call her for weeks.

Sometimes I would be a real jerk and try to manipulate her into feeling bad with my pointedly quiet and sullen behavior. It always worked. It did not get me into bed with her, however.

Gabe came by my parents' house the night before my wedding. I was in the kitchen with Sarah.

"I'm really proud of you, kiddo," Gabe said. "You've chosen well." She kissed me and then gave me a note Irene wanted me to read that night.

Honey
You support my struggle to grow
You hold me up when I feel down
You notice what I do and feel
You challenge me to try, to trust, to stretch

Honey
You make room for me in your life
You tell me if you think I'm wrong
You laugh with me
You give without expecting to receive
You give me honesty
You make me feel special in so many ways
You share your feelings and thoughts with me

Honey
You are endlessly fascinating to me
You are my sunshine
You are God's blessing on me
You are every woman's dream, but especially mine
I love you. Thank you. I love you.

Irene 6/70

Irene wanted three children, each two years apart. I agreed. Initially. And because I was going to have a year of internship and two or three years of residency training ahead of me, we would start our family in three years.

"I want children more than anything else in the world," she told me. "I want them to be beautiful and happy. I want to watch them grow, to show them things. I want to see them play in the snow and watch their faces the first time they see a butterfly. I can't wait to have kids, honey. I'm so excited. We have so much to look forward to."

I was becoming increasingly uncomfortable with the quantities of drugs I was taking in the first years of our marriage. And so was Irene. The medicine cabinet was full of sleeping pills and tranquilizers.

"All the guys take this stuff," I told her, "to handle the stress. Once I get out of my residency, I'll stop. I promise."

As years passed the number of sedative drugs I took increased, I started flirting with amphetamines. An amphetamine in the morning would increase my alertness and make me perform better. An amphetamine tablet, or even a half of one, would also cause me to have a migraine headache.

So I would drink a lot of coffee instead, each cup with four or five teaspoons of instant. My coffee intake was causing my stomach to burn. I was sure I was developing an ulcer. So I drank Maalox, which made me constipated as hell. So I took laxatives every night.

I cried when I had my vasectomy. I had it done in 1975, some time after Logan died. Irene was in Mexico.

The urologist saw me crying.

"I've got you numbed," he said. "This isn't supposed to hurt."

Irene would not have her children. I could not allow myself to be a father. And I would die before I ever told her about the vasectomy. I wouldn't want her to know I was capable of such deliberate cruelty.

I couldn't stop taking the drugs. I needed them to survive.

Irene had looked up from *Fiber Arts* twice during dinner and had seen me not eating. Finally she sat back in her chair, picked up her Vernors, and looked at me.

"What?" she asked.

I told her I was going into a hospital in Toronto in two weeks.

"Nothing in my life is working," I said. "I'm so awfully unhappy. I don't enjoy anything. I'm drowning and I'm taking you down with me. I've got to start making some changes in my life."

I picked up my cup of tea and spilled some of it on my lap. I put it back down.

"Pat." Irene moved forward, put her Vernors down, and held my hand.

"This hospital treats people with addictions—alcohol . . . pills."

"Is it the pills?"

I nodded.

"How many do you take, Pat?"

"More than I need."

"I know you take a tranquilizer now and then and . . ."

"I don't want to talk about the gruesome details. Do you mind?"

"You're trembling, Pat."

"I'm scared, Babes. I feel so alone, so isolated."

Irene moved closer to me and had a soft, approving smile.

"You're doing this for us, aren't you? You want to save our relationship."

"I can't imagine . . ." I took a deep breath to stop from crying ". . . living the rest of my life without you." My eyes were watering. "I've really screwed up."

I started wiping the tears away.

"How long will you be gone, honey?"

"It's a twenty-eight day program. I'll get Mary to cover my practice for me. She's young but very capable. I'll see if Jeff can give my lectures. I'll have to close the office, I guess."

"What about me?" Irene let go of my hand and sat back. "Who is going to cover for you with me?"

I felt anger surfacing. How could she think of herself at a time like this? I picked up my tea and walked to the sink and stared out the window. It was raining hard now. I hoped the kid in the wheelchair—did he tell me his name?—made it home before the rain started.

Irene stood next to me, looking at me. She slipped her hand into my back pocket.

"Irene, after I've gone, I want you to open the closet in my study. The key's in the top right drawer." I looked at her. She was uncertain, worried, but forcing a smile. "And I'm going to tell people that I'm at a month-long conference. O.K.?" She nodded. "I don't even want Gabe to know. This is the last time I'm going to be dishonest."

"I've got a lot of things going on inside right now, Pat. I'm worried about you. I'm scared. I'm angry. But I love you. That's my strongest feeling. And I'm proud of you. God, this must be so difficult for you." She kissed me, first on the cheek, then the mouth. She placed her head on my chest.

Irene's smell, late in the day, after the smell of soap was gone, was close to that of warming chestnuts. And I loved it and its familiarity. It was part of the thrill of being close to her.

"Honey." Her voice was barely audible. "Do you think that the drugs you took are responsible for your low sperm count? Maybe when you stop the drugs . . ."

"No. No. It's the X rays. I'm sure of that."

6

OUR CAB slowed as we approached the entrance to the hospital. Two pillars made of large gray stones stood on each side of the entrance. The iron gates were open. On top of each pillar was a white, stone lion in full mane sitting erect and poised. The lions faced each other, silently communicating invincibility.

Red brick walls, about five feet high, stretched away from each pillar for about one hundred feet. A large black sign with yellow, Gothic lettering was attached to the wall. The sign read:

HOGARTH HOSPITAL AND RESEARCH INSTITUTE

As we drove through the entrance, I noticed the asphalt on the drive came above the bottoms of the iron gates.

I felt Irene squeeze my hand and I looked at her, hoping for a warm smile. She was staring straight ahead, her eyes fixed on something. It was the hospital.

Hogarth was disappointingly plain. It looked like St. Timothy's, the grade school I had gone to. It was red brick, unadorned, functional, artless. Six stories. I was quick to note that there were no bars on the windows.

I had got my hair cut and was wearing my three-piece dark green suit. Irene said that color highlighted my green eyes. I had asked Irene not to wear blue jeans, and so she wore dark slacks and a light gray blazer. This was the outfit she wore to functions at school that required, she said, "maximum formality."

With Irene next to me and carrying one of my suitcases, we climbed the stairs and walked through the door. Inside there was only a desk with a small switch board and a woman's head in profile talking into a telephone headset. She did not look up when we walked in. There was no one else in the lobby.

I turned to Irene. "So far I am not impressed."

The head turned to look at us as we approached. It had the face of an attractive young woman with dark, generous eyebrows. On the desk next to her was a paperback, *The Cracker Factory*, with its cover missing.

"Can I help you?" She forced a look of interest complete with an insincere, although not unpleasant smile.

"I'm Patrick, ah, Dr. Patrick Reilly. I'm to be admitted today."

She looked down at her desk and scoured a clipboard with names on it.

"I don't see your name, Patrick."

Panic.

"Oh, wait, here it is. You're down as an emergency admission."

"Emergency admission?"

"Most doctors are emergency admissions. They get in faster."

"What do I do now?"

"Have a seat over there," she said and handed me a small pamphlet.

On the front of the pamphlet was written, in bold, black letters:

HOGARTH HOSPITAL AND RESEARCH INSTITUTE

and, in italics:

*For the in-patient treatment of people with addictions and
the study of the prevention of unhealthy dependencies.*

"This is pointedly vague," I said and handed the pamphlet to Irene as we sat on the couch. "I bet they say nothing in there about their success rate."

Across from us was a door. A glass pane ran vertically next to it. Through the glass I could see what was apparently a hospital ward. I started to envision the patients I would be with. Consumptive, emphysematous, cadaverous fifty-year-old males.

"I'm not looking forward to this," I said to Irene in what was my greatest understatement of all time.

The entrance door to the hospital opened, and in walked three people. One was a man in his middle fifties, thin and unhealthy-looking. He was carrying a suitcase. He was followed by a pudgy, sad-faced woman about the same age, and a taller, younger woman, about thirty, with strawberry blond hair that fell wavy and windblown to her shoulders. She wore a light blue warm-up suit, about one size too big, and a pair of old, high-top black tennis shoes. She was smiling, happy at the fact, I thought, that she was finally getting her father in for treatment. She walked to the switch board.

"I'm Melanie McLain," she said, in a loud, clear voice. "Where do I go to be admitted?"

The woman at the switch board, her institutional smile in place, pointed toward the large, overstuffed brown couch that was to the left and diagonally across from where Irene and I were sitting.

The blond walked slowly to the couch as the man and woman who came with her watched. As she walked in front of me, I noticed traces of a blue and white sweatband across her forehead, most of the sweatband obscured by soft blond curls that reached almost to her eyes.

She slouched in the middle of the couch and pulled off the sweatband which caused her hair to fly in all directions. She shook her head once and her hair, magically, became exactly as it had been.

She looked at me and then at my suitcases that were in front of me. When she glanced back at me, her lips were molded into an uncertain, Gioconda smile. She gave no indication of noticing Irene.

All of a sudden an effusion of people burst through a door to my left. Most were smiling and talking loudly. There must have been eight or ten of them, all ages and both sexes. They were wearing name tags. I had no idea who they were or why they were smiling.

A small Asian woman came around the corner, stopped, and looked directly at me.

"Patrick?"

"Yes."

"Come with me."

I left Irene and my suitcase and followed her. She was about five feet with heels and she walked with quick, short steps. I had to hurry to keep up with her. When we got to the admitting office, she sat behind her desk facing me. She pulled out a form and turned to her typewriter.

"Name?"

"Patrick David"—her typewriter began snapping—"Reilly."

"Age?"

"Thirty-six."

"Religion?"

"Catholic."

"Occupation?"

"Physician. Pediatrician."

She looked at me and smiled approvingly.

"Where do you practice?"

"Cleveland, Ohio."

"Oh, we had another doctor from Cleveland in here about three months ago."

"What was his name?"

"It was a *she*." She turned back to the typewriter, fingers ready, not quite touching the keys.

"Wife's name and age."

"Irene. Thirty-five."

"Call her in case of emergency?"

"Yes." What emergency?

"Number and ages of children."

"None."

Her eyebrows slightly raised.

"Insurance coverage?"

"I'm paying for this myself. Bill me."

She looked at me.

"You don't have insurance, Patrick?"

"I have insurance."

"Well . . ." she turned back to the typewriter.

"Referring physician?"

"I referred myself."

"How about your private doctor? His name and address."

"I don't have one."

She pulled the form out of the typewriter.

"I'll need you to sign this, Patrick. It's for release of information."

I tensed.

"I don't want any information released."

"You will," she said and smiled. "When you apply for disability insurance, this will allow us to tell your insurance company that you are here as a patient with a diagnosis of substance abuse and length of stay. We tell them nothing else unless you want us to."

She put the form on the desk facing me and handed me a pen.

"I'm not applying for disability insurance, and I would prefer not to sign anything."

She took the form and the pen.

"Come and see me again before you leave, Patrick. You might change your mind."

We finished the interview, and I was about to leave the room.

"Oh, wait, Patrick. Here's something you must wear all the time." She handed me a name tag.

I returned to my seat in the lobby. I was beginning to feel nervous. My palms were sweating, something I had never experienced before. I noticed some movement through the vertical pane of glass. Someone was approaching the door to the ward. The door opened, and out came a small white-haired fiftyish woman. She was reading something on a clipboard. She looked up.

"Patrick?"

"Yes." I stood up.

She smiled broadly and examined me with her brilliant blue eyes. "We're ready for you."

Irene, still sitting, reached up and grabbed my hand.

"Can my wife come?"

"In a few minutes."

I followed her to a room with 209 on the door. It was a plain room with a hospital bed and a night stand. It had a gray linoleum floor. A large mirror was above one of the two white dressers. The room had a private bathroom.

"My name is Edith, and I'm the head nurse on this floor. This is the detoxification floor. Many of our patients when they first come in here are very sick for the first few days. Several years ago some of the patients named this floor Happy Valley. We still call it that."

She closed the door, turned, and looked at me.

"Now, Patrick, I have to search you. I didn't think you would want your wife here for that."

"Thanks."

She was going through my clothes. I noticed she even felt inside my suit coat and looked to see if the lining was intact. She looked at me staring at her. There was a bit of a twinkle in her eye.

"You'd really be amazed at the ingenuity of some of our patients. I especially don't trust doctors."

"I don't understand," I said. "If someone comes here to free themselves of an addiction . . ."

"Not everyone is here by choice," she interrupted. "And many who do come here don't believe they can live without their chemical. When people come to us, they're pretty nervous. Now, will you put your suitcases on the bed and open them?"

She was going through my things rapidly but thoroughly. Obviously she had done this many times before.

"Can I leave the room while you're doing that?"

"That won't be necessary," she said, a bit too sternly. "I'm not trying to make you feel uncomfortable. The first purpose of this hospital is to physically remove you from whatever you're addicted to. Too many people try to slip things in with them."

She paused and looked out the window.

"I really don't enjoy doing this. It's such a severe invasion of privacy. But someone has to do it." She was apologizing.

"That's all right," I said.

I walked over to the window. I could see the entrance to the hospital. A well-dressed woman was stepping out of a cab. She paid the driver and he drove off. She climbed the stairs toward the entrance and stopped. She put her suitcase down, opened it, and took out a bottle. She opened it, threw her head back, and drank from the bottle until it was drained. She screwed the top back on and flipped the bottle into a bush. She then walked defiantly into the hospital.

I turned to see Edith giving me a disappointed look. She held out her hand.

"What are these?" she asked.

"Those are pills I take for my migraine attacks. Talwin, Equagesic, and Compazine."

She gave me a "you-should-know-better" look and put them in her pocket.

"Before I get your wife, there is one thing we have to talk about. When you came through the door this morning you surrendered for as long as you are a patient here the right to think of yourself as a doctor. Physicians are given no deferential treatment. It's so difficult for doctors to think of themselves as patients. I don't know why. But I can tell you from experience that until you start thinking of yourself as just another patient, your recovery will be that much delayed."

She paused, apparently to give me a chance to respond.

"Edith, you said that as if you had rehearsed it."

"I don't have to. I get a chance to say it often."

"You have many doctors as patients?"

"Quite a few."

"All right," I said. "I will regard myself as only a patient."

"Well . . ." she smiled, "at least try."

She walked toward the door. "I'll get Irene. You sit here and relax."

"Relax, hell. I've never been able to relax in my adult life."

"By the time you leave here, you'll be able to. I guarantee it."

She said it so convincingly I believed her.

Irene came in. She had been crying.

"When you left, Pat, I really got nervous."

"I was searched, for Christ's sake. Only the first of many indignities I'll experience, I'm sure."

One hour later I was being taken for a chest X ray with three other new arrivals. They were Steve, Gordon, and MacGregor. We were all nervous after our much-too-polite introductions. We sat quietly in the waiting area of the X ray department. Time was moving slowly. Gordon sat next to me. He had the demeanor of an executive. His prominent nose was bright red. He looked at me and grimaced in what I interpreted to be his smile. Steve sat across from me and had a vacant stare. He had a full head of wavy black hair, but no sideburns. MacGregor, about fifty and an Ontario policeman, sat chain smoking and, except for having no front teeth, was Howdy Doodyish in appearance. He talked incessantly about nothing in particular, and appropriately, no one was listening.

Steve began smiling.

"I was supposed to be in court this morning. Ten days ago I was picked up for impaired driving. That's the seventh time in three months. Christ, they'll throw away the book. My lawyer told me to get my ass in here and maybe the judge will consider that when I do get to court. I wasn't supposed to be admitted for another six weeks. They had a cancellation." Steve looked at me. "I hate this fucking place already."

"How many times you been in the can, Steve?" asked MacGregor.

"Twice for impaired driving and three times for disorderly conduct. I'm a bad ass when I'm drinking."

"What's the sentence in the States for impaired driving, Pat?"

"I have no idea."

"You've never been in jail?" MacGregor was incredulous.

"No."

It was only when someone else talked that I realized I was in another country. The X-ray technician came in and called our names.

". . . and Dr. Reilly."

"Goddamnit," I said to myself. I didn't want anyone to know. Not yet.

The three of them looked at me.

We returned to our rooms. Irene had gone but she had left a note.

Pat, leaving you here is one of the most difficult things I've ever had to do. I hurt for you and for me and for us. The only way I can face a separation this painful, knowing how difficult these following weeks will be for you, is to keep reminding myself that it's your only hope for a better life and our only chance to revive a relationship which I think was very special.

I admire your decision to admit yourself and know only too well all the fears and seemingly insurmountable problems that making such a decision presented. Seeing that you finally had the courage to stop the endless chain of cover-ups and excuses, regardless of the consequences, has given me a great deal of respect for you and in the process seemed to evaporate all my resentment.

My only concern now is for you to get well and to see you smile again. These next fews weeks will be as difficult for me as they will be for you because I love you so much that I feel your pain.

Remember that and it might help.

Irene

After ten years of marriage Irene and I had never been able to say good-bye, even if we were separated for only a short time. Except for our all-too-infrequent expressions of love, we both often withdrew into silence when we felt things deeply.

I now felt terribly alone and afraid.

At three-thirty I was ushered in for my interview with Dr. Michael Randolph, a tall thin man in his mid-forties and impeccably groomed. His thick hair was, prematurely, the same color as his white clinic coat. He smiled as I walked in the door. We shook hands. There was some small talk. Then:

"What were you into, Patrick, alcohol, pills, or both?"

"Pills."

"When did you start?"

"I took my first Valium fourteen years ago. I started seeing a psychiatrist about six months before I started medical school. I was so anxious about beginning school that I couldn't sleep and I lost my appetite. He started me on Valium."

"Did you take it regularly?"

"Three times a day. As prescribed. He told me that I shouldn't even consider medical school because I was being destroyed with anxiety and uncertainty. But I went, and when I started school, I doubled the amount of Valium I took."

"Did you get any psychiatric help while you were in med school?"

"Yeah. I saw an older, semiretired psychiatrist twice a week during my first year."

"What was his attitude toward your taking Valium?"

"He didn't like it. He told me medical school just wasn't worth it. He told me to go home. Of course, I didn't."

"Why didn't you follow the man's advice?"

"Well, as I told him, if I couldn't be a doctor, I didn't want to live. He could never understand that. And of course, he was concerned that I was on Valium and very depressed. He told me that could be a suicidal combination. I remember him explaining that if I became depressed enough to entertain thoughts of suicide, the Valium could decrease the normal anxiety I would feel about taking my life."

Randolph smiled a bit.

"Do you see the dilemma you created for yourself, Patrick?"

"Yes. I felt I would be suicidal if I didn't make it in medical school, and he felt I might actually kill myself if I stayed."

"Did you try to stop the Valium when you finished med school?"

"No."

"Why?"

"I guess I was most afraid of insomnia. I was about to begin my internship. I would be making decisions which, if wrong, could kill people. The few hours I would have to sleep I saw as precious and absolutely essential to my functioning optimally."

"Sounds as if you're trying to make a good case for Valium."

"I don't mean for this to sound as an apology for drug abuse."

"When did the polypharmacy begin, Patrick?"

"I got onto Dalmane, Doriden, Librium, Placidyl and the rest of them in increasing amounts over the past seven or eight years."

"Hmmm . . ." he said, "a chemical connoisseur. What about alcohol?"

"I'd usually drink two or three beers or several glasses of wine at night."

"You must have realized the danger in mixing pills and alcohol."

"I did. Sometimes at night before I reached oblivion, I wondered if I would ever wake up again."

"I find it remarkable, Patrick, that the fear of dying never stops an addict from taking what he thinks he needs. Do you drink and take pills as a nighttime cocktail, or do you take pills during the day, too?"

"I take pills all the time. I only drink at night."

"Did you ever do uppers?"

"I can't take amphetamines. They give me migraines. I took some Ritalin one time during medical school."

"And?"

"And I walked around with an erection for three days."

"Oh?" He gave me a quizzical look. "You actually had a turgid penis for three days?"

"No. No." I laughed. "I just meant I was sexually aroused."

"Well, that should have been easily remedied."

"It wasn't. It happened right in the middle of exam week. There wasn't time for a date, and my roommate was a fundamentalist Christian who prided himself on the fact that he never beat off. Which made him unique in the Western world. He'd even wear a tiny jockstrap at night under his boxer shorts. He said it prevented 'pudendal tumescence.'"

Randolph chuckled.

"We slept in the same room and I had the bed with the loud springs. One night the noise from my springs apparently became rhythmic, and he flipped on the light and frowned at me. He said he would leave if I were going to make a habit of violating myself. And all I was doing was scratching. So being sexually aroused by Ritalin only served to frustrate me. I never took it again."

Randolph got back to business.

"Demerol or morphine?"

"No. But I do take Talwin occasionally for a migraine. And maybe an Equagesic."

"Any other drugs? LSD, cocaine, grass, heroin?"

"I've smoked grass on occasion."

Randolph paused and reviewed his notes.

"So your story is that you have an obsessive dependence on sedative drugs and you take them all the time. And your alcohol consumption is limited to a few beers or glasses of wine at night."

"You don't believe me."

"Well, Patrick, let's just say that I think you're probably grossly underestimating what you're taking. Don't get me wrong. The drug dependence that you described would clearly be enough to get you in here. But I've treated many physicians for drug dependency and alcoholism and normally a physician's involvement with drugs and alcohol is much more total and complete that what you described. I believe there is more to your story."

"Hey, goddamnit, I'm not lying, nor am I underestimating. You're being unfair. I've tried to be as open and honest as I could possibly be, and it's not been easy. Do you have any idea of the disgrace, the inexpressible ignominy of being drug dependent? I've told you everything. What I told you, I never thought I could tell anyone. I feel foolish."

We stared at each other. He apparently unmoved, and me angry, breathing loudly through my nose.

"Patrick, the hallmark of addiction is dishonesty. Addiction is a disease that flourishes and progresses because the person is unable to be honest with himself. If you had ever stopped and thought what you were doing, you would have done something about it long ago. But you didn't. If you've been dishonest with yourself for so long, how can I expect that you're being honest with me now? You came here as an addict, and I'm fairly certain that you're still toxic from whatever drugs you were taking. Do you understand why I can't fully rely on your story? I'm not trying to humiliate you. That would serve no purpose."

I slumped back into my chair. He was kind enough to look away from me and occupied a few moments with lighting a cigarette.

"Did you ever try to stop?"

"Yes. But I couldn't. A couple of years ago I even went to a psychiatrist about the problem. He told me I was taking sedatives because I was anxious and depressed. He said that the anxiety and depression needed to be treated before I'd be able to get off the tranquilizers and sleeping pills."

"How did he treat your anxiety and depression?"

"He added Mellaril and Tofranil to my daily drug regimen."

Randolph closed his eyes and slowly shook his head.

"Well, Patrick, don't be angry with him. We only diagnose what we know, and we only know what we learn. About fifty percent of the alcoholics who are here have sought treatment from a physician before we get them. Invariably they've been put on Valium to, quote, calm them down so they won't drink so much. When we get them then, they're cross-addicted to alcohol and Valium. And that's tough to treat." Randolph shook his head again. "There's a lot of ignorance out there."

"What's your success rate here?"

"Just consider the fact that you have a hundred percent chance for recovery."

"So I have four weeks to change my life."

"No, Patrick, you'll have longer than that. Didn't you know we almost always keep doctors who are on drugs at least seven weeks?"

I jumped out of my chair.

"I didn't know that. How the hell was I supposed to know? No one told me. How am I going to support myself for seven weeks? I made plans to be away for only twenty-eight days. I'm trying to build a practice. I'll lose everything I worked for. I just cannot, will not stay longer than four weeks. No way."

He sat back in his chair and looked at the ceiling.

"Well, let me put it this way. With rare exception we recommend to all physicians that they stay longer than four weeks."

"How can I be a rare exception?"

"It will depend on the severity of your withdrawal, how well you sleep at night, and your participation in Group Therapy."

"How the hell severe can withdrawal be when I'm just coming off sedatives?"

"Valium withdrawal is notorious for causing seizures and sometimes hallucinations. Beginning tonight you'll be on Dilantin, and we'll give you decreasing amounts of Valium over the next three days. Your blood level of Dilantin should be sufficient in seventy-two hours to prevent you from having seizures."

"I won't take the Valium."

"We can't force you. But you're being foolish. Unless you have any more questions, it's time for your physical."

He was performing on me what was undoubtedly the finest physical examination I had ever had. He was, however, spending an inordinate amount of time percussing and palpating for my liver.

"Your liver's slightly enlarged . . . about two finger breadths."

"Goddamnit! You just have to believe that I'm an alcoholic. I don't drink any more than I told you. It's absolutely devastating to me not to be believed."

The physical exam was complete, and I started dressing.

"Being searched was my first humiliation. Now you are assuming that I'm dishonest. That's the second. How many more?"

The question was not meant to be rhetorical, but he either thought it was or disregarded it.

"Are you a psychiatrist?" I asked.

"No. I would soon become impatient with hand holding. I'm an internist. Fifty percent of my time here is spent on research. I'm trying to find a way to make the prescription sedative drugs non-addictive." He sighed. "That may not be possible."

I stood.

"Well, what is my admitting diagnosis?"

"Chemical dependency, Soft drugs, Voluntary admission. Also, Hepatomegaly, slight, Etiology uncertain."

"Then you do believe my story."

"I didn't say that. Your diagnosis isn't written in stone. I can change it." He inhaled deeply. "Patrick, you're a very sick man. But you'll get better if you do what we tell you. I promise you that."

When I got back to my room, daylight was vanishing. And so was my enthusiasm for this experience. Through my large window I could see past the entrance to the hospital. There were houses, small and very close together. Inside those houses people were living normal lives, surrounded by their families. I began to feel unregenerate envy for those people whom I had never met and could not even see. My mood was becoming dysphoric, and I was no longer comfortable being alone with myself. It was time to seek the company of my fellow addicts.

There they were, sitting in the Happy Valley lounge. The pretty blond who had come into the hospital at the same time I did looked up as I walked in. I could see her name tag. Melanie. MacGregor, Gordon, and Steve were playing cards and actually appearing to have a good time.

I sat down, and the bald guy to my right was looking at the black and white television and was smiling. *The Newlywed Game* was on and undoubtedly was delighting Canada and the United States into fits of hysteria. On the screen a brutally unattractive woman with large hands was reviling her small husband because he had made an oblique reference to her apparently enormous ass. The audience made noises of unrestrained glee. My bald friend was now convulsing with laughter. He looked at me hoping I, too, would be enjoying with him this moment of elegant humor. He instead caught me staring at him and making a value judgment. He reached out his hand to me.

"Hi, I'm Walter."

I reached for his hand, embarrassed because my palm was sweating. After we shook hands, I saw him unobtrusively wipe his palm off on his pants.

"When did you get here, Walter?"

"My wife, Lucy, came in this afternoon. Drunk as a skunk. She's the patient. She's in her room. I should be with her, but I just have to watch this program. It's my favorite. Do you ever watch *The Newlyweds?*"

"I sure don't."

"It's really a lot of fun. The wife, she don't like it. She says it's vulgar and profane. She always says that TV is directed at people who can't comprehend complexities or deal with abstractions. But hell, man, how would she know. She's in the booze most of the time."

I got up to leave.

"Hey, Pat, how's it goin'?" MacGregor was smiling.

"Just fine. I'm having a swell time," I said, going out the door.

I went back to my room and sat on my bed.

"This is bullshit," I said to no one.

A knock on the door, and in walked a thin, pretty brunette. She was dressed casually, and I had no idea who she was until I saw the medicine cup.

"I'm Reggie," she said. "I'm the evening nurse. How do you feel?"

"Suicidal."

"Really?" I had worried her.

"No, not yet."

"I have some medicine for you. I also brought some Valium along in case you changed your mind. Dr. Randolph told me to encourage you to take it."

"Nope."

She dropped a large white pill and a capsule onto my palm and handed me a cup of water.

I looked at them.

"The capsule is Dilantin," I said. "What's the white pill?"

"Antabuse. Dr. Randolph said you were supposed to be taking it before you came in here."

"I didn't. And I'm not taking it now. I'm not a goddamn alcoholic. Why should I take Antabuse?"

I felt smug.

"In here we like patients to develop good habits. For you, taking Antabuse is a good habit."

"I'm sorry," I said, "that's not good enough."

She took the Antabuse and put it back in the cup. I swallowed the Dilantin without water. I had become expert at taking pills dry.

"A nurse will be coming into your room at least every hour tonight. If you start having problems, talk to her. She's very good. If you need a doctor, we can get one. Have a good night, Patrick."

It was going to be difficult. I couldn't remember the last time I had tried to sleep without having reduced myself to oblivion with a handful of drugs. I have always been someone with an extremely critical conscience. This was clearly going to be a time for self-recrimination.

The night went slowly. The silence and the darkness were broken approximately every hour. At fifteen minutes past each hour, the door to my room would open, and the night nurse, the glow of the bright light from the hall behind her, presented herself as an apparition.

She would say something unintelligible and I would try to affect a smile and give a wave. And then the door would close, and the darkness and the silence would settle around me again.

7

I MUST have fallen asleep, because I woke abruptly when the door of my room crashed against the wall. Randolph was standing over me.

"You refused to take the Antabuse last night. Why?"

"I don't know why I should take it."

He assumed a defiant pose.

"Right now it's not important to me that you do know why. I don't have to explain to you everything I do. You aren't calling the shots here. I am."

"I'm not going to take it until I know why."

He glared at me.

"I'm not screwing around with you. Either agree to take the Antabuse or get out."

"You're a real sweetheart," I said. "Where did you learn your bedside manner, Auschwitz?"

"Well?" he asked, impatiently.

"I'll take it," I said. "Under protest."

He turned and blustered out of the room. I had just been humiliated for the third time in less than twenty-four hours.

Breakfast was at eight-thirty for those of us in Happy Valley. Mac-Gregor, his eyes red and hands shaking, sat across from me. With each attempt to drink from his cup, coffee spilled on his shirt. He was embarrassed.

"This is a lost cause. Every time I get off the sauce I get like this."

I helped him light his cigarette, and after several puffs he calmed down to a manageable state of agitation. He coughed spasmodically after every drag of his cigarette. The smoking and the coughing by most of the patients were annoying me. It seemed as if half the patients here had severe symptomatic emphysema.

"You know, MacGregor, those goddamn cigarettes will kill you just as dead as alcohol will."

"But they won't destroy my family."

Gordon and Steve joined us. The first night had not treated any of us gently. Steve was frowning and perspiring. It was hard not to look at him.

"I'm suffering from an acute lack of Valium," he said. "The nurse wanted to give me some Valium last night, but that's some of the shit that got me in here. Besides, I haven't taken any in a couple of days."

"Steve, you really ought to take some if they tell you to," said Gordon. "It's just possible they may know what they're talking about. What do you think, Pat?"

"You probably ought to do what they say, Steve," I said and felt like a hypocrite.

Gordon was looking at me and smiling. Apparently I had not been convincing.

"Pat, you don't look as bad as the rest of us." It was MacGregor, and he seemed upset by the fact that I was neither trembling nor perspiring.

"I don't feel bad at all, except for being tired."

"I was reading last night," said Gordon, "that withdrawal from drugs may not start for up to ten days after coming in here."

"Then Pat has something to look forward to," MacGregor said with some enjoyment.

"Today," said Gordon, "we have psychological testing, and if they find we are sufficiently crazy, we get to see the spook."

"The what?" I asked.

"The psychiatrist, Dr. Francis Xavier O'Malley. I saw him briefly yesterday. He's an inscrutable son of a bitch. Speaks in well-rehearsed aphorisms."

"You obviously don't like the man."

"It's not that I didn't like him. I just doubt that he's burdened with compassion. Detachment seems to come easy for him."

Steve became rigid and looked frightened. His face was wet, and his eyes had glazed over. He was biting his tongue, and blood mixed with saliva poured from his mouth. He gave a plaintive wail and fell to the floor. He became incontinent. The seizure was over in a few moments, and he lay on the floor unconscious. A hospital attendant was with him momentarily and turned his head to the side so he wouldn't aspirate. We were quickly marshaled out of the dining area.

We sat in the Happy Valley lounge in silence. Edith walked in. She was smiling.

"Steve's being examined by the doctor," she said. "We're pretty sure he'll be all right. What you just saw was not pleasant. But think how bad it would have been had it happened on the street somewhere."

"But that wouldn't have happened if he had still been on Valium." It was MacGregor.

"We offered him a tranquilizer last night," she said. "He wouldn't take it. But he may have had severe withdrawal anyway. He also drank very heavily."

MacGregor was still mad.

"Well, I bet he was better off before he came into the hospital than he is now."

Edith remained calm.

"When I saw Steve a few minutes ago, I told him all of you would be upset. He gave me his permission to tell you some general things about himself that might help relieve some of you." Edith was making eye contact with each of us.

"Yesterday Steve told me that he considered himself ineffectual as a husband, as a father, and in general as a person. He already attempted suicide once. In here, he will be given the opportunity to salvage the rest of his life. So no, I don't agree that he was better off before coming here, and I don't feel sorry for him now. He's had a temporary setback."

Edith had a soft manner and a genuine smile. She had effectively reduced the palpable sense of gloom.

"The first few days here are very difficult. But all of you did the right thing by coming here. I want you all to feel very good about yourselves because you made the decision to be admitted."

She paused.

"There are several things we need to talk about for a few minutes. It may not be necessary to say this, especially after what happened to Steve, but they must be said. You probably don't feel as if you're in a hospital. You walk around here in jeans and smoke and you can go around the grounds whenever you like. Many of you don't even feel acutely ill. But, folks, this *is* a hospital and you *are* sick in ways only each of you know best.

"You are here because you abused a chemical, alcohol or pills, and if any of you are found to have taken a drink or a pill not prescribed for you by a doctor here, you will be asked to leave. To help in that regard, any time you leave the hospital grounds, you will have your breath analyzed for alcohol when you return. And we will be doing spot urine checks on you to see if any drugs show that were not prescribed."

"Edith," said Melanie, "I'm getting the impression that you people are going to attempt to control our lives while we're here. I don't like being dominated by anybody."

"This may sound trite, Melanie, but our sole purpose in being here is to help you regain control of your life. So you must follow the rules. There will be no exceptions. We cannot negotiate with every new group of patients. The hospital has stood the test of time. We think we do a pretty good job."

Edith spoke without sounding imperious or judgmental.

"You'll be going for psychometric testing in a few minutes. If your tests indicate something that concerns us, you'll be asked to spend some time this afternoon with Dr. O'Malley, our psychiatrist."

She stood.

"If there are no questions, you better be off for your testing. Patrick, I want to see you a minute."

I went to her, and she waited to speak until everyone had gone.

"Patrick, you haven't got off to a good start. You tried to sneak drugs in with you, and you refused your Antabuse last night. I want you to remember about the urine screening that we will be doing on you periodically.

"After a few days most of the drugs that you took before you came in should be gone from your system. If any new drugs show up that Dr. Randolph did not prescribe, we will ask you to leave. Don't blow this opportunity, Patrick. As for not taking the Antabuse, I suspect Dr. Randolph chatted with you about that already."

"Chatted? Jesus Christ!"

"Dr. Randolph does not like to have his orders challenged. He can become indelicate when someone—a patient—questions his orders. It's best not to do that."

"No one told me I would be given Antabuse. Or why. So I refused to take it. I don't think it's unreasonable to ask for an explanation why I'm to take a drug that I don't feel is indicated."

"When you were admitted, you signed a consent form for treatment. That included Antabuse. The reason we want you to take

Antabuse is very simple. We have found that when people who have been on drugs leave the hospital, they sometimes turn to alcohol. You know that Antabuse will make you violently ill if you drink after taking it. So we ask all the drug patients to start taking Antabuse while they're in the hospital and for at least two years after they leave."

"Would it have been so goddamn difficult for someone to have told me that yesterday?"

"Most patients don't ask. They do what we tell them."

"Will I be considered a threat if I ask for reasons?"

"No," she smiled, "just a pain in the ass."

I joined my group around a rectangular table in a small room. A young woman with brown frizzy hair walked in and was carrying a bundle of papers. She looked at us and smiled.

"Hello, I'm Donna. I'm a psychologist, and we're going to do some testing, O.K.? The purpose of this testing is to give us some idea of your intelligence, your mood, your level of impairment, and your self-image, O.K.?"

MacGregor stood up.

"Lady," he said, "I can save you a lot of time. I'm dumb, depressed, fucked up, and an asshole. Now can I go?"

"You certainly think in basic terms," Donna said.

"I can be very basic," MacGregor said and leered at her.

Donna appeared bemused but unruffled. She looked away from MacGregor.

"Let's start now, O.K.?"

Gordon was sitting next to me and started chuckling.

"Donna," he said, "after everything you say you ask 'O.K.?' Why must you continually seek approval?"

"It's just a nervous habit. I'll try to stop, O.K.?"

First we completed a Personality Inventory Questionnaire. There were a lot of thinly disguised questions attempting to find out if we were depressed, sexually deviant, psychotic, or morons. That took two hours.

Next we had to draw a person. I finished and saw Donna looking at my drawing.

"Hmmm," she said.

I looked at her and smiled.

"O.K.?" she asked, meaning, I think, "Are you finished?"

She looked at my drawing again and then gave me a thoughtful look. I was finished but considered I might be giving something about myself away.

"I just want to touch it up before I turn it in," I said. "Give me a minute."

"Call me back when you're finished, then, O.K.?"

She walked away, and I grabbed Gordon's arm.

"Do you see anything about this drawing that's unusual?" I whispered.

Gordon made an exaggerated grimace and started laughing. Everyone looked.

"Pat, your person has no feet, only three fingers on the left hand, and no right ear. I can't tell what sex it is."

MacGregor began cackling.

"Pat's fucked up. Pat's fucked up."

Donna came running.

"Stop that now, O.K.?"

She grabbed the drawing out of Gordon's hand before I could. She had the evidence.

Dr. Francis Xavier O'Malley watched me as I entered his office. He greeted me, and I went to the chair in front of his desk. He settled into his chair and we stared at each other. His hair was long and parted in the middle, and he had a deep black beard and mustache. This face could have made the impression on the Shroud of Turin. He moved forward in his chair and took a pen and notebook from his desk. His eyes left me briefly, but then he resumed his stare. He crossed his legs and rested the notebook on his left knee. I was getting bored so I looked away.

The curtains were closed, and the only light came from four small aluminum fixtures that were in the ceiling above the desk. The light from each fixture spotlighted a certain area. One was on him, one on me sitting in front of his desk, one on a fish tank that had water but no fish, and the fourth highlighted his diplomas that hung on the wall off to my left.

"Why did you come to the hospital, Patrick?"

"Well," I said, "I take a lot of downers. And I didn't have the freedom to stop."

He wrote in his notebook.

"But why did you come in at this time? Were you found out by someone? Had you almost killed a patient? Has your wife left you?"

"I was very unhappy," I answered. "Nothing terribly violent had happened to me, though. I just slowly realized that I was doing something to myself that was very cruel. It was time to do something about it. It was a time to stop."

"A rare display of Ecclesiastical wisdom," he said.

"I took drugs for a long time. I don't know why it took me so long to see myself as an addict."

"That," he said, "is uncertain tribute to the mind and how it can prevent unpleasant self-scrutiny."

There were a few moments of silence in which he tried to appear casual. It didn't work.

"How do you feel right now?" he asked.

"Depressed."

"Your tests did show that. They also indicate that you have poor self-esteem, which is, of course, related to the depression. Your tests also show you to be intelligent, but that right now your judgment may be slightly impaired."

"And that," I said, "would suggest that I may be entertaining thoughts of suicide."

"That's right. Are you?"

"No."

"Can you tell me why you're depressed?"

"I'm depressed because yesterday Randolph told me I'd probably be asked to stay longer than I had anticipated. I'm not prepared to suspend my life for longer than four weeks. I figured when I came here I'd only be staying a month, and that I would leave a healthy, happy man and could go back and resume my life."

"We try to discourage magical thinking," he said.

"Can you tell me why I'm going to be required to stay longer?"

"Well, that decision hasn't been made and won't be until the beginning of your fourth week. But I can tell you that we normally recycle doctors who have a drug problem."

"Recycle?" I laughed. "Like an aluminum can?"

"Recycle as in making them repeat the program. We found that when we sent physicians who were on drugs home after four weeks, we would soon get reports that they were back into drugs. It's very difficult for doctors who have a drug problem."

"Why?"

"There's no protection from drugs. There's nothing similar to Antabuse for drug addiction. And physicians live and work in a high anxiety environment. Physicians have a constant reexposure to drugs and have such easy access."

"How will keeping me here longer make any difference?"

"It may not. But I think the longer we keep you, the angrier you'll get. You'll develop the habit of abstinence from drugs and a sense of outrage that hopefully will maintain you the rest of your life. When you get out of this place and go back home, you will find that the world has not changed. But you will have."

"I'm not sure I understand."

"You will."

"Why didn't Randolph try to explain this? Maybe if he did, I wouldn't be so depressed."

"Well, Patrick, Randolph is an internist. He deals in enlarged organs and abnormal laboratory tests. He doesn't have to deal with ideas."

There was silence, and then O'Malley started writing in his notebook.

"What I would like to do right now," I said, "is to ask someone to forgive me. I just don't know who to ask."

O'Malley continued writing and didn't look up.

"It's pretty common here in the first few days for people to do a number on themselves. Self-recrimination and consequent self-directed anger are to be expected. Once you've realized this is an illness like any other . . ."

"Bullshit," I said. O'Malley looked up. "How can you dignify addiction by calling it an illness? What I have done to myself is immoral. I have performed a travesty on myself. Addiction should be put in the same category as suicide. It's something that is totally reprehensible."

His eyes narrowed.

"You're really beating yourself up. Pretty soon you'll need to stop that."

O'Malley wrote in his notebook.

"Do you have any questions before I let you go, Patrick?"

"Will I be seeing you again?"

"Yes. I'll put you on my schedule. We'll meet regularly. You concern me."

We were being served liver for dinner, so I only drank coffee. I sat with Melanie and told her about my encounter with O'Malley. She was to see him the following morning, and it clearly bothered her.

"It's not that I've been happily exempt from psychic pain," she explained; "it's just that psychotherapy is one crutch I wanted to do without."

"I liked O'Malley," I said. "His style isn't calculated to soothe. But he's not a sponge. He talks. He explains things. When I left his office, I felt pretty good. That's always been my measure of a psychiatrist's worth. I've had some experience."

"I don't even know why I'm supposed to see him." She was upset. "But there's a list of things about this hospital I'm not sure of. How do you feel? Are you glad you came?"

"Well, Melanie, I seriously doubt I'll ever be able to get off the pills. Drugs were an integral part of my life, my daily routine. But I had to try. This will be my one and only attempt. If I fail this, I won't try again."

I had said that with such finality that I was stunned for a moment.

"Melanie," I said, "what was your problem?"

"Uppers, downers, coke . . . I love coke. . . . Darvon . . . wine—cheap wine—ludes . . . love those ludes. . . ."

"Why did you come here?"

"I don't like myself." She slowly shook her head. "Nothing in my life is working. I've always blamed everybody but me. My life has to drastically change. The first thing I decided to do was to try to get rid of the drugs. If this doesn't work . . . well . . . there's always suicide." She smiled. "I tried it once . . . failed at that, too." She bent toward me. "When you can't even do suicide right, you know you're fucked up."

Gordon and another patient whom I didn't recognize joined us. Introductions were made. The man's name was Boone. As usual, Gordon's introduction of me ended with: ". . . and Pat's a doctor."

Boone stared at me. His prognathic jaw became more prominent. Some small talk was made. Boone spoke in a whiskey baritone. He talked a lot and gave me an occasional glare. There was clearly something he wanted to say to me, and he was not hiding it well. Soon his glare became steadfast.

"Boone," I said, "why do I bother you?"

"You're a fucking doctor. A doctor, a psychiatrist, is the cause of my being here. He gave my wife so many goddamn pills that she is little more than a zombie. She's overdosed a dozen times, and he won't take the pills away."

"But that doesn't explain why you're here," I said.

"My wife has virtually been taken away from me. She's in a

chemical straitjacket, and she was put there by an incompetent. So I drink. A lot. I've lost my job and my daughter. I have nothing because of that doctor. I don't like doctors."

"Boone," I said, "I'm very sorry. But I will not accept the blame for what you say another doctor did to your wife."

"Be careful what you say to me, doctor." Boone stood and pointed at me. "Remember, I warned you."

That night, my second night of voluntary incarceration, the March nineteenth group, my group, was alone together for the first time in an unstructured activity. We sat in Happy Valley lounge. The television was turned on, but it was more an annoyance than an object of interest. We would glance at each other and then look furtively away when the glance was met. We all knew we had ahead of us at least four weeks of forced intimacy.

"Let's go see Steve," I said to Gordon.

As we approached Steve's room, we saw Reggie, dressed in jeans, coming out. She saw us and smiled.

"He's all right. He's sleeping now. He'll be back with you tomorrow."

I had noticed that Gordon had been looking increasingly disconsolate for most of the evening. I had wanted to ask him what was wrong, but I was learning quickly that some patients here liked to keep some of their misery private.

"Pat, I probably won't even be here tomorrow. I have a business transaction that will be worth close to four thousand dollars to me. It just came up, and I'll need to get out of here for several hours tomorrow. I doubt if Randolph will let me out."

"You know he won't."

"I'll have to sign myself out, then."

"Gordon, for Christ's sake, this has got to be worth more to you than a few thousand dollars."

He didn't answer.

"Couldn't you transact the business over the phone?"

"No, I'm a gemologist. I have to be there with the stones."

"Well, Gordon, good luck with Randolph. That seems to be your only hope."

"My only chance is that I never drank or took drugs until after five or six o'clock. Maybe if I promise to be back before dinner, he might let me do it."

"And if he doesn't?"

"I'm gone."

"Will you try to get back in here again?"

"I don't know. Maybe this isn't worth it. I'm fifty-six. I've been an alcoholic for the last twenty years. I've been taking heavy doses of Dilaudid for ten years."

"How did you get Dilaudid?"

"I told you I'm a gemologist. Pharmacists have what I want. I have what they want. It's simple. This probably wouldn't have worked for me anyway. I've tried A.A., psychiatric hospitals, Antabuse. Nothing's worked."

I couldn't say anything to help him.

"I'm depressing the hell out of myself and you," he said. "Let's go back to the lounge."

I sat in the Happy Valley lounge and tried to read. I couldn't. I remembered Randolph had said my liver was enlarged. So I tried to feel for it.

"What are you doing?" It was a voice from across the room.

"Trying to palpate my liver," I said without looking up.

"Would that fall into the same category as self-abuse?"

"Randolph's a jerk. My liver's not big."

I looked up to see who I was talking to. It startled me. It was a puffy, yellow-orange human being.

"Hello," he said, "they call me Pumpkin. For obvious reasons. I'm just beginning my third week. I was asked to come down here and welcome the new people. I think they chose me to scare the shit out of people."

"What do you mean?"

"Well, about the third or fourth day here most people want to leave. If they see me, maybe they'll want to stay so they won't become like me. They tell me I'm a walking textbook of alcohol abuse."

People in the lounge were beginning to notice Pumpkin. He looked at me.

"My appearance is attention getting, wouldn't you say?"

The television was turned off. He pointed at MacGregor.

"How old would you say I am?"

"Forty-six."

"Wrong. Thirty-four. And now I will show you more of the ravages of demon rum. I will point to parts of my body and annotate accordingly."

He stood.

"Notice my eyes," he said, pointing to them. "They're yellow.

· 55 ·

And the color of my skin disgusts most people. My hue is because only twenty-five percent of my liver is functional. The color, I am told, is due to something called bilirubin, which my liver, such as it is, cannot metabolize anymore. Any questions?"

He was smiling.

"I'll go on, but I must warn you, it gets worse."

He took off his shirt. He raised his arms to shoulder level and stretched them out.

"My arms. Look at them. Thin and small, out of proportion to the rest of my body. My thighs are the same. 'Why?' you ask. Because my major food source for the last eight years has been alcohol. All carbohydrate. I've taken in virtually no protein and therefore whatever muscle I had has atrophied."

He stood in profile.

"You see my belly is very big. Why is that, pretty lady?" He looked at Melanie.

"Fat."

"Wrong. Fluid in my abdomen. The explanation for that has something to do with my cirrhosis and my advanced state of malnutrition. Is everyone sufficiently depressed, or should I go on?"

"Go on," MacGregor shouted. "We've already eaten our dinner."

"Look at my ankles," he shouted, as he pulled up his pants to his knees.

"Enormous. I haven't been able to wear shoes in over six months. But it's not fat. And certainly not muscle. Fluid due to—you guessed it—cirrhosis and malnutrition."

"With all that extra fluid you have in you," Melanie shouted between short bursts of laughter, "if you ever fell down, you could conceivably drown yourself."

"How the hell do you live like that?" MacGregor asked.

"Well," Pumpkin said, "I don't wear green, and I try not to sneeze. Any more questions?"

There were none.

"I have," he continued, "a body clearly diseased by alcohol. And next year, if I am still alive, I have been asked to be the poster person for Alcoholics Anonymous."

He stretched out his arms and bowed. His performance met with standing applause. He walked out.

Later, alone in my room, I decided it was time to write to Irene. She was home alone hundreds of miles away. I was terribly lonely for her. But I could not tell her how miserable I was. So I wrote about Melanie, MacGregor, Steve, Gordon, Boone, and Pumpkin. I determined right there I could not ever write to her about anything substantial. Not while I was in here.

A knock on my door and Reggie breezed in with my Dilantin and Antabuse. She also offered me a Valium. I took the Dilantin and Antabuse and refused the Valium.

"Why didn't you warn me about Randolph?" I asked.

"Would you have believed me?"

"Probably not. But, God, did he have a serious case of red ass! I'll do what he says from now on."

"Two days without your drugs. Have you had any unusual dreams? Or any jerking movements?"

"No hallucinations or seizures, Reggie."

"How did you sleep last night?"

"I drifted off now and then, but it was pretty rough. I felt very lonely . . . and afraid."

"Nothing intolerable?" There was something ominous in her tone.

"Why do you ask?"

"Well . . . guilt has a way of menacing people in their first week. Especially when the lights go out. I want you to take this as cautionary advice, Patrick. You will experience guilt. But it is a kind of pain that can be dissipated by talking about it. O.K.?"

I nodded.

"So use us. Talk to us. . . . Tell us what's going on. . . . Tell us how lousy you feel. Listening to people is the part of my job I enjoy the most."

"Thanks, Reggie. Thanks for your concern."

"Since I'm the chairman of the department, I was asked to talk to you. I've heard some things."

"What things, Andy?"

"I've known you for ten years, Pat. I handpicked you to be chief pediatric resident seven years ago. You're a bright, capable man. A good doctor."

"What things, Andy? Who's been talking about me? What are they saying?"

"It's the nurses mostly. And a few of the medical students. They tell me you look pretty groggy in the morning. And they say you call them by the wrong names . . . you go to the wrong floors to see patients . . . you're drinking coffee all the time . . . you're very nervous during your lectures.

"And they're beginning to question some of your orders."

He put his glasses on and pushed some papers on his desk. He picked up an order sheet and looked at it for a few seconds. His eyes then moved to me.

"This order for Lanoxin that you wrote three weeks ago for the baby in congestive heart failure . . ."

"The Stevenson baby. I remember. A simple miscalculation."

"That miscalculation could have cost the baby his life."

"We all make mistakes, damnit. Remember the appendix you missed six or seven years ago?"

"Yes, I remember," Andy laughed and slapped the desk. "You saved my ass on that one."

"I suppose they think I'm drinking. Right?"

He nodded.

"Nope. Wrong. I drink maybe two glasses of wine at night. Or a couple beers. That's all. Ask Irene. You know she wouldn't lie.

"Has anyone ever smelled booze on me? Or seen me with the shakes?"

He shook his head.

"But I have noticed one thing, Pat. Your personability has seemed to flatten out in the past couple years. And your sense of humor isn't what it once was."

"Just a midlife crisis, Andy. Questioning things. No good answers. No absolutes."

"Yeah. I went through that when I was about forty-two, forty-three maybe."

"Anything else, Andy?"

"Will you see somebody?"

"I've been seeing Scott Walsh. I'm making some progress."

"Oh, good! I'm glad to hear that. Well, I'll tell people everything's all right. That I've talked to you."

"Thanks, Andy. You're a good friend. I appreciate this."

He smiled.

"I knew you weren't a boozer, Pat. Or one of those drug addicts. You couldn't fool me."

8

THE MORNING of the third day did not arrive quickly. I know, because I had been watching for it all night. I stood in front of the mirror brushing my teeth, when Randolph's smiling face appeared in the mirror over my right shoulder.

"Why the smile?" I asked.

"If you will look out the window, you'll see we have the makings of a very nice day."

"That so?"

"How do you feel?" His concern was unmistakably clinical.

"Fine."

"How did you sleep?"

"Pretty good."

"You don't lie well," he said.

He disappeared from the mirror and went in the direction of the window of my room. Both my legs felt weak. I could hardly stand. I grabbed the sink with both hands. I could see myself in the mirror. I was struck by the total lack of color in my face. I went to my knees.

Randolph was still in my room, his voice imperceptible to me now. I sat on the floor. I heard a loud sound. It was my scream. A thousand tiny explosions went off inside my head. I felt myself fall backwards. My tongue was slipping to the back of my throat and blocking my airway. I lost control of my bladder and my bowels. I was certain I was dying as I slipped into unconsciousness.

The ceiling light was so brilliant I had to look away. I first saw Edith. She was smiling, but there was obvious concern in her face. She was holding my hand. I was terribly confused and frightened.

"What happened?" I asked.

"You had a seizure."

"I remember talking to Dr. Randolph. He said it was a nice day. That's the last thing I remember."

"Squeeze my hand, Patrick."

"I can't. I feel drained."

"We've given you a drug intravenously so you won't have a

seizure again. It will make you very sleepy. We'll be checking on you every few minutes."

She went toward the door.

"Edith," I called, "did Randolph see this happen?"

"He found you. You were choking on your tongue and you were blue. He was able to get your tongue out."

She opened the door and left. I looked out the window. Randolph was right. It was a nice day.

When I woke I could hear Randolph urging me to squeeze his fingers. I squeezed the hell out of them. He tested my reflexes.

"Your reflexes are intact," he said to me.

"I guess you saved my life."

"I guess I did."

"I'm not sure you did me a favor," I said. "Don't feel pleased with yourself."

"I feel very pleased with myself."

"Why?"

"Patrick, I guess I owe you an apology. Your urine tests so far indicate that you were taking only the drugs you told me about. Also, your liver profile showed no abnormally high values. If you were telling me the truth, you will be the only physician I ever treated whose problem was only soft drugs."

"Does that mean I'll get out of here in four weeks?"

"We won't discuss that anymore until the final decision is made. Don't ask me again."

He stood to leave.

"Any more reasonable questions before I go?"

"Do people normally have seizures just coming off soft drugs?"

"Every individual has a different seizure threshold. It's impossible to predict if someone will have a seizure even when we know the type and amount of drugs previously taken. That's why we give everybody Dilantin.

"If you had let us bring you down slowly off Valium, you probably would never have had a seizure. I think I can promise you that you will not convulse again, if that's any consolation."

Randolph affectionately squeezed my hand but did not seem comfortable even with such a small gesture of intimacy. He left the room.

9

It was now twenty-four hours since I had had the seizure. I still felt enervated physically and emotionally. I tried to avoid O'Malley's chilling stare. Finally, he looked at my chart.

"Your skull X rays are negative. Your Dilantin blood level is sufficient to prevent you from having another seizure. Randolph says you're neurologically intact."

He looked up at me.

"But how do you feel, Patrick?"

"Humble. I think if anyone right now were to look at me with anything but total approval, I'd cry."

"Why?"

"I guess I'm starting to realize that I am drug dependent. Has anyone ever died of disgrace?"

"You are right in the middle of a mutually reinforcing cycle of negative self-image and despair of the future."

"How do we break the cycle?"

"We won't be able to. Not right away. Our ally here is time. As you progress in the next few weeks, your attitude about yourself and about the future will gradually change. And during that time you and I will talk. I'll monitor your progress, and I won't interfere with it.

"Distorted and confused thinking can be interrupted with a variety of techniques."

"And what will be your technique with me?"

"I have several options. With some patients I retreat into a stereotype and become detached and formal. That wouldn't work with you. Some people need a full measure of approval. They need continuous reaffirmation of their worth. But you, I think, function at a somewhat higher level.

"I need to make you understand and appreciate exactly what is happening to you. And with you I will be aggressively honest. I think you can take it. Whether you want to or not, I don't know. I'll work on giving you a balanced view of yourself."

There was something about his manner and forcefulness that was helping me to gain confidence in him. And I needed somebody to have confidence in.

"Are you always so intolerably certain about things?" I asked.

"No. But you're experiencing a nondelusional affective neurotic disorder. And I feel fairly confident dealing with anxiety and situational depression.

"I'm not saying it won't get better. Tincture of time alone would assure it got better.

"But remember after our first meeting I told you that you concern me? I think you feel things more deeply than most people. So I intend to watch you closely. As with most things there are degrees of severity with depression."

"How bad will it get?"

"I wasn't blessed with the gift of prophecy."

"You weren't taking notes today."

"You aren't being apprehensive and cautious with me. I won't have to analyze your words and attempt to determine what you're trying to tell me. That's easy to understand.

"The seizure, I'm sure, was a real jolt to your psyche. You must feel fairly defenseless and vulnerable, and that frees you to be honest without being circumspect."

I stood to go. I was feeling stronger. When I got to the door, O'Malley called out.

"Patrick, I'm glad we got you while you're salvageable."

Gordon was standing in the lobby. He had on his coat, and his bags were packed. I walked up to him, and we looked at each other.

"Randolph wouldn't let me go out for a few hours. I've signed out against medical advice. I'm going home."

"Gordon, you live alone. The liquor and pills will be there when you get home. How will you handle that?"

"I don't know. Maybe I won't be able to."

"Do you think you'll try again?"

"Probably not. You might say," he paused and exhaled softly, "that I'm a dead man."

He walked away. I felt incredibly sad for him. I didn't feel like being alone and went back to Happy Valley. Edith was at the Nurses' Station, and she motioned for me.

"Your wife called yesterday. I talked to her. I didn't tell her what happened. I thought I'd let you do that."

"I'm not going to tell her I had a seizure. I couldn't. I don't know how she would take it."

"That would be wrong. You must tell her. You have to begin the groundwork for honesty with your wife. This is the time."

I went to my room and stared at the phone. I was actually trembling at the thought of talking to my own wife. Although Irene and I had on almost every occasion been open and honest with each other, there was an undercurrent of dishonesty with us.

I had never admitted to her the number and infinite variety of pills I took. Some day soon I would have to confront that. But not now. Jesus, not now. I just was not ready to admit how severe my problem was. If I told her I had had a seizure, she would know.

My palms were ornamented with a shiny glaze of moisture. I held the receiver with both hands.

"Hello."

Her tone was expectant. As if she were waiting for good news.

"Hi, Babes."

"Pat! It's been days. Why haven't you called? Are you all right?"

"I'm fine."

"I called yesterday and talked to Edith. She's so nice. She told me you were sleeping. I couldn't figure why they would let you sleep in the middle of the day. She told me she would have you explain."

"Well, I've been having trouble with insomnia and . . ."

I couldn't lie.

"Babes, I had a seizure yesterday. I slept most of the day afterward. Seizures have a way of depleting you of energy. But I'm all right now. They said I wouldn't have a seizure again."

I could hear nothing. She was crying and didn't want me to know.

"My problem with drugs was worse than either of us thought. I'm sorry I've done this to you."

"Should I come?" she asked.

"No. There is nothing you could do for me here. This is something I have to do alone. I can't share this with you. I'm pretty depressed about everything that's happened. Randolph really blew me away the first day. He told me I might have to repeat the program. That would mean I'd be here an extra three weeks. I won't do that."

"I don't want you to stay any longer. I won't let you."

"Thanks. I'm glad you feel that way."

"How do you feel? What's your mood like? Have you made any friends?"

"I don't like being alone, so I constantly am seeking out other people. But then when I talk to them, I can't help getting involved in their sadness. Jesus, there's so much misery in here. As for my mood, my only available emotion lies somewhere between rage and oppressive gloom."

"God, Pat, you sound just awful."

"Things will get better. They have to. I just wasn't prepared for the violent mood swings."

She was crying again, and I was becoming less able to deal with that. We exchanged intimate reminders of how much we missed each other.

"Pat, would you mind terribly if I told some of our friends where you are? I can't keep lying. But worse than that, I need to talk to people about this. I want to be able to tell someone just how lonely I am. I'm not good at silent suffering. I need to tell some people that I hurt."

"No! Absolutely not. You're not to tell anyone. We've already discussed this. If the medical society found out, I'd be through. I'll tell Gabe when I get home. I don't want Adrian to ever find out. Or Sarah."

"I don't think you give people much credit. You're embarrassed because you developed a problem which is an occupational hazard many doctors . . ."

"I've already told you not to tell anyone. The discussion is *over*. You're upsetting me, and I don't need that."

"I didn't expect you would get so angry. I'm just so lonely. I'm sorry. I know it must be just dreadful for you. I wish I could be there. I care so much for you. Write me. Please."

"Good-bye, Babes."

I went to the Happy Valley lounge and sat alone. I was beginning to feel more unhappy than I ever had been in my life. I began to feel impatient and restless.

"Oh, God," I thought, "please don't let me have a seizure again."

I noticed over in the corner of the room a single figure sitting alone. She had been watching me. She was smiling timidly. She knew I was embarrassed by her presence. She lit a cigarette.

"I'm sorry," she said. "I should have spoken when you came in. You look like you're having a difficult time."

"I am. I don't know what the hell is going on."

I looked at her.

"Who are you?"

"My name is Lucy. I came in Monday. This is the first I've been out of my room. I celebrated my arrival here between the car and the hospital door with about eight ounces of scotch. I've been pretty sick. They told me I'm experiencing severe emotional and physical withdrawal symptoms.

"What do they expect? They've deprived me of my sole source of reassurance—scotch. Even my husband, Walter, is second to alcohol. I don't know how he stands me."

I began to feel a bit more self-possessed, but I still trembled perceptibly and perspired openly.

"You are starting to look a little better," she said. "How about some dinner?"

Lucy, MacGregor, and I sat with a short little man with close-cropped hair and an enormous belly. The little man assumed that since I was an American—a "foreigner"—I would be interested in discussing politics.

"We are in rather a unique position being so close to the States. It's like sleeping in bed with an elephant. We have no idea what you're thinking, but by God, when you roll, so do we."

When he saw I listened with something less than unqualified enthusiasm, he disregarded me and talked to Lucy about himself.

"I'll be getting out of here in a week, and I have all sorts of plans."

"What are they?" She obliged him.

"Because of the demands of my job, I went home and drank every night. I now have plans for getting out every night of the week. Four of those nights I'll be at A.A. meetings. I'm not married, so I can do that. And on weekends I will go up to my brother's cabin in the woods. That should help relieve some of the pressures."

"Jesus! What kind of work do you do?" MacGregor asked.

"I'm a librarian."

"Let me ask you a question," I said.

He gave me his total concentration.

"When and how do they make the decision who is going to have to repeat the program?"

"You mean be recycled."

"Yeah."

He thought for a moment. He was apparently beginning to feel important.

"On the Monday morning of your fourth week here, the doctors—Randolph and O'Malley—and your group therapist and all the nurses you've been involved with meet and discuss your progress. Obviously, the severity of your withdrawal and your attitude are important. Are you having much of a withdrawal?"

"My physical withdrawal was sudden and fairly dramatic. I threw a fit on my bathroom floor. Randolph saw it."

"You may be here into the next millennium," he said with a half-smile.

That was neither funny nor appreciated.

"I would suggest one thing," he continued in his much-too-serious tone. "Smile a lot. You can't bullshit Randolph or O'Malley. But we deal with the nurses on a fairly superficial level, yet their input is pretty important. Talk to them. Tell them how glad you are to be here."

I looked at Lucy.

"I never thought I'd have to scheme to get out of here," I said.

But I knew I'd do it.

A knock on my door and Reggie came in with my Dilantin and Antabuse. I had practiced looking relaxed and smiling. I was ready for her. She handed me the pills.

"Patrick, are you all right? You don't look good tonight."

"But I'm feeling beamish. I really am. No kidding. I feel relaxed, and my palms aren't sweating as much. Everything's just fine. Things are going well. I'm glad I'm here. This is a nice place."

She laughed.

"Most patients don't start contriving to look happy for several weeks. You've started early." She sat on my bed. "Would you like to talk for a while?"

"No. I just think I'll sit over here and gnash my teeth in frustration."

"There's probably very little I can say to make you less unhappy. But this is the fourth day of your first week. The days of your first week go very slowly. You're aware of every moment. You don't know what your mood will be in thirty seconds. Everything is new. Your nerves are raw. You're scared. You're angry, frustrated, and it looks like the end will never come. But things do get better.

"Look at the patients in their fourth week. Most of them are smiling and feel pretty good about themselves. This program works. I know."

"Were you a patient here, Reggie?"

"Eighteen months ago. Codeine. Six years before I came here as a patient I had a spinal fusion. I was prescribed codeine for pain. I just couldn't get off it. I knew I was addicted. My doctor knew I was addicted. But I'd keep asking for a prescription, and he would keep giving it to me. It was easier for him that way. He didn't have to deal with an iatrogenic codeine addiction. Finally the pharmacist refused to fill the prescription for codeine that he had been filling for five years.

"He called my doctor and told him he thought I was hooked. After five years. Can you believe it? So my doctor not only stopped writing prescriptions—he had to then—he stopped seeing me. I then went to a psychiatrist. She helped me and eventually got me in here as a patient."

"What made you decide to seek treatment?"

"Well, my husband left me and took our son. He saw that I had lost control of my life. I lived to take codeine. I thought if I came in for treatment I could get them back. Of course I only came in here as a gesture. I never thought it would work for me. But during the nine weeks in here, I gradually regained control. I never got my husband or my son back. I had hurt them too much. But I do have my self-esteem."

"Any relapses?"

"No. As trite as it sounds, I take one day at a time. That works for me. I used to go to A.A. meetings, and those really helped. But since I started working here, I have a nightly reminder of where I was, and I'll never take another codeine.

"I spend a few hours in the early evening while I'm on duty answering calls from former patients who are having problems. That may be a poor substitute for a husband and a son. But it's important. And I'm good at it.

"I never go home anymore and cry because of what might have been. That's in the past. There's nothing I can do about what has happened. But I can control what I will do each day if I just take one at a time. I know if I stay off drugs for that day that I will be productive with my life. And working here, I have daily opportunities to help people."

She paused, and I was afraid she was going to stop. But she didn't.

"Self-respect, like so many other things, is something you rarely think about until you find it has slipped away. I know what it's like to live without it. I have it now, and I'll never be without it again. That's the only thing in my future that I can predict with certainty."

She smiled at me.

"And you, my beamish boy, will one day soon have to stop looking back and get on with the business of your recovery. Our staff here is too good. We will not allow you to fail."

"Reggie, thanks for telling me about yourself. But you must be uniquely resilent."

"Every patient in here has a story just as bad or worse. Every patient in this hospital has his or her own personal agony and, like you, is fighting a very difficult, a very lonely battle. The battle we fight is never really won. Although I guess there is a certain victory in the fight itself."

I was beginning to feel for the first time since I'd been in the hospital that I was actually learning something about addiction. And there wasn't that unequal physician-patient relationship, with its implied omniscient-ignorant uneasiness. I was beginning to feel good. Here was a person—a young woman—who had a problem at least as serious as mine, and she beat it. And she was sitting there smiling.

"One more question, Reggie. How long does it take to develop that blatant, uncompromising honesty about yourself? You talk with so much openness and candor. I admire that, because I could never do it."

"It took me a long time. Too long. My addiction was destroying my life, but I kept denying it. Seeing a psychiatrist helped. Every time we met she made me talk about it. And we talked about every gruesome detail. That was the first step. I was then able to talk about it to one other person.

"Then I came here and found in Group Therapy that I had to talk about it in front of other people. At first that was almost impossible. But then other people began talking about themselves. It's such a release, such good therapy when you talk about your habit. Probably the best thing was that I found other people cared. I mean they really cared. You'll see what I'm talking about."

She stood.

"Well, Patrick, I have to go and push some pills and calm the multitudes. I've enjoyed talking to you."

I walked her to the door, and I put my arm around her. She felt so small and fragile, as if she could be easily broken. But of course she couldn't be. Not this lady.

"Patrick, I don't pretend to be an authority on addiction. But I am an authority on my addiction, because I lived the experience. Sometimes talking to someone who actually has been where you are makes a difference. I hope we can talk again."

We smiled at each other. There was something between us now—
a certain affection—that I guess could come only from sharing with
someone a common vulnerability.

10

INSOMNIA is a lonely, boring experience. And tiring. I wonder if anyone ever gets used to it if it is a chronic problem.

Conventional wisdom has it that no one ever died from insomnia.
But is there anything written or stated that is both traditional and
profound about what effect a consistent lack of sleep has on the
quality of one's life? Insomnia is so frustrating. I don't know how to
deal with it, how to fight it. But what weapons are there?

Of course, maybe there is a medical reason for my insomnia. This
could be a rebound phenomenon from having been sedated for so
long. Maybe my body is telling me that I need to become more aware
of the world.

"Stay awake," it tells me. "You missed too much. And what you
haven't missed, you were not able to react to appropriately. This is
not punitive. You have to catch up on so much. Stay awake. Think
and feel and learn. Don't waste this time. Read. Write. Talk. Listen."

Insomnia is unfair. It is too high a price to pay. Trying to fight
insomnia is totally preoccupying. I cannot pretend to be interested in
anything else but getting to sleep. Occasionally thoughts of other
things come. And I grasp for them because they are a temporary
pause in the battle. Although some of the thoughts are not ones I
would have chosen, given a choice.

At a little after three o'clock this morning, I started remembering
my patient Charlie, a little eight-year-old blond-haired boy with cystic
fibrosis and severe lung disease. He was terminal, and everyone including Charlie knew it. All he wanted was for people to smile at
him. It is hard to watch an eight-year-old boy die of emphysema, desperately struggling for every breath. You want to comfort him. You
want to do anything you can do for him. But a genuine smile was all
he wanted.

Since it was no longer possible for him to talk, he and I devised a means to let people know he wasn't afraid. And that he loved them. When someone would look at him and he knew it was more difficult for them than it was for him, he would flash a peace sign. It invariably worked. He would get his smile.

Charlie's parents and I were with him just before he died. We didn't think he was conscious. His blood oxygen level should not have allowed it. But I remember his eyes slowly, very slowly opening. His right hand moved. He brought it up in what must have taken all the strength and courage that was left for him in this life. Very weakly Charlie gave us the peace sign. Then he was gone.

I saw his parents smile. I knew Charlie would have liked that. His last gesture told us that it was all right. He was ready. He wasn't afraid.

We all then cried unashamedly. We hugged each other and talked about Charlie. I think he knew he lessened for us the impact of his death.

"It's the first time we ever had two members of one group have seizures. I'm glad they weren't synchronized."

We sat surrounding Edith in the Happy Valley lounge.

"We encourage you to get out and walk the hospital grounds Saturday and Sunday. We're having a fairly mild March in Toronto. It really is nice. Also, getting outside may be the only salvation for your lungs, which are constantly being abused by cigarette smoke.

"A physical therapist will be around to see each one of you today. She will be involved in teaching you the relaxation techniques that we employ. She will also begin to involve you in the physical exercise part of the program starting for you next week.

"On Sunday morning you will have a general meeting and a talk. The talk will not be religious, but I hope it will be inspirational. We want you to get better, but not for the wrong reason."

"God is not involved in the treatment program?" asked Lucy in a neutral tone.

"I'm glad they keep God out of it," said Boone. "I used to go to church. It didn't get me anywhere. So I stopped going. I think I'm better off."

"Yeah," said Steve. "Look where you are now."

"I didn't come here to save my soul," Boone fumed. "I came here to save my ass."

"We don't patently exclude God from the treatment program,"

said Edith. "If you want God's help, ask for it. We just do not specifically include religious activities. There are religious services all over Toronto. If you want to attend a church, we'll try to arrange that for you.

"Hogarth is a public hospital. We are not affiliated with any church."

"What about A.A.?" asked MacGregor. "Are there A.A. meetings here?"

"There are several Alcoholics Anonymous meetings here on Sunday and two every night of the week. There is one right after your general meeting on Sunday morning. You aren't forced to go. But we strongly suggest that you attend. We hope you are attracted to A.A., and we feel that involving yourself in A.A. is critical to sobriety once you leave us."

"A.A. didn't work for me either," said Boone. "I got nothing out of those meetings. And I won't go."

"You're a real pioneer, Boone," said MacGregor, obviously impatient.

"Hey, I know what works for me and what doesn't. I won't badmouth A.A. I know it's saved millions of lives. I'm responsible for my life. I'll make my own decisions."

"Boone does have a point," Edith said. "We are all responsible for ourselves. But I think there are very few people who could leave this hospital without having some support in their community and remain sober.

"I would caution you, Boone, not to summarily dismiss both God and A.A. without some serious reconsideration."

Edith seemed to be amused with herself.

"I think you will all be glad when you get into Group Therapy. You won't have to listen to my prattle."

"Edith," I asked, "when do we get out of Happy Valley? This floor not only has a bad name, it's joyless and oppressive."

"Well, I work on this floor every day, and I like it. And the floor was named Happy Valley by patients."

"Were they coming or leaving?" asked Melanie.

Edith disregarded the question. "All of you will be moving up to the fourth floor tomorrow morning."

It seemed the appropriate time to break up. We rustled in our chairs.

"One more item, people. You'll be getting a replacement for Gordon. He's flying in from up North and he'll be here this afternoon. We have a three-month waiting list. It wasn't difficult to get someone to come on short notice."

Steve and I shared in the disgrace of having had seizures. We jokingly agreed that in a hospital full of moral syphilitics, rakish and dissolute people, we were the nadir.

"Actually," I said, "I convulsed because I was overdosed on Antabuse."

Steve laughed.

"You know," he said, "I refused to take Antabuse. I've been on it before, and it gave me headaches and I became impotent. I also smelled like a garlic bulb. Randolph put me on Temposil, which will make you just as sick as Antabuse will if you drink."

"Garlic. That's it. I've noticed a certain unpleasant smell coming from some of the people who've been here a couple of weeks. One more damn humiliation they inflict on us."

I felt two quick jolts of pain on my right shoulder. I turned quickly and saw a long, dangerous-looking index finger zeroing in on my shoulder again. I readied myself for pain. But it did not strike a third time. I stood up and faced a tall, broad-shouldered woman. Her short red hair was wet and brushed back behind her ears.

"Patrick?"

"Yes."

"My name is Karren. That's with two *rs*. Follow me. We'll go to your room."

She turned, walked, and I followed, picking up the smell of soap.

Karren wore a white sleeveless blouse and black polyester pants which were tight enough to suggest definite firmness in the muscles of her legs. She walked silently, bent her knees slightly, and kept her spine erect.

In my room she sat in a manner suggesting royalty. She wore no makeup and had large eyes and a sensuous mouth. She was not beautiful, but her looks were intriguing. There was something about her face that suggested she was both complex and passionate, like a character in an Ingmar Bergman film.

"I'm a physical therapist," she said. "I have several purposes here. I am going to introduce you to relaxation techniques and an exercise program. How do you relax?"

"I don't. I can't."

"Do you exercise?"

"Yes. I swim regularly and I play racketball."

"Doesn't the exercise help you relax?"

"It used to."

"How's your sex life?" she asked as if it were the appropriate next question.

"Virually nonexistent."

"It sounds, Patrick, as if you have a lot of energy but very little exhilaration."

"I'd like to learn how to relax and enjoy things. I just can't. I guess I'm one of those type A personalities."

"That's bullshit," Karren said, a matter-of-fact tone to her voice. "Anyone can learn how to relax, how to respond to stress without using chemicals. And my job is to teach you some nonchemical coping skills. The first thing I'm going to expose you to is the relaxation response.

"We will have a relaxation class every afternoon, and you will practice alternately tensing and relaxing your muscles. You will have headphones in your room upstairs. Put them on every night when you go to bed. You will hear my voice telling you how to relax while trying to fall asleep."

"Then I will hopefully fall asleep every night with your mellifluous voice whispering in my ear. I'll bet there are some men in Toronto who would pay handsomely for that."

Karren responded to my attempt at casual humor with a quizzical look as if there were something deep implied.

"And what about my sex life?" I continued, still attempting levity.

She looked out the window and at something distant. Her lips parted ever so slightly.

"Are you impotent?"

The suddenness of the question and her directness stunned me.

"No," I said and hoped that my inflection suggested finality. I did not want to discuss it. Not with a physical therapist. Not with a woman.

She was staring at me again almost as if it were a challenge. I tried to summon some defiance, but she was clearly dominant. And we both knew it.

"I hope you will learn to trust me, Patrick."

"I'll need some time."

It was lunchtime but I wasn't hungry. The unrelenting unhappiness I had been experiencing since my admission was becoming acutely oppressive. I thought about Gordon. He had been good for me. We could talk. I started to feel panic. I couldn't be alone. Not now. My hands were quivering.

How does one prepare for a seizure?

I closed my eyes. I felt a sense of impending doom. It was like nothing I had ever experienced. I became terribly frightened. I needed to keep moving. I walked rapidly and fitfully toward the Nurses' Station. I saw Edith. She saw me and smiled. When I reached her, the smile was gone. She knew something was wrong.

I wanted to speak to her, but I couldn't. I was trembling more, and she grabbed my shoulder and directed me toward my room. Her grasp on my shoulder was comforting. I looked at her and tried again to talk. I couldn't.

She sat me on the bed and pushed the intercom button above the bed. Some static and then:

"Yes?"

"This is Edith in 209. Get Dr. Randolph."

I couldn't sit on the bed. I had never felt such extreme discomfort. I knew I couldn't help myself. I needed Randolph.

I continued to tremble, and pacing seemed to help. Edith was smiling at me but was not concealing her obvious concern. Her head turned toward the door. Randolph was there. It was good to see him.

"What's the matter?" He was talking to Edith but never took his eyes off me.

"He's been showing uncontrollable, undirected activity. He looks extremely distressed. I don't think he can talk."

"Yes, I can," I shouted, surprised that I was making sounds.

Randolph's presence was more comforting than I realized.

"Tell me what's going on, Patrick."

"I got extremely depressed very quickly. I feel that I have to keep moving. There is some relief when I move. What's the matter with me?"

I sat on the bed. The discomfort was lessening. I felt myself take some deep breaths. I was beginning to gain some control. Moments went by, and Randolph wisely said nothing. He apparently saw me getting stronger.

"I started to feel very lonely. Then I started to think about Gordon. He shouldn't have gone. . . . I'm terribly frightened. I want to go home. I want to be with my wife. . . . Nothing in my life has prepared me for this. I'm not ready for it. Maybe I should go home. . . . No. I can't do that. When I leave this place I'll never come back. I'll stay. . . . I've never felt such violent self-disgust."

I looked at Randolph, who was resolutely maintaining his clinical silence. His whole manner was axiomatic:

When the patient is getting better, say nothing. When you don't know what to say, say nothing. But appear omniscient.

The silence continued, and Edith squeezed my hand, smiled, and nodded in a manner that said:

"I like your courage."

Several silent minutes went by. I was terrified that Randolph would leave. I really needed him. But I could never let him know that.

"We have a weekend coming up. What'll I do if this happens again and you aren't around?"

"It won't happen again. I'm going to order some Haldol for you. It'll get you through the next couple of days."

"I won't take it."

"We can only psychologically mother you up to a point. The agitated depression could hit you again. I don't want you to go off the roof."

"I'll never take another fucking drug."

Randolph was both angered and dismayed. "This is the third time you've refused one of my orders. I ought to throw your ass out of this hospital."

"I'm not suicidal."

"No, I don't think you are. There's nothing in your past to suggest such self-destructive tendencies. If there were something, I'd have you in a closed psychiatric ward."

"I am afraid for my sanity though," I said. "It scares the hell out of me when I think that I could lose touch."

"You won't."

"How the hell do you know?"

"Let me put it in terms O'Malley would use. In your ego functioning, you are clearly mature and goal oriented. You'll not break with reality."

"I hope that's not an attempt at false reassurance."

"Give me credit for more than that," he said. "You're frightened because you're dealing with a very difficult feeling. You're now more psychologically stressed than you ever have been, and your ability to cope has been compromised."

"So this is what the textbooks mean by situational depression."

"Extreme situational depression. You're having a rough time. When most people get depressed, they don't want to get out of bed in the morning. They lose their appetite. They suffer insomnia. They withdraw. Few people, fortunately very few, experience agitation. That's what you experienced. And it may happen again. I'd like to prevent that by putting you on Haldol."

"If I get that bad again, I'll take the Haldol. I promise. Give me a chance."

"I don't negotiate with patients, Patrick. I want . . ." Randolph sighed, put his hand into his pocket, and took out his cigarettes. He looked to Edith. "Make the Haldol a give-as-needed order."

He lit his cigarette.

"If it weren't for lawyers and doctors . . ." Randolph slowly shook his head and looked to Edith, who nodded.

"The Good Lord doesn't want to make it too easy on us, Dr. Randolph," she said.

"Get out and walk the hospital grounds this weekend, Patrick," Randolph said. "Don't leave hospital property. Maybe I'll let you do that next weekend."

"You mean I can't even walk around the block?"

"No! You're still a very sick man."

I let the phone ring a dozen times. No answer.

"Oh, God," I thought, "please let Irene be there."

I was beginning to lose it again. Fear, frustration, anger. And I started to tremble. I headed for the Nurses' Station to ask for Haldol.

I passed the lounge and heard voices. It was my group. They were there. I walked in and saw them, and I didn't feel alone anymore.

"Hey, Pat, where have you been, man?" It was MacGregor.

"Decompensating."

I sat down and looked around. I felt relaxed. And I could talk.

The food, for a change, looked good. I hadn't tasted anything like it before.

"The meat is obviously beef. What are these little things shaped like kidneys?"

I looked up and Melanie was smiling.

"You're kidding me," I said.

"No. That's steak and kidney pie. It's a Canadian dish."

"That's awful. You people not only talk funny, you eat strange things. What's for breakfast tomorrow? Guinea worms and prostates?"

It was always nice to be with Melanie. She was quiet most of the time. Not out of shyness, but rather, I guess, because she had been wounded and was healing slowly. She did not volunteer much about herself and always tried to keep the conversation on something besides her personal life.

She had large, innocent eyes that made her appear vulnerable. She could not have been unaware of the fact that she had extraordinarily good looks. But her casual manner suggested that she was not preoccupied with the fact she was beautiful.

Lucy sat with us. She did not appear quite as nervous and timid as before. Smoking seemed to have a calming effect on her. And she was seldom without a cigarette.

"I'll bet the weekends are very long here," I said.

"Do you have any family in Toronto, Patrick?" asked Lucy.

"No. I'm from Ohio. My wife is back there. She's an assistant professor of art."

"Any children?"

"No."

"Have either of you seen the fellow who's replacing Gordon?" asked Melanie. "He's sitting over there."

We turned to look at him just as he stood. He was short with a round head and little hair. His back was slightly curved and his body was very thick, but more like a sausage than a tree stump. His stubby extremities were totally appropriate and logical extensions of his porcine torso.

"He calls himself Hog Body," said Melanie.

He walked by our table, and Lucy murmured quietly, "God does have an imagination."

"I hear you had a bad time today, Patrick. Do you feel any better?" asked Reggie.

"Yeah. I feel better. But I wonder what new emotion I'll have tomorrow."

"You'll soon even out. You learn a lot of new things about yourself here. I never knew how low I could sink. I found out during my first week when I was a patient. I remember the days I spent on Happy Valley so vividly. And they kept me here for two weeks. You'll be leaving this floor tomorrow. That's a good sign."

"Why did they keep you?"

"I got into the Nurses' Station one night looking for anything I could take that was mood altering. All I could find was a bottle of rubbing alcohol. So I drank it. They would have thrown me out, but I got too sick. After I was better from that episode, Edith intervened for me, and they let me stay."

"Reggie, tell me the truth. Did this experience really make a difference in your life? Was it that good?"

"Being a patient here was my most difficult experience. I don't think I could do it again. But being here helped me more than anything else ever. It was the singular experience of my life. It got me out of the gutter. I think I now have some dignity."

"Are you happy now?"

"I'm happy that I'm not a drug addict. But I have too many self-inflicted wounds that are not responding to just abstinence alone. I have not had a single moment of unqualified happiness since my husband left and took my son."

"Is there any chance of your getting back together? You seem to be doing so well."

"No. Apparently some things are unforgivable."

"I'm sorry."

"Well, Patrick, what are your plans for the weekend?"

"I'd like to discuss MUTINY with the other patients. We will rise up and take over the place. The asylum will be in the hands of the lunatics. And Monday morning at dawn we'll take Randolph and O'Malley outside and tranquilize them."

It was Friday night. I had survived the first five days. I had experienced fear, anger, loneliness, guilt, and depression bordering on despair. I could only hope that the past five days would be the nadir of my existence.

I did not feel in the mood for sober reflection, but of course, I couldn't sleep. Thoughts of a kind and gentle God would not come.

There is the joke about the poor Hispanic who dies and goes to heaven. He is assured that in heaven *all* people are treated equal, having been created that way.

But he sees a man with a white coat and a stethoscope around his neck receiving reverential treatment.

"Hey," he says to Saint Peter. "Why is that guy getting special treatment?"

"Oh," says Saint Peter, "that's just God. Sometimes He likes to play doctor."

With some surgeons being the exception, most physicians don't believe they rank with the divine. Sometimes, however, deity is thrust upon us. And it is uncomfortable.

On the second day of my internship I was working the trauma section of the emergency room. It was early in the morning when firemen wheeled in a teenage girl yelling: "We've got a bad one." The girl had been in a head-on collision on her way to school. Her neck had been damaged badly, and she was blue and having difficulty breathing. The girl needed an emergency tracheotomy or would certainly be dead in minutes. I had never done one. Trained surgeons were too many valuable minutes away.

The girl was calmly looking at me. She trusted that I was going to save her life. Her lips silently formed the words: "Help me."

I was overwhelmed, angry. This girl was going to die because I was untrained and inadequate.

"Get me some help," I called out.

The tracheotomy set was ready, and I reached for a scalpel, not sure what I was going to do with it.

There was a strong hand on my shoulder, and I turned to see the chief resident in Ear, Nose, and Throat Surgery.

"Can I help?" he asked as he looked at the girl. He had a confident smile.

"Thank God you're here," I said and moved to the side.

"I got your page," he said to me as he began to perform the tracheotomy.

"What page?"

"A few minutes ago the operator paged me and said I was needed in trauma."

"But this girl just got here, and she's the only patient. I didn't page you."

We shared a brief, stunned glance.

Many nice things happen in medicine. When a life that should be lost is unexplainably saved, we sometimes refer to it as third party involvement. An oblique reference to divine intervention.

Two weeks later the girl was discharged from the hospital. She came to see me with her parents. I was hugged by each of them. They said: "God Bless You. . . . Thank you. . . . You saved my daughter's life. . . . You're wonderful."

They didn't know.

I think each of us is given a single moment in time when we are to die. This girl's time had not arrived. I had nothing to do with her being alive. I stop considerably short of deity.

11

THE GRASS outside my window was wet and gleaming from the overnight moisture and cold. Saturday morning had eventually appeared. A dark squirrel was sitting up beneath a tree surveying the immediate world. A lone car was silently and unhurriedly moving into the parking area outside the hospital. Several smiling nurses were walking toward their cars.

It was Saturday morning and everything appeared to be in its place. Except me.

"You know that goddamn coffee doesn't have any caffeine in it." MacGregor was commenting on the state of things.

On our breakfast plates were something called cheese dreams. Two pieces of toast, each with a slice of cheese that someone had attempted but failed to melt. On top of that was a piece of bacon, mostly cooked.

I had weighed myself on the way to the dining room. In five days I had lost six pounds. Unhappiness can apparently burn calories.

Hog Body was sitting across from me. He sat impassively, having inhaled his cheese dreams. He was watching me eat as if he were hoping I would drop some food.

"Would you like to finish this?" I asked and pushed my plate toward him.

He said nothing but smiled showing only an occasional tooth. His broad hand grasped the toast, and he placed it unhurriedly but without pause into his mouth. His Adam's apple bobbed, and he smiled, satisfied. He had swallowed one entire piece of toast with cheese and bacon without chewing.

Boone and MacGregor had observed this along with me, and we looked at each other to make sure we all agreed on what we saw. There was agreement. We then turned to look at Hog Body and gave silent testimony.

On the Saturday morning at the end of the second week of hospitalization, each group puts on a skit for the other patients. We sat expectantly in the claustrophic gym awaiting the performance of the patients that had come in the week ahead of my group. Next week it would be my group's turn.

The lights dimmed. A figure moved toward the unlit center stage. Scattered applause. The figure was then bathed in light. What appeared can only be described in extremes. He was very tall, very thin, and very black. His look was serious. But then the corners of his mouth began spreading in the direction of each ear, and his somberness began dissolving away. Soon his face became alive with a broad, toothful grin. He had forgotten his lines.

Eventually the skit got under way. The tall guy was dressed as a witch doctor and patients would come to see him and tell of all the effects of Antabuse.

A man and a woman who were supposed to be married were talking to the witch doctor:

"Doc," said the man, "the Antabuse has really worked. My wife hasn't had a drink since she started taking it."

"Great," said the doctor, "that will be a thousand dollars."

"Just one problem," said the man. "My wife won't put out for me since she started taking it. She brings a bottle of gin to bed with her every night and—here, watch this."

He handed the woman a bottle of gin and she began simulating fellatio on the neck of the bottle.

When the cheering and applause quieted, the witch doctor spoke to the woman.

"Why do you do that?"

She put the bottle down.

"Well, doctor," she said, "look at my husband. Can you imagine having sex with him while you were sober?"

"Hey, Doc, I don't think you've cured her disease. You've only stopped her from drinking."

The doctor and the two patients froze, and a man walked on stage from the left. He was impeccably groomed and wore a white clinic coat. He had a serious expression. He was portraying Dr. Randolph.

"Alcoholism is more than just drinking too much," he lectured the audience. "Alcoholism is lying, hurting people, destroying ourselves and our families, and being insane. It's being spiritually and morally bankrupt.

"You don't treat alcoholism with just a pill."

Steve, who was sitting next to me, turned to me. "This sucks," he said.

"None of this means anything to me," I said to him. "I'm not an alcoholic. Maybe I don't beyong here."

"They treat junkies here, too," Steve reassured me. "They can help you."

There was a smattering of applause, and the married couple was walking offstage. The man paused and called back to the witch doctor: "Hey, Doc, is your ass as black as your face?" It was spoken with rancor and was obviously not in the script. And it was totally inappropriate. There were a few nervous laughs from the audience accompanied by a palpable sense of discomfort. However, the guy playing the witch doctor laughed, forcibly, loud and hard.

And I thought I was having problems with self-esteem.

After lunch I moved out of Happy Valley to the fourth floor. My first move up and eventually out.

My new room was small, but much less institutional in appearance than my room in Happy Valley. And it was carpeted. There was a large mirror in the room. I stood and could see myself full length. The weight I had lost was noticeable.

There was a knock on my door, and in walked the witch doctor from the skit.

"Hello, Patrick, welcome to the fourth floor. We're going to be neighbors." He spoke slowly and in a thick southern accent. There had been no trace of an accent while he was on stage.

He languidly strolled over to a chair and sat. He chuckled for no apparent reason. There was something about his mood which didn't seem appropriate. It wasn't that he was euphoric. He just seemed to be unaccountably jovial.

"I'm Lorenzo," he said and laughed. "Demerol and Ritalin. You?"

"Tranquilizers and sleeping pills. All different types and amounts."

"What do you do, Patrick?"

"I'm a shepherd."

He laughed and clapped his hands. He even bent at the waist. It just wasn't that funny.

"I know you're a pediatrician from Cleveland," he said in between chuckles. "I'm a surgeon. I practice in Detroit, now. I'm from Birmingham."

We talked more, but he never looked at my face. He only seemed comfortable when given something, however unfunny, to laugh at.

And his laugh was always exaggerated. He was dealing with his lack of self-respect with superficial joviality. Perhaps that worked for him. Maybe that got him through the day.

But I wanted to tell him that it was O.K. He didn't need to be that way with me. He could tell me how awful he felt. And I'd tell him the same. But there was a difference between us. He was black. Perhaps he considered that a liability now that I could never understand.

So I chose to let him use whatever defense he needed. Maybe he would eventually let me get close. I liked him. I hoped that we could soon tell each other how unhappy we were and how we had sabotaged our lives.

"How was your first week here, Lorenzo?"

"Bad, man, really bad." He appeared reflective for a moment, and I thought he was going to open up. "Would you like to come over and listen to some music?"

"No. I think I'll just stay right here and harbor resentment."

"At who?"

"The whole fucking world."

It was Saturday night. I sat in the fourth floor lounge engulfed in cigarette smoke. A small asthenic fellow sat slightly behind me. I was between him and the television. He would occasionally cough spasmodically, and I would feel small wet things on the back of my neck. I hoped they were not tiny pieces of lung. In between his spasms of coughing, he'd suck on a Player's cigarette.

Boone, Melanie, and Lucy were playing cards. MacGregor sat alone and snored loudly. Hog Body sat near the television and, with proptotic eyes, stared at it. Steve was in the lobby talking on the phone. There was an angry expression on his face, and he gestured wildly as he talked.

I heard a rumble emanate from the cougher behind me. It came from about mid-abdomen but began moving up. Chest, neck, and then his mouth opened, and out came a cough that filled the air with visceral debris. I tried to duck but was hit full square in the side of the face with little moist objects that came from somewhere in his body. He then sat back and smoked as if nothing had happened.

I got up and went to bathe. I felt unclean.

"Dr. Reilly, Dr. Striker's on the phone."

"Hello, Andy, what's up?"

"Couple of things, Pat. I've had two calls recently about you. One was about a pregnancy test you ordered."

"I order pregnancy tests on all my adolescent females. And I'll continue to."

"How about on a three-year-old?" Andy laughed. "And it was a boy."

"Oops. I guess I made a mistake. Sorry 'bout that."

"The other is kinda serious, Pat. You miscalculated a dose of insulin. A nurse caught it. You could've killed the kid. He would have convulsed for sure."

"Damnit! I'm so lousy with calculating doses."

"You didn't used to be. Pat . . . we've got to do something."

"No more mistakes, Andy. I promise. I'll check out those calculations with a nurse or a med student each time. Is that all right?"

"Super. That's good. That should solve the problem."

"I'll see you, Andy."

"One more thing." His voice became low and serious. "If there are any more mistakes, Pat. You know, with calculations . . . or anything, I'll have to have the resident on the floor cosign your orders.

"I'm sorry. I hate to do that. But I'm sure I won't have to."

"Thanks, Andy."

"Hey, Pat, while I have you on the phone, how many Golden Apple Awards have you got from the med students? Must be at least a couple."

"Three. I have them here on the wall of my office. 'Best Clinical Teacher 1975' . . . '1976' . . . '1977.' I'm really proud of those."

"Well, your evaluations by the students the past couple of years have been awful. If the evaluations are bad this year, I'll have to replace you with someone else. I'm sorry. I know how much you enjoy teaching. Times have really changed, haven't they? Students are evaluating us."

"Please don't take that teaching position away from me, Andy."

"I don't want to," he shouted. "But goddamnit, get well!"

"But I'm not sick. I'm not sick. Really."

God, I think, must avoid certain places. In here, in this microcosm of hell, we are separated from all things divine. There is nothing holy here.

Before coming into the hospital, I prayed all the time. I pleaded with God to help me get off drugs. And now that I was in treatment, I felt I had been abandoned. I'd tried to talk to God, but I just didn't feel a presence. I knew I was alone now more than I had ever been. I didn't understand God's withdrawal from my life. But it didn't anger or frighten me. I only knew that I was on my own. And maybe that is the way it should be.

Most mornings when I'd gotten out of bed, I'd shaved and showered hurriedly. I didn't want to give loneliness any more chances to engulf me. This morning I felt almost relaxed, even though I didn't sleep, and insomnia the night before was much less of a cataclysmic event than usual. I couldn't believed I'd ever experienced agitated depression, and it certainly could never happen again. This morning I was actually not afraid of being alone.

Ruthy, the weekend day nurse, strode into my room bringing my vitamin pill. Ruthy had not a trace of elegance. She was tall, maybe six feet, and at least a hundred pounds overweight. There was a forced erectness to her posture that suggested arrogance, and she did little to promote herself with her judgmental, unsmiling expression.

She gave me a disapproving look and handed me my vitamin pill.

"You know, Ruthy, you're not the most appealing thing to see this early. It's just not the best way to start the day."

Her tiny lips disappeared into her mouth. She inhaled deeply and tensed. The vitamin pill dropped to the floor. Her face registered incredulity and rage. She had been violated by a patient and didn't know how to respond. But she was clearly thinking of only one thing —retaliation.

"I'm going to report you," she snapped with some glee. "I don't have to take verbal abuse from *you people*."

Apparently satisfied that she had wounded me, she turned with some effort and trundled away with the sound of giant thighs slapping against each other.

God, will I miss Edith and Reggie.

The Sunday morning general meeting was forgettable. A small man with a large nose gave a talk on loneliness. It was unimaginative, uninspired, and unrewarding.

After the talk we were directed to go to one of the two A.A. meetings. I chose not to attend. I was feeling good, and since I was finally having a respite from unhappiness, I decided to go outside for the first time in a week.

Outside it was absolutely magnificent. The sun was illuminating the grounds of Hogarth, and the air was cold but exhilarating. I felt unburdened. I never wanted to go back inside. It was peaceful, and I felt good being alone.

After some time, the doors of the hospital opened, and a steady stream of people came out. The A.A. meetings were over. People stood in small groups smoking and talking. There were men and women of all ages. And they were smiling. Why were they all smiling?

Some of them noticed me and a few walked over and said hello. But I was not anxious to be with them. After all, I was not an alcoholic. I had nothing in common with them. I was different. My problem was only parallel to their problem. They wouldn't understand.

I saw Lorenzo admiring a sculpture outside the building, and I joined him. He grinned widely for no apparent reason.

I told him about my agitated depression two days before. As we talked, I saw him begin to look uncertain and mildly astonished. He was unprepared for anything that was not superficial. He didn't look at me when I spoke, and I could feel his discomfort. I stopped speaking, and we were silent for several minutes.

He wasn't smiling, and occasionally his lower lip would quiver. He was struggling with something.

"I had a laryngospasm again last night," he finally said, in a manner and with an inflection that said it was a devastating experience.

"You mean your larynx actually closed off? You couldn't breathe?"

He nodded.

"What happened?"

"Well, they watched me turn blue to make sure I wasn't faking and then injected me with Valium."

"This has happened to you before?" I was incredulous.

"Every time I try to get off Ritalin this happens. I admitted myself to a hospital six months ago as a gesture to stop my wife from leaving. I stayed in for a month."

"Any laryngospasms then?"

"Well, every time I started to have one . . . there was a nurse who helped me. She'd get me some Ritalin."

"And your wife?" I asked.

"Saw right through it. I should have told her I couldn't give up Ritalin because I was afraid I'd die. She never left me, but we might as well not have been married.

"She ran my office for me, sending patients to other doctors if she didn't think I could handle them. She lied for me."

I felt bad for Lorenzo. I was glad he could talk to me. But I knew there were things about my life I would never be able to tell anyone.

The fourth floor was filled with visitors. I had no one. Ruthy was at the Nurses' Station reading patients' charts. She seemed to enjoy wallowing in other people's misery. I looked closely and saw she was reading my chart. I felt violated. I began to hurt from anger. She saw me, but I was able to look away before her face formed an expression.

I went to my room, but before I got there I was trembling and felt what I thought to be irrevocable anguish. I looked out the window and felt myself getting short of breath. I needed the Haldol but I just couldn't ask Ruthy. I actually had some pride left. But it was costing me.

I felt a hand on my shoulder. I tensed. I didn't want anyone to see me like this.

"Patty?"

It was Hog Body.

I didn't attempt to answer. I didn't know if I could speak. His hand stayed on my shoulder. I felt my breathing get slower and deeper. I forced a cough to see if I could make noise. I could.

"Patty. Can I help?"

I turned to look at him. He was beautiful.

"You have helped, Hog. Thanks."

"What's the matter?"

"Sometimes unhappiness is uncontrollable."

"How about a coffee?"

"I have a son named Patty," Hog Body said, as we walked to the dining room. "I hope he becomes a doctor."

"Why? Being a physician is certainly no guarantee of happiness. Hog, sometime ask yourself if you want him to be a doctor just so you can reflect in his glory."

"No. I want him to be a doctor because then he has at least the opportunity to do something worthwhile. Me, I've worked in a mill all my life. I'm a nobody."

I was sorry that I had confronted him like that. And I apologized.

"That's all right, Patty. You know, I've never talked to a doctor like this before."

"You will have ample opportunity in the next three weeks."

The Cleveland Indians had lost another exhibition game. It felt good to know that could still upset me. I was actually able to pre-occupy myself with the Sunday morning sports page of the *Toronto Star*. That was a good feeling.

The lounge was filled with families and forced smiles. There was talking but no conversations.

Steve was with his parents and his two young sons. His wife had left him the day before. He was stoically refusing his parents' vain attempt at consolation. He was watching his boys play a game on the floor. He was looking at them with an intensity I had not seen in him before. Possibly he was looking at his only reasons for staying off drugs.

Boone and Lucy played cards. Lucy's husband, Walter, sat on the couch several feet away. This was the first time I'd seen Lucy and Walter in the same room. Occasionally he would look at his wife, and his face would register disapproval and then resignation. That upset me. I knew how Lucy felt.

You don't attempt to change the behavior pattern of someone you love by showing disapproval of them. Logan proved that to me. Over and over.

"Tell Lucy you love her, Walter. Tell her you'll help her in any way you can. That you'll always be there. You don't need to tell her she's disappointed you. She's acutely aware of that. Show her some affection. Give her a reason." I wanted to say that.

I was still uncomfortable just being in the same room with Boone. Every time I would speak, he would look at me and tense his lower jaw as if preparing for combat. I was still the hated doctor, somehow apparently responsible by the remotest of associations for the inability of his wife's psychiatrist to help with her emotional problems.

I hoped Boone and I could talk about that very soon. I didn't want to be disliked like this. We needed a resolution.

Hog Body was reading the comics and appeared to be a totally uncomplicated human being.

Melanie was with her parents. I could feel her embarrassment. She was the focus of their attention but clearly didn't want to be. I had not seen her smoke before, but now she was taking rapid puffs and exhaling the smoke without inhaling. Her manner was self-conscious and uneasy.

She crossed her legs, and I noticed her thigh through the split in her skirt. I then noticed something in me that was clear and unmistakable—heterosexual craving. Maybe that was an early but tangible sign of recovery.

I had not made love for a long time. I just could not make any sexual advances toward Irene the way things had been between us. And the fear of impotence was always there. Attempting to sustain a marriage without a working sexual relationship was becoming increasingly impossible. A certain coldness was developing. There were fewer affectionate moments. An indentifiable distance was between us. And it was growing wider.

Dear Pat,

I've thought about you most of today, and I couldn't wait to get home and write you. One of the nice things about looking back is that you can choose the things you want to think about. We have a lot of nice memories.

Remember Topsail? God, that was fun. Everything was perfect that week. The ocean, sailing, swimming, walking on the beach. We need to do things like that more often. It gives us the chance to think about why we are important to each other. You are the only thing in my life that is irreplaceable. I need you healthy to be happy. I just don't enjoy things without you.

I know you don't feel the same. You never have. That used to bother me. It took me a long time to realize that you can be happy when you are alone. You don't always require other people and close relationships.

We probably do need to spend some time away from each other. It seems that things have become so acute between us. Stupid, minor problems always become magnified. We have become very skilled at hurting each other. Sometimes I spend hours thinking up what I hope will be penetrating, clever sarcasm. I even practice the inflection that I'll say it with. Do you do that, too?

Unfortunately, it took this separation for me to realize, once again, how important you are to me. I hope some day you can honestly tell me that I am important to you. You used to tell me I was important. You haven't told me that in a long time. Although we have hurt each other during our long hours of arrow slinging, I don't think the damage we have done is irrevocable. I want to work on our marriage.

However, Pat, I will not stay with you if you go back to the drugs. I love you too much to watch you destroy yourself. But you have attained everything else you wanted and worked for, and I know that your getting off drugs is just one more thing you'll accomplish. Once again your single-mindedness will work for you. I hope when you get out of Hogarth, reconstructing our marriage will be a priority for you.

I'll be coming to Toronto in two weeks for the Family Program. I hope we'll be able to spend some time together *ALONE!* I'm about ready to start making obscene phone calls.

I love you.

Irene

This was Irene's first letter to me in which there was no element of pity. We both knew I was where I had to be. I knew she hurt for me. That's just the way she was. What attracted me first to her was her genuine concern for other people. And her gentleness. When other people hurt, she hurt too. And if she unwittingly ever inflicted a hurt, she would be devastated. She had a tremendous capacity to love and to forgive.

But during the years of our marriage she had learned how to play rough. She had learned how to turn an invective, but only for survival. And she rarely said anything to me meant to hurt. She was completely lacking in guile and never attempted to manipulate. She couldn't intimidate and, therefore, just never learned how to fight very well. She was honest all the time and was therefore unfair game in the marital battles. Although occasionally in an argument she would have a good offense, her defense was not good. I knew how to reduce her to tears with a well-placed remark. And I was doing it more often.

But she was getting tougher, and that was beginning to threaten me.

I was listening to Karren telling me to relax. I had on my headphones, and I lay naked on my bed. Unfortunately her voice was not sensuous as I had hoped. She spoke with gentle authority, and I did everything her voice told me to do. I would tense certain muscles and then relax them. I was too aware of trying to relax. But ten minutes into the tape, I noticed there were some brief moments when my eyes would almost close completely and I would start to drift off.

For some reason I strongly resisted falling asleep at such times. I just couldn't, as Karren suggested repeatedly, "let go, let go."

When the tape was over, I lay relaxed and limp but not sleepy. As Sundays go, this had not been too bad. Tomorrow would begin the active phase of the treatment program. For the past seven days we had only vegetated and allowed our bodies to detoxify themselves. It was probably good that we had not yet been forced into active therapy. In fact maybe, just maybe, the people who ran this place knew what they were doing.

I was not convinced of that yet.

"Dr. Reilly," Diane called as I was about to enter an examination room, "Dr. Striker's calling."

"I'll take it in my office, Diane."

I walked into my office, locked the door, and sat at my desk and unlocked my bottom right-hand drawer.

"Hello, Andy," I said and reached for the Valium bottle.

"Hi, Pat. Can you and Irene come over for dinner Sunday?"

I placed the bottle of Valium on the desk.

"Sure. We'd love to. We haven't seen Joan in months. How is she?"

"Well, Joan's been a little nervous lately. Must be change of life or something. Anyway, she's seeing Dave Gordon. He's got her on Librium. It really seems to help her. Especially in the morning. By the way, wasn't Dave in your class?"

"Yes. Graduated number one in the class. For a long time he actually wanted to be a surgeon. Can you imagine a smart guy like Dave being a surgeon? I remember Dr. Starr, he was chairman of internal medicine then, wanted Dave to intern under him. Dr. Starr used to tell us that he treated surgeons the same way he treated hemmorrhoids—with disdain. I don't know how Dave ever ended up in psych."

"Dave and his wife will be with us on Sunday. Maybe you can get together with him, Pat."

I opened the Valium bottle and dropped two ten-milligram tablets on my desk.

"Pat, there's something I have to talk to you about. You put that

· 91 ·

teenage girl with hepatitis on Valium yesterday. Do you think that was a good idea? Did she need a tranquilizer?"

"I put most of my teenagers on Valium when they come into the hospital. It's a stressful time for them, Andy."

"Pat, you've got to be careful what you order for kids with liver disease. Didn't we teach you that?"

"A simple mistake. That's hardly . . ."

"In the past year you've made more mistakes—and some weren't so simple—than in all the previous years I've known you. One of these days I'm afraid your name is going to come up in a Quality Assurance Committee meeting. I don't want that to happen. I like to . . . well . . . protect my medical staff. Know what I mean?"

"Yes, Andy. Thanks."

"You're an excellent pediatrician. I know that. But people are calling me about you. They tell me about your mistakes . . . and that you look nervous. Something's happened, Pat. Something's wrong. I wish you'd tell me."

"Well, Andy, I know what's wrong. I just didn't want to admit it. I'm . . . I'm sick. It's these migraine headaches. I'm getting five or six migraines a week. They're devastating." I scooped up the Valiums and swallowed them. "I'm not functioning very well. I've had a rough year with these headaches."

"Have you seen anybody?"

"No."

"We don't take care of ourselves very well, do we, Pat? Well, I think I'm going to insist that you go over and see Rudy Weiner. Will you do that?"

"Yes. I'll do that."

"Pat, until you get your headaches under control, how about not admitting patients for a while? If you get a kid that needs in, give him to Jimmy Fagan. O.K.?"

"That hurts, Andy. That really hurts."

"I think it's best. I'm sorry. But I am relieved. There are easy explanations for everything. I just wish you had told me before. We'll get this taken care of, and then you can start admitting patients again."

"I suppose you're right. I'll do whatever you think is best. I hope you know I'd never lie to you."

"I know that. I'll see you and Irene on Sunday. Until you see Rudy, why don't you take some Librium or Valium. Maybe it'll calm you down."

"Yeah. O.K. That's a good idea."

"Just be careful with that stuff. Don't drink when you start taking it."

"Hey, Andy, I'm no dummy."

13

INSOMNIA is uniquely enervating. When I am fatigued and angered by my inability to sleep, my defense mechanisms, especially repression, don't work very well. Unpleasant thoughts and memories surface, and I'm left alone with a person I don't like very much.

It would be difficult to overestimate the benefits of a shower after a sleepless night. I would not say that a shower renews my enthusiasm. That would be a grand overstatement. But I keep the water cold enough to make me shiver, and I tell myself it is invigorating.

When I came out of the shower, I saw evidence that a nurse had been in my room. There was my vitamin pill in a cup on my dresser along with an empty urine cup. Another urine sample was being asked for so it could be screened for drugs. These urine screenings were beginning to anger me. I had been searched when I came into the hospital and all my drugs taken away. I hadn't been able to leave the hospital grounds, and I had not had any visitors. There was no way I could have got drugs.

These bastards were unrelenting in their desire to continually humiliate me.

When I approached the Nurses' Station, I saw Randolph sitting reading a chart. A tall, thin black woman who I assumed was a nurse stood over him and looked at me as I came near. She was a handsome woman, in her early forties, I guessed, whose face became absolutely radiant when she smiled at me.

"Hi, Patrick," she said, smiling. Her name tag read: Charge Nurse Toni.

"How did you sleep?"

Randolph looked up to hear my answer.

"I had a fairly good night's sleep," I lied.

I saw Randolph shake his head slightly. The son of a bitch never believed me. I needed to tell him that I thought he was jaded by his close association with drug addicts and alcoholics. I was beginning to feel that although most of the patients are well practiced in deception when we come in here, we are trying to be honest, and it's difficult when the staff doesn't believe much of what we say. I would wait for a time when I wasn't lying to tell him that.

"Patrick," Toni continued, "if ever I can help you, please come and see me. You'll be on my floor for several weeks, so I'd like to get to know you." Toni was sustaining a genuine, expressive smile for an inordinately long time. And when she talked to me, I noticed her eyes searching my face, trying to determine what I was thinking.

Randolph came from behind the desk in the Nurses' Station, approached us, and stood facing me. Toni, still smiling, nodded and walked off. Randolph looked at my chart and then at me.

"You didn't need the Haldol?"

"Well, I didn't ask for it." I felt myself smile. I needed a drug and didn't take it. Possibly the first time in my adult life. I felt a little proud, and I wanted Randolph to compliment me.

"The order for Haldol is being canceled as of now," he said and remained expressionless. He reached out and touched my left forearm in a gesture meant to tell me to follow. We walked to my room.

"Patrick, from now on you'll be required to be an active participant in your treatment program. You won't have as much time to be angry. We'll all be glad for that. From what I've been told, you are becoming insufferable."

"I didn't know it was that obvious," I said.

He lit a cigarette and chuckled softly.

"Why were you so brutal with Ruthy?"

"I'm sorry I was unpleasant with her," I sighed. "She did nothing to provoke me. I'll apologize when I see her."

"It may bore you to hear it, but everyone on the staff here is interested primarily in your recovery."

"I'll try to remember that."

"Patrick, have you had any migraine headaches since admission? I didn't see any notes on your chart about headaches."

"I haven't had any. It's been at least a year since I went seven straight days without a migraine."

"It's not inconceivable that the drugs you were taking contributed to the frequency and severity of the headaches. Time will give us the answer to that."

He wrote something in my chart, then looked up.

"I want you to continue seeing Dr. O'Malley on a regular basis. If you want to see me for anything, grab me before breakfast or late in the afternoon. The only next scheduled meeting you and I will have will be two weeks from today, when we will discuss your discharge or being recycled."

When I heard the word *recycled* I experienced a few seconds of what had to be ventricular fibrillation. Randolph saw my discomfort.

"Jesus Christ, man," he said, obviously upset. "If we recommend that you stay several extra weeks, it will be only because we feel it will give you a better chance for recovery. It's not punitive."

He stood.

"Anyway," he continued, "talking about your being recycled is premature now. Get the most out of the program. We won't discuss your future here for another two weeks."

Monday mornings were always difficult for me because I drugged myself heavily on Sunday nights. There was something foreboding about Monday morning and the beginning of a new week. That feeling started in medical school, where there was day after day of treacherous anxiety.

In medical school I found myself battered with exams. I spent my time worrying, memorizing, hoping, and being chronically anxious. So I took heavy doses of Valium daily. I survived medical school almost drained of my enthusiasm to learn and with an addiction to Valium. Graduating medical school was, for me, an achievement that was Pyrrhic at best.

But during my internship and residency, I developed a new attitude and a more mature approach to learning medicine. I enjoyed the intimate exposure to clinical physicians and my involvement with patients who called me "doctor." I had a new self-image, and learning became more of a positive act, not motivated so much by a fear of failure as by a desire to learn.

But there was stress of another kind, which required, I thought, not only Valium, but also sleeping pills. There were unbelievably long hours and the constant need to prove that I was not only competent but that I read all the appropriate medical journals and could quote from them.

Many situations arose during residency training that my fellow residents and I were not prepared to deal with. Such as the dying patient. But we were never intellectually honest enough to admit we were inadequate. We just forged ahead and made our mistakes. No one ever told us we did not have the tools to alleviate all human misery.

It depressed me when there was suffering and I could do nothing about it.

But this Monday morning was different. If anything, this would not be a boring week.

As I walked down the hall toward the steps leading to the dining room, Toni stepped in beside me. She had a pleasing, soft, soapy fragrance. She gently grabbed my arm. I felt a twinge of sexual excitement. She was smiling again, but this time her smile was more sensual than cheerful. I stopped and looked in her eyes. She moved closer and put her mouth close to my ear.

"Patrick," she whispered, "you forgot to bring me a urine specimen."

I sat with Hog Body at breakfast. There was something unfamiliar about him. He was more refined and mannered. And he was even chewing his food. After a few minutes I realized that Hog Body had his teeth in place.

Steve and Lucy joined us.

"Did you hear that Randolph threw one of the patients out this morning?" asked Lucy.

"Yeah," said Steve. "The patient was a doctor, too."

"Lorenzo?" I asked, startled.

"No," said Lucy. "It was a man on the third floor. He went home yesterday, and while he was out took some Darvon. He told Randolph about it this morning, and Randolph told him to leave."

"And this was going to be his last week," added Steve.

This depressed and annoyed me. It just wasn't fair that you are not allowed one mistake.

"I guess there's a lesson there," I said.

"Yeah," exclaimed Steve. "Don't fuck with Randolph."

After breakfast my group, the March nineteenth group, gathered in the Auditorium. We viewed a movie in which the main character, a middle-aged man, husband and father, began a descent into alcoholism. The movie dramatized how he lost his friends, his job, his family, his health, and self-esteem.

As I watched the movie, I became terribly frightened. These things had not happened to me, but maybe they could have. My unwitting choice of self-destruction had been pills, not alcohol. But I could relate to what this man in the movie was doing to himself. It was hurting me to watch.

I was beginning to feel weak. I was perspiring, and my clothes were wet. When I tried to grab the metal surrounding the chair seat, my hands slid off. My breathing was becoming labored. I got up and left the Auditorium and went to the fourth floor lounge.

I sat on a couch and partially unbuttoned my shirt, which was wet. I took a few deep breaths.

"Patrick?" It was Toni. She saw I was having a difficult time. "Can I do anything?"

"No. But thanks. We were watching a movie about an alcoholic. I think it was too soon for me to see something that graphic. I'm still pretty fragile."

She approached me and sat down. Her eyes began searching my face again. I looked away from her. I could see out the window but chose not to focus on anything.

"I'm a doctor, Toni, I should be stronger than this. Christ! I'd hate for any of my patients to see me like this."

"You're sick, Patrick, not weak. Weak people don't come in here for treatment."

I forced a smile and nodded.

"Weak people with your disease stay out there"—she looked toward the window—"and die."

Steve was the last one to arrive in the lounge. It was almost ten A.M., time for Group Therapy. There were a few inane remarks, shallow pleasantries and nervous laughs. MacGregor spilled his coffee and filled the room with obscenities.

A woman with unnaturally light blond hair appeared in the doorway. She wore navy blue slacks, a gray blazer, and a frilly white blouse with a virginally high collar.

Her eyes moved quickly to each of us, counting us. MacGregor was the last person she looked at. She smiled at him, reached behind her, and closed the door to the lounge. The door had not been closed before. It wasn't supposed to be.

"We need to arrange these chairs in a circle," she said, as she walked to the center of the room. "This has got to be the worst room imaginable for Group Therapy. It's too big . . . windows without curtains . . . newspapers and magazines all over the place . . . a card table

". . . just too many distractions . . . and these overstuffed chairs . . . ," she shook her head, ". . . just too comfortable."

"How do you want it?" Boone asked impatiently and stood. Each of us got out of his or her chair.

"We'll use the couch," she said. "Two people on that. Leave the coffee table in front of it. Six chairs around the table."

Hog Body and I sat on the couch. He was to my left. Melanie was in a chair to my right. Lucy sat next to her. Then Steve and Mac-Gregor. Boone was to the left of the group therapist. She still had not told us her name.

"I'd like to have the seats arranged like this for each session," she said. She looked at Steve. "Would you take the responsibility for that?"

"No," he said. "Fuck, no. Get somebody else."

"I'll do it," Hog Body said. "I'll be glad to do it."

"Thank you," she said, smiling. She turned to Boone, who was glaring at her. He was in his prebattle, defiant posture. She looked at him for about ten seconds. He seemed to relax slightly, and his lower jaw became less prominent. She smiled at Boone, and her eyes then moved to Lucy. Lucy grabbed for her cigarettes.

In a few seconds she smiled at Lucy, and then she turned to Mac-Gregor. She continued on to Steve, Melanie, Hog Body, and then me. When she looked at me, I did not feel as uncomfortable as I'd thought I would. Her stare was more an observation than a challenge. Her pale blue eyes seemed to be tearing, causing her to blink frequently. That was distracting.

After a few seconds of her looking at me, her mouth broke into a warm, expressive smile that made her even more attractive. Her smile was clearly an offer of friendship.

She brought her left hand to her face and rubbed just above her eyes as if she were in some distress.

"I celebrated my thirtieth birthday two weeks ago," she said and slowly shook her head. "On my birthday I had my hair lightened and got fitted for my first pair of contacts. I've been wearing the contacts for three days. How long does it take to get used to these things?"

"Not long," offered Melanie.

So Melanie wasn't perfect.

"You going to tell us your name?" Boone asked.

"Christine," she said. "I'll be your group therapist for the next three weeks."

She looked slowly around the room.

"Have any of you ever been in Group Therapy before?"

"I have," snapped Boone. "When I was a patient here two years ago."

Steve raised his hand quickly and brought it down but didn't say anything.

"There are only two rules in my group," said Christine. "Show up on time and never repeat anything that's said in here outside this room. It's absolutely essential that we learn to trust each other."

Christine had spoken slowly, measuring her words. She was making sure she was understood. She sat back in her chair and crossed her legs.

"Before last Monday, I'm sure none of you had ever seen each other. And although you've spent the last seven days together, I'll bet you know very little about one another. I suspect that you have all been polite and tentative with one another. And that's all right. But now it's time to go beyond that.

"A certain amount of self-disclosure is going to be asked from all of us. Myself included. But we will only find out about each other what we each want the others to know. And we will start that slowly."

When I could see Christine in profile, I noticed that her nose was slightly upturned, and that it ended abruptly a short distance from her face. Her nose could legitimately be called cute.

"This morning we'll begin to tell each other who we are and why we're here. And you can tell us anything about yourself that you think will help us know you better.

"Who would like to begin?"

Silence. Nervous glances.

"I'll start," said Christine. "I'm thirty, and I have a master's degree in psychology. I'm about one year away from my Ph.D. I've worked at Hogarth for three years conducting Group Therapy sessions. I'm from Alberta. I'm not married, and I have no children.

"I always feel excited when I start with a new group. Most of my experiences with groups at Hogarth have been positive, and I expect and hope that this will be a good experience for all of you."

Christine smiled.

"That's all I would prefer to volunteer about myself right now," she said. "If anyone has any questions, though, I'll try to answer."

There was total silence for several minutes. Then Lucy lit a cigarette.

"I'll go," volunteered Boone. "I'm fifty-one, and this is my second admission here. I was here two years ago for the same problem—

booze. I did well for over a year after I got out of here. I took my Antabuse and even went to some A.A. meetings.

"But my wife has some psychiatric problems, and she's been on a lot of drugs prescribed by her psychiatrist. Eight months ago she overdosed and had to be hospitalized. I don't know if it was accidental or not. I went to her psychiatrist and told him to stop some of the medicine. He wouldn't, so I punched him. That cost me a thousand dollars, and I went to jail for two months."

Boone was getting angry again as he spoke, and he glanced at me.

"I've been out of work for six months and I drink a lot. But I don't touch drugs. I don't understand how people drug themselves up and walk around all day in a fog. At least I know how I'll feel when I wake up in the morning."

Boone began staring at me while he was talking. And he was being obvious.

"Taking drugs has got to be a coward's way of getting through the day. Drug users are just not able to be adults and accept any responsibility for themselves. As I said, they're cowards."

Boone had challenged me in front of the group. I was nervous, and my heart was pounding, but I was also angry.

"I'm Patrick, and I'm thirty-six. I'm a pediatrician and I practice in Cleveland; I'm married and have no children. I've taken sedative drugs in increasing amounts for the last fourteen years.

"I did my internship in adult medicine but found I didn't like working with the illnesses caused by obesity, smoking, and alcohol."

I was angry but still in control. I looked at Boone and continued.

"I especially didn't like alcoholics. I considered alcoholism a self-inflicted disease. A disease of indulgence. A disease, Boone, of incorrigible assholes."

Boone got out of his chair and pointed his finger at me.

"I warned you," he said and started toward me.

I stood.

Christine got in front of Boone.

'This is not the way to solve anything," she said. "Please. Let's talk about it."

"This is the way I solve things," he said and stepped around her.

Hog Body stepped in front of me and faced Boone.

"Come on, Boone," he said. "Sit down."

"Get out of the way, fat man," said Boone, as he continued to look at me.

Hog Body then spread his arms and took Boone in a bear hug.

Boone gave an incredulous look. He couldn't move. Hog Body must have had amazing strength.

Hog Body held him for a few seconds. Boone looked down at him. "O.K. Let me go. I'll sit down."

Boone sat down and put his head in his hands. He sighed audibly.

"Jesus Christ. Jesus fucking Christ. I don't understand why I got so mad. I have a temper but . . ."

He sighed again.

"I think I understand, Boone," said Lucy. "Whenever I stop drinking for a few days, I become hostile and belligerent. My husband usually knows when I try to quit." She started to laugh. "About six months ago I hit Walter from ten feet right between the eyes with a can of frozen orange juice. This was right after he got home from work. And do you know why I hit him? Because he hadn't thanked me for breakfast."

The tension in the room was dissolving. My heart had stopped pounding.

There were a few moments of silence.

"How do you all feel about what's happened here?" asked Christine.

"I found it very upsetting," said Melanie. "I didn't like it. Violence disgusts me."

"It didn't bother me," offered Steve. "I wish they had duked it out."

"I think this was all your fault," said MacGregor and pointed at Christine. "You should have seen it coming and stopped it. And just what are your credentials, anyway? A master's degree? A Ph.D.? That's bullshit. Thirty years old? What the hell could you know at thirty? What can you tell any of us about life?"

Christine looked directly at him.

"I'm glad you said those things if that's the way you really feel," said Christine. She did not appear threatened as she and MacGregor stared at each other.

"Well, you didn't answer any of my questions," Macgregor challenged.

"I'm just here as a facilitator," Christine finally answered. "I keep the conversation flowing." She smiled. "I wouldn't want any of you to fall asleep."

"You need a Ph.D. for that?" MacGregor shot back.

"You big fucking dumb ass, Mac," snapped Steve.

"Hold on," said Christine. "We're getting off track. Patrick and

Boone need to resolve their feelings toward each other before we go on." She looked at me. "Patrick?"

I looked at Christine.

"I've been unsure of him," I said and pointed at Boone, "ever since we met. It's not . . ."

"Patrick," Christine interrupted, "look at Boone and talk directly to him. Tell him how you feel."

I looked at Boone. He was looking back at me but appeared subdued.

"Boone," I said, "you're treating me unfairly. I have felt the anger you've directed at me since we first talked. That bothered me, but I didn't know what to do. I'm here as a patient, not as a doctor. The hatred you feel for doctors is your problem. I don't think I can help you with that.

"I'm a fellow addict, Boone. Nothing more. All I want from you is to treat me like any other patient. Being a patient here is difficult enough. I'm just as frightened as everyone else."

Christine looked at Boone. He began a smile but stopped and covered his face again and started to cry silently. He didn't need to say anything.

"That will be enough for this morning," Christine said, as she smiled and looked around the room. "But I feel I need to comment on two things that were said.

"I was asked a few minutes ago, 'What can you tell any of us about life?' It is not my purpose to tell you how to live your lives or to comment in a judgmental way on how you have lived. I've been given the title group therapist. That's inaccurate.

"You will see as we go on that all of you are the therapists. As I said, I'm the facilitator."

Christine stopped and looked at Melanie.

"You look like you want to say something."

"Are the things we say in here *really* confidential, Christine?" Melanie said with a half-smile. "I'm sorry. I don't feel right now that I trust you."

"Thanks for saying that, Melanie, if that's how you feel. That was very honest. I will occasionally write on your chart how I see you progressing in group. But all I report on is your participation. It would be professional misconduct if I ever repeated anything you said in here. And I wouldn't do it. I also would be fired immediately.

"It's absolutely critical that you believe me."

She looked at each of us.

"We believe you, Chrissie," Hog Body said, and he smiled. He had taken his teeth out again.

"The other thing that was said that I need to comment on was said by Patrick." She turned to me. "You spoke pejoratively about alcoholism as a disease. I think you said 'a disease of assholes.' You probably upset some people. Do you really feel that way?"

I looked back at Christine. I knew their eyes were on me.

"I used to think that," I said. "I don't anymore." I hoped I sounded convincing.

"I know you're supposed to be in your exercise class now, but this was the only free time I had today. I wanted to see how you were."

O'Malley was speaking to me but was reading my chart. He hadn't looked at me since I came in the room. His eyes widened slightly as he read something. I knew what it was. He looked up at me.

"Had you ever experienced any agitation along with depression before?"

"No."

"How bad was it, Patrick? Tell me how you felt."

"Confused. Frightened. Intense. Very intense. I was aware of every second. It was awful. And I'm afraid of its happening again."

"Did you experience any unusual emotional turmoil over the weekend? Did the agitation come back?" He was reading the progress notes again.

"The weekend wasn't too bad. I started to feel pretty bad a couple of times, though. But not so bad that I had to take the Haldol."

O'Malley looked up at me. He turned his head slightly to the left and his eyes narrowed as he continued to measure me. After a few seconds he opened his eyes slightly, and it almost appeared as if he were going to smile. Of course, he didn't.

"You may have humped it, Patrick," he said in a congratulatory tone.

I felt incredibly good. It was the first hopeful thing he had said to me, and I wished he would shake my hand and smile at me. Of course, he didn't.

"Remember, Patrick, that I did not say it was going to be easy. I'm just expecting that it will not get any worse."

I rejoined my group for the exercise session. Karren was on a raised platform leading the group. They were running in place. I took a position in the group standing between Hog Body and Melanie. Hog

Body was giving it his all but was breathing hard and appeared to be nearing florid congestive heart failure.

Melanie was enthusiastic and was dressed in a baggy sweat suit which obscured all points and places of interest.

"On the floor," barked Karren ". . . now on your backs . . . spread your legs apart . . . far, far apart. . . . lift your hips off the floor . . . slowly and hold. . . . now go down and repeat. . . ."

I looked over and saw Hog Body looking at me, smiling.

"Gotta teach the wife this one, Patty," he said in a stage whisper.

Everyone heard him. Within seconds everyone in the room except Karren was laughing without restraint. We looked at each other and continued laughing. We knew we were sharing with each other a rare moment. One that was genuinely without pain.

Before the relaxation class we were all given warm hot packs to be placed around the backs of our necks. We lay on mats on the floor and were instructed to place pillows under our knees so that as much tension as possible was removed from our legs.

Karren played a tape of a woman's gentle, melodious voice explaining the importance of setting aside times during the day for conscious relaxation.

Then the voice took on an ethereal quality and began to take us through the steps for total body relaxation beginning with our feet.

But I began to think of Irene, and I rapidly began feeling lonely. I wanted to be with her so badly it was beginning to hurt. I didn't want to cry, but my eyes were getting moist and I was losing control of my lower lip.

A sudden silence brought me back harshly to where I was. Karren had stopped the tape and went over and woke up MacGregor. She then turned on the lights. She was not happy.

"While the tape was playing," she said, "I walked around the room. There did not seem to be a lot of interest in what we're trying to do." As she talked, her voice became lower and she spoke more slowly. She was trying not to show her anger.

"Learning relaxation techniques is a priority for the patients while in this hospital. And it is my job to teach you those techniques. You people must learn to respond to stress in different ways than you probably did before. And I will see to it that you do."

She looked directly at me.

"It's easy to preoccupy yourselves with other thoughts when the lights are down, listening to a very soothing voice while lying on your backs."

She then looked at MacGregor, who was yawning.

"It's also very easy to fall asleep." She looked at each of us. "It's up to each of you to bring yourselves back to the voice. You must do that, or you'll be wasting your time. And we only have three more weeks to prepare you for the rest of your lives."

As we left the gymnasium to go back to our rooms to shower, I noticed a man and a woman sitting on the couch where Irene and I had sat when we first arrived. There were two bags in front of the man, who was about my age.

The two sat silently and looked straight ahead. They were holding hands and they both looked frightened. I remembered sitting there one week before. I had no idea then of the emotional turbulence ahead.

Edith came out from Happy Valley carrying a clipboard and called the man's name. He stood and followed Edith into Happy Valley and the door closed behind them. The woman remained sitting and stared at the entrance.

I went to the couch and sat beside her. She glanced at me suspiciously. I would have reached for her hand, but I was still conscious about my sweating palms.

"I'm Patrick. I came in here a week ago. Is that your husband?"

She nodded.

"He'll be all right. We'll take care of him," I said.

A tear appeared and gently but rapidly descended over her left cheek. Her expression never changed.

"I don't want him to see me cry," she said. She paused and wiped her cheek. "Was it very difficult for you?"

"The only requirement for the first week is that you survive. And I did. It gets better. It really does."

After dinner most of the patients headed for the television to watch the hockey game between Toronto and Montreal. That didn't interest me, and as I headed for my room, I was jolted into unhappiness. Depression had never hit me so suddenly and unexpectedly. I leaned against the wall. I began despairing of my sanity. How could I ever function being this unhappy? I hated this place and what it was doing to me. I wasn't getting any better.

I needed to start moving.

I walked quickly toward the stairs, and when I got to the top, I ran down them two at a time. I headed for the door and went outside. I stared down the driveway. If I knew anyone in Toronto, if I knew where to go, I'd leave. I'd put this place and this experience behind me.

I needed very badly to cry. But I was too angry.

I went back in and headed for Happy Valley. Reggie would be there. But there was a stranger at the Nurses' Station.

"Is Reggie here tonight?" I asked.

The nurse looked at me.

"Who are you?" She put on her glasses to get a better look.

"Patrick Reilly. Fourth floor. Second week."

"No. She's not here. I'm working in her place."

I was disappointed and turned and started to walk away.

"Wait, Patrick."

I turned and saw the nurse get up, take off her glasses and smile.

"Reggie called me at home this afternoon. She asked me if I'd work for her tonight. She said something about having one of her rare bursts of enthusiasm and that she wanted to go out. I asked what she was going to do, and all she did was let out a whoop."

"A whoop?"

"Yes. And it was carnal. Decidedly carnal."

I walked away feeling very good. It was comforting to know that there was sex after Hogarth.

"Does anyone have anything to say before we begin this morning?" asked Christine after she had made eye contact with each of us.

"Yes," said Lucy. "I do. I . . ." she hesitated and looked down. There were a few seconds of silence. "I'm sorry," she continued, "I'm not used to talking in a group without a drink in my hand."

"I know how you feel," said Melanie. "And I'm an actress. I'm supposed to enjoy being the center of attention. But not in here."

Lucy inhaled deeply, exhaled slightly and continued. "The thing that bothers me is that no one here seems to be as unhappy as me.

I'm terribly depressed. I don't have an appetite, and I can't sleep. I think that maybe I'm in the wrong place. Maybe I should be in a psychiatric hospital."

I almost fell out of my chair when I heard this. Hadn't she noticed how depressed I was? Nobody in the hospital could be as unhappy as I. How could she say that?

"Lucy," cried Melanie, "you've got to be kidding. I'm more depressed now than I've ever been. The only thing I think about is getting out of here. I've almost gone over the wall a dozen times. I didn't think that you were so bad."

I started to speak, but Boone and Steve spoke just as I did. We then looked at each other, each waiting for the other to speak.

Christine laughed and slapped her hands together.

"Excuse me for laughing. But I've never seen so many people anxious to speak at once during group. Does that tell you anything, Lucy? Do you still feel alone?"

Lucy shook her head.

"None of you has a monopoly on unhappiness," continued Christine. "No patient in this hospital is not depressed. But the depression becomes less acute as you go along. Have you talked to Dr. O'Malley, Lucy?"

"Yes. But he hardly ever says anything. He just stares at me. The second time I saw him, he didn't blink once. I thought he was sleeping with his eyes open."

"He's not helping you?" I asked.

"I didn't say that," Lucy snapped. "But he just doesn't volunteer much."

We made small talk for a few minutes, hoping to put off for as long as possible the self-disclosure that we had begun the day before. Christine reminded us that we needed to continue what we had started during the first session. She asked for someone to begin.

"Everybody calls me Hog Body, Chrissie. Well, my wife doesn't." He smiled. "When she's mad, I'm Herman.

"I'm forty-eight now. I have two kids. My son, Patty, is twenty. I want him to be a doctor. My daughter, Angeline, is thirteen. I work in a mill. I'm a foreman."

"Why are you in Hogarth?" asked Christine.

"I drink too much rye."

"Is there anything else you'd like to tell us?"

"Well," smiled Hog Body, "that's everything."

There were a few uncomfortable minutes of silence.

"I'm a mechanic," said Steve, finally. "You might say I'm between jobs. The last time I worked was eight months ago. I got fired because I was always late for work. I have bad insomnia, and I take Valium and Placidyls every night." He grinned widely. "So I sleep late. And I drink like a fucking fish . . . Molsons. . . . I get into a lot of fights when I drink. I also have a lot of citations for impaired driving."

"Any family, Steve?"

"I am divorced as of three days ago." He paused and looked at the floor. "She divorced me. The bitch."

"Would you like to talk about it?" Christine asked.

Steve shook his head.

Christine looked at Lucy. "Next."

"I've been an alcoholic for at least twelve years," said Lucy in a trembling voice. "My husband has been in the navy for twenty-five years. He loves it. Especially the dinner parties. I get very nervous at cocktail and dinner parties. I'm uncomfortable with small talk.

"But Walter has always been very ambitious. He loved rubbing elbows with higher-ranking officers. So we went to a lot of parties and we hosted a lot.

"I found about fifteen years ago that if I had a few drinks before the party, I'd function without being nervous. Of course, I'd only have one or two glasses of wine during the party. I always wanted people to think of me as delicate.

"As the years went by I'd drink more and more scotch before the parties. I thought I needed more. And I was drinking earlier and earlier during the day. Then I began sneaking drinks during the party. And again after the party.

"About six or seven years ago, I was drinking continuously. Walter threatened to leave me because I was becoming a liability. So I tried A.A."

Lucy looked startled for a moment.

"Am I saying too much, Christine? Should I be saving some of this?"

"Your story is very interesting. Why don't you go on? Did A.A. help you?"

"I thought the people in A.A. were terribly rigid, and I didn't like the way they ritualized humility. But the reason I quit A.A. was because of all the honesty I encountered.

"When you're an alcoholic, it takes an extraordinary amount of courage not to lie. I couldn't even admit that I had a problem."

"Why are you here, Lucy? Did something happen?" asked Boone.

Lucy folded her hands on her lap and closed her eyes.

"God, I wish I had a drink now," she said. "Walter can be disapproving in ways that really hurt. He's been seeing another woman for at least six months. And I don't blame him. I'm a drunk.

"So I came here hoping this would be my first step toward sobriety."

"We appreciate very much your sharing your story with us," said Christine. "You volunteered more about yourself than most people do this early into group."

"I find it difficult, Lucy," I said, "to believe that you've ever had trouble with honesty."

Melanie appeared nervous. Only she and MacGregor remained to tell the group something about themselves. MacGregor appeared bored.

"I'm twenty-six," said Melanie. "I have a master's degree in drama. I'm a good actress. There's no greater feeling in the world than being on stage in a good part with everyone's eyes on you, and you know you're being convincing.

"I drank a lot. Vodka mostly. But I started substituting tranquilizers for vodka about a year ago, when somebody told me alcohol had a lot of calories. I do cocaine, too, when I can afford it. I've done ludes. And"—she shrugged her shoulders—"speed. I've been drinking a lot of cheap wine lately. I'll tell you, cheap wine and some codeine can really hit the spot."

"I've never shot up," she announced proudly. "But . . . I want to stop all the shit I'm doing. I don't think I ever will, though. I don't know what's wrong with me. I think I would be a good study for a psychologist—Melanie, the inadequate person."

"We'll want to know more about you," Christine said. "I seriously doubt you are as inadequate as you think you are. You judge yourself too harshly."

We all turned to MacGregor, who was beginning to look uncomfortable.

"I'm not sure I want to tell a group of people about my private life," MacGregor finally said. "It's no one's business."

"Let's not fuck around with him," Steve said, annoyance in his voice. "Boone, let's throw his ass out of here."

"Wait a minute," Christine said. She pointed a finger at MacGregor. "If you won't talk, you have to leave. It's your decision."

"C'mon, Mac," Hog Body said. "We're all equals in here. Nobody's better than anybody else. Tell us about yourself. Didn't you say you were an Ontario cop?"

"I lied, Hog," MacGregor said. He sat back in his chair and crossed his legs. After a few seconds he uncrossed his legs and took a deep breath. "I used to be a policeman. Now I work in the dispatch office. Ten years ago they took me off the street because I sometimes came to work sauced. In the last ten years I've been shuffled around to all the really shitty jobs.

"I don't know what the fuck is wrong with me. One drink and I'm a social problem. Every cop in the province knows I'm a drunk. They think they've been helping me by covering up for me. I should've been in here ten years ago."

"Your problem is just with alcohol then, MacGregor?" asked Christine, obviously glad that he had finally opened up.

"Call me Mac, will ya? I thought it was just booze until I talked to Randolph. But he says I'm hooked on Librium, too. The family doctor put me on tranquilizers a few years ago. He told me that would help me stop drinking. Randolph says I'm cross-addicted. I'll talk to that doctor when I get out of here."

Christine looked satisfied.

"I'm beginning to feel good about this group. You seem to be serious people. And I like your honesty. As I'm sure each of you know by now, these sessions can be stressful. In the next few weeks you will be quite surprised, I think, at the intimate and sometimes unfortunate details of your life you'll be talking about.

"See you tomorrow."

"Is this more Canadian food, Lorenzo? What the hell is this we're eating?"

"Penis tips and hog warts," he said, unsmiling.

"What?" I started to spit out my mouthful of food.

"Hold it, man. I'm just kidding," he said through bursts of laughter. "It's hot dogs cut up in raisin sauce."

For the first time, Lorenzo's laugh appeared to be genuine and not forced. It was nice to hear him make a joke.

"You look pretty good today, Lorenzo. Are you feeling better?"

"Yeah. I am. I had a long talk with Toni this morning."

"I was having a rough time yesterday morning," I said. "She helped. I like her gentleness."

He laughed.

"She's gentle all right. She told me if I didn't straighten up soon she'd kick my black ass from here to Montreal. She can really get an attitude."

"Has she helped ease your depression?"

Lorenzo looked surprised. I wanted him to know that his constant show of brave good humor wasn't always necessary.

His smile went away as he slowly shook his head.

During exercise class, Karren took off her cotton exercise suit and wore only a loose-fitting sleeveless top and running shorts. She had statuesque upper thighs and buttocks. Soft music with rhythmic drum beating was playing and was made sensual by the way she moved. We were supposed to be following her as she gave forward thrusts of her hips.

But I stood and watched as she moved. So did Melanie. Everyone else appeared to be trying. Karren sustained a long look at Melanie, who was still wearing her baggy sweat suit.

When the class was over and the music stopped, Karren barked out:

"Sit."

Karren sat cross-legged on the floor facing us.

"Exercise for me is the best treatment for stress. I run," she said, without seeming boastful. "Running works for me. I run in the morning before work. I try to think about all the things that anger me when I run. That way all the energy I would normally exhaust in anger is going into the exercise. And I can think about the difficult things unemotionally."

"Why aren't we running then," asked Steve. "Why the dry fuck routine?"

"We'll start walking in a few days. It's important now that you first start exercising muscles in your upper thighs and hips that many of you probably haven't used in a long time." She looked at me when she said that.

"This will just take a few minutes," Toni said to us, as we sat in the fourth floor lounge. There was a carton of pamphlets on the floor next to her. "I would like to give each of you a schedule of A.A. meetings that are held at Hogarth. We have two meetings each night and three on Sunday. You should go to as many of these as you can. I also have some information here about Alcoholics Anonymous and about each of the twelve steps.

"Also, we would like to contact an A.A. group in your home city so they can arrange a sponsor for you. We'll need your permission for that. I'll call each of your names. Tell me yes or no. Lucy?"

"Well . . . I don't know. All right."

"Hog Body?"

"Sure."

"Steve?"

"Yeah."

"Patrick?"

"No."

Toni took that as an affront.

"Are you sure, Patrick?"

"I'm a physician. I don't want anyone in Cleveland to know. I'd be too ashamed. Besides, I don't want the medical society to find out."

"Cleveland is a big city. Surely there are parts of the city where no one knows you. The medical society won't find out about you being here if you don't want them to know."

"Please, Toni. I don't want to discuss it. My answer is no."

"Patrick, when you leave here, you will be tempted to take drugs again. What will you do? Sit in a chair somewhere and grit your teeth and tough it out by yourself? That won't work. If you're in A.A., you'll be able to call someone for help."

Toni's face took on a plaintive look. It was difficult to disagree with her. But I did. I shook my head.

"Patrick," she said, "you're being foolish."

She shook her head. She was disappointed.

"Melanie?"

"No."

"MacGregor?"

"Yeah."

"Boone?"

"Yes. I'll give it another try."

"I hope those of you who said no will reconsider before you leave Hogarth," Toni said in an impersonal, slightly angry tone. She did not handle disappointment well.

Dear Irene:

My ninth day of captivity and counting. Nineteen more to go.

The violent mood swings I've been experiencing and the ambivalence I'm feeling have me confused and disoriented. This morning for a short time I was so proud of myself for coming to Hogarth. I was almost euphoric. But this evening I'm depressed and angry. I'm on an emotional roller coaster and I can't slow down and I seem to have no control.

I feel as if I'm playing out a role in a soap opera. I just wish there were some goddamn commercials.

I've had plenty of time to reflect. Things seem to get reduced to their basic importance and unimportance in here. Being with you and seeing my patients are the only tangible things of significance in my life.

You know what I miss most? You and I reading to each other. Listening to you read is the most pleasant thing I can think of.

We're supposed to be learning some relaxation techniques here. And I'll need some. My stress tolerance is nonexistent. I'm responding to anxious situations now with only visible anger which is an unfamiliar phenomenon for me. I'm not used to showing my anger.

Maybe without being sedated I'm more like Logan. His blind, unfocused rage used to frighten me so much. And it got worse as he got older. In the last few years before he died, he was pathetic. How do I know that anger won't consume me now as it did him?

Do you realize these past nine days is the first time I've been off drugs in fourteen years? You never knew me when I was not taking sedatives. That means that my adrenaline will now be flowing unopposed. I might change drastically. That worries me. I don't know what it will do to us. I suspect that some parts of my personality may emerge that neither of us is familiar with. One more thing to worry about.

I know I'm becoming more aware of people and sensitive to their feelings. Remember how intolerant of alcoholics I was? When I was an intern, I hated to see an alcoholic come in as a patient. We would only dry them out, give them vitamins, feed them, and release them as soon as possible.

I guess I never had contact with alcoholics before they were terminal. But I know alcoholics now, and they are intelligent, kind people who are, like me, crying for help. When I remember what my attitude was, I'm embarrassed.

I am finding it difficult acclimating to unhappiness. The staff here is aware of how difficult this time is for us. They really seem to care and are effective in dealing with anger. The other day I was mad as hell about the food here. I went to Toni, the charge nurse on my floor, and told her if they tried to feed me one more goddamn visceral organ I was going to go on a hunger strike. She told me to be prepared to be hungry because our next meal was going to be a pancreas soufflé. I got so mad, I started pulling at myself. She was putting me on, of course. I will get her for that.

Tonight we had our first practice for our skit we'll be doing Saturday morning. It should be a disaster. We have really been fumbling with ideas. Mac suggested we use a porno movie theme, and he described some scenes. Mac does not mess around with subtleties. Hog Body doesn't care what we do as long as he can dress up as a woman.

Melanie won't tell us exactly what she's going to do but has recruited me, Steve, and Boone to do a scene with her. She said it would be "something like Cinderella." She needs a prop someone is going to bring her. It should be interesting.

I think about you all the time, and I can't wait to see you again. I miss your smile, your smell, and your taste.

Love,
Pat

Preparing for bed at night was not terribly exciting anymore. I never had to be concerned about the possibility of overdosing and accidentally killing myself.

I lay naked on the bed with my earphones on listening to Karren's voice attempting to direct me into tranquility. It wasn't working. And although her voice was sounding sensuous, and I could place the voice with the face and the face with the nice thighs and buttocks, I remained unaroused.

15

LORENZO and I were finishing a last cup of coffee before beginning the day. For the first time we were discussing the practice of medicine, and I for a few moments had forgotten where I was. A member of Lorenzo's group joined us. It was Presswood, the guy who'd made the racial remark during the past Saturday's skit.

"Hi, Docs," he said very loudly. "What are we talking about?"

"We were just leaving," said Lorenzo.

"Hey, I hear you're from Cleveland," he said to me. "I spent a month there one day." He laughed loudly. "Colored people and Polacks. That's all you got there."

"I happen to like Cleveland," I said.

"Sorry pal," he said, without a hint of remorse.

Presswood looked at my plate. I had eaten about half of my pancakes. I enjoy mixing ketchup with my syrup. It doesn't look appealing, but I like it. He continued to look at my plate, and I readied myself for an inane remark. I told him what it was. He laughed derisively as he poured a huge amount of syrup on his pancakes.

"Jesus H. Christ," he proclaimed loudly. "You don't eat like a white man."

Lorenzo stiffened slightly. I hoped he would say something. But he just slowly stood and walked away.

Presswood smiled broadly, unaware of inflicting a hurt. He watched Lorenzo go, and while his head was turned, I reached over and with one finger flipped his plate onto his lap. He turned quickly and gasped. He looked down, then at me.

I stood slowly and looked down at him.

"Asshole," I said.

"I have found in working with previous groups that some people have had to experience a shock situation before they begin to realize that they have had a problem with alcohol or drugs. Maybe it was their wife leaving them or they got fired." As Christine talked, she looked slowly around the group.

"Usually it's an event that is very painful or embarrassing. But people often feel better once they've brought these things out in group. I'd like to open the session up this morning, and I hope you'll each tell the rest of us what happened to you to make you come into Hogarth when you did.

"I realize this may be very difficult."

No one spoke for several minutes. Then Christine finally said:

"Steve, would you like to volunteer?"

Steve stared at the floor and shook his head.

"Is it very painful?"

Steve nodded.

"Does it have something to do with having to go to jail?"

"No."

"Your wife?"

"Three months ago I came home and found my wife in bed with my brother. I didn't know which one to kill first." Steve's voice was shaking.

"My wife got out of the bed and laughed at me. She said: 'What do you expect? You're not a man anymore!' I turned around and my two sons were there. They saw it all, and they heard what she said."

Steve stopped abruptly and looked momentarily surprised. He then gave Christine a piercing, severe look.

"You shouldn't have made me do that," he said with restrained but obvious anger.

"Steve," Lucy interjected, "maybe the next time you talk about it, it won't hurt so much."

There was more silence.

"Melanie, what about you? Any shock situations?"

"My whole life's a shock situation. I have jolts every day."

"How about sharing one of those with us?"

"Well, a few months ago I was out buying some wine. Sometimes when I was low on money the guy who owned the store, Mr. Benson, would give me a bottle free. I wasn't working then, and he gave me a bottle . . . the cheapest stuff he had. Then he started leering at me . . . then . . . then he touched me. . . . the son of a bitch actually put his hand on my breast." Melanie's chest was heaving. "I wanted to spit in his face . . . but I needed him . . . I needed his wine . . . so I said nothing. He only gave me one bottle so he knew I'd be in the next day . . . and I came in. But this time his wife was there. He gave me a bottle of wine and whispered to me: 'You owe me.' I waited until his wife got close to us, and I said to him in my Scarlett O'Hara voice: 'Mr. Benson, I *just* love the things you do to me with your tongue. I want to thank you so much.' "

"Beautiful, Melanie. Beautiful!" shrieked Lucy.

"I left the store and I heard things crashing. She must have been throwing things at him. I never went back."

"I had six or seven different stores where I bought alcohol," said Lucy. "I never went to the same store more than once a month. I even kept a list." She sighed. "Even us drunks must keep up appearances."

Christine's eyes moved to me, and I looked at the floor.

There were a few moments of silence.

"Patrick," Christine said, "I'm still looking at you."

"A lot of bad things have happened in the past year," I said and looked at her. "I've had some definite shock situations. Some professional . . . some personal."

"Tell us the one that hurts the most."

I sat up in my chair, took a deep breath, and looked out the window. I couldn't look at anyone.

"About three months ago I was asked to lecture at the Friday morning Grand Rounds at the hospital. I was going to talk on the need for a mandatory child-safety restraint law in Ohio. I was on a committee that was trying to get a bill introduced in the legislature that would require all children to be protected while riding in cars.

"I get pretty nervous before any type of public speaking. So the night before the talk I took more drugs than usual. And I knew I would. So I put an amphetamine tablet, my only one, on the sink in the bathroom. I was going to take it as soon as I got up. Even though those damn amphetamines give me a migraine, I'd still need the pill to get through the talk."

My hands were dripping wet, and I smiled weakly at Christine.

"Go ahead," she said. "You're doing fine."

"No, I'm not. But"—I looked out the window again—"well, when I got up that Friday morning, the pill wasn't there. It was gone! I panicked. I couldn't get up in front of people and talk the way I was . . . groggy, slurring my words. I'd make a fool of myself.

"Irene had got up during the night and had accidentally dropped the pill into the sink. Most of the pill dissolved, and she threw what was left in the wastebasket.

"When she told me that, I ran into the bathroom and threw everything out of the wastebasket onto the floor so I could find what was left."

I stopped and took a deep breath. I glanced at the members of my group. They were staring at me. I didn't want to go on. I didn't want them to know. Why did I start this? I looked out the window again and exhaled.

"Irene saw me on the floor going through the trash. She yelled at me . . . said I looked like a bum rummaging for food. She screamed at me again and again . . . told me to get up. I couldn't find the pill. . . . She kept screaming at me. I needed that damn pill. . . . She said I was acting like a drug addict."

"You hit her," Melanie said, her inflection mirroring her disappointment.

"With my fist . . . I hit her with my fist. Christ, it was awful. . . ." I started to cry, and Christine handed me the always-present box of Kleenex. "Her nose started to bleed . . . her eye turned red . . . Irene looked so hurt, so helpless. . . ." I took a Kleenex and wiped the tears away and blew my nose. "I had never hit her before. I felt such disgust. I've apologized to her a thousand times . . . but I still feel so awful, so guilty."

"Patrick," Christine said, and I looked at her as she moved forward in her chair and put her elbows on her knees. "The Fifth Step of A.A. is admitting to the exact nature of your wrongs with complete honesty. Someday when Irene understands that you were physically and psychologically addicted to drugs and that you felt helpless, terrified, and out of control when you were looking for that pill, she'll forgive you. And you won't feel quite so guilty."

Christine gave me a reassuring smile.

"Irene is either a saint or a fool," Melanie said. There was disgust in her voice. "Didn't she ever confront you about all the drugs you take? Why does she stay with you?"

"Irene has never known me when I wasn't taking drugs. She has no idea how many drugs I take. I keep one bottle of tranquilizers and one bottle of sleeping pills in the medicine chest. Occasionally I'll let her see me take a drug from one of the bottles. That's all she thinks I take.

"I keep most of my drugs locked in a closet in my study. And some at my office."

"Sounds to me," Christine said, "as if Irene is working overtime on denial."

"That story must have been very difficult to tell us," Melanie said.

"Thanks for sharing that with us, Patrick," Christine said and then slowly turned her head and looked at Hog Body. "And what about you?"

Hog chuckled.

"Chrissie, you haven't called me by name once. It's O.K. to call me Hog Body. I like it. And nobody ever forgets my name."

Christin nodded and smiled.

"Any shock situations, Hog Body?"

"No. Not really," he said pleasantly.

"C'mon, Hog," snapped Steve. "Don't bullshit us."

Hog's smile disappeared and the look on his face became serious and then sad. He stared at the floor. We had not seen him like this before.

"I'm usually pretty easygoing, and when I drink, my wife tells me I act like a buffoon. I get foolish. When I drink a lot, I sometimes wrestle with my son. He's a tough kid. But I always beat him.

"About two months ago I had drunk about half of a bottle of rye. He wasn't home. But my daughter was. She's thirteen. I started to wrestle with her. I . . ." Hog Body stopped. He made no sounds as if he were crying, but tears were forming in his eyes and rolling down his cheeks.

"I accidently touched her." He looked at Christine. "You know, down there." He pointed to his groin. "I started to get excited. I touched her again. I think she knew it was wrong, but she didn't stop me. I started to kiss her. My own daughter. Then I took off her clothes.

"I put my hands all over her. Then I put my tongue in her . . . I think she had an orgasm. I was so drunk . . . I couldn't get it up or I would have done that, too."

He began sobbing.

"I love my daughter. But not that way. I would never have done that if I hadn't been drinking. Please believe me . . . please."

Hog Body was bent at the waist and had his face in his hands. He was crying silently.

"Will any of you . . . ever speak to me again?" He was desolate.

Melanie got out of her chair slowly and walked to Hog Body. She knelt beside him and very softly kissed him on the cheek. She then put her arm around his broad back.

"We love you, Hog," she said.

Simply put, I didn't like O'Malley's style. To be sure, the physician-patient interaction has a certain ceremony and required rituals. But I found him to be unnecessarily formal, and that made it difficult to be comfortable with him. And I hated those stupid spotlights.

I wanted to ask O'Malley if he were as inured to other people's psychic pain as he appeared to be. I was sitting across from him and pouring out to him how terrible I felt. He sat listening intently but giving no evidence of compassion.

"I'm afraid that I'll feel this desperate and unhappy when I eventually get out of here. How could I ever function like this when I try to resume my life?"

"Despairing of the future is fairly characteristic of acute depression."

I was becoming disappointed with O'Malley. I didn't want any more reassurances that I was not intractably unhappy. I wanted to feel better immediately. I slouched in my chair, folded my arms across my chest, and rolled my eyes toward the ceiling. I wanted him to know I was bored and that he wasn't helping me.

"Patrick, situational depression is by definition self-limited. This will pass. And there is nothing in your premorbid personality profile to suggest that you will not rebound from this." He was being pointedly patient and instructive.

"Your thinking is in the irrational spectrum right now," he continued. "Try not to think about the future for a while. I know that might be difficult, but planning and making decisions are two things that you shouldn't be doing when you feel like this."

"What upsets and frightens me," I said finally, "is that I don't want to stay like this. And I don't understand why I'm so angry all the time."

O'Malley began stroking his beard as he stared at me.

"There may be a fairly simple explanation for your anger. Most of our patients have reached the cowering and desperate stage before we get them. Their lives are in ruin and they have very little left. For most of them, coming to Hogarth is their only remaining survival maneuver. When they come in here, they are fairly submissive and are accepting of whatever we ask them to do.

"You, on the other hand, came here with still a lot to lose. Although I know you are convinced you had a serious problem, you probably feel that coming to Hogarth may have been too drastic a step. You are becoming a more cooperative patient, but I think you are still attempting to deal with an inner conflict about the necessity of your being here."

O'Malley was finally beginning to make some sense. I gave a nod to let him know that he had made a point.

"I hate to see a doctor come in here as a patient," he said, shaking his head. "Physicians don't accept the role reversal very well. They normally are two weeks behind the other patients in their progress.

"Lawyers are worse, though. They want to challenge and negotiate everything."

I was beginning to feel more comfortable with O'Malley, but I still could take him in only small doses. The self-revelation he required of me was too concentrated. At least in Group Therapy I could sit back most of the time and listen to other people reveal things about themselves. I got up to leave.

"Sit down," he said with abruptness. "We have a lot more to talk about."

"More than twenty minutes with you is counterproductive," I said but sat down as ordered.

He smiled. O'Malley actually smiled.

"We need to talk about your feelings of guilt for a few minutes."

"Are we going to jump from one problem to another without resolving anything?"

"*We* will not resolve your problems," he said, emphasizing the *we*. "You have to do that. Hopefully I'm just giving you some things to think about."

"What about guilt?" I asked impatiently.

"Guilt is something that you will soon have to put aside. It severely limits your capacity for insight. Remember last week when I called addiction an illness? You got livid. How do you feel about it now?"

"Illness is such a soft word. But I haven't really thought about it since then."

"I would like you to think about your addiction as a behavior problem, not a moral problem. Your involvement with the sedative drugs is something that you started unwittingly. You never made a decision to be a drug addict. It was a behavior that became ritualized and obsessive and something that you could not control. Taking sedatives became as much an integral part of your life as eating. You were unable to make the decision not to take the pills. Addiction for you, then, was simply a bad habit out of control.

"The point that I'm trying to make, Patrick, is that you came here with a behavior problem." He leaned forward and pointed his pen at me. "It's a behavior that *you* can change."

"You have a call, Patrick."

"Is it my wife, Toni?"

"It's a man."

"But my wife is the only one who knows I'm in here. Did he say who it is?"

"No. But it's a local call."

I walked slowly to the phone and picked up the receiver.

"Hello."

"Hi, Pat. It's me, Gordon."

"Jesus, Gordon, you scared me. Until Toni told me this was a local call I thought the medical society back home had found out."

"Are you doing all right? You sound better."

"I do? Well, maybe there's been some progress. I've had some good sessions with O'Malley. And Group Therapy is quite an experience.

"Tell me about yourself, Gordon. How are you doing?"

"I'm back on the waiting list for Hogarth. I'll come back in as soon as I can. They said maybe I could get back in five or six weeks. I've been taking Antabuse every day."

"Are you staying off the drugs, too?"

"No. One thing at a time, Pat. At least I probably won't kill myself as long as I can't drink. By the way, don't ever drink when you're on Antabuse. They had to take me to Emergency."

"Why do you want to come back here, Gordon? You seemed pretty unhappy when you left."

"I was unhappy when I left. I had never developed such a fondness for people so quickly as when I was in Hogarth. I miss you and Melanie and Lucy and the others. I liked the atmosphere of people trying to help each other—and themselves. I want to try again."

"I'm really glad to hear this, Gordon. I miss you, too."

"There's something else. I was off all drugs and alcohol for a week. I realized during that time that I still had some passion left. There are things I want to do. So I'm going to come back to Hogarth as soon as I can. I want to save my life."

Late in the afternoon we met with Reggie and Toni. Although Toni worked days and Reggie evenings, their shifts did overlap for one hour. Reggie and Toni appeared to have a warm friendship.

"We weren't always friends," Reggie said, smiling. "When I was a patient here, I couldn't stand Toni. I was always angry with her because I thought she didn't trust me."

"I didn't trust you. Nobody did. Not after that trick you pulled the first week of drinking the rubbing alcohol. I had all the men hide their after-shave lotion."

"C'mon, Toni, I'd never drink after-shave lotion. It's too sweet."

"I never knew a patient who talked as much as you," Toni said, vainly attempting to hide a smile. "And, girl, you never said one worthwhile thing for the longest time."

"I thought you were judgmental and arrogant," Reggie shot back. "But now that I know you better, I can tell your patients that you're not judgmental. Arrogant, yes. But not judgmental."

Reggie then told the group of her codeine addiction and what she had lost.

"Toni can tell you that for my first six weeks I was something less than the ideal patient. I groused around here feeling guilty and angry. I thought I was wasting my time.

"After six weeks Dr. Randolph let me go home for an afternoon.

When I got to my apartment, I found I was completely alone. My husband and child were gone. It was the loneliest I have ever been. I found a bottle of codeine pills that I had hid before I came to Hogarth. I stared at it for a few seconds; then I took the bottle and emptied it into the toilet. I realized then that I had regained a freedom that I had surrendered five years before. I had the freedom to choose not to take codeine. I once again had control of my life."

"We need to start making plans for the Family Program next week," said Toni. "Having members of your family spend a few days here learning about alcoholism and drug addiction is an integral part of our program."

"Your spouses need to know about substance abuse and how they should deal with it just like you do. I think that if my husband had come here for this program, it would have saved my marriage."

"Reggie," I said, "I'm a little afraid of having Irene come. I know she'll find out just how much I lied and how calculating I was."

"She already knows, Patrick. Now it's time for her to find out that your lying was probably something that you had virtually no control over. She needs to understand so that she won't dwell on it, because that would be destructive.

"When your wife is here, she'll learn some harsh truths about you. Don't be afraid of that. She'll learn some difficult things about herself, too."

"Will I be able to spend some time alone with my wife?" Mac-Gregor winked at Steve. "We have a lot to talk about."

"A little ficky-ficky with a warm fuzzy," I said, quoting an old Irish uncle of mine. "That's long overdue." I hoped this would imply to the group that I was sexually well adjusted and functional.

Toni then asked each of us if any relatives would be coming.

"Melanie?"

She shook her head.

"Hog Body?"

"My wife."

"Steve?"

"My mother."

"MacGregor?"

"Just the wife." MacGregor had a way of referring to his wife as if she were property. I found it interesting if not appealing.

"Patrick?"

"Just the wife." I tried to capture MacGregor's inflection.

Reggie gave me a severe look. I had been successful in sounding proprietary. I smiled at Reggie to let her know I was joking. She did not smile back.

"Boone?"

"No one."

"Lucy?"

"Walter will be here."

I made arrangements with Hog Body to have our wives share a motel room. This arrangement would give Irene and me the least privacy, I reasoned. I was terrified of being alone with her. Being unable to perform again sexually was a torturing thought.

Melanie was more subdued during skit practice than ever before. We were all concerned, but no one said anything. After practice I went to my room, but I couldn't help thinking about her. Of all of us in the group, she seemed the most vulnerable.

She was surprised when she opened her door and saw me.

"C'mon in, Patrick. This is a nice surprise."

I went into her room and she closed the door.

"I hope you don't mind my coming here this late."

"Not at all." She was a little unsure of my motive.

"Normally when I pass your room at night, I pause for a few seconds and pant. Tonight I mustered up enough courage to knock."

She laughed.

"Melanie, you looked so unhappy tonight. Is something wrong?"

"When we were talking with Reggie and Toni about the Family Program, I got very upset."

"Because no one is coming for you?"

She nodded.

"What about your parents?"

"I don't want them here," she said.

"How about close friends?"

"You mean lovers. No. At least not one that could come."

"Are you lonely?"

She nodded. "Every close relationship I've had has been destructive for me in one way or another. I have only one real friend—a woman."

I wondered if Melanie was admitting something. My expression must have shown my uncertainty.

"No. I'm heterosexual." She smiled. "And right now I'm desperately heterosexual."

"You mean horny."

She nodded. "God, I get so horny just before my period."

She turned away but then looked at me with an expression that was unmistakably alluring.

"I like you a lot, Patrick. And I find you very attractive." She moved toward me.

This was totally unexpected, and I didn't know what to do. How would Bogart react in this situation? Casual? Jaunty? Evasive? Mildly interested? Amused? And how would he react if he were impotent?

Melanie put her arms over my shoulders. I felt her firm breasts against my chest. I hugged her, and she put her head on my shoulder. Her hair was gentle against my face.

She had the soft scent of lilac.

"Are you nervous?" she whispered.

"Terrified. In a few seconds my ears will start to move up and down uncontrollably."

She backed away and gave me a questioning look.

"Is this the way you respond to a seduction?"

"Right now it's the only way I can respond."

She didn't understand and looked expectant. Then her eyes widened slightly. She gave me a small, apologetic smile.

"I hope I didn't embarrass you, Patrick."

"No. I'm flattered that you find me attractive."

I placed my hand along the side of her face. "You're very nice, Melanie."

She reached up and gently began smoothing down the hairs on the back of my hand. Her touch was exquisite.

"Are you sure I can't help? I'll do anything."

She moved in close to me and put her arms over my shoulders again. "Anything," she whispered. She pressed her upper thighs and pelvis against me. Her hands slipped down my back and rested on my hips. She pulled me closer. She kissed me and slipped her tongue into my mouth.

She was going too fast. She would demand too much. My heart was beating fast. I wanted so much to be aroused. I wanted to make love to her. But I didn't want to fail again. I didn't want to be humiliated.

I stood back from her. I was embarrassed.

"I'm sorry," she said.

"It's my problem. I'll have to solve it. And I'll start tonight by fantasizing about what might have happened between us. I'm sorry if I'm leaving you in heat, Melanie."

"That's all right," she said. "I can take care of that myself."

I'm fucking impotent, O'Malley. What am I going to do about that? You're full of shit. This is more than just an illness. It's a loss of self-respect, self-control, self-determination, self-assurance.

And I'm not getting any better. If you or that miserable bastard Randolph don't start helping me soon, I'll put this goddamn place behind me. I'm not going to give you much more time.

I LAY AWAKE all night and prayed for an erection. I tried every fantasy I could think of. A friend in medical school, an aggressive heterosexual, had told me that his favorite fantasy was having sex with fat little boys. He later became a psychiatrist.

My fantasies did not have much range. They included only me, in various situations with adult women. And I had one favorite lady. I had seen her in a cheap black and white silent stag film when I was fifteen. She must have been in her forties and overweight. And she perspired heavily. Her moves were acrobatic, and she performed with the single-mindedness and enthusiasm of someone who loved her work.

And I remember vividly her look of exquisite pain when her various orifices were penetrated.

She would come whenever I needed her, silent, heavy, and perspiring. We would do unspeakable, marvelous things to each other, and then she would go. We never spoke.

I think I loved her.

I had finished showering and was standing in my room with only a towel around my waist when Toni breezed in with my vitamin pill.

"Hey, you should knock first. I could have been doing unnatural things to myself."

"That might have been interesting. I always like to learn new things."

Toni was looking particularly good this morning.

"You have an appointment to see Dr. O'Malley after breakfast."

I nodded, and she headed for the door.

"Wait a minute, Toni. Now that you've seen me almost naked, what do you think? Not a bad body for a thirty-six-year-old. Right?" I was joking, but a compliment would have been nice.

She looked me over.

"Hmmm . . . shoulders are pretty good . . . sagging around the middle . . . legs are O.K. . . . butt's too small."

"If I were to be auctioned off for stud service, Toni, how much would someone like you pay?"

"Someone like me wouldn't be buying."

"Don't be too sure, Toni. You haven't seen what's under the towel."

"I wish I had time this morning, Patrick. I need a good laugh."

I quickly pulled off my towel and tossed it at her as she shrieked and darted out the door.

O'Malley was unusually uncommunicative. He appeared to be somewhat disconsolate and definitely preoccupied as we talked.

"There's a physician's support group that meets here on Thursday evenings," he said. "I think you should go to it. These are physicians from the area who have come through Hogarth and are now back in the community."

"Sure. I'd like to go."

"It can get a little rough."

"How do you mean?"

"You will find that recovering impaired physicians can be pretty uncompromising with each other. And some of their stories might shock you. I know you're still depressed, and this meeting could be a difficult experience. But at least you'll see other doctors who are making it. Just like you will."

"I'd like to go," I repeated. "I would like to have gone last week."

O'Malley shook his head.

"You weren't ready. I'm not sure you're ready now. But if you start feeling distressed, I want you to get up and leave."

I nodded.

O'Malley was clearly not one who had a natural impulse for wit and casual good humor. But this morning he spoke without inflection and was unquestionably dispirited. I had to ask.

"What's the matter? You really seem unhappy."

He looked away from me and rested his chin on his fist. After a few seconds his eyes moved back to me.

"Sometimes working in this field can be discouraging."

He opened a top desk drawer and pulled out a hospital chart.

"I was reading this before you came in," he said, looking discouraged. "It's the chart of a doctor we had in here eight months ago. He was cross-addicted. Alcohol and Valium. We kept him four weeks. We didn't make him stay longer."

He looked at me and saw me cringe. Even a hint of the possibility of my being recycled was upsetting.

"He called me last week and was very agitated because he had relapsed. The hospital where he was applying for reinstatement to the staff rejected him. So he started drinking again.

"I made arrangements for him to be admitted next Monday."

I was surprised to see O'Malley so discouraged about a relapse.

"So you'll have to work with him again?"

He shook his head.

"He overdosed on Seconal yesterday. He's dead."

O'Malley slammed his fist on the desk.

"He shouldn't have done that," he shouted angrily. "He could have called me."

He then sank back into his chair and for the first time looked defenseless. I wished I could help him.

"I had spent a lot of time with him both while he was in Hogarth and after he got out. I felt I had helped him." O'Malley smiled. "I had put his chart in my ego file."

O'Malley was suffering from the *this patient would not have gotten better if it were not for me* syndrome. That attitude was not only wrong, it was dangerous.

"This is one more vivid and terrible example," he said, "that one is never *cured* of alcoholism or drug addiction. You might recover from the ill effects of substance abuse. But never speak of a cure.

"And it requires an extraordinary vigilance not to relapse back into an addiction. Remember that, Patrick. Please."

Christine had a devilish grin and seemed somewhat tentative. It was as if she were going to play a dirty trick on us and was not sure how we would respond.

"What we are going to do today will be very difficult for most of you." She kept her grin and made eye contact with each of us. "I want each of you to select two other people in the group and ask them their opinion of you."

"Chrissie, I don't want to ask anybody how they feel about me. Please don't make me do this."

"You may be pleasantly surprised, Hog Body."

There was a barely audible "Fuck this shit" from Steve. It was said with more discomfort than defiance. MacGregor then cackled loudly because he enjoyed obscenities.

"Any other comments?"

Christine glanced at me, and I looked quickly to the floor. I didn't want to go first.

"I'll begin," said Christine. "Steve, what is your opinion of me? Say it any way you'd like. Just be honest."

Steve glanced at Christine and didn't move. There was silence. It appeared as if he were not going to respond. The silence was becoming long and uncomfortable.

"My first impression of you was that you were not the person for this job," Steve said slowly and angrily. "You look too young and inexperienced. I figured you were a rookie, and I didn't think you'd be able to handle yourself."

"Has your opinion of me changed?"

"Yeah. I think you're a tough broad. And you're doing O.K." Steve slowly began to smile.

"Is there something else, Steve?"

"The first time we met, I thought of you only as a lady who was very pretty. And you have a nice body. I had sexual feelings." Steve paused as if trying to choose his words. "I don't feel that way anymore. You're very professional. Too professional."

"Maybe you're not used to being around a woman who's in a position of responsibility and authority."

"I'm not used to it," Steve snapped. "And I'm not sure I like it."

"You've been very open and honest, Steve. I think we all appreciate that. It saves us a lot of time." Christine began looking at each of us again. "Lucy, how do you feel about me?"

Lucy began taking short, quick puffs of her cigarette and looked at the floor.

"This is difficult, Christine," she finally said.

"Take your time."

"I hate to admit this, but I felt similar to the way Steve felt. I was disappointed when I found out you were our group therapist. You didn't appear strong enough to deal with us drunks and drug addicts. You look like you could be intimidated." Lucy smiled. "So much for first impressions. . . . You're obviously in complete control here without being obtrusive. I think you are an extremely capable young woman, and I admire you. I also like you."

"Thank you. That was nice. Is it getting any easier for you to speak in a group without a drink in your hand, Lucy?"

"No." Lucy smiled and lit another cigarette. "But at least I'm doing it."

"Who would like to be next?" Christine asked and slowly looked at each of us.

More silence.

"What the hell, I'll go next." Predictably it was Boone who spoke. "Melanie, what's your opinion of me?"

Melanie was lighting a cigarette she had borrowed from Lucy. She closed her eyes tightly when she lit the cigarette, and she coughed when she exhaled. Melanie sat back in her chair.

"I think you can be cruel and violent and insensitive, Boone. You frighten me. I wouldn't want to be alone with you. I've seen you angry several times, and it's an anger that makes me think that you could become violent very quickly.

"I hate violence.

"But when you cried the other day, I started to think that maybe you aren't as insensitive as I thought. I guess you are as vulnerable as the rest of us. You're just afraid to show it. You're a person with very strong emotions and passions that you don't have good control of. I don't envy your wife."

"You really don't like me, do you?" Boone said to her.

"I don't dislike you, Boone. I'm just not comfortable with someone I'm afraid of. If I hurt you, I'm sorry."

"I asked for your opinion, and I got an honest answer. Thank you." Boone spoke courteously, but he had been hurt.

"Patrick," he said, "I want to hear how you feel about me." He then looked at Christine. "I'm feeling unusually masochistic this morning."

"Haven't we done this before, Boone?" It was a rhetorical question. I sat up in my chair. "You are not an easy person to get to know. You hide behind your strong opinions and anger, and those are obstacles that are difficult to get through.

"Maybe you've had some bad experiences, I don't know. But

you're missing a lot. Your tendency to violence bothers me, too. That's very unpleasant. I feel sorry for you. I wish you would put your guard down and be less combative. Sometimes it seems that you don't want anyone to like you."

Boone was staring at me and was not missing a word. His lower jaw was becoming more prominent as he clenched his teeth.

"If I'm so fucking awful to be around, maybe you people would prefer that I go. You all would like that." He stared at me. "Especially you."

He got up and walked impulsively toward the door. I reached him just as he was about to open the door. I put my hand on his shoulder as firmly as I could and turned him toward me.

He was surprised, but rapidly a look of contempt crept in and molded his face into a look of maniacal rage. He was trembling. We stood face to face.

"I could kill you," he said with such emphasis that I was shocked. But I wasn't afraid.

"We don't want you to go."

His look of rage began slowly dissolving.

"Why do you want me to stay? What difference does it make if I go?"

"Because we all have an investment in each other. We started out together, and we want to finish together. We've already lost one person. We don't want to lose anyone else. It weakened all of us when Gorden left."

Boone began to look embarrassed as he slowly walked back to his chair. He sat down and I returned to my seat.

"I owe all of you an apology," he said.

"I have noticed that some people in here are afraid of you." Christine was speaking pointedly to Boone. "That's taking an unfair toll on the group. Occasionally a group can't function because of one person, and that person will be asked to leave. I think it speaks well of the individuals here that they want you to stay. We all care about you, Boone. I hope that makes you feel good."

Boone nodded, and he gave a small, hopeful smile.

"You must feel those hysterical attacks of extreme anger coming on," said Lucy. "Can't you stop them?"

"I've never tried. But I'm not usually this bad. It's just when I'm trying to stop drinking, like now. I have this feeling that all things are conspiring to fuck me. And I feel helpless. But when I'm drinking, I'm a pussycat. I never fight, never argue. Everybody loves me."

He shook his head. "Could somebody else talk now? I don't want to say any more."

"I'd like to go next, Christine." It was the first time Lucy had volunteered for anything.

She looked at Steve and nodded. Steve was not as challenged as he was when Christine had first asked him.

"We didn't see you for the first few days. You were sick in your room. You and I have talked a couple of times and you're so intelligent and so honest. I can really talk to you.

"I'm sorry your husband is seeing another woman. You deserve better than that. I'd never do that to you."

Lucy was looking at Steve intently. There was a closeness between these two I had not realized.

"Do you have sexual feelings toward Lucy?" Melanie asked.
Steve nodded.

"Do you know I'm fifteen years older than you, Steve?"

"I think you're beautiful."

"Thank you. You're very kind."

"Would you like to ask someone else, Lucy?" asked Christine.

"No. If you don't mind, I'd like to enjoy a few moments of puffery. It's been a long time."

"Mac, it's your turn."

Mac folded his arms across his chest and assumed a disinterested posture.

"Hog. I'll start with you."

"Mac, I think you're a fool." Hog Body was sitting bent at the waist with his elbows on his knees. He stared at the floor. "You're wasting everybody's time. I don't think you want to be here, and I'd like to know why you came to Hogarth."

"I don't have to explain anything to you. Who in the hell do you think you are?"

"I feel the same way Hog does, Mac," I said. "I'm getting very impatient with your boredom and lack of involvement in what we're doing. Why did you come? And why are you staying?"

"Fuck you, pill head."

Hog jumped to his feet.

"Don't talk to Patty that way. Take it back."

"Forget it, Hog. There's nothing Mac could say that would hurt me."

Hog sat down slowly and pointed his finger at Mac. "Be careful how you talk to people."

"You are perilously close to being ostracized from the group, Mac," said Christine. "Your lack of interest in what we're doing is becoming tedious."

"I'm not bored," Mac snapped angrily. "I'm so royally fucked up, there's nothing that can be done for me. I can't live without alcohol. I've been a patient in a psychiatric ward six times in the past ten years. I was never helped. This won't be any different.

"I came here because the wife said she'd leave if I didn't come and stay for the entire program. And she'll take the kids. That's why I'm staying. I'm hopeless. I can't be helped. I can't live without booze, and I don't want to live without the wife. I can't have both."

"Psychiatric wards are notorious for their incompetence in dealing with alcoholic patients," said Christine. "Don't attach much significance to the fact that you weren't helped."

Mac began to look interested.

"You mean I wasted my time?"

"What do you think?"

Mac responded with a questioning look.

Christine bent forward, knees on her elbows.

"It sounds to me, Mac, that you have a hidden agenda. You've come here only so your wife won't leave you. I can tell you that will not be a good enough reason to maintain sobriety. There has to come a time in your life when you want to be sober for yourself, when *you* become your first priority."

"How long has your wife been threatening to leave you?" Lucy asked.

"Ten years."

"What makes you think she'll really leave you now?" Lucy had a skeptical smile.

"Because," Mac sighed deeply, "I'm about to lose my job. There'll be no reason for her to stay around anymore."

"Don't bet on that," Christine said, and smiled and nodded to Lucy.

"What I'm getting at," Lucy said, "is that disappointment can become a way of life for some people. Maybe your wife is comfortable with you being a drunk. Maybe she likes being needed the way you need her. I doubt if she'll leave you now."

"I doubt it, too," Melanie added.

"Priorities, Mac. Think in terms of priorities. You have got to want to do this for yourself." Christine smiled. "One of life's few absolutes."

Steve interrupted. "I've been to a couple of A.A. meetings with you, Mac. You don't seem bored during the meetings."

"I'm not bored," Mac said with a hint of surprise. "I like to listen to the talks and see how bad off other guys were and were able to stop drinking."

"That's good." Christine was emphatic. "A.A. meetings are a form of group therapy that doesn't require a lot of self-disclosure. Many people are comfortable in that setting. I hope you continue to go to meetings."

"I will," he said.

I felt sorry for Mac. I couldn't think of anything more unpleasant than attending Alocohlic Anonymous meetings for the rest of one's life.

"Why are you two just drinking coffee?" Lorenzo asked as he sat down with Melanie and me. "You aren't going to eat?"

"We had a rough Group Therapy session this morning," I said. "It took away my appetite."

"They're all rough," he said. "And they don't get any easier."

"Two members of our group really were abusive to Patrick," Melanie said.

"I don't think these people like to see their healers wounded," I said. "I wish we could somehow hide the fact that we're doctors, Lorenzo."

"People do have a tendency to overestimate us. You and I, Patrick, are walking testimony to the fact that we're as afraid and insecure as anyone else."

"What happened to that certain specialness and elevation that is supposed to come with being a doctor?"

Lorenzo smiled at me. "Myths, Patrick. All myths."

"Well, you two are really feeling sorry for yourselves," Melanie said, looking from me to Lorenzo.

We disregarded Melanie's comment.

Lorenzo explained that O'Malley had told him about the doctor's group that met on Thursday nights. Lorenzo was going for the first time, too.

"You and I are supposed to meet with someone at six-thirty in O'Malley's office."

Presswood came to our table, sat down, and smiled lecherously at Melanie.

"When are you going to invite me to your room, Melanie?" he asked. "I've seen you looking at me."

"Invite you to my room? To do what?"

Presswood opened his mouth wide, stuck out his tongue, and wiggled it up and down.

Melanie looked at me. "Do you believe this guy?"

Melanie and I got up to go, and as I turned away from the table, I heard Lorenzo:

"Presswood," he said, "you make white people look bad."

All afternoon I had been looking forward to meeting the doctors who had been through Hogarth. I felt I would capture some hope when I saw successfully treated people with whom I shared at least one thing—a profession. That seemed so important now. It was my first experience at Hogarth which I looked forward to with some positive anticipation.

The door to O'Malley's office was slightly ajar, and I heard an unfamiliar voice. I opened the door slowly and saw Lorenzo and a man I had not met before. He was sitting in O'Malley's chair. The man stood as I came into the room. He was about six feet five, at least two hundred fifty pounds. His shoulders were enormous, and his muscular biceps were not well contained inside his suit coat.

He came toward me ponderously and with authority. I thought I felt the floor tremble. He moved in close to me, and I felt as if I were surrounded. He smelled like roast beef, medium rare.

His large head and thick neck took up my entire field of vision as I looked up. I continued to stare at him and lifted my right hand, assuming he would like to shake hands.

Something large and forceful grasped my hand, and the pain was instantaneous. I was disappointed when I winced.

"Name's Bossy," he announced.

He continued to compress my hand for several seconds while he stared at me, never blinking. When he freed my hand, I finally exhaled. He turned and walked back toward the desk.

I had been thoroughly intimidated.

I sat next to Lorenzo in front of the desk. Bossy sat in O'Malley's chair. He spoke with a commanding, sturdy voice, while he explained he had been a patient at Hogarth ten years before. He was now forty-four. As he spoke, a Byronic recalcitrant shock of copper red hair occasionally would fall and cover his left eye.

He had been an alcoholic and also addicted to Valium. He pronounced it "Val-yum." Somehow it seemed appropriate that he was an orthopedic surgeon.

It was difficult to imagine Bossy as an alcoholic. He appeared invincible.

"Besides my practice, I do confrontations and interventions with impaired physicians. That's the most difficult thing I do."

Bossy explained that when the medical society in Toronto suspects a physician is compromised due to substance abuse, they call him to intervene.

"I usually get to the impaired physician during the denial phase of the illness. But they can't bullshit me, because I was where they are. They get very angry with me. They don't appreciate the fact I'm only trying to save their lives."

Bossy's voice grew passionate when he spoke of physicians not taking care of each other and how we "turn our back on our colleagues when they need us most. When they're obliterating themselves and destroying their families."

He moved his massive hulk forward in the chair. He was angry.

"Do you realize that ten to fifteen percent of physicians are impaired because of alcoholism or drug abuse? We're talking fifty-five, sixty thousand doctors in the United States and Canada, gentlemen, and many of them are performing surgery and making life and death decisions." He shook his head. "Frightening, isn't it?"

Bossy got up and moved slowly around the desk. He came in front of us and sat on O'Malley's desk. He folded his arms and peered down at us. His large blue eyes were powerful and challenging. I was both afraid and in awe of him. I would never give him cause to be angry at me. He was indestructible.

He smiled in a conscious attempt to reduce our discomfort.

"There are over fifty physicians in the Toronto area who have come through Hogarth. A few years ago we decided to meet once a week and try to help each other. This is not an A.A. meeting for doctors. There are no speakers. We usually have twenty or thirty show up. We let people talk about anything they'd like. It can be fairly discursive at times. People usually come here looking for practical solutions on how to lead their lives."

"Will we be asked to say anything?" Lorenzo asked timorously.

"You can talk if you want. But except for introducing yourselves, you won't be asked to say anything. Neither of you is probably strong enough."

"Strong enough?" I asked.

Bossy's eyes narrowed, and I immediately wanted to apologize for sounding questioning.

"You have a terminal illness," he said. "You were destroying yourself, and if you didn't stop, you would have died."

The impact of that was sudden and severe. I felt nauseated and weak and I momentarily lost the rhythm of my breathing. He was right.

Many of the doctors were sitting around the long rectangular table which took up most of the room. Others sat away from the table, along the walls. A few were dressed casually, and one of the younger women wore jeans. But most seemed to believe in the maxim that one dressed according to one's station and were well-appointed, dressed in expensive clothes.

Many were self-conscious and uncomfortable. There were no spontaneous, relaxed conversations. Those who were at the table sat stiffly, and the people who sat near the walls seemed to do so in a vain attempt at being less obvious.

There was one middle-aged guy near the back who kept a sadistic snarl. It was the face of a urologist, of someone who loves to massage inflamed prostates.

Lorenzo and I sat along the wall and tried to be inconspicuous, but everyone noticed us. Bossy had not come in with us, and I felt unprotected. Many of the doctors came to us and smiled warmly and shook our hands. A fiftyish gentleman with graying hair asked me how I liked Toronto. I had not seen any of the city, but I smiled and told him how pretty it was.

"Everybody calls me Doc," he said. "I hope you will, too."

I called him Doc as I answered his many questions, which required personal and detailed answers. His smile was mocking as he looked at the people in the room.

He leaned close to me.

"When you can appreciate the irony of this," his hand gestured at the other doctors, "then you know you're well into recovery."

There was an abrupt, reverential silence. Everyone looked toward the front of the room. Bossy was standing at the head of the table. Unquestionably, he had a presence which commanded attention.

"Shall we begin," he said. It was not a question. It was a command.

Everyone bowed their head. They spoke in unison:

God grant me the serenity to accept the things I cannot change, the courage to change the things I can, and the wisdom to know the difference.

"Margaret, tell these two young doctors what the serenity prayer means to you."

Margaret was probably near sixty, and had pure white hair. Her eyes seemed iridescent as they moved from Lorenzo to me. She had the seasoned, expressive face more characteristic of the artist than the physician, suggesting she preferred creating to fixing things.

"Eleven years ago I delivered a baby after I had been drinking heavily. The baby developed respiratory problems right after delivery. It died a few minutes later. If I hadn't been drunk, I might have saved the baby's life.

"There is nothing I can do about the dead baby or the incredible sorrow I caused the parents." Margaret stopped and appeared as if she were going to weep. But she didn't. "I will not allow the fact that I was probably responsible for the baby's death to devastate me as it used to. Guilt is no longer rewarding or productive. I cannot change my past. But I can influence the present and to a certain degree my future in a positive way. I must make the right decision, always considering what will benefit the most people."

As Margaret spoke, I felt deeply moved and elevated. I knew I was learning something that I would never forget. Margaret was not living an unexamined life.

Bossy turned toward Lorenzo and me.

"Learn the Serenity Prayer. When you're feeling guilty, say it. Over and over."

Bossy talked briefly about the doctor who had overdosed on Seconal but would not allow any discussion of the man or his suicide.

"We can't dwell on it," he said. "He's gone. There's nothing we can do now. He made a choice." Bossy had tried to sound stern but was unable to hide a genuine sadness.

"We have two guests tonight. Would you introduce yourselves?"

"Patrick. Cleveland, Ohio."

"Lorenzo. Detroit."

"There are three other doctors in the house," said Bossy. "But Frank O'Malley didn't think they were ready. Lorenzo, you and Patrick can leave the meeting at any time."

Bossy asked if there was anything anyone wanted to discuss. He turned to a small man on his left.

"Arthur, you look like you have something to say."

Arthur was in his sixties and wore a dark suit and tie, a white shirt and a hemorrhoidal expression. His white hair was cut short. Surely this man was never intemperate. He looked at Bossy.

"I've been sober for two years. I had a lot more fun when I was drinking. Sobriety isn't so great."

"You've chosen to be sober for two years. You must be getting something out of it."

"I don't know what it is."

"You old fart," snapped Margaret from across the room. "Arthur, I've known you for thirty years. For a good part of that time you were a drunk, a misfit. You received nothing from your colleagues but ridicule. A lot of people admire you for staying sober the past two years. You have their respect. Doesn't that mean anything?"

"We do difficult things only because there is a reward," explained Bossy. "How is staying sober benefiting you?"

"I'm not enjoying sobriety. I'm tolerating it. I needed to prove to myself I could do it." Arthur still had an unpleasant look.

"Are we going to lose you?" Margaret asked with a touch of anguish.

Arthur didn't answer.

I looked at Lorenzo, who appeared as shocked and upset as I was. We had both hoped for cheerful encouragement that the agony we were experiencing at Hogarth would be well worth it. The exchange with Arthur was not good for either of us.

Bossy addressed the man to the left of Arthur.

"Gerald, you've had some good news in the past week."

Gerald had dark hair and was several years younger than me.

"I've been reinstated. I can practice medicine again." He smiled proudly.

Bossy looked to Lorenzo and me.

"Gerald had a long battle with Demerol and he had many relapses. We had to protect him from himself, so we got his license to practice medicine pulled two years ago."

Two years!

"What did you do in that time?" Margaret asked. "How did you support yourself?"

"My wife worked for the first year. Then she left me. For the past year I've helped embalm bodies."

"Aren't you overtrained for something like that?"

"Not really. I'm a radiologist."

Bossy continued asking people around the table about difficulties they were having in their personal or professional lives. Most admitted to marital discords, and many in the room were in the Family Aftercare Program at Hogarth.

"Stacey, are you and your wife still seeing Karren?" Bossy asked of a man who bore a striking resemblance to Marlon Brando.

Stacey nodded. "Once a month."

"Karren is not only a superb physical therapist," Bossy announced and then looked at me. "She is a well-trained sex therapist."

"Why did he look at me when he said that?" I whispered to Lorenzo.

"Man, you look like someone who hasn't had an orgasm in a long time," Lorenzo murmured and then moved quickly as I prepared to elbow him savagely in the ribs.

A small young woman standing in the back had her hand timorously raised.

"Katie!" Bossy boomed.

Katie had the amorphic shape of a twelve-year-old prepubescent boy.

"As some of you know," she said in a barely audible voice, "I work in an emergency room. Last week some morphine was missing. They're questioning everyone. The hospital administrator knows I had a problem with drugs. Guess who he suspects?"

"Did you take the morphine, Katie?" asked Margaret sharply.

"No."

"What drugs were you doing before you came to Hogarth?" Bossy asked but obviously knew the answer.

"Demerol. Talwin. And morphine."

"Have you taken any drugs in the last three days?"

"No."

Bossy moved forward in his chair.

"Katie, will you give us a urine specimen?" he asked.

"Now?"

"Yes. We'll send it to the lab tonight."

"I'm hurt that you don't believe me."

No one spoke, and all eyes were on Katie.

"Where is the goddamn specimen bottle?" she snapped. She got up and started toward the door defiantly.

"There's a bottle in the bathroom," said Bossy. "Margaret, go with her."

Katie stopped abruptly as if shot with an arrow and bowed her head. She then glared at him.

"You bastard."

Katie and Margaret left the room.

I again felt weakened. This was not what I had expected. There was no cheerfulness here. No encouragement. I was now seeing the ravages of drug abuse and alcoholism in my peers.

I knew I should leave the room, but I couldn't. I didn't want anyone thinking that I couldn't cope with this. I wasn't an alcoholic or addicted to hard drugs. I hoped they knew that I wasn't as bad as they were. I had just taken tranquilizers and sleeping pills.

Lorenzo stood and walked past me out of the room.

Bossy looked at me with surprise. I knew he wanted me to go, too. But I wouldn't.

He began talking to David, the man on my left, when Margaret and Katie came back. There was a sense of awkwardness in the room.

"I'm sorry, Katie," Bossy said to her. "There's no other way."

She stood with her hands on her hips and faced him.

"Why did you send Margaret with me? How would I fake a urine specimen? With apple juice?"

"The last time I asked someone for a urine specimen, he went up to the fourth floor and had a patient fill the container."

"Don't you know me better than that?" she pleaded.

Bossy didn't answer.

"You really enjoy the power you have here, don't you?" Katie was beginning to cry. "You bastard," she said to him again, but this time in a voice not sufficiently loud to sound contemptuous.

There was a general discomfort in the room. I doubt if people were used to having Bossy challenged.

Katie and Margaret returned to their seats. Bossy once again addressed himself to David. I had noticed him throughout the meeting. David was overweight, and there was a small tear on the back of his suit coat where the sleeve meets the shoulder. His shirt was unbuttoned at the collar. He smelled like a stale, cut onion.

David smoked continuously and nervously. The index and middle fingers on his right hand were dark orange from nicotine. His entire upper torso moved as he breathed.

David appeared to be the perfect candidate for a myocardial infarction.

He did not look at Bossy while they talked. He had been in Hogarth twice as a patient, both times for cross-addiction. David referred to his wife as a "practicing alcoholic."

"She's drunk all the time," he said with great irritation.

"Why do you continue in that relationship?" asked Margaret. "Neither you nor your wife seems to benefit from your staying together."

"I'm seeing my lawyer tomorrow."

"Bullshit!" Bossy exclaimed loudly. "You've said that before. You and your wife seem to feed off unhappiness. I think you two are determined to reinforce each other's lack of self-worth.

"Get out of that relationship, David. You're dying."

David lit another cigarette and glanced at me. I didn't belong at this meeting. It was too soon. I wasn't ready, and I started to stand to go. But Bossy spoke to David again.

"What drugs have you taken today?"

David looked at Bossy as if he were facing an executioner.

"Valium. Some this morning. A couple this afternoon. I couldn't have got through today without Valium."

"You've relapsed again," Bossy said tersely and with an inflection that hid neither his anger nor disappointment.

"If David's actively taking drugs," Margaret said, "he shouldn't be here. I think he should leave."

Several people nodded in agreement.

"Wait a minute," said Doc. "He probably needs us more now than he ever has. If we censure him, he may leave here without hope. He could do something drastic. We've just lost one of us to Seconal."

"Let him stay," Katie offered from the back of the room. "But he shouldn't be allowed to say anything."

Margaret agreed and pointedly looked away from David.

There was no more discussion of the matter. Bossy, his face scarlet, turned to David.

"You can stay if you like. But don't talk."

Bossy's eyes were wide and his expression maniacal.

"Goddamn you, David." He slammed his fist to the table. Ashtrays bounced and Styrofoam cups filled with coffee fell over. "You're destroying a person I like. And you remind all of us how vulnerable we are."

There was silence as I walked toward the door. I was profoundly disillusioned. My thinking was clear now. I knew what I had to do.

I smiled at the lady who was at the switchboard as I walked past her toward the front door. Outside, I quickly went down the stairs, and when I got to the driveway, started to run. When I reached the street, I was running as fast as I had ever run. My experience at Hogarth was now over. There would be no more pain.

I was free.

17

"WHERE are you, Patrick?"

"The bus station. There's a bus leaving for Cleveland in twenty minutes."

"You ran all the way? That's about eight miles."

"I want to go home, Reggie. I wasn't ready for Hogarth. Maybe I'll try to come back when I've thought things through a little better. My coming to Hogarth was not a well-thought-out decision. I just called to say good-bye."

"You're making a terrible mistake, Patrick. You were in Hogarth for almost two weeks, and you've suffered a lot. But you've survived it. There's a phrase that we use in A.A., 'Don't waste your pain.' If you leave now, you'll never come back. You would never relive those first two weeks.

"Come back. Please."

"No. I can't face another two weeks of this. Or will it be five weeks? I kept thinking that the worst was behind me, and that sustained me. But tonight was the worst night of my life. When I met with the doctors' group, I saw so much unhappiness. And these people were supposed to be cured."

"Not cured. Recovering. There's a significant difference. You've made such good progress. . . ."

"Progress? What progress?"

"We had a staff dinner on Wednesday night. Dr. O'Malley said he was very pleased with your involvement in the program. He said that you have shown significant improvement."

"O'Malley said that about me? He's never given me any indication that I was getting better."

"And Dr. Randolph said that you have been a real challenge, but he has seen improvement, too. He also said he likes you."

"Randolph likes me?"

"And I've seen a dramatic difference, Patrick. You're less angry, and you're not as depressed as you were. I'm watching you become a friendly, warm person."

I was beginning to regret having run away. If only O'Malley and Randolph had given me some encouragement, some approval, I would never have left.

"Patrick, get a taxi and come back. You have an hour before the doors are locked."

"I need to think about this, Reggie."

"Think about it here. Come back and we'll talk. You have an hour."

Reggie was talking on the phone when she saw me coming down the hall. She waved her left hand excitedly. When I got to the Nurses' Station, she hung up the receiver and came out and hugged me. That gave me a nice, warm, welcome feeling.

She looked over her shoulder at the clock. It was ten fifty-five.

"I wish you had come and talked to me before you ran away," she said with real disappointment.

She was right. I should have.

"I'll be off in five minutes."

"We don't need to talk, Reggie. I just made a mistake. I need to stay here. I don't need to be convinced."

Reggie smiled, but there was uncertainty in her face.

"Had Dr. Randolph given you permission to leave the hospital grounds yet?"

"No." I had not thought of that. I had broken a rule. "Does he have to know?" Only Reggie and I knew I had been off the grounds.

Without hesitation, Reggie nodded. I would do nothing to compromise what she had to do.

"Will you at least let me tell him?" I asked.

"Sure. Tell him in the morning, Patrick. I'll need to collect a urine from you and do a breathalyzer, O.K.? I'm part of the system here, you know."

I didn't even attempt to sleep. A couple of Valiums and a glass of wine would have been nice. I turned the lights out in my room but stayed in my clothes. I thought of Randolph, and I detested him because of the power he had now. It would be his decision and his decision alone whether I stayed at Hogarth or was discharged. I didn't like anyone else making pivotal decisions about my health.

Outside my window the morning light gradually appeared as expected, but sooner than I had hoped. The trees and the tall shrubs wearily but resolutely presented themselves again as our protection against a world that preferred to ignore drug addicts and alcoholics. We were the misfits, the obvious failures, who had shown that we were not capable of living in a manner that was not destructive. We were embarrassments, emotional lepers.

A few early spring flowers dotted the landscape. They appeared so delicate, fragile, and sensitive. They were courageous but foolish. They had come too soon and would be battered mercilessly by the harsh weather still to come. They would live a short, pitiable existence in which they would know only adversity.

Nature has its own way of dealing with things that are dysynchronous.

Although the carpet in the hall muffled footsteps, there was someone coming in the direction of my room who walked confidently and with a purpose. I was ready for him.

There was a knock on my door, and Randolph walked in, holding my chart.

"You wanted to see me?" Randolph looked at my bed, which had not been slept in, and then back at me. "I guess I better sit down."

Randolph lit a cigarette, crossed his legs, and assumed his best clinical manner. I remained standing, looking down at him. I felt less vulnerable that way.

"I bolted last night."

His expression didn't change as I told him what had happened.

"I didn't drink or take drugs while I was out. Reggie analyzed my breath and took a urine specimen when I got back. I'll submit another urine this morning."

His eyes narrowed, but he remained silent.

"I'm sure what I did is sufficient cause for my being thrown out. But I hope you'll let me stay. I'm presuming on your patience again."

He nodded. I would say no more. I would not give the son of a bitch the satisfaction of seeing me squirm.

He put his cigarette out, opened my chart, and began writing in it. He spoke without looking up.

"I won't dismiss you for one impulsive act that wasn't too flagrant. And I'm sure your running away was at least partly motivated by your continuing need to show me gratuitous defiance." He looked at me. "You are a challenge, Patrick. But that's because you're still a sick man."

He stood and held up my chart.

"I've just written an order in here that you have permission to leave the hospital grounds. I put yesterday's date on the order." He turned abruptly and walked out of my room.

I had wanted desperately to ask him if my running away would influence his decision concerning my leaving after twenty-eight days. But even discussions of that seemed to anger him, so I didn't bring it up. I felt that coming back as I did would speak well of my intentions and sincerity. I'm sure he realized that I did not need an extra three weeks in Hogarth. I wasn't *that* sick.

He was an intelligent man. He could see I wouldn't need to repeat the program. Randolph would exercise good judgment and send me home in two weeks. It would be counterproductive for me to stay longer.

And if he did suggest I be recycled, I would see his mistake and refuse to stay.

"Patrick, you look awful this morning." Lucy had her head tilted and was looking at me with concern. "Is there something wrong?"

"I didn't sleep. And I had about an hour of unexpected vigorous exercise last night. My body feels like it was used as a tackling dummy by the Cleveland Browns."

I was getting inquiring looks from the group. So I told them what had happened.

"Why did you come back? Was Reggie really that convincing?" asked Lucy.

"Or did you want to be convinced?" added Melanie.

"While I was running away, I was sure I was doing the right thing. But I began to feel very sad, because"—my voice was cracking—"because I wouldn't be seeing any of you again. I would miss you all, and I also felt I'd be letting you down." I had to stop talking and try to gain some control. "You're right, Melanie. When I called Reggie, it was a cry for help."

"I'm glad you came back." I was surprised to hear Steve say that.

"I'm glad, too, Patty."

"We would have missed you."

"Thanks, Boone."

Christine looked pleased and satisfied. There had been evidence of concern and trust among us before. And now, once again, there was a suggestion of love.

"Steve, why don't you start off this morning?"

"The same thing as yesterday?"

Christine nodded.

"How do you feel about me?" Steve asked Boone as if he were challenging him. And they stared at each other like two boxers just before the bell, anticipating violence and not shrinking from it.

"I think you're a tough guy, Steve. I bet you've mixed it up a lot and have probably never lost a fight—with a person. You really feel bad about losing to drugs and booze, don't you?"

Steve nodded.

"And you're embarrassed and hurt because your wife left you. And you find that difficult to deal with because you can't solve it with your fists."

Steve was fuming.

"I know you want to stay out of trouble, Steve. But I'm not sure you want to stay sober."

Steve jumped from his chair.

"Get out of my face, Boone," he said in a quiet, threatening voice.

Boone sat back in his chair and smiled knowingly.

"You and I are very much like each other, Steve. Similar emotions. Similar attitudes." He stopped smiling. "And that's unfortunate for both of us."

Steve remained standing for a few seconds. His anger had been controlled but extreme, and he was not embarrassed. Anger was an emotion he enjoyed. When mad, he was indomitable. Steve could kill.

He looked at me.

"Patrick."

I decided to give Steve a few more moments to relax. I rustled in my chair, put my hand through my hair, and tried to look pensive. I saw him getting impatient.

"I like you, Steve. I think you're trying very hard to be responsible. Two weeks ago you were trying to impress us with your cavalier attitude. You said you were in Hogarth only to avoid jail. And maybe that was your initial motive. I don't think it is anymore. You're interested in what is going on."

"I've noticed that, too," interrupted Lucy, smiling and sitting forward in her chair.

"But, Steve," I continued, "I think you're a person who does not easily accept advice or criticism. And I doubt you were ever responsive to discipline."

"I've been restless all my life," he said. "I've never been able to keep a job. I have a difficult time with bosses."

"What about your marriage, Steve?" asked Christine.

"I wanted that to work. I never touched another woman."

"There's got to be more to a marriage working than just not being unfaithful," charged Melanie.

"I did my best," Steve shot back. "I never hit her. She got everything she wanted."

"What about love, Steve?" Melanie said. "You haven't mentioned the word. Did you love your wife? Have you even been in love?"

"Fuck you, Melanie," Steve said and folded his arms across his chest. He was finished talking.

Christine looked at me, then Hog Body, then Melanie.

"I'll go next," said Melanie, with little enthusiasm. She looked at me for a few seconds and then turned to Christine.

"What's your opinion of me, Christine?"

Christine looked both surprised and pleased that she had been asked.

"You've done a lot of talking in these sessions, Melanie. But I still feel I don't know you very well. You're evasive but not in an obvious way. I think you're a lovely, sensitive woman, and a very private person. And I feel that privacy is a protective strategy you use to avoid being hurt. And I think you've been hurt. You're a genuinely honest person, Melanie, and I feel you really care about people. You would be a good friend."

Melanie smiled and began to speak, but Christine interrupted.

"And, God, are you beautiful," she said with exaggerated emphasis. "Do you realize, Melanie, that I always try not to sit too close to you? I'd suffer in the comparison. I guess I use distance to nullify the competition."

Melanie was slightly flushed with embarrassment and gave a self-conscious smile. Her modesty was unaffected.

Christine looked at me with a bemused expression.

"Do you know of an easy cure for vanity?"

"Yeah," Steve blurted. "You could take some of Mac's ugly pills."

Mac laughed loudly and slapped his thigh.

"Or you can become an alcoholic," offered Lucy. "I guarantee that you would never suffer conceit again."

Melanie looked tentatively at Lucy, who for the first time in memory, was not smoking.

"We have spent a lot of time alone together," Lucy said. She groped for her cigarettes but kept looking at Melanie. "We've shared intimacies and I feel I know you fairly well. I have a tremendous affection for you. But I've noticed on occasion that you will pull back as if you don't want me to get too close. Sometimes I think I understand you, Melanie. Then there are times I feel I don't know you at all."

Melanie smiled, as if apologizing.

"Maybe I'm being too cautious. I hope I haven't offended you." Melanie looked at me. "I don't ask for commitments from anyone. Nor will I give any."

Melanie asked Lucy for a cigarette, lit it awkwardly, and the smoke burned her right eye. She squeezed her eye closed and gingerly rubbed her eye.

"Don't anyone ever give me another goddamn cigarette," she said, frustrated. "Not even if I get on my knees and lick your ankles."

The look on her face suddenly became very serious.

"People think acting is difficult. Speaking someone else's thoughts is a snap compared to what we're doing here. I feel so naked in here." She looked at Christine. "I don't like this."

It was now down to me and Hog Body, who was putting his teeth in. I had to get it over with, and I nodded to Christine.

"Mac, let me start with you," I said and wiped my wet palms off on my pants.

"I like you, Pat. I'm sorry I called you a pill head. You're a nice guy and really intelligent. And, boy, are you funny when you get mad!"

"Funny?"

"Yeah. You get so highfalutin."

"Highfalutin? Whadda ya mean?"

"He means arrogant," said Lucy with an impish grin.

"Arrogant? Bullshit. I'm not arrogant. Randolph is arrogant."

"It's not arrogance," said Melanie. "It's more . . . a self-righteousness."

"What? Melanie, how can you say that about me?"

"It's arrogance," said Steve, as if he were making the final statement on the matter.

"Definitely arrogance," added Boone.

"Highfalutin," said Hog Body loudly and raised his right hand as if at an auction. Then he winked at me and smiled.

"Wait a minute," said Lucy. She picked up a pencil and licked the top. "Let's get this down on paper. We got two for highfalutin, one for self-righteous, and three for arrogance." She looked up in mock seriousness. "We'll have to go with arrogance."

I placed my hands behind my neck and sat back in my chair.

"Well," I said, "if it is arrogance, I come by it honestly."

That brought scoffs and snickers, and Lucy's pencil hit me in the chest.

I turned to Christine.

"Because of my lofty station in life," I said, attempting to sound haughty and contemptuous, "I'm not used to being around unregenerates and being savaged like this. I refuse to ask anyone else from among *them* for their opinion of me. That only leaves you."

"Nail his ass, Christine," blurted Steve.

"I assume," she said smiling, "you want me to be honest."

"Yes. And gentle."

"Initially I found you difficult to interpret, Patrick. I think you're experiencing unfamiliar feelings and some fairly toxic emotions that have obscured your personality."

"You should have seen him during the first week," said Melanie. "He was so quiet and polite with us."

"And formal," added Boone.

"But your identity is beginning to emerge," Christine continued. "You're a kind, sincere, friendly person. I hope you'll give us the opportunity to know you better."

"I did try to keep a certain distance from all of you during the first week," I said. "I hope that wasn't misinterpreted. Normally when I'm unhappy, I prefer to be alone. But I'm finding that, when I can be with you people and share my feelings, I'm less unhappy. I've learned a lot about myself in the past two weeks."

"Most of the physicians I've dealt with in the past," Christine added, "don't open up for two or three weeks into the program. It seems to take them longer to appreciate the very real benefits of our therapeutic community. You're doing better than most of them at this point."

"I hope you'll write that in my chart, Christine. Give Randolph some evidence that I'm improving."

"I think he knows. Don't underestimate Dr. Randolph."

Christine turned to Hog Body.

He shook his head.

"I can't do this, Chrissie."

"We've all fucked up, Hog," snapped Steve. "That's why we're here. We're all equal, remember?"

"Hog Body," said Lucy, moving to the edge of her chair again, "would you have come in for treatment if you had never had that incident with your daughter?"

"No. Hell, no."

"It's important that you think about Lucy's question and your answer." There was a command in Christine's inflection.

"If that thing with your daughter hadn't happened, you'd still be out there drinking," offered Mac. "Now you're in here and you may be able to turn everything around."

"I'd like to add something," said Lucy. "The one thing that has impressed me about you, Hog Body, is that you are someone who will accept nothing less than complete honesty from people. You caught me a couple of times when I was less than candid. You will do well in A.A."

"You really helped me one day when I was having a difficult time with agitated depression," I said. "If it hadn't been for you, I would have had to ask for a drug. Where did you go to medical school, Hog?"

He was smiling now, and his abdomen began to move as he laughed silently.

"You're the only person in this whole goddamn hospital who seems to understand me, Hog," said Mac. "You're the only one I can talk to."

Hog Body was now beaming. He had been restored.

"I was surprised when I heard you ran away last night. You aren't the type of person who does things on impulse. You must have really been hurting." There was a suggestion of compassion in O'Malley's tone.

"I don't think it's something that warrants deep discussion. And I'm really embarrassed that I did it."

"Just one question. Why didn't you leave the meeting if it was too much? I told you to."

"I guess I want people to think that I'm stronger than I really am."

"Patrick, it seems that you have to pay a heavy price to gain precious little insight." He sat back and hooked his thumbs in the small pockets in his vest. "How are things otherwise?"

"I'm not quite as restless and impatient as before, but I'm still very unhappy."

"You have a right to be unhappy." O'Malley looked and sounded as if I were boring him. "This is a difficult experience. Every patient in here is depressed."

"Hey, goddamnit, I'm experiencing pathological depression, and you're trivializing it. I take little consolation in the fact that other people are unhappy."

"You're as irascible as ever." O'Malley paused and shook his head. "I spend half my time talking to patients about the depressions they're experiencing."

"I hope you're helping them more than you're helping me."

"You're not benefiting from these sessions with me?"

"Well, you must be fulfilling a need, because I do feel better after talking to you. I'm just not improving."

"You've measurably improved, Patrick. Believe me. And a week from now, you'll be more improved."

"Then I wish I could slip into catatonia and just vegetate for the next week."

"O'Malley laughed without appearing to be amused.

"I won't need to see you as frequently for the next few weeks. But we still have a lot to discuss."

"There is one thing I need to talk to you about," I said. My face was becoming warm, and I knew I was starting to blush. "I'm not comfortable talking about this. It's . . ."

"You're impotent." He blurted that as a statement. At least he could have made it a question.

"Yes," I said louder than I had wanted to say it. "Now I suppose you're going to say, 'You have a right to be impotent. Every patient here is impotent.' I need some help with this. My wife's coming next week."

"Karren does our sex counseling. Talk to her."

"She's a woman."

"That's been well documented."

"Why can't you help me? Is sex counseling outside your range of confidence? I'd be very embarrassed discussing my impotence with a woman."

"Then talking to her will be therapeutic for you in several ways."

I closed the door to O'Malley's office and started walking toward the elevator. But there was something I needed to say to him. I walked back to his office and opened the door. He was sitting in his chair and looked quickly at me. He was both startled and annoyed. He had his hand in a large brown paper bag.

"I'm sorry," I said. "I should have knocked." I started to back out into the hall and close the door.

"That's O.K. Come in."

I walked slowly over to the chair in front of the desk. We were both embarrassed.

"You caught me in the middle of a dietary indiscretion," he said sheepishly. "This bag is filled with popcorn." He tilted the bag so I could see.

"That's a lot of popcorn."

"I love the stuff. But eating it is not something I can do in polite society. It's pretty bad. When I eat popcorn, I become a gorilla."

"I'll leave in a second," I said. "I just want to apologize to you. It seems that whenever I'm with you or Randolph, I get contentious and almost insulting. I'm usually not like this. I'm sorry."

"Why are you so angry, Patrick? Tell me."

I sat in the chair, but I didn't look at him.

"I'm trying to escape from my addiction to drugs. I know I have to, because those pills are destroying me. But I don't think I can do it. It's putting me in real conflict with myself, and it's making me very angry. And I project a lot of this anger onto you and Randolph. It's because you two are my peers and, at the same time, my doctors."

"Patrick, I want you to do something for me. I want you to tell me your name and tell me what disease you have."

I sat back and took a deep breath.

"Patrick Reilly . . . sedativism."

"Say it again. Make it a sentence." He moved forward in his chair.

"My name is Patrick Reilly and I'm experiencing a disease . . . sedativism."

"I don't like 'sedativism.'" His arms were folded on the desk in front of him. His eyes widened. "Say what it really is."

I looked directly up into the spotlight that was shining on me. The light burned my eyes.

"My name is Patrick Reilly and I have . . ." I looked at him but could see only his silhouette. . . . "I'm a drug addict."

In a few seconds his face came into focus. He was smiling.

Melanie and I lingered in the dining room after dinner and had a second cup of coffee. We had hardly spoken during dinner, but that did not make me uncomfortable. I felt safe with her, and I trusted her.

"When will your wife be coming?"

"She'll be here next Tuesday night. The Family Program starts Wednesday morning."

"I don't want to meet her, Patrick." Melanie slid her hand next to mine and touched the back of my hand.

"You'd really like Irene. She's the only person I know who has never been unkind. I'm very lucky."

"What about your . . . problem?"

"O'Malley told me to talk to Karren. She does the sex counseling here. Can you believe it? A psychiatrist referring me to a physical therapist for sex counseling."

"Maybe he realizes she can do it better. That's not so hard to believe. You're just upset because you'll be talking to a woman." She raised her eyebrows. "Correct?"

"Correct."

"Could you talk to me about it, Patrick?"

Was she kidding?

I shook my head very slowly for dramatic emphasis. I was not equivocating.

"I hope Karren can help you," Melanie said with a slight, mischievous grin. "I have a selfish reason for saying that."

"If she can help me, you'll be the first to know."

I was not sure if I meant that. It had been long years since I had made love to anyone but Irene. It would not be humanly possible to resist the advances of someone like Melanie. But still, it would be adultery, and adultery, like sodomy, has an awful sound. No one ever has anything good to say about it.

I suspected I would feel guilty if I had made love to Melanie. But I wasn't sure. I would think about guilt at another time. Hopefully, in retrospect.

"Hi, Babes."

"Pat. I was hoping you'd call. Evenings are very difficult without you. God, I miss you."

I would never take Irene for granted again. I told her that I missed her, too. I had never meant it more.

Irene was a requirement in my life. I needed her if I were ever going to be happy again. She was my support, my security.

"What have you been doing, Babes?"

"I've spent the last two hours emptying your bottles of pills down the toilet. And there are plenty more."

"Wait a minute. Don't go throwing all those pills away. I'll need some of them."

"No, Pat. They're all going." There was a strength and certainty in her voice.

"But I was addicted to only the sleeping pills and tranquilizers."

"You could become addicted to something else."

"That will never happen. I'm telling you, don't throw away the Equagesic or Talwin. And keep the Compazine and Darvon. I need all those things for my migraines."

"Are you sure, Pat?"

"Yeah. Believe me."

"I won't throw them away yet. But I'll ask somebody when I get to Hogarth next week. Who's your doctor?"

"I don't want you talking to my doctor. Forget that. This is my problem, and I'll have to deal with it."

"No, Pat, this is *our* problem. It's affected my life, too. I won't know what to do when you get home. How will I make sure you're not taking drugs again?"

"You'll have to trust me."

There was a long silence. Then: "I'll need to learn how to do that again."

Irene had spoken softly, and there was pain in her voice. I knew she had always trusted me. But now she was realizing how I had deceived and been evasive with her concerning my taking drugs.

She was hurt, but I couldn't detect any resentment as she talked.

I told Irene about the doctor's group I had met with and about my grave disappointment. I had hoped to be comforted and consoled by them.

"It was like a wake, a group of unhappy people grieving over their loss of self-esteem."

"Maybe you expected too much, Pat. You seem desperate for some good news."

"You'll be coming next Tuesday. That's good news."

"Can we spend the night together?"

"No. I have to be in bed here at eleven o'clock."

"We will be able to spend some time alone, won't we?"

"I don't know . . . probably not. . . . you'll be kept too busy. . . . we'll always be in a group. . . ."

"Why is your voice getting so high, Pat?"

"A young nurse just walked by and squeezed my testicles."

"What?" Irene began to laugh.

"Yeah. I'm not kidding. Every night she has a different way of telling us it's time for bed. Sometimes she points. Or she might flip off the lights. Sometimes she squeezes testicles."

Irene had a rich, almost hysterical laugh. I loved to hear it.

"I gotta go, Babes. Our skit's tomorrow, and I want to go over my lines one more time. I have a long soliliquy, at which time I will make a total ass of myself."

"Pat, there's something I have to tell you." Her voice was tentative. "Gabe called and wanted to talk to you. I told her where you are. Don't get angry, please. She's your sister."

"I told you not to tell anybody." The muscles in the back of my neck stiffened. "Why did you do it?"

"Because she loves you and cares about you. And because I'm not going to lie anymore."

There was a desperation in Irene's voice. I realized for the first time how lonely she must be. She was suffering, too.

"I'm sorry I got angry. It's just that I'm so embarrassed by what's happened to me. Please don't tell anyone else."

"You shouldn't be embarrassed. I'm more proud of you now than I've ever been. You're doing something very difficult that will help both of us. I love you, Pat, so much. I need you to be healthy."

"I'll see you next week, Irene. I love you, too. By the way, why did Gabe call?"

"She's getting divorced again and . . . she wanted a prescription for Valium."

I often regretted that I would never be a parent. Some kids, especially Adrian, made me feel this regret deeply. Molly Casey was another.

Molly was blond and small and had exactly eight freckles symmetrically situated around her nose. She had misty blue eyes, and the middle of her upper lip was pinched just a little and turned up as if she were preparing to kiss someone. Molly had been my patient since she was twelve.

Molly had a way of getting things she wanted. She called them her routines. Her Camille routine was used when she was sick. It was a series of emotive posturings that made it seem as if her death was imminent. I saw her use it convincingly once in my office in front of her mother. I never saw her Cagney routine, her Mary Poppins routine, or after she read *The Catcher in the Rye*, her Holden Caulfield routine.

During one of Molly's office visits when she was fifteen, her mother complained that she couldn't get Molly "out of blue jeans and T-shirts. That's all she'll wear. We make good money."

Molly responded to parental pressure with passive resistance— her Mahatma Gandhi routine.

As Molly got older, it was apparent she was going to stay a small person. At seventeen she was five feet one and ninety-five pounds, slightly smaller than her mother. Her brother at age eighteen was over six feet.

"When you're five feet one, no one takes you seriously, Dr. Reilly. People tell me I'm cute. I don't want to be cute. I want to be pretty. I want to be beautiful. When I get mad, they want to pat me on the head. I'm everybody's kid sister. My brother calls me 'Shortness.' I'm going to punch him the next time he calls me that. I really will."

As young adulthood approached, Molly began to observe the rites of passage of that awkward time. She used a few drugs, smoked marijuana, drank.

A few days after her seventeenth birthday, Molly asked me for a prescription for birth control pills.

"I didn't know you were sexually active, Molly."

"I'm not," she said angrily. "But I'm scouting around. Virginity is about as much fun as starvation."

"You know," she said, as she was about to leave my office, "you're one of the few people who listen to me. I mean you really listen. I like that."

Three months before her graduation from Saint Bernadette High School, Molly charged into my office.

"I'm leaving home," she proclaimed. "I'm getting out of here. I'm not getting along with my parents or my brother. Everybody has an idea of what I should be. They tell me what to say, how to act, what school to go to. They don't like my friends.

"I'm leaving. I'm going to California. They let you be a person out there."

I tried to talk her out of going. But she had her mind made up.

"I have my plane ticket for L.A. I'm leaving tonight."

As she started to leave my office, I called out to her.

"Molly, promise you'll call me at least once a month while you're gone."

She hesitated for a moment, nodded her head, and left.

Molly kept her promise for the next four months. The third time she called her mood was euphoric. She was high on something. The fourth and last time she called, Molly was slurring her words and said something about "living with a guy." I pleaded with her to come home, and she laughed and hung up on me.

Six months passed, and no one heard from her. It was an early December evening, and we were getting our first snowfall in Cleveland. Irene and I were just starting to have dinner. Lucifer and Macbeth had themselves positioned so that they could watch us eat and so that we could see their plaintive expressions.

There was a knock on the door. Macbeth dashed furiously to the front door and barked angrily. Lucifer sauntered over toward the door and a few feet away from it laid on his back and spread his legs.

When I opened the door, Macbeth stopped barking and sat down. It was Molly. Her face was thin and drawn and had a pained expression. I put my arm around her and brought her in the house. She felt warm.

Her blond hair was longer and matted. She had no coat and wore a stained blue dress and shoes with inordinately high heels.

"I'm sick, Dr. Reilly," she said in a weak voice. "I feel awful."

Irene and I took Molly to the emergency room, and Irene called Molly's parents while I examined her.

She was sick.

I admitted her to the hospital with the diagnoses: (1) Gonorrhea with pelvic inflammatory disease and (2) Secondary syphilis.

I came into her room after her family had gone. She was sitting up in bed, holding on, tenuously, to whatever defiance she still had.

I sat in a chair by her bed and we stared at each other. She looked so small and vulnerable to the point of defeat.

"We're glad you're back, Molly. A lot of people around here love you."

"After what I've done?" She snapped. "I doubt it."

"You don't stop loving someone because they make a mistake."

"You know what my brother called me," she said, trying to sound angry. "He called me"—her hand went to her eyes . . . her chest started heaving as she cried—"he called me 'Shortness.' I've . . . missed him . . . so much. My mom brought me some . . . of my old jeans . . . and T-shirts. . . . I've missed my folks. . . ."

I put my arm around her and she looked up at me. I could see her eight freckles under her tears.

"Dr. Reilly . . . do you think . . . God . . . still loves me?"

"Now more than ever, Molly. Please don't leave us again."

"Never . . . never . . . I promise." She wiped the tears from her eyes and blew her nose. "I guess this is my 'Molly Casey routine.' "

I kissed her on the cheek.

"Molly," I said, "I'll probably never have a daughter. But if I did, I hope she'll be just like you."

"Thanks, Dr. Reilly, for always being there when I needed you. And thanks . . . for now."

Molly never realized that I needed her more than she needed me. The world is full of pediatricians. There are precious few Molly Caseys.

As I stepped out of the shower, I heard someone walking in my room. There was a frequent loud, bored sigh and the sounds of swishing nylons.

"Morning, Ruthy," I called out.

No answer.

I opened the bathroom door, stuck my head out, and saw Ruthy assume a defensive pose. She was sure I was going to attack. Ruthy was the only nurse at Hogarth who wore all white, including a cap, which made her stand out as an anachronism.

"Ruthy, I'm sorry I was so abusive last week. I was in bad shape."

I pulled a towel around my waist and walked out of the bathroom. Her eyes widened. I walked up to her and held out my hand.

"Let's be friends."

She shook my hand tentatively and made a pathetic attempt at a smile. This was an uncertain situation for her.

I stood back.

"Whaddaya think, Ruthy, not a bad body for a thirty-six-year-old pediatrician, eh?"

Her eyes widened again, and her lower jaw dropped.

I inhaled deeply. "If I were being auctioned off for stud service . . ." My towel fell off. "Oh, damn!"

I grabbed the towel and started to tie it around my waist again. I was terribly embarrassed. Ruthy was trembling, and her eyes were closed tight.

"You're disgusting," she screamed. She opened her eyes and pointed at me. "All you men from the States are vulgar and conceited."

"Oh?" I let the towel fall away, and I stood facing her. "I know some women who would kill if they could be where you are right now, Ruthy."

She snarled and headed for the door, her body making dissonant sounds. Her large buttocks seemed to move independently of the rest of her body. Her giant right hip crashed into the door handle, but she didn't seem to notice any pain.

Nurses are some of my favorite people, Ruthy notwithstanding. I get a curious delight out of baiting nurses whom I have not met before. It seems that barriers come down more quickly that way.

Several months before Hogarth, I was holding forth with a group of recently graduated nurses on how nurses have an exaggerated opinion of themselves.

"Let's face it," I said and tried not to laugh, "nurses are only glorified technicians."

One of them, a brunette with fire in her eyes, stepped forward.

"Dr. Reilly," she said. "Fuck off."

From behind the curtain, I could see O'Malley sitting among the patients and trying to look comfortable. All of the staff was in the audience. Randolph. Christine. Edith. Toni and Lorenzo were standing in the back, and she had her finger in his face and appeared to be lecturing him.

Reggie and Presswood sat on adjoining chairs in the front row. He was talking loudly to her, and she was earnestly attempting to look interested.

Karren, always the enigma, sat alone and was immersed in her own thoughts. Ruthy sat commandingly on two chairs in the second row and was chewing strenuously on something and grimacing, annoyed that the calories were not going down effortlessly.

Some of the patients started to clap and whistle, wanting us to start the skit.

Presswood chanted: "Give us Melanie. . . . We want Melanie. . . ." He started to clap his hands and look around. He hoped others would pick up the chant. He was ignored.

Melanie was standing next to me. She had on a white tight-fitting dress that showed her breasts to be larger than I had fantasized. She was smoking nervously and appeared uncertain and frightened.

The lights went down, and the spotlight was turned on. Melanie dropped her cigarette and stepped on it. She began to smile and look confident. I had not seen her appear so self-assured.

I squeezed her hand, but I don't think she was aware of me.

She strode briskly out to center stage and into the spotlight.

"Hello, scoundrels," she yelled to the audience. "Welcome to Junk City."

She explained that our skit would be a series of totally unrelated scenes, each written by a different person.

"All of the scenes have only one thing in common—bad taste."

"All right!" Presswood yelled and clapped loudly.

Melanie turned and walked offstage as the lights dimmed.

"Hey, guys," Presswood hollered. "Don't ya think Melanie has the nicest ass in North America? That ass could sell blue jeans to the queen."

When the lights came back up, Steve, Boone, and I sat in chairs on the right of the stage. Melanie stood in center stage and kept her right arm behind her back. She was holding something in her right hand. She smiled slightly and had a distant, ethereal look.

"Ever since I was a teenager, I've dreamed of a certain man with a special quality. He would be my prince. I think I've found him here in Junk City.

"I don't know which of you it is yet. But I've found an article of clothing here. I want each of these three"—she looked at the three of us who were sitting—"to try it on first. Whoever fits into this"— she brought her right arm from behind her back and held up a jock strap with a cup size that was large enough to hold a three-foot penis —"whoever fits into this will be my prince."

Hoots. Hollers. Whistles.

"I wondered where I left that," Steve said loudly above the noise as he walked up to Melanie. This was not in the script. Melanie was surprised but delighted. "I'm your prince. Let's go."

"Oh, no," she said. "You'll have to try this on. Right here. Right now. Pants off."

"You mean you don't believe me? What do you think that lump is down in my sock? And can't you tell by the way I walk? You know, the way I have to kick out my right leg."

"Drop 'em, Stud," a woman yelled from the audience.

"Do you realize what will happen if I take my pants off? All the women will rush the stage and want to touch me. I won't have one moment of peace for the next few weeks. I'm sorry, Melanie, not here. Up in your room later?"

"That's a deal," said Melanie, and she and Steve started walking offstage with Steve kicking out his right leg.

Above the applause, Presswood yelled:

"Hey, Melanie, do you take it in the poop chute?"

She stopped and looked over her shoulder at him.

"Maybe . . . do you?"

Presswood had gone too far. I jumped off the stage and went toward him. He saw me coming, stood, and started laughing maniacally. I wanted desperately to hurt him.

"No. No." Reggie stood in my way. "Don't Patrick. He's still sick. He can't help himself."

"I don't give a shit. I'm gonna knock him on his ass."

A pair of very strong arms grabbed me from behind.

"C'mon, Pat. Let them handle it." It was Boone.

Presswood continued to laugh, but with increasing intensity. He was sick. Very sick. Reggie and Toni led him out of the auditorium.

Boone and I returned backstage. *He* had stopped me from committing violence. The irony of that was not lost on either of us.

The last time I had actually fought with another person was when I was seven and in the second grade. It had been a totally unpleasant experience. There had been a large group of kids watching us fight. Gabe, who was ten then, was in the crowd. I remember glancing at her while I was fighting and seeing her disapproving look.

I knocked one of the kid's front teeth out, and then he started to cry and ran away. I felt awful and started to run after him. I wanted to tell him I was sorry. The other kids stopped me. They thought I was running after him so I could hit him again.

But Gabe knew. She took me and we found him and I told him I was sorry and we shook hands.

Later when Gabe and I were walking home, I made a promise to her that I would never hurt anyone else again. In twenty-nine years I had not forgotten how distasteful hurting someone was. But if I had reached Presswood . . .

"Patrick, I know you care for me. But don't think you have to protect my virtue." Melanie was upset with me. "And I don't have tender ears."

She then smiled.

"Are you ready? It's about time for us to go on."

All my sphincters went into spasm.

"I'm terrified."

"I'll be out there with you. It's O.K."

All the others were on stage.

Hog Body was impersonating Karren. He had on a red wig and some things under his T-shirt to make it appear he had enormous boobs. And he had on very brief shorts. He was supposed to be leading exercises.

"And now, finally, we'll exercise the things you'll need for sex. Mac, what would that be for you?"

"Well, I guess I'll need to strengthen the muscles of my right hand. I need to work on a better stroke."

There were a few titters and some perfunctory applause, and they ran off stage. Hog Body stopped just before he reached the curtain, pulled down his shorts, flapped his hairy ass, and mooned the audience.

Melanie once again walked back on stage to the sound of whistles and feet stomping. She was enjoying herself immensely.

She introduced me as "Dr. P. D. Attrition from Cleveland, Ohio. He has a pharmacy in his basement. He makes all his own drugs.

"What drugs do you make?" she asked me.

"Only the ones I consume. I spend a lot of time in my basement."

"What's your drug of choice?"

("When I ask you the question," Melanie had told me in rehearsal, "take a deep breath and move to the center of the stage. Be loose but be convincing," she said. "Remember Burt Lancaster in *Elmer Gantry*. Use gestures, be expansive, talk with passion.")

A spotlight followed me to center stage.

"My drug of choice," I said, "is Valium.

" 'Cause Valium is magic.

"It is calomel washed in the amnion of a virgin.

"It is good for alcoholic dissipation and hardness of the liver.

"It is a certain cure for decadence and hedonism . . .

"A salve for melancholy.

"It is made from saffron, quicksilver and vermilion . . .

"And can help with persistent engorgement, excessive emissions, and sexual frenzy.

"It will cure dimness of sight and tightness of the breath . . .

"And can help with low esteem.

"Valium is the absolute panacea, the universal remedy.

"It is from the tear of the Paraclete and like a smile of the Comforter.

"It will give surcease to all discomfort . . .

" 'Cause Valium is magic."

I made a sweeping bow and almost fell on my face. The applause was nice and I felt a momentary rush of exhilaration.

The skit was over, and the others from our group joined Melanie and me onstage. As the applause got louder, we started hugging each other. We had survived and conquered this difficult experience. And we had done it together.

As we left the stage, Melanie moved in close to me.

"You did a super job, Patrick."

I put my arm around her shoulder and noticed, once again, her breasts. I would have to include them more in my fantasies.

As we were leaving the auditorium, I noticed Randolph and O'Malley talking. Neither of them gestured, and they both wore clinical expressions. They were being formal, probably discussing a case.

Randolph saw me and motioned for me to come to them.

O'Malley had an unusually stern look, but it was made almost comical because of a small piece of popcorn in the lower corner of his beard.

"I'm glad you could talk humorously about something that was destroying you," O'Malley said with a disinterested tone. There was obviously a problem that needed to be addressed, and he was making small talk.

Maybe something had happened to Irene! They were afraid to tell me. I started to panic. I couldn't live without Irene. Or maybe the medical society in Cleveland had found out. They would pull my license. I would never be able to practice medicine again!

· 164 ·

They looked at each other as if they were unsure which one should tell me. I needed to know what was wrong. I tensed, ready to be devastated.

"Patrick," Randolph said, "we've just heard something that we need to talk to you about."

I froze with fear and uncertainty.

"Why did you expose yourself to Ruthy this morning? She told us that . . ."

Randolph stopped when he saw me start to laugh. I wanted to stop and explain, but I couldn't. I had to laugh this one out. I could respond in no other way. The absurdity of that accusation was so extreme, so unbelievable that it was not deserving of an answer. I continued to laugh uncontrollably.

O'Malley looked from me to Randolph and smiled.

"I think we have our answer," he said.

"Our patients have enough grief," Randolph said disgustedly, "without this type of accusation."

I explained what had happened while I wiped away the tears.

"I got pissed when she said all men from the States are conceited. I wanted to show her what conceit really was."

"I guess you showed her." O'Malley smiled and turned to go.

"Wait," I said. "Can I ask you a question? This is probably none of my business, but what's the matter with Presswood?"

O'Malley looked at Randolph, who appeared uncertain for a moment. Randolph then nodded.

"Go ahead and tell him, Frank. He understands this will be told in confidence. There may be a lesson in this for Patrick."

"Presswood came to us about four months ago." O'Malley spoke formally as if presenting a case for discussion. "He had been addicted to Valium for seven or eight years. On the advice of his family doctor, he stopped taking Valium abruptly about two weeks before coming here. That was bad advice.

"A week after coming here, he started to actively hallucinate. We couldn't handle him, and we transferred him out to a psychiatric hospital." O'Malley shook his head. "He had a tough time. He had to be restrained in bed for several weeks and was fed intravenously and given heavy doses of antipsychotics."

"Wait a minute!" I was starting to breathe rapidly. "Presswood was only taking Valium?"

O'Malley nodded.

"A lot of Valium," Randolph said.

"Hallucinations . . . restraints . . . antipsychotics . . . holy shit! Do you see this . . . very often?"

They stared at me.

"We took Presswood back three weeks ago," O'Malley continued. "He doesn't need drugs anymore, and he hasn't exhibited any psychotic tendencies. He continues to show some psychopathic behavior, and that makes it difficult for all of us. We don't like his inappropriate comments any more than you do. But he is getting better, and he's definitely salvageable. We're going to continue to work with him."

"We all need to be patient with him," Randolph said pointedly and looked at me.

"We know he can be offensive," O'Malley said.

"Our most interesting patients are the ones that are the most challenging," Randolph said, smiling, and looked to O'Malley for agreement. O'Malley nodded.

I was sure that was a reference to me, and it was not funny. Randolph could piss me off without trying. Before I left Hogarth, I would have to sit down with him and tell him of his need for personality adjustment.

O'Malley and Randolph walked off, but quickly separated and went out different doors.

Melanie was in the hall waiting for me.

"What were you laughing about in there?"

I told her of my encounter with Ruthy.

"I wish I could catch you in your room with just a towel around you," she laughed. "You wouldn't have the towel on for long."

"Patrick," she said and lowered her voice. "You know I really think I could help you if you'd just let me try. I could do some things that maybe you haven't experienced before. Has any woman ever . . ."

"I don't want to talk about it, Melanie. It's really embarrassing." In my attempt to be emphatic, I was also showing anger.

"All right. I'm sorry. But just one more question. Have you tried masturbating? It might . . ."

"Melanie! Goddamnit!"

". . . help. You'd be surprised the things you can learn about yourself."

"Will you please stop!"

"I won't say any more. But you know where my room is." She lowered her eyes and pretended to look hurt. "You haven't invited me to your room."

"Pat! . . . telephone . . . long distance."

"Thanks, Boone. Is it a man, woman, or child?"

"A lady with a very sexy voice." He winked at me as I breezed by him. "Can I get on the extension? You won't hear my heavy breathing. I promise."

"Hell, no. I'm not going to add to the delinquency of an alcoholic. . . ." I picked up the receiver. "I know what *you people* are . . . a bunch of sexual deviates . . . can't be trusted . . . hello . . ."

"Sexual deviates! Sounds interesting . . . can I come?"

"Gabe!"

"Hi, kiddo. How ya doin'?"

"Good . . . well . . . pretty good. How about you?

"I suppose Irene told you that Martin and I are getting divorced. I'm a two-time loser, Pat."

"It's about time you dropped that creep, Gabe. I don't know . . ."

"He's dropping me. This time he got involved with a law student. He got her pregnant, and he's going to marry her. She's twenty-three. Martin's forty-five going on sixty."

"I'm sorry Gabe. I didn't know."

"That's all right. But I didn't call to talk about me. I want you to know I have here a letter I've written to you. It's an angry letter, Pat. That's why I haven't sent it. I'm really hurt that you didn't tell me that you had a problem and were going to a hospital in Toronto. I love you, kiddo, and I care about you. You shouldn't be so disregarding of people that love you."

"I would have told you—eventually. I'm so goddamn embarrassed by this. Please understand that."

"I bet you haven't told Sarah either."

"No. Please don't tell her, Gabe. Not now."

"All right. But she'll be offended, too."

"And don't tell Number Eighty-two. I don't want him to know. I haven't seen Adrian in a long time. How is he?"

"Growing like a weed and just as recalcitrant. He misses you, Pat. You've been more of a father to him than Martin ever was or ever will be. Remember that old stethoscope of yours you gave him a few months ago? He sleeps with it."

"I love that kid, Gabe. You've done a good job with him."

"Thanks, Pat. I wish you and Irene could have had some kids. Both of you would be terrific parents. It's so tragic you had that heavy exposure to the X rays."

"Yeah . . . I wish I could change a lot of things in my past."

"Now, would you please tell me what in the hell you're doing in a hospital, in another country? You have sedativism? Is that the word?"

"I've been taking tranquilizers and sleeping pills for about fourteen years. I started taking pills about six months before I went to med school. And I haven't been able to stop."

"This is Logan's fault, Pat. He pushed you into medicine."

"No, Gabe. This is *my* fault. It's too easy to blame him. I'm a responsible adult. *I* made the decision to take the drugs. And I became addicted to them. . . . I took more and more . . . I couldn't stop. I had to do this."

"Irene wouldn't tell me very much about what was happening. And she was crying, Pat."

"Well, I was screwing up everything. I was making stupid mistakes with my patients. I was losing friends. Losing my memory. And I would've lost Irene."

"Don't lose her, kiddo."

"I don't want to."

"Good. By the way, Pat, Sarah's coming to spend a week with Adrian and me in about two weeks. Will you be home by then? The last time you, me, and Sarah were together is when she married Vic. That's five or six years ago."

"That will be great. They should be releasing me in two weeks. There's been some talk of keeping me an extra three weeks here. But I wouldn't stay."

"You do what they tell you to do, Pat! Let them make the decisions."

"Bullshit! And don't go pulling that caring big sister crap on me, Gabe. I know what I need and what I don't need."

My outburst was met with silence.

"Sorry, Gabe."

"You've never talked to me like that before. I didn't like it, Pat. You sounded like Logan."

That was a frightening thought. I apologized again.

"That's O.K., Pat. By the way, did Irene tell you why I called the other night?"

"Yeah. She said you wanted a prescription for Valium."

"How do you feel about that?"

"I'll never take it again. I can't. And I'll never write a prescription for it again. Absolutely never!"

"I need something, Pat. I'm having a pretty rough time."

"You won't get Valium from me. It won't be difficult getting it from just about any doctor, though."

"I know. I've been taking Valium on and off for about eight years."

"I didn't know that, Gabe. That's awful. You're probably addicted, too. Stop taking it!"

She laughed.

"I don't take it by the handful, Pat. And I don't take it every day."

"You shouldn't take it at all. That's a poor way of dealing with stress. I know. Now I've got to learn at age thirty-six how to deal with stress like an adult."

"Well . . . we can talk about it when you get home. Right now, I'm going to call my gynecologist and get a prescription."

"I'm sure the turkey will give you one."

"You, my dear brother, were the first one to give me a prescription for Valium. Don't you remember?"

"I . . . don't remember. I'm sorry I did that. Very sorry."

"I feel I'm upsetting you. I'm sorry. Listen, if something happens and you have to stay in the hospital longer than you think, Sarah and I will come up and see you. I love Toronto."

"Thanks for calling, Gabe. Tell Adrian I said hello and that I'll take him to see the Indians this summer."

"Good-bye, kiddo. I'm proud of you."

The first time I met Martin, I knew Gabe was making a mistake. He was loud, got drunk, and grabbed Gabe's ass several times. And I mean grabbed! I found him not only unappealing, but offensive.

The next day I called Gabe.

"Drop him," I said. "He's awful."

"You're being unkind to me," she bristled, "and cruel. I'm going to marry Martin. You have no right to say those things."

"But, Gabe . . ."

"It's my life, Pat."

I got drunk the morning of Gabe's wedding and didn't attend. I did not want to see Sarah cry again.

I saw Gabe and Martin only on holidays for the next several years. The air would be thick with discomfort. Martin would get drunk and be loud. I would lie about having "to see a patient" and leave early.

Martin was not at Adrian's baptism.

"I'm not sure where he is," Gabe said. "But I think I know."

Apparently that was the beginning of Martin's not-well-concealed affairs.

During one of her separations from Martin, Gabe sent me a poem.

> Inching along with no direction
> Fulfillment no longer a goal
> Having no function anymore
> But to be a protectress.
> Burning,
> But not with passion
> And not with intensity
> But with grief over
> A life corrupted with
> Banalities.
> Fatiguing
> With a mind
> No longer cluttered with dreams.

"Do you ever write a poem when you're happy?" I asked her once.

"No," she said. "It's not necessary."

Adrian and I were near ecstasy late one Sunday afternoon. We had seen the Indians sweep a doubleheader from the Yankees. After the game, Adrian was able to get the autographs of Bucky Dent and Rick Manning.

He ran screaming into his house holding his scorecard with both signatures. Adrian was anticipating that the autographs would bring his mother incredible happiness. He stopped when he saw Gabe sitting at the kitchen table smoking a cigarette. Her right eye was red and swollen.

Adrian sat at the table across from his mother and stared at her.

"Where's Martin?" I asked her. "I've got to at least tell him what I think of him."

"You have no right to do that, Pat," she said, not looking at me. "I am where I choose to be."

I walked to the door.

"Gabe, don't ever again show me your poems detailing how unhappy you are. I won't feel sorry for you anymore. But I do pity you."

"Gabe's staying with Martin is insane," Irene told me. "But it's her life. You can't make decisions for her and you can't share her pain. Just be her brother, Pat, and love her. And be there for her whenever she needs you. That's what she'd do for you."

I called Gabe and I apologized for the way I had talked to her.

"Thanks, kiddo," she said. "Things will get better. And one of these days when I'm feeling good, I'll write a poem and send it to you."

Gabe never sent me another poem.

"You've never been on the subway, Patty? We'll take you on it today."

Boone, Steve, and Hog Body were making plans to go into downtown Toronto and invited me along.

Melanie did not have permission to leave the hospital grounds yet. Mac wanted to stay at Hogarth because he expected a call from "the wife." Lucy said she preferred to stay and read.

"Dr. Randolph said he wasn't going to let me go out," Melanie said, "until I agree to let my mother get the drugs and alcohol out of my apartment. I have some problems with that."

"It would be a lot more interesting if you came with us."

"I could make it interesting for you if you stayed here with me," Melanie said. She moved her mouth close to my ear. "I'll be lonely."

"See you later, Melanie."

As I signed out, I felt something ominous and massive behind me and a judgmental expression glaring at me.

"We'll be back in a few hours, Ruthy," I said, without turning around.

"You have permission?"

"Yeah."

"I better check." She trundled off to get my chart.

"Did you ever smell Ruthy?" Steve asked as he came up to sign out.

"She smells like she's been dipped in perfume."

"That's called a Newfie bath," he said.

Boone had moved in to sign out and heard us.

"Maybe because she knows she's so awful to look at, she figures she'll work on one of our other senses."

We met Hog Body and the four of us walked past the Nurses' Station.

"O.K. The four of you can go," Ruthy yelled. "Where are you going?"

"It's none of her fucking business," Steve said.

"We're going looking for intelligent life," Boone called back.

· 171 ·

"I'm going out to buy a long black raincoat, Ruthy." I yelled. "One that I can pull open quickly."

The last time I had gone down the driveway, I'd had no intention of coming back. I had been angry, frustrated, afraid. But as we headed for the street, I knew I would be coming back. Running away was no longer a consideration. But I was nervous and confused.

When we reached the street, cars were going by so fast. And they were so loud. I began to tremble. I felt unprotected and vulnerable. I didn't want to go anywhere but back to Hogarth. Hogarth was safe. I wouldn't be hurt there.

"C'mon, Patty." Hog Body put his arm around my back and urged me to keep going. He could see my fear. I tried to break away from him so I could run back, but he wouldn't let me go.

I felt terror. If those goddamn fucking cars would only slow down! Everything was so impersonal. Strangers who didn't care. The buildings were so tall, and I was frightened when I looked up. I couldn't sort things out.

"Help me, Hog," I gasped.

"I gotcha, Patty. Nothing's gonna happen."

"I need to go back. Please." I looked to Boone. "Please take me back."

"I'll take care of him," Hog shouted. "You two go on up to the station."

Hog Body moved me into a small drugstore and we stood near the magazine rack.

"Number one, Patty, you're not going back. You're going downtown on the subway with us. Number two, I'll be next to you all the time. Nothing is gonna hurt you. I promise."

He had a reassuring look, and I believed him.

"O.K. Now take a few deep breaths like Karren taught us. C'mon."

After several minutes things seemed manageable again. We walked around the store. I nonchalantly but with direction walked to the back of the store and looked at the drugs on the pharmacist's shelves. I always did this when I was in a drugstore. It was exciting.

The subway train was arriving as we got to the station. Boone and Steve were annoyed that we had almost missed it.

"Where the fuck were you guys?" Steve called to us. "We could've taken the train before this one. We should have. That would have fixed your ass but good." Steve and Boone both lived in Toronto, and without them we would have been lost.

"You O.K., Pat? What happened?" Boone was concerned.

"Panic attack. A bad one. But it wasn't anything the good Doctor Hog couldn't handle."

Hog and I sat behind Steve and Boone, but they turned around in their seats so we could talk.

"We've noticed you and Melanie," Steve said to me. "You get in her pants yet?"

I frowned to let him know that the question was inappropriate.

"You've been in her room at night. You gotta be gettin' something."

"Steve wants to know so that the next time you go see her, he can stand outside the door and beat off," laughed Boone.

"Speaking of beating off," said Steve. "Let's go see some strippers. There's a place down off Yonge Street."

There was tacit agreement to that proposal.

"What about you and Lucy?" Boone asked Steve. "You two seem pretty friendly."

"I like her very much. We've talked a lot. No touching so far. But soon."

"If you get a chance to score with her, where would you go?" Hog asked. "There aren't any locks on the doors."

"What about the shower?" I asked. "Couldn't you screw in the shower? Even Ruthy wouldn't come peeking in the john."

Steve looked at me as if I had said something incredibly dumb.

"The johns at Hogarth would only be good for meat and potatoes stuff," Steve explained, as if he were telling me the facts of life. "I got moves I like to use. I need room.

"I could teach you some things," he said to me. "I bet you doctors don't know shit about technique."

"Hey, goddamnit," I said, "my wife has told me I'm good in bed."

"Maybe she doesn't know any better."

"Or maybe," added Boone, "she just has a good sense of humor."

We got off the subway at Yonge Street and began walking east. At first I was frightened by the crowds of people but soon got used to it. Hog Body kept watching me.

Steve stopped in front of an old, unattractive building that advertised strippers and went in. The three of us followed. Inside we began walking up a long flight of stairs. We could hear the bump-and-grind music.

On the stairs coming down were two disgruntled guys in work clothes.

"Hey, lads," one of them shouted to us, "they don't show no pussy."

The four of us turned as one and climbed back down the stairs.

We walked the streets for hours. We were getting a taste of freedom that we needed badly. No one seemd to notice us. There were no suspicious glances. Apparently we were not conspicuous by our lack of self-esteem.

Toronto definitely had majesty. In some ways it reminded me of Chicago. It had the same elegance of proportions and flavor of greatness. Toronto had shape and dignity and sovereignty. It was solid and manifestly proud. And it was unbelievably clean.

"I wish we could keep Cleveland this clean," I said to Boone.

"Canadians have more respect for themselves than Americans do," he answered pointedly and without hesitation. "And we're more considerate of each other."

"Gratuitous remarks which I'll let pass," I thought.

"I lived in the States for ten years," Boone said. "I know."

As we approached the subway station to go back to Hogarth, Boone and Steve began talking in hushed tones.

Steve turned to us.

"Boone and I aren't going back just yet. We'll eat dinner downtown and see you back at the hospital tonight."

"Are you guys gonna drink?" Hog Body was challenging them.

"I drank once before when I was taking Antabuse. I never will again. Steve won't drink either."

"I'd feel better if you came back with us," said Hog.

"Don't worry about us," said Steve. "We have a friend we . . . ah . . . share . . . and we thought we'd pay her a visit."

"She's sort of in the entertainment business," Boone added, smiling.

"C'mon, Patty, let's go back." We started to walk away, but Hog stopped and turned around. "Hey, don't forget that they'll be testing you guys back at Hogarth to see if you've taken anything. "

There were only a few people on the train with Hog and me and no one was sitting near us. But Hog bent toward me and whispered:

"Have you ever been with a prostitute?"

"Yeah. Once. You?"

Hog nodded. "Once a month." He lowered his voice even more.

"There are things that I want to do . . . you know . . . in bed . . . that I can't ask my wife to do. So I do those things with this prostitute. Is that wrong?"

"You're asking the wrong person."

"Do you ever want to do some things in bed with your wife that you just can't ask her to do?"

"Yeah."

He smiled knowingly. "Frustrating, isn't it? Maybe you should get yourself a lady."

"My only experience with a prostitute was not very good."

I was eighteen and I had never kissed a girl. And a kiss was all I really wanted. "Paddlin' Madelyn" was what everyone called her. Her apartment was a few blocks from the high school.

"Ten bucks for a blow job . . . fifteen for a straight fuck . . . twenty for both. And ten bucks added for anything else. You look nervous . . . you ever done this before?"

"Oh, yes," I said. I wanted to ask how much it would be for just a kiss.

"Well, what do you want?"

"Straight." I couldn't say "fuck" in front of a woman.

"You don't have a drip, do you?"

"No." A drip?

"Come here and kiss me, John," she said.

"Pat. My name's Pat."

When I was about a foot from her, I closed my eyes as I thought you were supposed to do, and I lunged toward her face. When I opened my eyes, my lips were on the bottom of her jaw and my nose landed squarely in her open mouth.

"This is going to be terrific," she said. "I can tell right now."

She stood back and undressed. Her breasts were small and she had long nipples. I was getting excited. She took her panties off, and I tried not to stare at her black, curly pubic hair. The guys at school had said that area smelled like clam juice.

I had seen one stag film and some women naked from the waist up in *Playboy*. That was hardly sufficient preparation for this.

We lay in bed naked, and I turned to kiss her. She shook her head.

"We've already kissed. You only get one. If you want more, it will cost you. Are you sure you've done this before?"

"Yeah. I'm sure. But it's been a long time. I may have forgotten a few things."

She smiled. She knew.

"I'll get your cock hard, John, and then we can fuck."

"Pat. Call me Pat."

As she worked on me, she said: "Well, Madelyn, you're deflowering another one."

As soon as I was in her, she started moaning loudly.

"Your cock feels so good . . . I like you young guys. . . . fuck me. . . ." She yawned. ". . . yeah, this is good . . . say something, John. . . . talk . . . tell me how it feels. . . . is it good. . . ."

Her tone was becoming increasingly urgent. And she wasn't yawning anymore.

". . . fuck me. . . . oh, shit . . . fuck me. . . . oh, that's good. . . ."

"She's having more fun than I am," I thought.

"Keep going . . . I'm going to try and come. . . ."

"How will I know?"

Her eyes widened and she smiled derisively.

"I'll start . . . singing . . . 'The Star Spangled Banner' . . . you turkey. . . . keep going. . . ."

It was over for me in a few seconds, but Madelyn kept moving, more and more violently. Her legs went further and further apart, and I felt as if I were going to be swallowed up.

". . . fuck me. . . . oh yeah . . . fuck me harder. . . . shit . . ."

I was getting tired and losing interest, so I stopped.

"What's the matter, John?"

"Oh, say can you see . . ."

"Did you come? You didn't make any noise?"

"Am I supposed to?"

As I got dressed, I felt almost nothing. Not guilt or shame. I wasn't happy or sad. The guys at school talked about sex all the time. There had to be more to it than this.

"Good-bye, John," Paddlin' Madelyn called to me as I was going out the door. "I was your first. You'll never forget me."

"See ya, Mildred."

"I wish the train was taking me home, Hog. I miss Irene so much."

"Why don't you have kids, Patty? You love your wife, and you're a baby doctor. You must like kids."

I didn't feel like lying again. But I wasn't ready to tell the truth.

"Look at the people on this train, Hog. Don't you envy them? They're going home to their families. No problems with alcohol or drugs."

Hog's look showed annoyance.

"Nobody's perfect. Everybody has something to hide. We have a problem and we're doing something about it. I'm starting to feel good. You should, too, Patty."

We got off the train and walked back toward Hogarth. Several blocks from the hospital, I began to feel some anticipation.

"Hey, Patty, slow down."

I kept walking faster.

About one block away I finally saw the entrance to Hogarth. And the sight of it made me feel good. When we reached the driveway, I was five steps ahead of Hog Body. I wanted to be inside where it would be warm and comfortable. A place without hazards, where everything was predictable. It was an environment where, now, I could survive without apprehension, without shame. I was among my peers, my equals in the most important, most basic ways.

I had found an environment where I could live without taking drugs. I had no choice anymore. However distasteful, I had to accept the fact that I needed Hogarth.

God grant me the serenity to accept the things I cannot change. . . .

19

A LIGHT SNOW powdered the ground as if someone with an eye for beauty had selectively and with a delicate hand dusted the landscape with white sand. The spring flowers had not been touched by the snow and appeared undaunted by the cold.

There was a quietness and peace and symmetry out there that seemed to balance all the emotional turmoil I had experienced.

I became acutely aware of a much-too-sweet, overpowering smell.

Ruthy was somewhere near. I turned from the window and saw her, in all her whiteness, occluding the doorway.

"Morning, Ruthy. You look nice."

"Here's your vitamin pill, *doctor*."

She spit out *doctor* with an inflection that dripped with ridicule.

I walked to her slowly so she wouldn't run. She didn't trust me. When I got close enough, I put my arms around her and hugged her and kissed her on the cheek. Although her breasts were mammoth, they seemed to collapse as I squeezed close to her.

I stood back from her. She had been surprised to the point of being paralyzed. Finally she breathed. "Why did you do that?"

"Most people think I'm a pretty nice guy. I don't like your treating me with such disdain. I don't think I deserve it."

"Oh, yes, you do! You men from the States think you can get away with anything. You're as bad as the rest of them, and you're a doctor. I would expect more from you. I run a tight ship here on weekends."

She pointed her finger at me. "You straighten up, or I'll see that you're dismissed. I have some power here, you know. They listen to me."

"Sure, Ruthy."

"Toni lets you people do what you want during the week, and I've reported her for it. I'm sure that they'll want me to replace her as charge nurse on this floor soon. I've heard that she even flirts with the male patients."

Ruthy looked expectant, hoping I could give her some ammunition.

"Toni's a hell of a woman. I wish she would flirt with me."

Ruthy snarled and handed me the vitamin pill.

"Don't you ever touch me again, or I'll report you. Remember, *doctor*, I have an advantage over you here. So watch your step."

She turned with as much flair as possible and moved away, apparently thinking that she had left me frightened, with an admonition resounding in my ears.

Ruthy was unmistakably and unalterably a fool. She wasn't clever enough to use invective as a weapon. She could only assault from a position of what she considered authority. It is sad that witless people repeatedly proclaim loudly what they lack.

"You're not going to eat any breakfast?" Melanie asked.

"Just coffee. Any time they serve something here I don't recognize immediately, I'm not going to eat it."

· 178 ·

Melanie looked at her plate.

"Scrambled eggs and toast. What don't you recognize?"

"Look closely at your scrambled eggs. Looks like somebody mixed little green pubic hairs in with the eggs."

Melanie moved her plate forward and dropped her napkin on top of the scrambled eggs.

"Damnit, Patrick. I was hungry this morning. You're disgusting.

"You're the second person in two days to tell me I'm disgusting. Ruthy told me yesterday."

"I must give Ruthy more credit for being observant. You're not too bright either, Patrick. Pubic hairs. Really!"

"I've seen you people eat kidneys. How do I know you wouldn't eat pubic hairs?"

Melanie raised her right hand.

"C'mon, Patrick. This is Sunday morning. Don't talk like that."

"I'm sorry."

"You're in rare form this morning. What's the matter?"

I told her of my encounter with Ruthy.

"You actually put your arms around her?"

"Yeah. It was like hugging a giant marshmallow. And just about as rewarding."

Melanie leaned forward.

"You smell like Ruthy, Patrick. You must have squeezed her good. You better change clothes and shower."

"Hell. I've already showered once. But if it's that bad, I'll go shower again. Want to join me?"

"Sure."

"I'm just kidding, Melanie. Maybe if things were different."

"You know we'll never see each other again after we leave this place," Melanie said, with an inordinate, desperate sadness.

At our Sunday morning general meeting, a minister spoke about alcoholism and addiction with the authority of someone who had had the problem.

"Many times in prayer we ask the Lord to 'forgive us our trespasses.' And many of us work hard at forgiving others. But when have we ever asked for help in forgiving ourselves? You must learn how to forgive yourself.

"You're the number one priority in your life. And when you leave here, you'll have a new relationship with yourself. But you will never acquire self-esteem until you have forgiven yourself for the mistakes that brought you here.

"And until you have self-esteem again, you will be of no real value to anyone."

Forgive myself? I think this guy had a point. But how does one forgive himself? That would take more insight into myself than I was capable of. At least at this time.

A new relationship with myself? I had thought of that before, and it frightened me. How would I be different if I were alert all the time? How would Irene and my patients respond to the unsedated Patrick Reilly?

So often people had commented on my being calm and passive and aloof. But I couldn't be any other way. I was toxic from the heavy doses of drugs I consumed. But what would I be like without drugs? Irritable? Impatient? Restless? Agitated? Angry?

Oh, God, what have I done to myself?

We had a buffet lunch for a change, and I scrutinized everything I put on my plate.

"Man, you smell just fine."

I wanted to tell Lorenzo to go to hell. But it was Sunday.

"You're smelling Ruthy," I said.

"Oh? You and Ruthy been rubbing up against each other?"

A vision of that popped into my mind, and I let go with a genuine belly laugh.

"You'll stop laughing when you see who's motioning for us."

Bossy sat at a table near a window and was gesturing for us. Sitting with him was Doc, who had introduced himself to me at the physicians' support group meeting.

When we got to the table, we shook hands, which I thought was unnecessary. Bossy looked at his palm after shaking hands with me.

"You're still in withdrawal," he said. He looked at Doc. "Sweaty palms."

"Well," I said, "it looks like winter has come back."

Bossy disregarded my small talk and glared at me as we sat.

"Did you go to an A.A. meeting this morning?" Bossy asked me.

"No."

"Why not?" He moved closer to me, and his lips formed an unpleasant smile. He was preparing to become forceful on an issue over which he had certain and clear feelings. He was going to slaughter me, and all four of us knew it.

"Damnit. I'm not an alcoholic." My temerity surprised me. "I'm not going to waste my time . . ."

"Waste your time? Did you say waste your time?" Bossy spoke through clenched teeth. He was furious but did not raise his voice.

I tried to appear calm, but I was shrinking rapidly.

"Let me tell these young doctors why I'm in A.A.," Doc said. Bossy continued to stare at me. He was attacking, in pursuit of my fragile ego, and he was annoyed that Doc was trying to stop him.

Bossy moved back in his chair and continued to stare. Then he pointed at me. "Just talk to this guy. The other one doesn't need to be convinced."

Doc moved his cup toward Bossy.

"How about getting me a coffee?"

Bossy took the cup and lumbered off.

"Don't let Bossy frighten you," Doc said to Lorenzo and me. "Sometimes he shows more zeal than wisdom. He cares so much and he doesn't want anyone to make the mistakes he's made. He appears invincible. But he's not. Bossy's relapsed once. About six years ago." Doc shook his head in disappointment. "He just is not able to see the irony in all of this yet."

Bossy returned, handed Doc the cup of coffee, and sat down. Doc stared at him as if he were trying to read his mood. After several seconds Bossy looked at Doc, smiled pleasantly, and with some embarrassment said:

"Thanks."

Doc looked at Lorenzo and me.

"Lads," he said, "my story may shock you. I still get nervous when I tell it. I'm fifty-three. Twenty-three years ago I finished my residency in obstetrics and gynecology. I spent two years in the army and then went into a private practice in Buffalo."

As Doc talked, he looked at us less often and more at his hands, which encircled tightly around the coffee cup. Steam was coming from the coffee. He was burning his hands, but his face remained expressionless.

During his years in the service, he had started to drink.

"I don't think I was an alcoholic then," he said and looked at Bossy. "I'm not really clear where to draw the line between my social drinking and my uncontrolled drinking."

He drank while in the army because he was "completely unstimulated."

"About all I did was snatch uteruses out of career officers' wives after they had had all the children they wanted."

Watching Doc with his hands around the very hot cup disturbed me. Lorenzo began moving in his chair. He must have been bothered by it, too.

"Doctors choose their specialties for different reasons," he said. "I chose obstetrics and gynecology because I liked working with young, healthy women during their pregnancies. I never liked working with serious illness."

He smiled.

"As you know, gynecologists work where other men play."

He relaxed his grip on the cup and took several drinks from it. His palms were an angry red.

"I noticed during my residency that I would get a little excited when I was examining young women." He looked at us. "Sexually excited. When a woman gets on the table to be examined, she's so vulnerable, so trusting. It aroused me. Even thinking of it now still excites me. I should have gotten out of the field and into another specialty, but I enjoyed being aroused. It became an addiction.

"I started having erections when I was examining my patients in about my second year in private practice. No one, including my nurse, ever noticed, because I would wear an oversized white coat that I kept buttoned. Sometimes I even ejaculated in my pants."

He looked at us again as if he were asking for understanding.

"Can either of you ever begin to imagine how this made me feel? The embarrassment? The disgust? But I couldn't stop."

He took a large drink of coffee.

"I couldn't talk to anyone about this. So I started to drink again. Mainly in the evening. But after a year, I'd have a couple of drinks in the morning and even between patients." He shook his head. "I drank a lot of Listerine, too."

"How about some more coffee, Doc?" Bossy asked.

Doc nodded.

Bossy took the cup and looked at Lorenzo and me.

"Either of you?"

Lorenzo nodded and handed his cup to Bossy.

"I'm going to continue, Bossy," Doc said. "You've heard this before."

This story was not only shocking, it was depressing the hell out of me.

"After a while I found that if I masturbated in between seeing patients," Doc continued, "I could get through the day all right.

"One day about fifteen years ago I had a young woman up in the stirrups and I started to get an erection. I excused myself and went back into my office, drank a shot of vodka, pulled down my pants, and masturbated.

"I turned to go back and saw my nurse looking at me and crying. She had seen me for the first time."

Bossy returned with the cups of coffee.

"Are you two doing all right?" Bossy asked. "Lorenzo, you don't look so good."

"I'm starting to feel the same way I felt last Thursday night," Lorenzo said with an unmistakable trace of anger. "I just want to get up and leave." He looked at me.

"I'm depressed again, too," I said. "I don't want to hear any more."

Doc leaned forward and rested his hand on Lorenzo's forearm. He was smiling, almost glowing.

"You don't understand," he said. "This story has a happy ending. I'm alive and I'm healthy and I'm in control of my life. Isn't that what you lads want?"

"Are you happy, Doc?" Lorenzo asked pointedly. "That's what I want. Happiness."

There was a long, awkward silence while Doc sipped his coffee. He did not look at Lorenzo or me.

"Things have never been better for me," Doc said slowly.

"That wasn't an answer."

"Let me finish my story," he said to Lorenzo. "Then see if you need an answer."

He gripped his cup again.

"My nurse quit and reported me to the hospital. The administration took away my privileges, and then word got around. Everybody knew. I closed my office and started drinking continuously. I was in and out of psychiatric hospitals for eighteen months. That was a complete waste of time.

"My wife went to work. She had to. Back in those days, disability insurance didn't cover alcoholism. She said she'd leave me if I didn't stop drinking. I took Antabuse every morning in front of her, and I stopped drinking. But Antabuse wasn't the only drug I took. I got into amphetamines and Demerol. I could hide those better than I could alcohol. I was a mess.

"I got up every morning with my wife and ate breakfast. She'd go off to work, and I'd get dressed in my best suit and drive to the hospital. Sometimes I'd even speed so that the police would stop me and I'd tell them I was a physician and had an emergency at the hospital. Then they'd escort me. That would make me feel so important.

"I was delusional and all my colleagues knew it. But they covered for me. The fools."

Doc sipped his coffee and then looked at Lorenzo and me. He tried to smile but couldn't.

"I don't know if it's harder to tell this story or to hear it," he said.

"They're doing O.K., Doc," Bossy said. "Go on."

"I'd sit in the doctors' lounge in the morning and drink coffee and start up conversations with anybody who'd talk to me. I even knew each doctor's favorite topic." He smiled. "I could always start a conversation with any of them when I would bring up the topic of governmental interference with medicine.

"I'd get home around noon and take some drugs. I had an office set up in my basement, and I'd spend the afternoon pretending I was talking to patients. I'd actually have conversations with patients who weren't there.

"When my wife got home from work, I'd tell her about the patients I saw that day. It's incredible the amount of love that woman had for me then. She stayed . . . for a while."

Doc got involved in A.A. when his wife called A.A. and asked for help. She didn't know what else to do. She had asked the medical society for help and they referred her to a psychiatrist who, in turn, only prescribed more medication for Doc. I was beginning to relate to Doc's story.

"At first I didn't like A.A.," he said. "I only had a drug problem. I didn't think they would understand or be able to help me. Boy, was I wrong."

I didn't have to look at Bossy. I could feel his glacial stare.

There was a hand on my shoulder and I turned to see Lucy standing behind me.

"Patrick, your wife is on the phone."

"Thanks, Lucy." And thank you, God.

Bossy gripped my upper arm.

"He'll call her back," Bossy said and glowered at Lucy.

"Hey, I want to talk to my wife."

I started to get up, but Bossy tightened his grip. I couldn't move.

"We're trying to save your life, fella. Sit down." He looked back at Lucy. "He'll call her back."

I hated myself for being so thoroughly overwhelmed by Bossy.

"The worst is over, Patrick," Doc said. "Just a couple more minutes."

Doc was looking at Lorenzo and me now and he relaxed his grip on the hot cup.

"Two men from A.A. visited me at my home. They saw I was sick and needed professional help. One of them—he called himself Brownie—had been a patient in Hogarth. He advised me to come here. I laughed at the idea.

"Then my wife left me. She thought I was hopeless. I attempted suicide when she left. I overdosed and woke up two days later in Intensive Care. I was in the hospital two weeks, and people from A.A. visited me every day. I didn't even know them. They'd stay and talk for hours. They were beautiful people."

When Doc got out of the hospital, he came right to Hogarth.

"I stayed in Hogarth nine weeks, and I never went back to Buffalo. I'll stay in Toronto for the rest of my life. I need Hogarth and I need A.A. Sometimes at night I walk over here and just sit around this place. I get strength from it. And I go to A.A. meetings four times a week."

"Why?" I asked. "How can you waste . . . ah . . . how can you afford to go to meetings four times a week?"

He looked me in the eyes.

"Without A.A. I would die. You see, I've become very good at feeling sorry for myself. An expert. I think you're probably good at it, too. The people in A.A. won't let you feel sorry for yourself. They remind me of how much I lost and how far I've come. Because of A.A. and Hogarth, I'm as strong as I can possibly be."

Doc looked at Lorenzo.

"I lost my wife, and I can never practice obstetrics and gynecology again. Living with my past is like living with an inoperable cancer that I know won't kill me as long as I don't think about it. When I do think about it, the cancer starts to grow and is quite painful. And I've lived with it long enough to know I don't have to think about it.

"Son, I can't give you a yes or no answer to your question about my being happy. It's not that easy."

Bossy moved forward and folded both arms on the table. He looked at me, then Lorenzo.

"You probably don't appreciate this yet," Bossy said. "You're still early in treatment. But alcoholism and drug abuse are uniquely devastating illnesses. You can recover—from a strictly medical standpoint. But we are all left with wounds that may bleed forever.

"We've hurt ourselves and we've hurt the ones we love the most. You will see that your relationship with your wife will never be the same. There are resentments that have built up over the years. These resentments really never go away. They may remain unspoken, but they'll never go away."

I felt a little smug. I was sure of Irene. I had never detected any strong resentment from her. She loved me. I would always have her.

"We don't pray for happiness in A.A.," Bossy continued. "We pray for serenity so that we can accept things—our past included—that we can't change. And serenity is absolutely crucial to your existence if you want to remain away from alcohol and drugs."

"No one is saying you'll never be happy again," Doc said. "Happiness is such a personal thing. And it can be so elusive."

Bossy looked at me.

"Have we made any points with you? Do you understand what we're saying?"

I nodded.

"It's possible you can make it without A.A.," Doc said to me. "But it's unlikely."

"What were you doing that you couldn't come to the phone, Pat?"

"Two doctors, both former patients, were telling me I needed A.A."

"But you aren't an alcoholic. You never drank much . . . or did you? Did you drink, too, and never tell me?" Irene's tone was indignant. "Was that one more thing you lied to me about?"

"You don't need to talk to me like that, Irene. I feel bad enough about what I've done."

"You feel bad! What about me? I'm alone. . . ." There was silence, and I knew she was starting to cry. "I've been so depressed today," she said, her voice breaking. "And I've been blaming you for everything."

I didn't want Irene to be depressed. She had no right to be. I wanted her to be happy and to love me and give me encouragement.

"I think I've been experiencing enough depression for both of us, Babes. This is the worst experience of my life. Absolutely the worst."

"It will be over soon, Pat. In less than two weeks you'll be home again with me, and everything will be all right. I won't let this happen to you again."

Irene's voice was gaining strength, and she continued to be optimistic as we talked. This is the way I wanted her to be. Strong and optimistic.

I listened as she told me about school and the politics and manipulating inside the art department. It bored me, of course. I was totally preoccupied with myself and what was happening to me. But it sounded as if she needed to talk.

Her problems seemed so insignificant.

As she talked, my thoughts wandered back to Doc and Bossy and their insistence on the importance of A.A. for recovery. Maybe I should go to meetings. I had nothing to lose.

". . . and I won't even be considered for tenure for another year."

"I'm going to try A.A., Irene. I'm going to go to meetings. At least that will get some people off my back."

"You weren't even listening to me, Pat."

"I'm sorry. I can't really think about anything else but myself. I guess that isn't unusual for me, though."

"Tell me what's been happening. Have you got out at all?"

I told her all about Saturday, and how refreshing it was to find that the world was still going about its business without me.

"Somehow the world is managing without you, Pat. I'm not, but the rest of the world is carrying on." Irene laughed softly. "By the way, I'd like to meet this nurse who walks around squeezing testicles."

"You'll know her by her handshake. Good, strong hands."

"Think she'll let me help her? I need to start squeezing something."

"You can squeeze me, Irene."

"You said we wouldn't have any time alone together."

"That's right." I needed to end this discussion.

"I'm going out tomorrow and buy some devices . . . personal devices. Gabe said there was an adult bookstore down on Prospect that has some nice vibrators."

"Irene!"

"These are tough times, Pat. I've got to do something."

"I don't believe you. This doesn't sound like you at all. I want you to stay the hell away from Gabe. She . . ."

I could hear Irene attempting to muffle a laugh.

"C'mon, Pat, you've got to know that I'm kidding. Could you see me walking into an adult bookstore on Prospect?"

The thought of it was amusing.

"No," I laughed. "That isn't you."

"It would be a different story if the adult bookstore was at Shaker Square."

I would not be baited a second time.

It was very difficult being without Irene on Sunday. It was our favorite day together. After early mass we would come home, and I would prepare breakfast. I loved to cook, although I had absolutely no talent in the kitchen.

Irene would always indulge me and eat whatever I made and tell me how good it was. And I always believed her. Until about midnight when flatulence would set in.

After breakfast we would spread out on the living room floor with the *Plain Dealer* and read ravenously while the Cleveland Orchestra's recordings of Beethoven and Mozart played on the stereo.

We would stay on the floor for hours and hardly ever speak. But occasionally I would reach out and touch her to make sure she was still there. It was a constant source of amazement to me that this beautiful, kind woman could be in love with me.

I absolutely adored her, and my Sundays with her were so precious to me.

"I'll be driving into Toronto very late on Tuesday night," she said. I'll see you at Hogarth for lunch on Wednesday."

I told Irene which motel to go to. "You'll be sharing a room with Hog Body's wife."

"I'd rather be sharing it with you."

"We'll be sharing the rest of our lives, Irene. I look forward to that."

"Good night, Pat. I love you."

It was eight o'clock, and visitors were leaving the fourth floor lounge as I arrived. Coming toward the door as I entered were Melanie and a man about my age.

They were holding hands!

"Patrick, I'd like you to meet a friend. Scooter, this is Patrick."

Scooter was about five feet seven and balding. And he wore a wedding ring. When we shook hands, he did not smile, and he looked at me suspiciously.

"Patrick and I have become pretty close in the last two weeks. We're good friends."

Scooter firmly pulled Melanie by the hand, and they walked off together. A few feet away from me, she put her arm around his waist.

"Hey, Patrick." Lorenzo was slouching in the overstuffed chair several feet from the television. "C'mon in."

"No visitors today?" I asked as I approached him.

He shook his head slowly as he continued to watch television.

"Where's your wife?" I asked.

"Detroit," he said tersely. "With her parents." Clearly, he didn't want to talk about his wife.

"Who was the guy with Melanie?" I tried to sound unconcerned.

"Some little dude who looked very uncomfortable. She introduced us . . . can't remember his name." Lorenzo continued to stare, as if mesmerized, at the television screen. A news program was ending. "I love to watch white folks screw up," he said. "You should have seen this program."

"His name is Scooter," I said. "What an awful name for an adult."

"They looked pretty tight."

"Melanie can do better than that."

"Slack off, man. You sound jealous."

"Jealous? Me? Bullshit. I'm not jealous. Why should I be jealous? I'm just saying that she can do better."

"You're protesting too much," he said in a barely audible, bored voice and reached for the TV listings. "Wonder if there's anything worthwhile on tonight."

"I don't care who she goes with. It's none of my business."

"That's right. You don't have papers on her," he said and appeared to be memorizing the TV page.

"All I'm saying is that the guy is too short and he doesn't have much hair and . . ."

"And he's not a pediatrician from Cleveland." Lorenzo reached for the TV switch and started turning.

"Did you see him smile at all? He looked pretty sour."

Lorenzo finally looked at me.

"Let it go, Patrick. You're just complicating things for yourself."

"Hey, goddammit, I didn't ask for any advice from you." I was surprised at my anger. "And what's been the matter with you lately?

You've been as much fun as a fecal impaction. Where's the shallow good humor that we were accustomed to?"

"You want me to start rolling my eyes and shuffling my feet, too?"

I had hurt him and for a moment I was glad. But quickly I felt a passionate remorse.

"I'm very sorry for what I said, Lorenzo. That was awful. I'm just not able to control my anger. I hope you'll forgive me."

"Forget it. But thanks for the apology."

Lorenzo explained that he had experienced laryngospasms three times in the past week.

"Always thinking I'm about to die has done something to my sense of humor. And I don't know when I'll see my wife again . . . or *if* I will. And tomorrow they make the decisions about the people in my group. It's unlikely that they'll let me go. But maybe . . ." His voice trailed off.

It would be criminal malpractice to recommend that Lorenzo return to society. He must realize that.

I got up and walked to Lorenzo and put my hand on his shoulder.

"Sounds like you're going to have a tough night. If I can help you in any way, you know where my room is."

Lorenzo's lips formed a faint smile. It did little to mask his unhappiness.

"Thanks, Patrick."

I should not have left Lorenzo, but it was depressing to be with him now. I cared for him very much, but he was an open, bleeding wound, and I felt I needed to protect myself from becoming any more depressed. Sunday evenings had historically been bad for me. And I was anticipating one week ahead when I would be worrying about the next day's decision on my being recycled. But that decision would be academic. No way was I going to stay longer than two more weeks.

I had survived two weeks at Hogarth, and I would survive two more weeks. I had been scarred and bloodied, but I would persevere and win, however winning is measured.

Surely, the worst was over.

I ALMOST didn't recognize Christine.

She had her hair pulled back and had no makeup on. She wore a Quiana blouse and a pair of tight-fitting cords. Except for being slightly full in the hips, she had a trim, lean figure.

She was also wearing glasses.

"O.K., so I'm thirty," she said as she sat. "I'm back to the 'essential me' look."

"I like it," I said. I wanted to add that she looked positively sexy.

"Thank you, Patrick."

"That comes from a man who is not exactly generous with his compliments," said Melanie. There was a message somewhere in that statement.

Christine turned to Lucy.

"Did you flounder when you turned thirty? Was it traumatic for you?"

"No. Not at all. I was sober most of the time then." Lucy paused and a self-effacing smile appeared. "Turning forty was tough, though. That's when I started to get depressed and forgetful. My doctor called it 'middle age melancholy.' I was a certifiable drunk and having blackouts, and the guy slapped on me his best euphemism."

"Were any of you men jolted when you turned thirty?" Christine turned to me. "Patrick?"

"Well . . . no." Actually I had no memories of turning thirty. There had been a lot of drugs in the past six years. "I reached an acute state of perfection at age thirty, and as you all can see, it's become a chronic condition."

"If you people let him get away with that, I'm leaving." Christine sat back and folded her arms across her chest.

"Why don't we just ignore Patrick today?" Lucy said to the group. "He's having an arrogance attack."

Steve was shaking his head. "Every doctor I've ever met had his head up his ass. What the hell do you people learn in medical school?"

"Let's see . . . in the first year we had courses in how to be evasive and obscure, golf, and bad handwriting. Oh, yes, there was also Arrogance 101. If you pass these, then you can go on to Anatomy and Biochemistry and other less important things."

"You know," said Melanie to the group, "there was a time when I never thought I'd see Patrick smile, much less tell a joke." She looked at me. "I'm happy for you. You've come a long way."

"That was a very nice thing to say, Melanie. I'm sure Patrick appreciated your saying that." Christine's voice now carried a professional tone. It was time to get on with the session.

Christine made eye contact with each of us.

"I'm happy with the openness and honesty you have all shown so far. It's been refreshing. But my feeling about this group is that we still have a lot to learn about each other. Probably the quickest way we can get to know more about each other is the 'hot seat' approach. In the next several sessions, each of us will take turns as the focus of group. We will try to tell each other how we have become what we are.

"Anyone can ask the person on the hot seat any question. And every question must be answered with unswerving honesty."

"What if the question is unfair?" Melanie asked.

"There are no unfair questions. Not if you trust each other and . . ."

Mac yawned loudly as a statement.

"That's not impressive, Mac." Christine was irate. "If you don't want to do this, leave." She was raising her voice. "And if you have something to say, say it. Don't make sounds to show disapproval. That's what monkeys do."

"Well, the little lady's got a temper."

"Anyone who doesn't want to do this should leave the room. Now."

Mac stood and started walking to the door.

"I gotta go take a piss. I'll be back."

Steve stood up slowly and pointed a finger at Mac.

"You can do one of two things, Mac. Either sit down and shut the fuck up, or just keep walking when you get out the door. You won't get back in if you leave."

"Steve's talking for all of us," Hog Body said.

"I guess I can hold it for a while." Mac went back to his chair.

"If you screw up one more time," Boone said, "I'll suggest that we keep you out of group from now on."

"The group is telling you that your behavior is unacceptable," Christine said and looked sternly at Mac. "And don't ever refer to me as the 'little lady' again. I don't care what you get away with at home. They don't pay me enough to be patronized."

Mac was embarrassed and angry. He had been bludgeoned, and he wanted to strike back. But he chose, wisely, to be silent.

Christine looked away from Mac and began to smile.

"Let's go on with what we have to do. Who would like to go first?"

Silence.

"All right, then I'll start," Christine said. "If you can think of any question that will help you get to know me better, ask. Or if you think I'm being evasive, tell me."

Christine was born and grew up in Alberta.

"No child ever had better parents. My sister and I were always included in any discussions that would affect us. And our parents always listened. They would read to us every night before bed when we were young. I was a happy child until I was about seven. That's when I was molested by an uncle who was an alcoholic."

"How can you say that in such a matter-of-fact way?" I asked. "It must have been terrible."

"I've told this story before. The shock of saying it to a group has worn off. But sometimes when I think back . . ."

"How did it affect you, Chrissie?" Hog Body was subdued and had a concerned, worried look.

"I was terribly scarred by it. You see, because I loved and trusted my father, I trusted all men. But my uncle told me never to tell my parents, because they would get mad at me. I believed him. He molested me several times, and the only way my parents found out was one time he had rectal intercourse with me and I bled.

"The experience with my uncle has had a profound effect on my relationship with men. Whenever I started to get close to a man and intimacy was near, I would pull back. I had, and still have, a difficult time trusting men. Although I'm vey close to someone right now. He's helped me quite a bit."

"Why don't you tell us about him?" Melanie asked. "What does he do?"

"Well," Christine looked at the floor as if she were embarrassed, "you people probably won't think much of me when I tell you. I was hoping you wouldn't ask. He's . . . ," she sighed, ". . . a doctor. But he's unique. He doesn't have a monumental ego."

Christine looked at me and had a small, devilish grin. I smiled at her and nodded. She had scored.

"For many years I had a difficult time being sexually responsive.

I was in therapy for a while. But now he's all the therapy I need. He's kind, gentle, tender, and affectionate. And I trust him."

Christine always did well in school and "gravitated into psychology because I'm fascinated by people and learning why we act the way we do. I never knew what I was going to do with my degree in psychology until about five years ago. I found out that my sister, Jenny, was a drug addict. Demerol. Morphine. And now heroin. She's in terrible shape."

"That's awful," Lucy said, as she lit up. "Can't you help her?"

"Well, I talk to her about once a week by phone. She lives in Hamilton. All I can do is tell her that I love her and that I'm here if she ever wants help. I won't let this destroy me. It almost did several years ago.

"I can't be responsible for her life and her mistakes. I'll do anything I can for her, and she knows that. But I think I've lost her. Every time the phone rings, I expect it to be someone telling me Jenny is dead.

"So you can see I have both a professional and personal interest in addiction."

"Does your personal interest ever get in the way?"

"Yes, Patrick, sometimes. I relate too much with the people in your lives who care for you. I still approach some patients with an urgency and a desperation that are unprofessional. I can get emotionally involved with patients if I'm not careful. And that's when I'm ineffective."

"You've never been married? You're a very attractive woman."

"Thanks, Boone. No. I've never been married. About three years ago I became very close to a man, and he wanted me to live with him. But I couldn't do that. I guess I'm more insecure than you, Melanie. You said you didn't need commitments. I couldn't share that much with someone *without* a commitment."

"Were you frigid with him?" Steve asked.

Christine's face molded into an uncertain expression.

"I think that's an inappropriate question," she said. "I . . ." she paused and appeared self-conscious. "I had some problems responding to him. He was somewhat of a . . . sexual acrobat . . . and was more often concerned with technique than feelings. But we could have worked things out. We loved each other."

"If you loved each other, why did you need something on paper?" Melanie was slightly agitated and near anger. "I don't understand that."

"I loved him, but he was emotionally immature. I think there was a good chance he would have walked out when we started having problems. If we had had a formal commitment, he probably would have been more responsible, more likely to try to work things out."

Melanie moved forward in her chair.

"Would you live with the doctor without being married to him?"

Christine pressed her lips together in an embarrassed, feeble smile, and shook her head.

"I need that piece of paper, Melanie. I suppose you think that's absurd."

"No. I think it's your business."

"Well," said Lucy, "I think it's refreshing."

"Any more questions?"

"What happened to your uncle?" Hog Body still had a worried look.

"Jail. But that was twenty-three years ago, don't forget. That was virtually the Dark Ages in terms of our understanding of alcoholism and its attendant poor impulse control. We also know more about deviant behavior as a consequence of alcoholism."

"How do you feel about him now? Do you hate him?"

"I try not to, Hog Body. I know that he couldn't help himself. But I still dream about his touching me and forcing himself in me. I remember the look on his face . . . how he smelled . . . the sounds he made. . . . God, it was so awful."

Christine shook her head briskly as if trying to purge her memory. She sat silently and looked out the window. For the first time she looked vulnerable and small.

"You will find," she said in a soft voice, "that exposing yourself to people who care is exceptionally good therapy. I"—she paused and smiled warmly—"I feel so close to all of you now.

"I hope you're all left with the same good feeling when you've finished opening up to the group."

How could I discuss my sexual inadequacy with a woman and retain my composure and appear confident? It is important always to appear in control. And how could I discuss being impotent without abandoning all semblance of whatever dignity I had left? And with a woman who wasn't even a doctor!

This might be asking too much.

The relaxation exercises weren't helping at all. I was preoccupied with seeing Karren as a threat rather than a therapist. And I was near exhaustion from anticipating humiliation.

Our relaxation class was over, and my appointment with Karren was in fifteen minutes. I had time for a shower. A long, warm shower can occasionally be relaxing. I would have preferred, however, about thirty milligrams of Valium and a glass of wine.

The shower did seem to be helping a little. I kept the water as hot as I could stand it and soaped and shampooed all over. I wanted to choose my words carefully, but this would be a totally new experience. I needed Irene now. She was always so good at easing my apprehension.

There are some things for which one cannot prepare. Talking with a female physical therapist about being impotent must be one of those things.

When I got out of the shower, I walked out of the bathroom without drying off and sat on my bed. I cursed my flaccid penis and began to tell myself how unfair all of this was, when I saw the note and the flower.

Dear Patrick,

You have looked so frightened all day that I have wanted to hug you and tell you everything is going to work out. I know you are nervous about talking to Karren. I wish I could do this for you.

Take the flower with you when you see her and think of me and know that I care about you. Maybe it will help a little.

I am sitting here listening to you in the shower. I would love to come in and look at you, but I am afraid you would get mad.

I know I could help you if you would only trust me and let me try.

Love,
Mel

Some day, given the opportunity and lacking impotency . . .

"Someone's been picking our tulips."
"Melanie thought it might help fortify me through this."
"Is it helping?"
I shook my head.
Karren's office was similar to mine back in Cleveland. It was small and cluttered with books and magazines. Precision and the appearance of neatness were not important to her either. But there was a method somewhere in this confusion.

She was sitting at her desk, which faced a wall, and the chair I sat in was to the side and slightly behind her desk. There were no barriers between us. She had on a tank top which she had worn in our exercise class, but she had put on a wraparound skirt over her running shorts.

She sat with her feet up on a lower drawer that was slightly pulled out, and her knees were bent.

I pointedly continued to notice things in her office so that she would think I could be distracted. It was impossible not to stare at the bed to my immediate left and against the wall opposite her desk.

There were no windows.

"I'm going to develop rickets if I stay in this office much longer," she said. "They keep promising me an office with windows. I call this my 'mole hole.' " She looked at the bed. "Some people call this room other things."

Hanging on the wall behind Karren and directly in my view was a large print that had to be focused on because it was busy with seemingly unrelated detail. In a sea of black and orange and gray, arranged in a mosaic pattern, floated the head and long, thin nude torso of a woman. Her nipples were erect, and the right arm ran obliquely toward mid-pelvis, where the figure became serpentine. Her face was nearly lost in a mane of rolling gold hair. Her eyes were closed, and her lips were parted slightly in a spirited, rapturous smile.

"You look very solemn, Patrick. This isn't confession, you know."

I tried to smile and immediately felt foolish.

"Have you ever had a discussion with a woman about sex?"

I shook my head.

"How about your wife?"

I shook my head again.

"Patrick, if I'm going to help you, I need you to talk to me. This has to be a conversation."

I nodded.

"How long have you been impotent?"

"Six months."

"Have you had an erection in the past six months?"

"Yeah."

"Feel free to volunteer as much as you like," she said and began to smile. "Or else we'll be here for a long time. When was your last erection?"

"I woke up with one this morning. I also had one yesterday morning."

"What did you do with it?"

"With what?"

"Your erection. Did you masturbate?"

"Hell, no. I'm not going to beat off when I know Toni might come in anytime. No one in this goddamn hospital knocks before they come in your room."

"Yes, I understand that. That's a problem here. One should only masturbate in secure solitude."

"That sounds poetic."

"Have you brought yourself to climax in the past six months?"

"Yeah. Twice."

"Did you have full erections each time?"

"No."

"How many times have you masturbated without ejaculating in the last few months?"

"Many times."

"It sounds as though masturbating has become an anxiety-provoking experience for you."

I nodded.

"Tell me why. Tell me what happens and what you think about when you're preparing to masturbate." She smiled. "I'll get you to talk yet."

"First of all," I said, "I don't like the idea of masturbating, because I'm married. It shouldn't be necessary. Do you know what I mean?"

"Many married people masturbate."

We stared at each other for a few seconds, and I felt my face warm.

"I was married for six years, Patrick. I stimulated myself and brought myself to orgasm often while I was married. And I had intercourse regularly." She smiled, finally. "The first step is to give yourself permission to do it."

"I always felt guilty when I masturbated," I said. "I was brought up a Catholic and was taught that it was a mortal sin. And after I got married, I still felt guilty, because I thought it was insulting to Irene—that I would prefer masturbating to making love to her."

"I'm sure I don't have to remind you of the pleasure principle, Patrick. Much of human behavior, including sexual behavior, is motivated by what pleases us. If masturbating is a pleasurable experience —as it should be—then there is no reason to give it up just because you have a regular sex partner. I knew my husband masturbated and I wasn't insulted.

"By the way, I've talked to Dr. Randolph, and he told me that there is no organic cause for your impotence."

"Randolph knows? Shit! Why don't we get a goddamn loudspeaker and . . ."

"What happened six months ago?" She interrupted. "Tell me everything."

Karren placed her feet on the floor and bent toward me. Her closeness made me feel uncomfortable.

"Well, I had taken my usual handful of pills and kissed Irene good night and turned off the light. A few minutes later she came over to me and we started to make love. I had an erection and lost it. Then I fell asleep.

"I had lost an erection twice before since we were married, but I had never fallen asleep on her. She didn't know how many drugs I took.

"I tried to make love to her for the next three nights, and I couldn't. Each time she became more frustrated, and I got more embarrassed. So I stopped trying. I was afraid of failing."

"There are other ways to make love besides intercourse."

"I know that."

"Well?"

"If I couldn't perform, I didn't want to do anything. I would have been terribly embarrassed for Irene to see me without an erection trying to make love. I just couldn't do it."

"Have you been involved with another woman in the past year?"

"No. Why do you ask?"

"Often married men will become impotent after a liaison. That's a way guilt takes its toll. And unfortunately, when a man is sexually incompetent, it's hard to hide it."

"Performance failure is fairly obvious for men," I said.

"Impotence is more a failure of response than performance," she corrected. "Now I need to ask you two other questions. First, do you find Irene physically attractive?"

"Yes."

"How is she as a lover?"

"Super. Sometimes my mouth would water just anticipating making love to her. I sure miss concupiscence."

"Did you ever try to talk to Irene about the problem?"

"No. I knew what the problem was. I took too many drugs. I didn't want her to know. Besides, we don't talk about sex. We just do it."

"Patrick, think about that for a minute. Sex is one of the most important parts of a marriage, and you and your wife don't even talk about it. We need to examine that. Will Irene be here?"

"She's coming tomorrow night."

"Good. Then all three of us can talk."

"Absolutely not. You can talk to me alone."

Karren shook her head and moved back in her chair.

"I never do sex counseling with only one partner in a marriage. It's useless. A sexual dysfunction is a mutual problem and should be dealt with as such. With both partners."

"I don't think I could do that, Karren. This is hard enough, just talking to you. I don't think Irene would want to do it either. Neither of us is very open on sexual matters."

"That's quite apparent, Patrick. But if you want to solve this problem, you need to start talking about it."

Karren placed both hands behind her head and leaned back and stretched. She had unusually muscular biceps.

"Well," I asked, "what do I do now? I want to get this resolved."

"Don't be so impatient, Patrick. That will work against you." She folded her arms across her chest and stared at me. "Let's identify the problem. You're experiencing functional impotence, and you've gotten into a pattern of sexual avoidance, because of the fear of failing to respond adequately. Masturbating has not been a satisfying experience for you because of the guilt feelings you've discussed.

"I suspect that, even when you're stimulating yourself, you have some anxiety about reaching climax."

I nodded.

"This is routine stuff, Patrick."

"Routine for who?"

"Being on drugs, don't forget, was the initial cause of your sexual disability. As long as you stay off drugs, and if you and Irene really care about each other and are willing to work on this, you'll have an excellent outcome."

"How much time are we talking about?"

Karren sighed.

"We'll begin the process here, and then you'll need to follow up with a therapist in Cleveland."

"Well, let me think about this, Karren. I'm not sure what to do. I'll let you know. Do you realize that we've talked about sex all this time and you've never mentioned the word *love* once?"

"Yes. I know."

Karren handed me a key that was attached by a chain to a slice of pineapple. It was plastic, but looked remarkably real.

"That's a key to this office. I leave at six. You can be alone in here and lock the door. There are some erotic pictures in a box under the bed. There's also a bottle of coconut oil under the bed. I want you to use the oil while you're stimulating yourself."

"Thanks." I was shocked. "You know, I've consciously tried to have an erection several times late at night since I've been here. But nothing has worked."

"How have you tried?"

"After the evening nurse gives me the Antabuse and Dilantin, it's about three hours before the night nurse comes in. So I lie naked on the bed sometimes and listen to your relaxation tape."

"You're misusing the tape, Patrick. The relaxation tape is supposed to bring you to a low arousal state so . . ."

"I've been in a low arousal state for fourteen goddamn years."

"But you haven't learned how to relax or go to sleep without drugs. Those are the things you have got to learn. How are you sleeping now?"

"I'm averaging about three or four hours every night. Insomnia is rough."

Karren smiled pleasantly, but without warmth. She had a certain remoteness, which I found interesting if not appealing.

"You've done well, Patrick. I know this isn't easy for you. But we've only scratched the surface. I hope you'll bring Irene to see me so that the three of us can talk. I know we can work things out. Trust me."

It was July and I had finished my internship. Fifty weeks of working one hundred hours per week and taking home three hundred and fifty dollars a month.

The world, by God, owed me something.

Getting married just before the start of internship was a mistake. It was impossible for me to be kind and generous and loving and affectionate when I was chronically tired, overworked, and underpaid. Irene never complained. But I knew she was disappointed.

I wished I had someone to talk to, someone who understood me, someone who wouldn't look so hurt.

Keri Smith was a nurse's aide in the internal medicine clinic. As a purely physical specimen, she was near perfect. Well, maybe a little too tall. With her Afro, she was about six feet. And maybe her breasts were a little too big. Hardly a liability, however. She had deep black skin, large innocent brown eyes, and a totally engaging smile. And I loved the way she walked. Actually, she seemed to glide.

I loved to be near Keri, but I was uncomfortable being close to her. I fumbled with words. I would become formal and forget what I had planned to say to her. And then I would be angry with myself for blowing another opportunity.

I sent her a Beatles' album anonymously, and I circled the song *Something.*

One day, driving home from the hospital, I saw her standing at a bus stop. I pulled to the curb and waved for her to come over. As she came toward my car, I pulled off my wedding ring.

While I was driving her home, she told me she had been a professional singer. She had done backup singing on albums with Isaac Hayes, Barbara Streisand, James Brown, and Elvis Presley.

"That was nice for a while," she said, "but it couldn't go on forever. I needed to get out of that business. I learned some hard lessons. I really let myself be used. But no more. I'm very careful now.

"Want to come in for some coffee?" She asked me as we sat in her parking lot.

"No. I better not. I was on call last night. I'm pretty tired."

She nodded and was about to get out of the car, but turned and looked at me.

"You sent me the album, didn't you?"

"Yes."

"You married, Dr. Reilly?"

"Yes, Keri, I am."

"Do you love your wife?"

I nodded.

"Would you leave her?"

"No, I wouldn't."

She said good-bye and got out of the car. I put my wedding ring back on and drove home to Irene.

I avoided seeing Keri at work. But I thought a lot about her in the next two weeks. Several times while making love to Irene, I fantasized about Keri.

One night while I was on call at the hospital, I was paged. It was Keri.

"I want to invite you to a party, Dr. Reilly. This Friday at my apartment. Can you come?"

"Sure. I'd like to. Thanks for inviting me."

"I want you to be my date, Patrick."

I didn't know what to say.

"I'll expect you at seven. Bye."

I came home from work on Friday and told Irene I had to work that night.

"One of the other residents got sick. I'll have to cover neonatology tonight."

I showered and dressed. As I was about to leave, Irene hugged me.

"I really wanted to spend tonight with you," she said. "I love you, Pat, and I need you."

I was the only white person at Keri's party. Some of the men were not happy with her spending so much time with me. But no one said anything.

I got drunk on Boone's Farm Strawberry Wine and smoked some grass and took a Valium.

Before I passed out, I remember Keri telling me that she didn't want anything "too heavy . . . no serious involvements."

I woke up some time during the middle of the night. I was in her bed, my clothes still on. Keri was lying there, her back to me, her bare right shoulder above the covers.

I lay there silently for a few minutes and then I touched her on the shoulder. She began to move and then turned toward me.

"Keri," I whispered, "I don't think I can do this."

I smiled at her . . . and hoped to be persuaded.

She sighed deeply.

"Then go home, Patrick . . . and let me sleep." She turned her back to me. "I forgot you were here."

I sat on the side of the bed.

"You forgot I was here? Good Lord . . ."

I got out of her bed and walked toward the bedroom door.

"You wouldn't have been so hot anyway," she said disgustedly.

"Well, Keri, you will never know."

I felt hurt and angry and foolish for weeks after my episode with Keri.

It was about a month later when I met Keri in the hallway of the hospital. We stood face to face.

"Thanks for the lesson," I said.

She kissed the index and middle fingers of her right hand, flashed me the peace sign, and walked . . . glided away.

My only dalliance with adultery had not been one of my life's glorious moments. But now, now there was Melanie . . .

Lorenzo sat motionless in the lounge. His face was expressionless, a mask of despair.

I pulled up a chair and sat directly in front of him. He gave no indication of being aware of me. I put my hand on his knee.

"What's wrong?"

After a few seconds, he looked at me. But his eyes were vacant and didn't register any sense of awareness.

"C'mon, man, talk to me," I said.

"They want to transfer me to a hospital in Georgia." His tone reflected his manner. Morbid and flat. "There's a hospital there for doctors only. . . . they can keep patients up to twelve months. . . . Randolph says I need extended treatment."

"Will you go?"

He shrugged and looked away from me. He wanted me to go away. I searched for something to say, but everything seemed so trite.

"I probably won't commit suicide," he said in a barely audible voice. "But I sure am thinking about it."

"Have you talked to your wife about this?"

He shook his head.

"I'll call her tomorrow. She probably won't care."

Once again being around Lorenzo was depressing me, and I wanted to get away. But I was worried about him. He looked so unhappy. And while watching him, I felt what little equanimity I did have begin to drain away. But I wouldn't run this time. I would stay. I wanted him to know that I cared even if I couldn't help.

He eyed me suspiciously for a moment, and then looked away. After a few seconds, he turned back to me.

"What will you do," he challenged, "when they recommend that you go to the hospital in Georgia?"

21

"YOU'RE LOOKING almost cheerful this morning, Patrick. Has something good happened?"

Toni handed me a vitamin pill and began her routine of searching my face with her eyes as if the answer to her question would be found somewhere in my expression.

"Well . . . let's just say that . . . ah . . . I've had a release."

She smiled, but continued to look at me intently and with obvious uncertainty.

"Should I congratulate you?"

"I wish somebody would."

"You have an appointment with Dr. O'Malley at eleven, Patrick. Don't be late." Toni turned and walked toward the door. She had on a pair of designer jeans and looked fantastic. She turned her head quickly back to me and saw me looking lasciviously at her ass.

"Caught ya!" she laughed.

"Do you mind being leered at by us sex-starved male patients?"

She stared pensively out the window for a moment. Then a little grin appeared.

"Well, I could wear a potato sack, you know."

"I'd still stare at you."

She smiled, but I was being too forward and we both knew it.

"Sorry, Toni."

"Isn't your wife coming tonight?"

"Yeah."

"Thank God."

"She's going to be sharing a room at the Holiday Inn with Mrs. Hog Body. We won't have much privacy."

"When there's a will, there's a way," she said as she left the room.

The thought of seeing Irene again excited me to the point of distraction. I could think of nothing else.

Except for the two orgasms I had had in Karren's office.

"Who would like to be on the hot seat first?"

"What the hell," Boone said and took a deep breath. "I'll start. I'm not afraid of this."

Boone's voice trembled as he talked of his early life in Toronto.

"After I got my degree in chemical engineering, my wife and I settled in Halifax." Boone looked at me. "If you spent one hour in Halifax, you'd never go back to Cleveland."

"It rains too much there," Mac said. "It's not so great."

"You fucking moron," Boone said to Mac. "You're too simple and dumb to know anything about beauty."

Mac stood up.

"I'm not taking that."

Boone held up his hand.

"I'm sorry. I was out of line." Boone wasn't backing down. He *was* sorry.

"What you said to Mac was terribly inappropriate, Boone," Lucy said. "That offended all of us."

"I'm sorry. He looked at Christine. "I don't know why I get so angry every time I stop drinking."

Boone continued with his story.

"In twenty-five years I've worked for only one company. But in the last twelve years, they've moved me six different times. I've spent ten of the last twelve years in the States. When my drinking got out of control, they would transfer me to another city. They knew I was the best engineer they had when I was sober. A lot of people in the company knew I was a drunk. But no one ever confronted me. They just kept moving me, so I would be someone else's problem."

When Boone started talking about his family life, his mood became morose.

"My wife and I had a great marriage. When we started out, we were so poor and so happy. After being married for eight years, we had our first child, Vicki."

Boone explained that his wife began to change after she delivered Vicki.

"She'd cry easily, and her moods were so unpredictable. She became suspicious of me. She accused me of being unfaithful. I never touched another woman."

"What the hell was the matter with her?" Steve was indignant. "You were good to her, and all she did was fuck you over. You should have thrown her ass out."

"I love her, Steve."

"Love"—Steve sat back in his chair—"all you do is get hurt."

"Her obstetrician said it was postpartum depression and referred her to a shrink. She's been bouncing around to psychiatrists and hospitals for seventeen years. She's attempted suicide four times. All with drugs . . . prescription drugs." Boone looked at me, a plaintive expression on his face. "My wife could have been helped. I know that. But all the doctors have done is give her more and more drugs." Boone started to cry. "I don't want to live like this anymore. I just want to die. When I drink, I don't feel like this. I don't get angry. I don't hate anybody . . . not doctors, not my wife. . . ." He began sobbing.

Boone stopped trying to talk and wept openly. There was no sense of uneasiness or embarrassment in the room as we watched him. There was trust among us. Showing each other our wounds and our brittleness was no longer something we avoided.

"Tell us about your daughter," Melanie said to Boone.

Boone began to smile as he talked about his daughter, Vicki, as "a beautiful kid. Fortunately she looks like her mother." But his mood became somber as he told how he had hurt her.

"About six years ago Vicki stopped bringing her friends to the house. She was afraid I'd be drunk and embarrass her. She had no respect for me. And that's why I came here as a patient two years ago. I wanted my daughter to love me again."

Boone spoke with mixed feelings about his previous hospitalization at Hogarth.

"I learned a lot about myself. It was a good experience. But it didn't work because I came here for the wrong reason. I wanted to end my drinking problem so that my *daughter* would respect me. I never thought about ending my drinking so that I would respect myself. And that's why it didn't last."

"That's a very significant awareness," Christine said. "When did you realize that you have to put yourself first?"

"Well, they used to tell me that when I was here two years ago. And they told me that when I was in A.A. But I angrily reject things I don't want to hear. But when Vicki went away to school last fall, and she wasn't around to give me approval, I started drinking again. I guess I just have to make my own mistakes."

When Vicki left to go to school, Boone's focus changed back to his wife.

"I feel so helpless. There's nothing I can do to help her. She's always depressed and cries a lot. And she's frigid. We make love once a year. On my birthday. I've spent thousands of dollars in the last fifteen years buying sex. I just wish I could buy some woman's emotions that easy."

Boone started crying again but continued to talk.

"It's the sense of helplessness that kills me. I started drinking again about eight months ago."

"Are you saying you use alcohol as an anesthetic—to numb the pain?" Christine asked.

"No. When I drink I begin to feel strong, in control. Nothing is too hard."

"Alcohol is a poor substitute for personal strength, Boone," Lucy said and smiled at him. "I know. Believe me, I know."

"I can relate to your sense of helplessness," I said to Boone. "I'm sometimes overwhelmed by those same feelings. That's when I start taking more drugs."

Boone looked at me and clutched his hands in front of him as if pleading to be understood.

"The more helpless I feel, the angrier I get. Six months ago I tried to stop drinking and my world fell apart. I beat up my wife's doctor, lost my job, and went to jail."

"Boone," I said, "what you're describing is this: When you start feeling overwhelmed by things in your life, you start to drink, and you describe gaining strength when you drink. Then when you try to stop, you get angry and out of control. It seems to me that somehow you need to change things in your life so you won't feel so overwhelmed."

"Why don't you leave your wife?" Hog Body asked. "I don't understand why you stay with her. For sex you go to prostitutes. For strength you go to the bottle. It sounds to me as if your marriage is poison for you."

"I can't leave her, Hog. I married her for better or worse. I took my vows seriously. And she became sick through no fault of her own. I won't leave her. I have a responsibility to her."

Christine bent at the waist and put her elbows on her knees. Her instructive position.

"You are primarily responsible for yourself, Boone. You have to put yourself first. If you're drinking, you're of no use to anyone. Not your wife. Not your daughter. And not yourself. I'm impressed with your sense of duty. But if that relationship is destructive—and it appears to be—then I think you need to reexamine things and make a decision. And you must put your health first."

"How have you helped yourself or your wife by staying with her?" Melanie asked. "She's still depressed and trying to kill herself. You've become an alcoholic and you've lost your job and maybe even your daughter's respect. C'mon, Boone, you're smarter than that."

Boone looked slowly at each of us.

"Thanks," he said. "You guys have given me something to think about."

Christine sat up in her chair and gave each of us a complimentary smile.

"Sometimes the solution to *other people's* problems is painfully evident. Thanks for sharing your story with us, Boone. How do you feel?"

He smiled.

"I'm waiting for someone to give me absolution."

"Boone," Melanie said, "I really feel close to you now. And I like you."

"Well," Christine said and looked at Lucy, "your time has come. The hot seat is yours. Unless someone else would prefer to go next."

Silence.

Lucy lit a cigarette as she prepared to tell her story. She already had one smoldering in the ashtray.

"I was an only child," Lucy started, "and a profound disappointment to my parents. My father wanted sons and my mother wanted a daughter to lavish things on and who would be refined and beautiful."

Melanie picked up Lucy's first-lit cigarette as if it were hers.

"What they got was a daughter who was shy and who preferred to be alone and read. I'd rather stay home on a Saturday night and read Keats than go to a party.

"I did like to dance, but parties always required inane conversations. I had a terrible time in college. I was so bored and impatient with people. Everyone was into success.

"I wanted to be Emily Dickinson. I wanted to live alone, dress in white, and write poetry. And I was going to be a virgin. However," she smiled, "I got pregnant. The first time . . . the very first time. Nineteen fifty-two. So," she sighed, "Walter and I got married. He was in the navy."

Lucy put her cigarette out and lit another one.

"He's still in the goddamn navy. I've raised three kids, gone to a thousand boring parties, and haven't written a poem."

"You can start writing poetry now," Christine interrupted. "Your best and most productive years are probably ahead of you."

"It would be nice to think that," Lucy said and shook her head. "Thanks anyway."

"Then why are you here?" Boone asked angrily. "Why are you wasting our time?"

"Because I want my husband back. And I want my kids to start talking to me again. Everybody's turned their backs on me . . . because I'm a drunk. A goddamn, worthless drunk."

Lucy sat back in her chair.

"I can't even cry anymore," she said with disgust. "Do any of you know what it's like not to be loved by anyone? To be abandoned by your family?"

"C'mon, Lucy," Steve challenged. "You hear what my wife did. Do you really think you hurt worse than me?"

"Comparing scars," Christine murmured, "is usually unrewarding."

"There's a certain delicious pleasure in self-pity," Lucy said with a smile. "Don't take that away from me."

Lucy was quiet for a few moments, she smiled, and then a look of disappointment appeared.

"I love Walter, but he'll lick an ass in a minute if it will advance his career. And the parties . . . all those damn parties. The drinking got me through them.

"But then the alcohol started working against me. I couldn't remember people's names. I'd get lost in the middle of a conversation. I'd forget what people told me. So we stopped having parties, and Walter started leaving me home when he went out socially. He'd cover up for me, make excuses. The poor bastard didn't know that only reinforced my drinking. I've spent so much of the past few years in a fog."

Lucy stared at Christine.

"You know," she said, "this is the first time I've ever said these things to anybody."

"Join the club," I said.

"Several years ago," Lucy said smiling, "I was a happy drunk. Everything was going the way I wanted. At least I thought so. Everyone was moving in harmony. It was like a grand waltz. And I was the choreographer. It was beautiful.

"But a couple of years ago Walter stopped dancing. Or maybe he just started dancing faster and with less rhythm. He started doing the fast shuffle out the door every night, while I stayed home and did the soft shoe. He wouldn't stay home. I even tried to recruit him as a drinking partner."

"You said Walter was seeing another woman," Melanie said. "For how long?"

"At least six months. That really hurts. And what makes it hurt worse is that he flaunts it. He wants me to know he disapproves of me and that he's involved in another relationship.

"Walter is something like you, Boone. He has a strange sense of duty. He won't divorce me. But he'll stay married to me and watch me destroy myself. I don't understand."

"I'm tired of hearing you put yourself down," Steve said to Lucy. "You're a beautiful woman. . . . you're nice . . . and . . . and I like you. I have some real strong feelings about you. You know what I mean."

Lucy reached for her cigarettes and then stopped and sat up in her chair. She looked at the table for a few moments and a smile developed on her face. She looked at Steve with a grateful, pleased expression.

"I haven't been wanted by a man in a long time, Steve. It feels good to know that someone who knows me desires me. I'm not going to reject your feelings. And I won't reject you."

Steve's eyes were riveted on Lucy, his expression leering, puerilely intense.

Christine had a disapproving look, but said nothing.

"What do you want, Lucy?" Melanie asked.

"I want my kids to respect me again. And to love me. And . . . I think I want to have a better relationship with Walter . . . if we're going to stay married."

"Do you love Walter?" Christine asked.

"No."

"Do you make love to him?" Steve asked, still intense.

"Sometimes. But he never initiates. I practically have to beg the bastard." She pointed to the Kleenex that was next to me. As I handed the box to her, she began sobbing. "I can cry. . . . I can cry. . . ." She put the Kleenex to her eyes. "I want . . ." The Kleenex dropped from her hand, and she clutched her breasts. "I want to be treated like a woman."

I found it difficult paying attention to O'Malley. I was fatigued from the Group Therapy session and preoccupied with thoughts of food. I had never been so hungry. And from somewhere deep inside the recesses of my bowels, various intestinal juices were loudly burbling and trilling along in search of food to digest.

O'Malley talked on, apparently oblivious to the fact that Armageddon was happening in my stomach.

"Had you ever been agrophobic before Saturday?"

"No."

"Tell me how you felt, Patrick. What were your feelings?"

"It was a paralyzing, overwhelming fear. I couldn't move. I could hardly breathe. The cars were going by so fast, and they were so loud. And when I looked up, I thought the buildings were going to fall on me. I was terrified. I think Hog Body saved my life."

"With just simple reassurance?"

"Yeah."

"And you spent the rest of the time downtown with no more attacks?"

"That's right."

O'Malley bent his left arm and rested his chin on his left fist. He looked away from me, deep in thought. After a few seconds, he nodded his head in agreement to some unspoken conclusion. He looked at me.

"You're the eighth patient I've had in the last three years who has experienced agoraphobia. All eight of you used Valium." He shook his head. "Those minor tranquilizers are deadly comforts."

I wanted to ask him if agoraphobia would recur. Would it be a permanent problem? But I was afraid what his answer might be.

"No, Patrick, I don't think you'll experience terror in open spaces anymore."

"How did you know I wanted to ask you that?"

"You always anticipate disaster."

"Didn't you say something once about not being a prophet? How can you say with any certainty that I won't be phobic again?"

He looked at me and pursed his lips. I had tried his patience.

"You had a minor attack that responded to simple reassurance. My clinical impression is that agoraphobia will not be a problem for you in the near future. As for other phobias, I can't say. No one ever chooses to be phobic, nor do we select our phobias."

We stared at each other for a few moments, and then I started to move in my chair to let him know I was ready to go. The dissonance from my abdomen was getting louder and was reverberating off the walls. I needed food.

"You look better today, Patrick. I told you you'd improve. Are you aware of feeling better?"

I tried unsuccessfully not to smile as I nodded my head.

"You never hesitate to tell me when you're miserable," he said. "I wish you'd tell me when you're feeling good. I like good news."

"I'll remember that," I said as I stood. "I need to get something to eat."

"Karren told me you spoke with her yesterday. How did it go?"

"It wasn't too bad."

"Any results?"

My face warmed as I nodded my head.

"You can go, Patrick. Make an appointment to see me in a couple of days."

"But when I'm feeling like this, I don't need to see you. Maybe I'll continue to improve."

He smiled weakly.

"Maybe." He moved forward in his chair. "Say it, Patrick."

I took a deep breath and looked in his eyes.

"I'm Patrick Reilly and I'm a drug addict."

"I'm assuming this is beef stew. Please don't tell me if it's something else."

Melanie sat across from me, smiling deviously. She turned to Lucy.

"Should we tell him?"

"Wait till he's finished," Lucy said. "You know he doesn't appreciate our delicacies."

"Why aren't you two eating? What's the matter?" I put my fork down. "What is this stuff?"

"He's getting nervous, Lucy. Look at him. He's beginning to perspire."

"Stop screwing around, Melanie. I want to know what this is."

"It's a delicacy, Patrick," Lucy said and patted my hand. "That's all you need to know. A lot of people like it."

"People who aren't concerned with aesthetics," Melanie added.

"This is beef stew," I said. "I know it is. You guys are putting me on."

"Go ahead and eat then," Lucy said. "We'll watch you."

"Well, damnit, you've ruined my lunch. I can't eat this now. I hope you're both happy about that."

Melanie moved her face close to me.

"Consider this partial payment for ruining my breakfast on Sunday." There was revenge in her voice. "It's been fun watching you squirm. Let's go, Lucy. Let's leave Patrick to himself."

They walked off and Lorenzo came strolling up to my table with his lunch tray and sat down.

"What is this stuff they're serving for lunch?" I asked him.

"Beef stew," he said. "What does it look like?"

I had been had. Melanie had avenged herself and was probably feeling smug and satisfied.

Lorenzo smiled.

"Who got you this time?"

"Melanie. With able assistance from Lucy. I hope they won't underestimate my need for retaliation."

The last time I had seen Lorenzo, he was sullen and resentful. But now he was smiling.

"You look about a thousand percent better than you did last night," I said. "What happened?"

"Last night I didn't know what to do. The indecision was killing me, and I got depressed and angry. You know depression has a way of distorting reality. And my anger was exaggerating what I had distorted. I saw suicide as the only answer." He smiled. "They don't make it easy to kill yourself in this place."

"How did you get through the night?"

"I called Toni and she came in. She sat with me the whole night. I realized that if my wife would support me through this, I'd go to the Georgia program. Toni called Janice in Detroit and talked to her for almost an hour. Then I talked to her." Lorenzo's lower lip began to tremble, and he put his hand to his face and covered his eyes. "She still loves me, Patrick. She wants me to get well." He paused and wiped the tears off his cheeks. "Janice is coming, and we'll fly to Atlanta early Sunday morning. I'll go right into the hospital in Georgia as soon as I get there."

"This is the best you've looked since I met you."

"It's because of Janice. I know she's on my side. I know she loves me. I'll beat this drug problem, Patrick. And I'll never hurt that woman again."

"We're even, O.K.?" Melanie held out her hand. "Let's shake."

"Bullshit. We're not even. I'm going to enjoy calculating my revenge. Maybe I'll wait until you're taking a nice warm bath. I'm deadly at six feet with a bucket of ice water. Or maybe I'll jump you and force-feed you something that will give you explosive diarrhea for a week."

"That really sounds violent, Patrick. Are you into bondage and discipline, too?"

"Or I could wait until you think you're secure in your bed in the middle of the night. Have you ever been ravaged by an insane pediatrician?"

"So he's finally admitting to insanity," Lucy said, as she walked up from behind me and moved next to Melanie.

"And you, Lucy! I'm going to have you pilloried for complicity."

Karren entered the Auditorium and took her place on the platform, where she would lead the exercises. We arranged ourselves and were about to begin when I noticed Melanie standing off to my right. She had taken off the baggy sweat suit and wore a tight yellow T-shirt and white shorts partially slit up the side.

I tried not to stare at her as we did the exercises. Fortunately, I, like most male physicians, am adept at appreciating and consuming beautiful women with only furtive glances. This is a skill learned while making hospital rounds and having lust strike.

Melanie must have had a recent and significant weight loss, because her upper arms and thighs were unexpectedly thin and gave her a fragile appearance. Her shorts were slightly too big and unfortunately obscured the contour of her buttocks. Except when she bent forward. When she did bend, there was sufficient indication that she had a firm, smooth, well-rounded ass.

Her waist was trim, and even when she bent forward, no redundant skin folds appeared. Melanie's breasts, with erect nipples, were crying out to be fondled. And they moved with a pliancy that was causing me to have an erection.

I would soon need an emergency visit to Karren's "mole hole."

By the time the exercise class was over, I was in serious pain. My penis was preparing to explode, and I felt that my testicles were the size of grapefruits. The extreme pain was making it difficult to walk, so I had to move gingerly. It had been many years since I had attempted the "blue ball shuffle."

"Patrick!" Karren's tone was commanding as she called out and approached me. I took a deep breath, but it did nothing to relieve the pain. Potency was returning with a vengeance.

"Will you and your wife be coming to see me? I would like to see both of you together."

I waited to answer until all of my group was out of the Auditorium.

"I'm not impotent anymore, Karren. I don't think we'll need to see you."

She looked at me in obvious disagreement.

"Successfully masturbating is only the first step. You haven't been in a demand situation, yet, where you have to perform with another person. You could be setting yourself up to fail again. I don't want that to happen."

"I want to try. I feel I'm ready to be alone with Irene."

Karren saw that I was resolute.

"Well, everything may work out just fine. I hope so." She turned to go.

"Karren. Ah . . . I wonder if . . . ah . . . if I could . . . I need to be alone. . . . you know . . . secure solitude. . . ."

She unpinned the key attached to the pineapple from her running shorts and handed it to me.

"You have fifteen minutes," she said to me as I painfully shuffled off.

"What are you doing in the lounge by yourself, Patrick? It's almost eleven o'clock. Bedtime, you know."

"Hi, Reggie. Can you sit down for a minute?"

Reggie sat next to me and she took my hand.

"I feel so good tonight, Reggie. Everything seems to be working out. I'm starting to sleep better. The depression seems to be easing up. Over two weeks without any drugs. And Irene's in town. I just talked to her for a few minutes. That lady's my rock."

"You've come a long way, Patrick." She smiled and squeezed my hand. "At times I didn't think you'd make it. But ever since you came back that night after you had run away, I've felt very positive about you. Sometimes we still have to drag you along, but at least you're not kicking and screaming anymore. You're tougher and more resilient than you think you are."

I thanked her with a smile, and she gave my hand a gentle squeeze.

"My beamish boy," she said.

Reggie started to get up, but paused. She had a worried, happy look.

"I've had some good news, Patrick. My ex-husband—God, I hate to use that term—called me last night. I haven't seen him or our son in almost two years. We talked for over an hour. And it was pleasant. There were no accusations, no screaming. He told me about our son, Jason. He's five now."

Reggie reached into a pocket of her jeans and pulled out a handful of used kleenex.

"Damnit," she said. "I've gone through a box of these today." Her eyes were wet, but tears had not formed yet. "All I am hoping for is to see my son again on a regular basis. I want Jason to know that his mother cares about him." Tears began to fall from both her eyes. "I want him to know that his mother is strong and is a responsible person."

"Will you see them again, Reggie?"

"I'm having dinner with Jim tomorow night. He doesn't want me to see Jason just yet. I guess he wants to see for himself that I'm clean. And responsible."

"Do you think there's any hope of a reconciliation?"

"I can't think in those terms, Patrick. I just can't."

Reggie wiped away some more tears, and then blew her nose.

"It took me a long time," she said, "but I think I've finally adjusted to being a single woman. I don't want to get my hopes up. I'm not going to fill my mind with a lot of romantic nonsense about resuming my role as a wife and mother. I've done that too much in the past. I'm going to resist thinking that Jim will forgive me. I know he won't. And I don't blame him. Some resentments are justified."

"Maybe you're underestimating him. He knew you when you weren't addicted to drugs. He loved you then. I don't understand why he won't forgive you."

"Jim has a difficult time forgiving dishonesty. We used to pride ourselves on the fact that we never lied to each other. But then I got into codeine, and honesty wasn't important to me anymore. Getting my supply of drugs was all I thought of."

"Doesn't he know that lying is part of the illness? My God, I learned that the first day I was here. I don't understand. . . ."

Reggie put her hand on my arm in a gesture meant to silence me.

"There's more," she said. "Remember when I said some things may be unforgivable. Well . . ." She squeezed her eyes closed and grimaced. She looked directly into my eyes. "I began a sexual relationship with a pharmacist after my doctor stopped writing prescriptions for me. I had to get my codeine somehow. The pharmacist and I usually met at a motel. He was married, too. Jim was supposed to be away on a four-day business trip. I couldn't leave the house, because Jason was sick. So he came over to our house at night.

"Jim came home a day early. He was going to surprise me. He surprised me, all right. I'll never forget the look on his face when he opened the bedroom door. And he had a dozen roses in his hand."

I was jolted by Reggie's story, but I tried to appear undisturbed.

"Could you forgive your wife if she did that?"

"It would hurt. But I'd like to think I could forgive anything."

"I won't expect him to forgive me. That's asking too much." Reggie let go of my hand and stood slowly. "I've spent a lot of time trying to rationalize my sexual involvement with that guy. I used to tell Jim—and myself—that I needed those drugs in order to live. That I would have killed myself if I couldn't get my supply of codeine. But the bottom line is that I betrayed Jim and I violated probably the most precious thing we had—trust."

Reggie was trembling. I wanted to help her. I wished I could say something to take her pain away.

"I'm so disappointed in myself," she said. "And I get so angry when I remember what I did. I hurt Jim so much, and I hate myself for that. But I hurt myself more than I hurt him. Jim is a very special, caring, loving man, and I've lost him forever. And I have to live the rest of my life remembering what I did."

I stood and put my arms around Reggie and held her close. I could feel her trembling.

"Patrick," she whispered, "say the Serenity Prayer with me."

God grant me the serenity to accept the things I cannot change, the courage to change the things I can, and the wisdom to know the difference.

As we spoke the prayer, Reggie's trembling stopped. We continued to hug each other for a few moments, and then she stood back and looked at me.

"Is it any comfort at all," she asked, "to know that you could never do anything as cruel and unforgivable as what I've done?"

"Reggie, I've done something that's just as bad. Maybe worse. Irene doesn't know yet. God, I'm afraid of what she'll do when she finds out."

22

THE DOOR opened a few inches, and an unusually bright light from the hall pierced the comfortable darkness of my room. A thin, yellow mist with the pleasant aroma of smoldering incense began billowing in, as if heralding the arrival of an ethereal messenger.

I decided to reject whatever was going on, and I turned slowly and faced the wall with my back toward the door.

There were a few moments of uneventful silence. Then my body jerked, and I started falling asleep. Denial was working.

"Would he please wake up!" It was a voice speaking in a shrill falsetto.

I started loudly whistling *Waltzing Matilda*.

"Would Patrick please stop whistling and turn around! We have some things to discuss." The tone was now urgent and demanding.

Somewhere in my past I had heard this voice, and so I turned, more curious than frightened.

I switched on the lamp by my bed, and that is when I saw him.

He was about sixteen inches tall and wore a high, peaked red hat. He had a magnificent white beard and mustache, and he wore a three-quarter-length blue smock. A large brown belt tightened the smock to his waist. The bottoms of his blue pants were tucked into his black fur boots.

A leather bag was attached to his belt, and a stethoscope protruded slightly from the bag.

The stethoscope had gold earpieces. It was Eugene Starr, the chairman of the Department of Medicine where I had done my internship.

Dr. Starr was a physician of rare brilliance and precise thinking. But because of his overwhelming intensity and the forcefulness of his personality, he was more feared than respected. And he was, of course, intolerably arrogant.

"Patrick has suffered enough here," he said to me. "Although he does not yet know what pain really is. He should come back to Cleveland with me now. It is important to suffer where one has sinned."

"Normally, I'd do whatever you say, Dr. Starr. But I know Randolph won't let me go just yet. Still, I appreciate you coming to see me."

He held up his arms as if adoring me.

"Would he put me on the bed? I don't feel like jumping. Although I jump well."

He was amazingly heavy for a miniature person. I sat him next to me and near the edge of the bed so he could sit comfortably and dangle his feet over the side.

He turned his head and looked up at me.

"There will be no discussion of this. I'm taking him back."

"I'll have to check this out with Randolph and see if he'll let me go back with you. I'll tell him that you're here from Cleveland and that you're disguised as a gnome.

"Randolph's a suspicious son of a bitch, though. He'll probably think I'm trying to escape. Unless . . . would you come to see him with me?"

Dr. Starr put his palms on either side of his hat and pulled it down so it fit more snugly. He then shook his head violently.

"No! No! No! No! No! Patrick is on his own. I will not get involved. And I would suggest he does not tell Dr. Randolph about me."

"I'll never lie again, sir."

"Speaking of lying. Was he taking drugs when he interned under me?"

"Oh, hell, yes. Before morning report I'd pop some Valium. We were all so afraid of presenting cases to you. You would really destroy us when we made a mistake. Or if you asked a question and we didn't know the answer. Remember, Dr. Starr, we always started morning report at seven o'clock, whether you were there or not. Some guys would actually get into a fight so they could present their case if you were late."

Dr. Starr smiled and began patting his abdomen with both hands. A gesture of self-approval.

"The fear of being embarrassed in front of one's peers," he said as if lecturing me, "is a singular motivation for learning."

"You didn't need to be so insufferable, Dr. Starr."

"Arrogance breeds arrogance. We must sustain ourselves."

"There is a difference between honest arrogance and aggressive conceit."

"I have a brilliant mind and incredible powers of observation." His voice was now strident. "And I know more medicine than anyone. Those are not unwarranted claims. I have every right to be smug and self-satisfied."

"If you're so remarkably observant, why didn't you know I was taking drugs? You could have helped me then. And I wouldn't be here now."

His face twisted into an angry look, and he slapped both his thighs. He began moving his little feet.

"There has been enough talk. He should come back to Cleveland with us now."

"Us? Who else is there?"

He slowly raised his right arm and pointed toward the door. There were three little men grouped near the door. They were dressed in hospital whites, and I recognized them. They were guys I had been in training with.

They spoke to each other in muffled tones. Several were gesturing to me as if to come join them. All of them appeared to be angry at me.

"What do you little fuckers want?" I screamed, feeling terror.

"He should be more quiet," Dr. Starr admonished. "He shouldn't scream so loud."

"They have no right to talk about me." I was shaking. "Look at Mark pointing at me. He was an alcoholic and we all knew it. We used to laugh about it.

"Max did uppers. Christ, he was always high. He'd come into work on his tiptoes. He used to joke about lacing his chewing gum with speed so he could chew gum and stay high all day.

"And Henry was addicted to the female pelvis. He had to have a different woman every night. God, the way he used people!"

"They're all dead."

"What! Dead? How?"

"Mark was a suicide. Age twenty-eight. Max stroked out at age thirty-one. The amphetamines killed him. Henry died of a sustained erection. All of the poor lad's blood went to his penis." He slowly shook his head. "A slow death from intractable arousal."

"Dr. Starr, what do they want? Why are they here?"

"They're angry because Patrick is not with them. But they still want him."

"They won't get me. I'm alive, and I'm going to stay this way. I'm doing something about my addiction. I'm escaping it. I'm one of the lucky ones."

Dr. Starr fell abruptly back on the bed and kicked his feet in the air and laughed frenetically. I had never imagined him so uncontrolled. He tried to talk several times, but his frenzied laughing prohibited it.

"Please don't laugh at me, Dr. Starr. Please! You're upsetting me."

He began to slowly push himself up into a sitting position and dangled his feet over the side. He made no sound, but his rotund little body shook as he tried to conceal the fact he was still laughing.

Dr. Starr began struggling to stand.

"He thinks he's one of the lucky ones, eh?"

"Yes."

He stood firm on the mattress and faced me. All traces of amusement were gone from his face.

"Patrick should consider suicide."

"Don't say that! Please . . ."

"Patrick has betrayed the noble tradition of the medical profession. He has been contemptuous of the Hippocratic oath. Others have done this"—he paused and looked at the group of little people by the door—"and paid for it with their lives."

He took a step toward me.

"If Patrick chooses to live, and this is his apparent, present course, he should know what is ahead for him." He shook his head in disgust. "He has lost forever the dignity that comes with being a physician."

He began pointing at me and stepped closer. I edged back away from him.

"He will be scorned and taunted by his peers. He will be made a mockery of and be ridiculed, reproached, and insulted. He will be treated with disdain. We are so disappointed in him. Being a physician should have been more sacred to him. He is a betrayer."

He took a step back and placed his hands behind his back. He was going to make a pronouncement.

"The punishment will fit the crime. He can choose between death and disgrace. I want him to come to Cleveland now and feel the rejection. He can then choose better between the options."

"Please go away, Dr. Starr, and take your little friends. I don't like this. I wish you hadn't come."

He began smiling at me with unmistakable disdain.

"Did Patrick really think he would come here and then sneak back into Cleveland without anyone knowing? Ha!"

"If you won't go away, then I will." I got up and walked briskly toward the door of my room. The door was closed!

I looked down and the group of little doctors was gone. I turned around and Dr. Starr was gone. There was no yellow mist. And no aroma of incense.

"You look like shit," Steve said to me.

"I had a rough night."

"Why don't you tell us about it?" Christine seemed pleased that we could start off the session with something different.

"It was . . . sort of a . . . dream I had."

"Sort of a dream? What do you mean?"

"I'd rather not talk about it, Christine. It's too painful."

"I'm not going to let you get away with being evasive, Patrick. You have a contract with us to be open and honest at all times in group."

"What are you afraid of, Patrick?" There was genuine concern on Melanie's face.

"I just don't want to talk about it now. I'll tell you about it before the end of the week."

"That's not good enough," Christine said with authority. "You have to tell us now."

"I'm not going to."

Christine sat forward in her chair and looked around the group.

"If Patrick won't tell us what's bothering him, he should leave group. Does anyone disagree with that?"

I looked at each of them. Surely they wouldn't agree with Christine. Melanie frowned with uncertainty and then looked away from me as she reached for Lucy's cigarettes.

Lucy moved back in her chair and looked at Christine. Steve and Boone continued to stare impassively at me. Mac was smiling. Hog Body had a painful, worried look. He started to say something but stopped.

A minute. Two minutes. Silence.

Melanie reached toward the ashtray and tapped the ashes off her cigarette.

"Patrick," she said. "You better tell us what's going on with you." She sat up in her chair and had a frighteningly impersonal look. "Or leave."

"I'm disappointed that you don't trust us," Lucy said.

"It makes me angry," Boone said and tensed his lower jaw. "Really angry."

"Patty, if I could tell the group about what I did to my daughter, you should be able to tell us anything."

"I don't think we should fuck around with him anymore. If he . . ."

I held up my hand to stop Steve from talking.

"I don't like all this disapproval," I said. "I hope you will forgive me for insulting you like this."

"I've felt somewhat insulted since day one with you, Patrick." Christine sat forward. "You've exposed precious little of yourself to us." She sat back and nodded for me to begin.

"It wasn't a dream." I told them about my encounter with Dr. Starr and what he said to me. "I'm trying to quote him accurately." Anxious looks were being exchanged as I related my story. I told about the little doctors and how each of them died. "I knew those guys. They were my friends."

"You're telling us this story as if it really happened." Melanie was uncertain and annoyed.

"Patty, are you joking with us?"

"No, Hog. I know it didn't happen. But . . . I smelled the incense. I talked to Dr. Starr. I touched him." I looked to Christine. "I know it couldn't have happened. But it was so real."

"That translates into a hallucination, Patrick. But I think you already knew that. And that's why you didn't want to tell us about it."

I sank back into my chair and stared at the floor.

"What are you thinking, Patrick?" Christine's voice was soft.

"I've hallucinated for Christ's sake! Randolph's right. I am sick."

"We're all sick, Patty."

"I don't want Randolph or O'Malley to find out about this. They'll keep me here forever."

"You should tell them."

"No, Christine, I won't. I want to go home at the end of next week. I don't need to stay. I'm not that sick!"

A long silence followed, and my group patronized me with expressionless faces. And allowed me to feel foolish.

After several minutes I stood and walked to the door. I turned and faced them.

"I'm not that sick, goddamnit! I'm really not."

"Why are you in bed at ten-thirty in the morning?" Toni was leaning against the door of my room with arms folded across her chest. "Aren't you supposed to be in group?"

"They pissed me off. So I left."

"What happened? What did they say?"

"It's what they didn't say. Christine is good at engineering a silence to make a point. I'm not going to let her manipulate me like that."

"So you got angry and left. That's childish." She shook her head. "You have a lot of room to grow, Patrick." She started to leave the room but stopped. "I put a container in here this morning. You forgot to leave a urine specimen."

"I didn't forget."

She walked to the dresser, picked up the plastic container, and flipped it on the bed.

"I want that filled by noon."

"Maybe."

"It's going to be one of *those* days, I see. Patrick, I wish you'd tell me why you're so angry."

"I don't want to talk about it."

How is one supposed to react after hallucinating? Only a fucking moron would be smiling after an experience like that.

"You know where I am if you'd like to talk," Toni said as she left the room.

I came out of the john with my urine container filled and quickly put it back on the bathroom sink when I saw Melanie sitting on my bed.

"You O.K.?" she asked.

"Yeah. I'm better now. How did group go?"

"We've lost another one from our group. Mac is leaving today."

"Didn't you guys try to talk him out of it?"

"He said he simply couldn't live without drinking. He was wasting everybody's time here."

"I'll talk to him, Melanie. I won't let him go. It's certain death if he leaves Hogarth."

"He knows that. He's made his decision. You know how they keep telling us that we are only responsible for ourselves. And that we make our choices and that we have to live with them. He's made a choice, Patrick."

I sat on the bed next to her and held her hand. My hands were perspiring again but I didn't care.

"At this time yesterday, Melanie, I was feeling so good. I even had a few periods when I thought I was happy. Then Reggie upset me when she told me some of her story last night. I've hallucinated. We're losing someone from our group. Goddamnit! How much unhappiness do they expect me to tolerate?"

"I was a lot more unhappy before I came here than I am now, Patrick. I just didn't know it. And they didn't promise us smiles."

Melanie moved closer to me and placed her hand on the inside of my thigh.

"There are things we could do to make this less unpleasant."

Irene and I saw each other at the same time. We met in the middle of the dining room and hugged. The feeling of her breasts against me . . . her smile . . . her hair against my face . . . her smell . . . her hands on me . . . there was a special familiarity and an immediate closeness as if we had not been apart.

She kissed me on the cheek, and I felt warm and comfortable and secure and wanted.

When we separated, she raised her right eyebrow and smiled. There would be closer and more sustained intimacy later.

And I was ready.

She stood back and looked at my waist.

"You must have lost ten pounds, Pat. Haven't you been eating?"

"They've been feeding us a steady diet of entrails. I don't eat much." Actually I had lost eleven pounds in seventeen days and I had eaten most of the meals.

I got my lunch and was about to join Irene when I noticed Mac sitting at a table with a woman, probably "the wife." It upset me to see him. But I had to talk to him. Maybe I could say something that he hadn't heard.

I sat at the table with him.

"Hi, Patrick! Meet the wife, Janine." Mac sounded almost euphoric.

Janine had long, dark hair parted in the middle and large brown eyes. She was markedly overweight, but her face had been spared any traces of obesity.

"You're the doctor," she said and smiled. Nicotine-stained teeth nullified her pretty face.

"How do you feel about Mac leaving Hogarth?" I asked her.

"I guess I wouldn't know how to live with him if he was always sober. We know how to live together this way." She kept an uneasy smile.

"Patrick, people like me have a place," Mac said and grinned foolishly. "We give everyone else someone to look down at."

"Janine, two weeks ago Mac told me he came here only to please you. He said you would leave him if he didn't do something about his drinking. Now you're letting him come home?"

Janine stopped smiling and looked to her husband. Mac glared at me.

"This is none of your business anymore," Mac said with a mouthful of food.

"Janine, don't take him back. You're just letting him kill himself. You may be the only thing that can keep him sober."

"Shut the fuck up, Patrick. Go away." Mac started getting out of his chair.

"Janine, don't let him come home."

Mac was standing, his right arm cocked, his large hand tightened into a fist.

"I won't let him drink as much. . . . he'll be all right. . . . I'll watch him."

I stood and looked at Mac and Janine. Their faces showed no fear, only anger. I had made a terrible mistake. They had, in their own way, accepted the fact that Mac was a dying man, and I had interfered. I had caused them unnecessary pain.

I had done harm.

"I'm sorry," I said. "Please forgive me."

I took my lunch tray and headed for Irene's table. Two women were with her. One I didn't recognize. The other was Melanie!

"Pat," Irene said, "this is Helen."

"Hog Body is Helen's husband," Melanie added. "I came over and said hello to these ladies when I saw Presswood approach them. It's a good thing I did."

"When I told him I was from Cleveland," Irene said, smiling, "he asked me where my babushka was and how I kept the hair off my face." Irene looked at Helen. "Tell them what he said to you."

Helen started to laugh.

"When I went to take a bite of my sandwich, he said: 'Do you know what your asshole will look like in the morning if you eat that?' "

"His name's Presswood," I said. "He's one of Melanie's close friends."

Melanie kicked me under the table and then looked at Irene.

"How do you put up with this guy? How can you possibly live with his smart mouth and his arrogance?"

"It hasn't been easy."

"Obviously you're a lot younger than Patrick. Maybe that . . ."

"Hey, goddamnit, Irene's only a year younger than me. She's thirty-five."

"You're only thirty-six?" Melanie's eyes were wide as she looked at me and feigned incredulity. "Hmmm. Maybe it's your glands, Patrick. You must have old glands."

"What glands! Melanie, come back here. Don't say something like that and walk away."

Irene and Helen were laughing as they watched Melanie walk off. "I like her, Pat."

"I do, too," Helen said. "And what a beauty."

Helen was a beauty, too. She was probably in her mid-forties and slightly built. She had light brown hair and an unflawed, bronzed complexion. As Helen talked, I could sense a strong similarity to Hog Body—a sturdy common sense, and incapable of deception.

I was glad for Hog Body.

I told Helen how much Hog had helped me and how important he had been to me. That left her slightly amused. And proud.

Hog Body finally appeared and came toward the table, walking slowly and with a tentative smile. Helen appeared uncertain. But as Hog got closer, she brightened and sat erect. Her smile became warm and unreserved.

When he was next to her, she stood, and they hugged excitedly, connecting like magnets. Irene slipped her hand into mine.

Hog noticed me staring at them.

"Patty, this is my wife," he said in a tone suggesting total commitment.

Irene squeezed my hand.

Helen reached for her purse and smiled at Irene.

"I'll see you later," she said to Irene. "Nice meeting you, Patty."

I smiled at Helen, and saw Hog Body looking at her with a venerative expression. As they turned to walk off, I heard Hog Body ask her: "How are the kids? How's Angeline?"

"Maybe I'll just take the afternoon off," I said to Irene, "and we can go for a long walk."

"I'd love to, Pat. The grounds here are beautiful. And I've never seen so many blue jays. But I have an appointment with Dr. Randolph in twenty minutes. Isn't he your doctor?"

"Yeah."

"You don't like him, do you?"

"No, I don't."

"Why?"

"Well . . . he's a jerk."

Irene smiled. "Your bruised ego is showing, Pat. You just don't like being a patient."

"He's the son of a bitch that will decide if they're going to keep me another three weeks."

"I don't want you to stay another three weeks, Pat. I couldn't stand it. This is too hard."

It was good to hear Irene say that, to know that she was on my side.

"Be careful what you say to Randolph."

"I won't lie, Pat. I'm really looking forward to talking with him. I have a lot to learn about addiction. I want to find out everything I can. I learned some things this morning."

"Like what?"

"We saw a movie on alcoholism and had a lecture on chemical dependency. Then we broke into small groups. I was in a group with Edith. I remembered her from the first day.

"Each of us had to tell the group why we were here. When I told the group about you, Edith asked me if I knew that every night when you took your drugs and had a drink, that you risked never waking up." Irene looked at me with astonishment. "I didn't know that."

"But you didn't know how many drugs I took."

"I told her that. But she said I must have suspected something. And by choosing to be ignorant, I was being dishonest. She said that if you really love someone, you don't stand idly by as the person kills himself.

"Edith told me that I should have found out what you were doing, confronted you with it, and left you if you didn't try to get help. She said I was a silent partner in your addiction. And that I was responsible for you being an addict for so long, because you couldn't help yourself."

"Sounds like she was pretty rough on you."

"I started to cry, Pat. She told me not to feel sorry for myself because my husband was a drug addict. I'm not supposed to see myself as an innocent victim. Because, she said, I was part of the problem. She called me an enabler."

"Babes, I'm sorry you were brutalized like that. It seems unfair."

"Edith came up to me after our group session and apologized for being so ruthless with me in front of everyone. But she said this is a life-and-death situation. So she plays hardball."

"Well, you won't have to see her again, will you?"

"I'm meeting her for coffee later this afternoon."

"You're a glutton for punishment."

"Pat, I hope you don't mind, but they want us to attend an Al-Anon meeting tonight. From eight to ten."

"I have to be in bed by eleven. Alone."

"I know, honey. But I want to go."

"Well, at least we can have dinner together. We can go to a restaurant and have an honest-to-God steak."

Irene started to slowly shake her head.

"I've already accepted an invitation to have dinner with Denise Bossy. She said you know her husband. She's going to pick me up at the motel at six."

"They're surrounding you," I said and tried not to hide my disappointment.

"God, I have so much to learn and so little time. We have the rest of our lives. I don't want this to happen to us again. And if you get involved with drugs again, I need to know what to do."

"This won't happen again, Babes."

"But it might. You could relapse. And if you do, I won't be a spectator."

"I haven't gotten out of the goddamn hospital, and you're talking relapse. What the fuck's wrong with you, Irene?"

I had stung Irene with my anger, and she looked hurt.

"Pat . . . what's wrong?"

"I'm sorry. Really. Please forgive me. I'm just annoyed that we can't be alone tonight."

She forced a smile through her hurt and squeezed my hand. I felt myself becoming erect.

"I want you, too," she whispered.

"I can wait one more day, I guess."

Irene looked surprised.

"Don't you have a doctors' group meeting tomorrow night?"

"Nuts! I forgot. I'll skip it."

Irene shook her head.

"No, you won't."

"Irene, don't tell me what to do."

"I'm going to be meeting with the spouses of the doctors that you'll be with. It's at the same time."

"Sometimes they meet until midnight. When the hell are we going to be alone?"

Irene smiled. "Friday night."

I was crushed with disappointment. Then anger surfaced. I forced myself to remain silent. I didn't want to inflict my anger on her again. She didn't deserve it.

"Irene, I've got to tell you something. I'm trying to make a habit of honesty. I had another catastrophe last night."

Feeling embarrassment and with an unsteady voice, I told Irene about my encounter with Dr. Starr. I did not mention the word *hallucination*. But she knew.

"Oh, my God, that's awful, Patrick," she said as she rubbed my hand, consoling me. "What does it mean? Are you permanently damaged? Will this happen again? Did they put you on any medicine?"

"I didn't tell Randolph, and I'm not going to. I'm afraid he'd recycle me for sure if he found out."

"I think you should tell him. He should know, honey. He's your doctor."

I shook my head. "Nope. And don't you tell him."

Irene looked away from me abruptly as if something had caught her attention. She looked back at me, and there was compassion in her expression. Then uncertainty.

She pulled her hand slowly away from mine and sat back in her chair. I didn't like her manner. She was becoming impersonal, detached, distant.

"I have to see Dr. Randolph now," she said in a formal tone. She stood. She was different. She was decisive, determined. She briskly strode away.

"Gabe, it's Pat."

"Hi, kiddo. How are things? Is Irene there?"

"Irene's here. I've spent a grand total of one hour with her. It's as if they're trying to keep her away from me."

"Maybe they are. Maybe they need to."

"And she's different, Gabe. I don't like it. One minute she's affectionate, the next she's impersonal and cold. I want to be with her, talk to her."

"Sounds like you need some reassurance, Pat."

"Not you, too! Why does everybody feel they have to be a fucking analyst? I just want to be alone with my wife."

Silence.

"I'm sorry, Gabe."

"That's twice now, Pat. That same raw, unprovoked anger Logan had. Please don't become like him."

"Maybe I'm predestined to be like him, Gabe. I just never showed it before because I was sedated."

"That's unadulterated bullshit, Pat. And you know it."

"Yeah . . . probably."

"Irene stopped by two days ago. We talked. I didn't notice any dramatic difference. She's been jolted by this. She said she was upset mostly because you were dishonest with her."

"Was she angry, Gabe?"

"A little. But once you two get things out in the open, everything will be all right. You still have her, kiddo. She's not going anywhere. Consider yourself a lucky man. I wish I had been so fortunate in my choice of partners."

"What do you mean, 'get things out in the open'?"

"No more lying, Pat. Tell her everything. That way she'll trust you again. That shouldn't be too difficult now. Should it?"

"Yes, Gabe, telling Irene *everything* will be very difficult."

My voice trembled as I told her about the vasectomy.

"You're the first person I've told, Gabe."

"That's a rough one, Pat. I'm sorry for you. But you've got to tell Irene. She *has* to know. And you've got to tell her now."

"That's easy for you to say."

"No, it isn't. Can't you get vasectomies reversed?"

"I can try. And I will if Irene wants me to."

"Make sure you tell her that. See, it won't be so bad."

"Gabe"—I started to cry—"I've screwed up so badly. . . . I'm sure Irene will leave me."

"I seriously doubt that. Don't underestimate Irene. She's a tough lady. And she loves you."

"I don't know why . . . I've really made a mess of things. . . ."

"Stop feeling sorry for yourself, Pat. I don't like to hear you like this. You need to get your buns goin' and do what you have to do."

"I suppose so."

"It sounds to me that when you get some of this stuff behind you, you will be better than you ever were before.

"And that was pretty good, kiddo."

"Thanks, Gabe. How are you feeling?"

"Well . . . not too bad. I've seen Scott Walsh twice now. Irene recommended him. She said you were a patient of his."

"He's a good man. I'm glad you're seeing him."

"So far he's been an advocate for me. He tells me that I'm worthwhile and that it's O.K. to be unhappy when you're going through a divorce. And"—Gabe sighed—"he told me that I'm intelligent and that, at age thirty-nine, I'm still quite attractive. That kind of stuff."

"All of that sounds fairly accurate, Gabe."

"By the way, Pat . . . and don't ever tell him I asked you this . . . is Scott married?"

"No. He's been divorced for about two years."

"Hmmm . . . I will definitely continue to see him. Oh! You know what else he told me? He said I had to stop taking Valium or he wouldn't see me anymore. He said that was one of his new rules . . . something about not getting burned again."

"Do what he tells you, Gabe."

"All right . . . I miss you, kiddo, and so does Eighty-two. He keeps asking for you. Get well for us . . . please."

"I'm doing my best . . . really."

"You're on the hot seat this morning, Patrick." Christine spoke in a magistral tone for the first time that defined her role and separated her from us.

She was pointedly exercising her authority, and that annoyed and upset me. And she knew it.

"I think Patrick owes us an apology first," Lucy said to Christine. "Walking out on us yesterday was . . . well, I found it offensive." Lucy looked at me, and I could see she was hurt. "I thought you cared about us too much to do something like that."

"The person who should be offended most is Steve," Melanie said. "He told his story yesterday, and you weren't here."

"I didn't give a shit," Steve said. He wasn't convincing. I had hurt him, too.

"We had a bad day yesterday with Patty walking out on us like that and then Mac leaving. I got pretty nervous yesterday."

"People should think more about the consequences of their actions," Christine said and then looked at me. "Especially people who are supposed to be intelligent."

"You know," Boone said, "Mac's leaving didn't bother me too much. As a matter of fact, I feel relieved in a way. He didn't belong here. He wasn't ready for this. And I don't think he'll ever be ready. I feel sorry for him, though."

"Mac came to say good-bye to me yesterday afternoon," Christine said. There was sadness and disappointment in her voice. "There was an aura of death about him. It really made me feel uncomfortable. I thought about him last night. I was pretty rough on him a couple of times." She looked around the room. "Does anybody think I was unfair with him?"

"No." Melanie was the first to answer.

"Hell, no!" Boone added.

"Unless anyone wants to talk about Mac anymore, I think we should not discuss him further. We don't really have much to learn from that experience."

Christine looked around the room to give each of us a chance to talk. There was only silence. She then stared at me, her eyes narrowed.

"You better start talking," she said to me. It was a threat.

I looked at each member of my group and I could feel their disappointment coming at me like daggers.

I started to apologize, but the urge to cry came suddenly and intensely. I closed my eyes and resisted crying. I didn't want to appear that vulnerable.

"We're glad you're back, Patty. It's not the same without you."

"I'm sorry I walked out like that. I won't do it again. I promise. Toni said it was a childish thing to do. It was also boorish. I . . . I need you guys."

I saw smiles and felt an air of acceptance. I felt good again.

"Any little people visit you last night?" Melanie asked, smiling, but with concern.

"No."

"Did you tell anybody about the hallucination?" Christine was assuming she already knew the answer.

"I told Irene."

"Well, I'm glad you did that. But you know who I mean."

"I didn't tell Randolph or O'Malley. And I'm not going to."

"I wish you'd be more concerned with your health," Christine snapped, "and less concerned with your length of stay. I think you need to refocus on what's important here. You seem to think this is an exercise in white knucklery. And I'm getting impatient with that.

Goddamnit, Patrick, I'm so angry with you. You're an intelligent person. But you're not acting like it.

My face was warming and I pushed myself back into my chair.

"You've shown definite improvement since we first started in group," she said. "But, Patrick, your attitude stinks."

Christine moved into her instructive position, but she wasn't going to teach. She was assaulting.

"Your priorities are all screwed up," she said. "You still haven't accepted the program, and you continue to resist all advice that you don't like.

"This isn't prison, Patrick. You're not *doing time*. This is a rehabilitation program. We're trying to help reconvert you to a life that's free of drugs. And this program works. But you've got to do it our way.

"Dr. Randolph and Dr. O'Malley are not your adversaries. They care about you. And so do I."

Christine sat back and slouched in her chair. She took off her glasses and began rubbing the bridge of her nose.

"I met Irene yesterday, Patrick. I was impressed with her. She loves you and would do anything for you. I guess I've lost my objective posture with you that I try to keep with members of my group.

"I've done this before. It causes me to be more intense and blunt than I have a right to be. I owe you an apology."

"Is it wrong to care too much?" Melanie asked her.

"Yes. For me it is."

"Thanks for the apology, Christine. Unfortunately there's more than a grain of truth in what you say."

"Are you ready to tell us your story?" she asked and gave me a conciliatory smile.

I started to talk but then paused and looked at Lucy.

"Can I have a cigarette?" I asked.

She handed me her pack of Players and a lighter and then turned to Melanie.

"He *is* becoming one of us," she said.

"One less thing he can be judgmental about," Melanie stated.

I inhaled deeply on the first puff, and I felt as if molten lead had been poured into my lungs.

"I thought this damn thing would calm me down," I said and coughed. "You don't mess around when you smoke these things. I can feel the cancer cells growing in my lungs already."

I told the group about Logan and how afraid of him I was because of his anger. And how he dominated me.

"I succeeded in everything I attempted because I wanted him to be proud of me. That was my only motivation. He wanted me to become a doctor. So I went to medical school. The thought of failing in medical school would paralyze me at times. If it hadn't been for tranquilizers and sleeping pills I would have never made it. But . . . damn! I'd rather be cleaning sewers than what I am now—a doctor without self-esteem . . . a drug addict."

"How long have you been taking drugs, Patty?"

"Fourteen years. This cigarette is starting to taste better."

"All downers?"

"Yeah. Mostly."

"Well, how could you be seeing patients, kids, all day and make decisions, you know, life-and-death decisions, when you had all those drugs in you?" Hog Body was shaking his head. "I don't understand how you could be a very good doctor when you were taking that many drugs."

"I'm glad I wasn't taking my kids to you," Steve added.

"Fuck you, Steve." I moved forward in my chair. "I went through three years of pediatric residency, and my last year I was chief resident. I'm a board-certified pediatrician, for Christ's sake."

"No one is questioning your education or training," Lucy said.

"I may not have functioned at a hundred percent," I yelled. "But I'm damn good." I vigorously crushed my cigarette into the ashtray.

My outburst was met with silence, and I began to feel foolish.

"I'm sorry," I said.

More silence.

"It sounds like you have an issue here you better deal with, Patrick," Christine said.

I looked at Christine and nodded.

"It's painful to think of myself as a statistic . . . as an impaired physician. That is so humbling."

The urge to cry came, and I took a deep breath and cleared my throat.

"I'm pretty sure I never killed anybody. But it's only by the grace of God. I've written orders on the wrong charts. . . . I miscalculated a dose of digitalis on a three-month-old that would have killed him" —my eyes were watering—"I ordered penicillin for a kid who was allergic to it. . . . I wrote fluid orders on a newborn that would have put her into congestive heart failure. . . . I missed a case of meningococcal meningitis that a second year medical student could have

· 2 3 6 ·

diagnosed." I was crying and couldn't talk anymore. Christine passed the box of Kleenex to me.

I wished someone else would speak, but there was only silence and astonished expressions.

"Patty, didn't the other doctors see you making these mistakes? They should have helped you."

"Before you fucking murdered somebody," Steve added.

"Doctors don't"—I took a deep breath—"scrutinize each other very well. . . . It's so easy to kill . . . I owe all my patients an apology." I covered my face with my hands. "Oh, God, please forgive me . . . they trusted me . . . I betrayed them . . . God, I'm so sorry."

I felt a hand fall softly on my shoulder. I knew it was Melanie, and I reached for her hand. But I couldn't look at anyone.

They let me cry for a few moments.

"Patrick, look at me," Christine softly commanded. She was smiling at me. "You've just taken a giant forward step. I'm proud of you. I know it was very hard."

"I'm proud of you, too, Patty."

"How do you feel, Patrick?" Lucy said and handed me her pack of Players and the lighter. "I think I saw you start to smile."

I felt myself gaining strength as I lit a cigarette.

"I feel so much better . . . like, I've been freed. For so long I've felt trapped inside a giant lie. Being dishonest is so uncomfortable. And keeping a certain facade when you're decaying inside takes a lot of energy. And I'm tired. Being a drug addict is hard work."

Melanie squeezed my shoulder, smiled at me, and walked back to her chair. She left behind that nice fragrance of lilac. And as I watched her walk off, I felt a warm rush of blood into my groin.

"I would spend hours—sometimes days—planning lies," Lucy said. "Talk about expending energy!"

"I wonder if I fooled the people I was lying to," Melanie added. "I'm a pretty good liar. A pro, you might say."

Christine sat forward, elbows on her knees.

"Normally what happens is the people who are closest to you are fooled the longest. Some of this has to do with them *not wanting* to believe you're not in control." She looked at me. "Irene is a glaring example of what I'm talking about. She told me she thought you only took an occasional sleeping pill and one or two tranquilizers every day."

"Maybe *I* could learn some things from *you* about lying," Melanie said to me. "I thought I was good."

"I think Irene was unconsciously choosing not to know," Christine added. "She was just blocking out your drug taking." Her expression became serious. "You and Irene will need to tread softly for a while. You're going to need to renegotiate a new relationship. But from what I've seen this morning, I feel good about you, Patrick."

"Tell us about Irene," Lucy said.

"I met her when I was a sophomore in med school. She was a graduate student in art. Irene opened up a whole new world for me. Before I met her I had never been to the Cleveland Museum of Art. I had never been to a performance by the Cleveland Orchestra. I had never been to an arboretum.

"Irene's added so much to my life. I've benefited more from the marriage than she has."

"C'mon, Pat," Steve said angrily. "She's married to a doctor. I'll bet she's happier than a hog in shit."

"If you really believe that, Steve," Melanie bristled, "you're a complete asshole."

"That was a pretty shallow remark," Lucy said to Steve.

"Horse shit! I know what I'm talking about. You fucking women . . ." Steve looked at the floor and his anger began leaving, being replaced by sadness.

I finished my second cigarette, which I had enjoyed immensely.

"Do you have any more comments before we take a break?" Christine said to me.

"Yes. I now know what you mean about feeling close to people when you expose yourself."

"People who care about you," Lucy added.

During the break I stood looking out the window. I was feeling stronger than I had felt since entering the hospital.

Melanie's hand reached in front of me and offered me a lighted cigarette.

"I forgot how delicious these damn things were," I said, as I took the cigarette.

"Patrick, was Karren able to help you? You never told me."

I nodded.

"You mean . . . you're cured?"

I nodded and smiled proudly.

She moved closer to me, and I became aware of her smell again, which brought on my Pavlovian response of a primitive urging and the dawnings of an erection.

We stood quietly looking out the window and then she sighed deeply.

"Patrick, I care so much about you. When you were crying before, I wanted to hold you and make all your pain go away."

I glanced at her, and she turned toward me, her expression intense. After a few seconds she softened, and an earnest, small smile appeared.

"I want to go to bed with you, Patrick. Making love is an experience I want to share with you." She looked toward the window. "I've never thought of making love to someone in those terms before. I've never come on to a man like this." She looked up at me. "I don't have to." She touched my arm. "I'm sorry. I hope this doesn't complicate things for you. We have such little time."

"I can honestly say . . . I've never been happy." Melanie was staring at her hands, which were folded on her lap. Her thumbs were moving furiously in a circle. "My parents loved me . . . I think. But I'm sure they didn't want me. And I was their only child."

Melanie looked at me, a joyless smile on her face. "I was a mistake," she said and seemed close to crying.

Christine passed her the box of Kleenex, and Melanie put it on the table.

"My parents made me feel worthless . . . . they acted as if I wasn't good enough to be their child. They never told me I was pretty . . . or even cute." Melanie reached for her cigarettes. "Aren't fathers supposed to tell their daughters they're beautiful?"

She lit her cigarette with quick, flashy moves, and bent her head back dramatically and exhaled the smoke. "That was Bette Davis," she said and then slouched in the chair.

"I remember seeing a picture of myself at age seven or eight. The dress I had on was so ugly and the haircut I had . . . so awful." Melanie looked at me. "I think what my parents did to me was a form of child abuse."

I nodded and reached for Lucy's cigarettes.

"I retreated into a fantasy world when I was about eight. I fantasized that I had an older brother. His name was Dusty. He treated me so nice, and told me I was pretty. Sometimes I talked to him out loud. My parents didn't like that.

"When I was twelve," Melanie continued, "we moved from Ottawa to Toronto. My parents brought me to a child psychiatrist, and it was a good thing. I think I was becoming schizophrenic, or something. The psychiatrist tried to get my parents to come in with me. But they wouldn't. They thought they were perfect . . . the ideal parents."

Melanie sat up abruptly and nervously mashed her cigarette in the ashtray.

"By the time I was fifteen I had invested a lot of time in feeling worthless and pretending to be beautiful. I wanted to feel loved and be attractive, and I met somebody . . . he was twenty-four . . . a truck driver. He told me I was pretty, and that he loved me. I ran off with him."

Melanie reached for her cigarettes and lit one slowly.

"I was gone with him for three months. He sent me back . . . promising to come back and get me. He never came back, of course."

Melanie slouched in her chair and fell silent. She looked only at her cigarette as she smoked it.

"That was my first taste," she said slowly, "of feeling loved, and I started to think I was attractive."

"You're a beautiful woman," Boone interrupted. "You must have been beautiful then, too."

Melanie looked at Boone. She was annoyed.

"I don't like compliments," she said. "They make me uncomfortable. I don't know what to do with them."

"Why don't you just say 'thanks,' " Christine said.

Melanie smiled weakly and shrugged her shoulders.

"My running away was a real shock to my parents. I guess for the first time they realized that I was fucked up and that they weren't perfect. They stopped putting me down all the time. And they started to spend some money on me for clothes. And I started dating like mad.

"When I was in high school my psychiatrist suggested I try acting. My first meaty part was as Emily in *Our Town*. I loved playing Emily. God, she was so happy to be alive. So in love with life. So unlike me.

"After I did *Spoon River* when I was a senior I knew I was hooked. I knew what I wanted to do with the rest of my life. I liked playing someone else all the time. That way, I thought, I wouldn't have to worry about who I was."

Melanie sat up with a self-effacing smile. "I feel very self-conscious," she said. "I've never talked about myself like this in a group."

"We're finally getting to know you," Lucy said. "Go on."

"I've talked to Dr. O'Malley about myself. He told me that I've designed a life-style based on failure and defeat, probably because I grew up in an atmosphere of—he called it—emotional poverty. He said that I just didn't have the proper tools to develop into a responsible adult. And that's why I've used alcohol and drugs like I have."

"Melanie," Lucy said, "I think you're very lonely. I think you need people."

"I'm terribly lonely. But I'm rarely alone. And up until six months ago, I never slept alone. God! I've been through dozens of men . . . my drama teacher in high school . . . he was married . . . most of the group in drama in college . . . almost every acting instructor . . . a couple of directors . . ."

"Melanie!" I blurted. "How could you let yourself be used like that? How could you let yourself be treated like a piece of meat?"

Melanie glared at me, her eyes cold.

"Patrick, you damn fool, you don't understand. I was using them."

"Oh . . . but why so many?"

"A lot of reasons. Some were married and couldn't stay around long. Some, or maybe I should say most, didn't satisfy me sexually." She smiled. "I have a long history of faking orgasms. I've done some of my best acting in bed. Most men, I think, are pretty selfish in bed. They're only concerned with *their* orgasm."

"Maybe you're choosing the wrong men," I said. "And I don't like you summarily dismissing all men as being selfish in bed."

"I didn't say *all* men, Patrick."

"Melanie," Lucy had a disappointed expression, "there has got to be more to making love than just having great orgasms."

"This guy Scooter you introduced me to," I said, still angry, he's married?"

Melanie nodded.

"Why in the hell are you messing around with a married man, for Christ's sake?"

"Well, let's see; he's got a nice ass. That's the first thing that attracted me to him. And he's great in bed. You look like you're going to explode, Patrick."

Melanie looked at Christine.

"I know I need to make a lot of changes. But I'm not sure I'm ready to make them. I'll tell you why. When I'm sober, I'm dull and plodding and unexciting. I'm too serious . . . and guilt-ridden. . . . almost never climax. I can't look a man in the face when I'm screwing him. But when I'm loose, like when I have a buzz on, or when

I'm drinking, I'm lively and witty . . . daring, willing to take chances. And I feel sexy and passionate . . . and promiscuous. And as for men . . . well, I like intimacy, too. I need it. And the only way I can be close to a man . . . you know . . . be sexually intimate . . . is when I'm loose."

"Damn!" Boone said. "You really do have a lousy opinion of yourself."

"What do you mean?" Melaine asked and reached for her cigarettes.

"We've only known you when you've been sober," Boone said. "I find you very attractive. And you're bright and spontaneous and you have a good sense of humor."

"Boone's telling it to you straight," Steve said. "Any man in the world would love to have you the way you are now. I don't mean just in bed."

"I'll bet you're not as great as you think you are when you're drinking," Lucy said. "Listen to what these guys are telling you, Melanie."

"I'd like to comment on what you said about intimacy." Christine moved to the edge of her seat. "Being sexually involved with someone without first being emotionally close is not intimacy, Melanie. It's fucking, and that's all it is." Christine sat back and, unblinking, continued to stare at Melanie. "Have you ever spent some time getting to know a man, I mean really getting to know him, before you went to bed with him?"

"No," Melanie stated without hesitation. She then looked at me. "But I'm ready to."

O'Malley had a little piece of popcorn on his left eyebrow, and I found it distracting.

"When you eat your popcorn," I asked, "do you just stick your whole head into the bag and grind away?"

He paused for a few seconds, uncertain.

"I'm not sure why you're asking me that."

I lightly tapped my left eyebrow. His eyes moved up and out to the left as he pulled the particle off, held it, looked at, it and then flipped it away.

"You must really get it on when you eat that stuff," I said and laughed.

His expression became dour.

"We're not here to discuss my eating habits," he said and then moved forward and folded his arms on his desk. "I don't have any other pieces on me, do I?"

I shook my head.

"How are you and Irene doing?"

"We're not doing anything. You people have her surrounded. I won't be alone with her until tomorrow night. This is not what I was expecting."

"We try to bring family members to a certain level of awareness in a very short time. For some of them it's a road-to-Damascus awakening. And many experience some rather discordant emotions. We only have a few days, so we have to inundate them with a lot of stuff.

"Have you and Karren talked any more about your sexual disability?"

"No. I'm not impotent anymore."

"How do you know?"

"Concupiscence has returned!" I exclaimed, emphasizing the dramatic. "And I'm responding to it appropriately."

"You've had intercourse?"

"No. Hell, no. Where and when have I had the opportunity?"

"So you've just had erections and masturbated? Is that all?"

I nodded.

"What has Karren said?"

"Well, Karren wants to meet with me and Irene and talk about it. I told her I didn't need to."

O'Malley sat back and laid his head over the back of his seat and stared at the ceiling. I could see his mouth moving, but he was making no sounds.

"What are you doing?" I asked.

"Praying for patience," he said, as he brought himself into a sitting position.

"You think I'm stubborn?"

"No. I'd call it flagrant noncompliance."

"Noncompliant? Whadda ya mean? I've done almost everything." He moved forward, smiling, ready to score.

"Number one. You practically had to be crucified before you'd take the Antabuse."

"That's an overstatement."

"Number two. We wanted to wean you slowly off the Valium. You refused and had a seizure."

"I . . . O.K. I'll give you that one."

"Number three. You're still not going to A.A. meetings."

"I'm not convinced I need A.A."

"Patrick, you weren't convinced you needed a slow withdrawal from Valium, either. May I go on? What number am I on?"

"I think you've made your point."

"Number four. I told you to leave the doctors' group meeting if you were feeling shaky. But you didn't and ran away and almost blew this entire hospitalization."

I slouched in my chair and looked to the wall and started reading some of his diplomas.

"And now you're resisting Karren's advice—I know you're listening to me—about having a joint session with your wife."

I heard him sit back in his chair, and so I looked at him. He was glaring at me.

"Your obstinacy is not serving you well, Patrick."

"You hardly looked at me during dinner, Irene. You talked to Helen and Hog Body, damnit, but you virtually ignored me. What's going on?"

Irene kept looking at the ground as we walked. It was getting dark, but I could still see my breath spiriting in front of me. Irene was engulfed in my jacket, and had her arms tightly wrapped in front of her.

"Talk to me, Irene."

I put my arm around her and our walking slowed.

"I'm having a difficult time with some things," she said, still looking down. "I just can't get my emotions straightened out. I love you, Pat. You know that. But I resent you, too. For this. And I'm angry at you for making us go through this.

"But yet"—she looked up at me—"I'm proud of you for coming here. And I keep wondering if this isn't all my fault."

"Irene, damnit, this is not your fault! I don't care what these people are telling you."

"Remember about four months ago when you got that call from the emergency room in the middle of the night?"

"Sure . . . no. No, I don't remember."

"Well, it was the resident who was taking your calls that night. He was going to admit one of your patients. I tried to wake you up. I pushed you . . . poked you . . . screamed in your ear. And you hardly moved. I had to tell him you were sick and couldn't come to the phone. When I slammed the phone down, you woke up. You said something about needing to go to the bathroom. Remember what you did?"

"No."

"You got up and stumbled to the closet. Pat, you started to pee in the closet."

"I don't remember that at all."

"I got up and took you to the bathroom. Later after I got you into the bed, I remember looking at you and"—she inhaled deeply—"wishing you were dead."

I stopped walking and squeezed Irene closer to me.

"I'm not trying to hurt you, Pat. My point is that I should have known. You walked like you were taking drugs; you talked and acted like you were taking drugs. Edith was right. I was choosing not to know. I was choosing to be ignorant."

"I'm sorry, Babes. I don't know what to say."

We started walking back to the hospital.

"Dr. Randolph told me that over ten percent of physicians are either drug addicts or alcoholics or both. Some day I want to get involved in helping the wives and husbands of addicted physicians. I want to help them confront the problem. I'll tell them they aren't doing anyone a favor by remaining silent."

She looked up at me, enthusiasm in her expression.

"This is something that excites me, Pat. I could put a lot of energy into it."

I smiled at Irene to let her know that I liked the idea, too.

"How was your conversation with Randolph? I hope you didn't let him talk you into anything."

"It was a good conversation. I learned some things." Irene stopped, and we stood facing each other. She put her arms around my waist. "Pat, if they suggest you stay, I think you should do it. I . . ."

I stood back from Irene and pushed her arms off of me.

"No! I will not stay. And don't say that to me again. I thought you were on my side."

Bossy sat in his place at the head of the long rectangular table. The seat to his immediate left was empty, but all other seats were taken. And like the week before, more chairs had been brought in and placed against the walls. There were about forty people in the room, which was probably twice a comfortable capacity.

Lorenzo and I sat in chairs against the wall and were joined by three other doctors who were also inpatients.

After the Serenity Prayer, the new people were asked to introduce themselves.

"Joseph. I'm an anesthesiologist from Denver." Joseph was a large man and, like Bossy, had enormous shoulders. His head was shaved, but he had multiple small scars, about a week old, all over the top of his head.

"Nancy Mary . . . psychiatrist . . . Ottawa." Nancy Mary spoke in a dull voice. She was about my age but with a little more neglect could pass for fifty. Her eyes were lifeless, her expression vacuous, giving almost no indication of awareness.

"Charles. I'm an anesthesiologist, too. And, as most of you know, I pass gas downtown." Charles was thin and had hollow cheeks. He slouched casually in his chair, and he smiled a lot, as if he were among friends, which, apparently, he was.

Bossy admonished the three of them to leave the meeting "any time you need to. Only each of you will know when that is. Don't screw around if you start getting nervous. Leave!" Bossy looked at me.

"Patrick"—he began laughing—"do you want to tell these folks what happened to you last week because you didn't leave soon enough."

"No." What's so goddamn funny, you big son of a bitch?

"Lorenzo," Bossy continued, "you certainly look a hundred percent better than you did last week."

"Well . . . I'm leaving Sunday. They're sending me to the Georgia program."

"Why is that any cause for joy?" The male voice came from the back of the room. "They can keep you for up to a year down there."

Lorenzo, smiling broadly, looking in the direction of the voice.

"My wife's flying down there with me, man. . . . my wife's coming with me."

Congratulatory smiles appeared on faces as they looked at Lorenzo.

"Has anybody heard from Arthur?" Bossy boomed. "This is the first meeting he's missed in two years."

"I called him last night." The elderly lady with the white hair spoke. I couldn't remember her name. "He said he wasn't coming, and that he didn't need to come here anymore just so you could punch his ticket."

"Thanks, Margaret," Bossy said. "Did he sound sober?"

Margaret nodded.

Bossy slowly shook his head and wrote something.

"*Punch his ticket,*" Bossy murmured. "I'll talk to him tomorrow."

Bossy sat up in his chair and started looking around the room.

"Is Katie here?"

Two thin arms started waving in the back of the room.

"Why don't you smaller folks get around the table?" Bossy yelled to her.

No answer.

"Your urine was negative, Katie."

"No kidding!" Katie yelled with feigned surprise. "You could have just asked me, you know."

"Did they find who was stealing the morphine in your emergency department?" Margaret asked her.

"No. And the hospital administrator is still giving me the evil eye. I'm not sure what to do."

"Want me to come talk to him?" Bossy yelled.

"Yeah." Katie's voice was softer. "Would you?"

"Give me his name and phone number after the meeting. I'll ring him up in the morning."

Bossy looked at the overweight guy who had taken Valium before the last meeting. He was sitting to my right about three chairs over.

"David," Bossy said. "Have you taken anything today?"

"No. I haven't used anything in three days."

"Will you give us a urine specimen?"

David nodded.

"As a matter of fact, I'll be asking for a urine from you periodically."

"What if I don't want to give you one?"

"Well . . . I'll have to assume you're using drugs again. And steps will have to be taken to protect your patients from you."

"C'mon, Bossy," David asked, reaching for courage, "what difference can a couple of Valiums make?"

Bossy slammed his fist on the table. His eyes were wide, his face red. He pointed at David.

"Don't you ever offend us by asking a question like that again."

Nancy Mary and Charles stood and walked to the door. Nancy Mary opened the door and left. Charles turned toward the group, an angry smile on his face.

"Fuck this!" he said, turned, and hurried out the door.

Bossy looked at Joseph, who was still sitting. He was rubbing the top of his head. He tried hard to smile at Bossy.

"You know where the door is when you need to go, eh?" Bossy said.

Joseph nodded.

"Doc, how are things going?"

Doc was sitting near the opposite end of the table.

"I'm still battling cynicism, Bossy. Sometimes I win. . . . Sometimes I don't. That's a major issue for me now. I'm working on it."

Stacey, the Marlon Brando look-alike, was sitting at the opposite end of the table, next to Doc. Bossy looked at him.

"Stacey, you and Linda still seeing Karren?"

"No!" Stacey said bitterly. "I'm not doing anything with Linda."

"Problems?" Doc asked.

"Yeah," Stacey snarled. "I got problems. I just found out that Linda's pregnant." He shook his head slowly. "It's not mine."

"Joseph, I want you to leave," Bossy commanded. "Now."

Joseph stood as directed and left the room.

Bossy looked at me.

"Maybe you better go, too."

"No. I'm staying."

Bossy stared at me and his eyes widened. His look became intense. There were a few seconds of silence and then he looked back to Stacey.

Stacey was sitting forward with his arms folded on the table. He was staring at an ashtray a few inches in front of him.

I reached over and borrowed a cigarette from David.

"All right, Stacey," Bossy said, "bleed on us."

"Linda told me Sunday morning after I got home from making rounds at the hospital. She told me she loved him. She said we still had too many problems . . . that I was boring . . . I wasn't getting any better . . . I had become an Albatross around her neck . . . She needed to think of herself first." Stacey, a look of anguish on his face, stared at Bossy. " 'Albatross.' She really called me that. Can you believe it?"

"Take it easy, Stacey," Doc said and reached over and touched his forearm.

"Linda had her bags packed and in the car. Before she left, she told me she'd always have fond memories of me. She started to cry.

The last thing she said to me was, 'Please don't be hurt by this.' "
Stacey slumped in his chair.

" 'Don't be hurt . . .' "

"Need a coffee, Stacey?" Margaret asked. "Or a glass of water?"

"No! I don't want anything except . . . to stop hurting."

I noticed Margaret share a worried glance with Bossy.

"I keep wondering how long this has been going on. And why it happened . . . Linda and I had been seeing Karren as some of you know." Stacey had an angry, embarrassed look. "I've been having some problems in the past year or so. I . . . I haven't been able to get it up very often. But it's been better the past three or four weeks."

"What did you do on Sunday after you found out about them?" There was disappointment in Bossy's voice.

"I went home but I couldn't stand to be there . . . not after I looked at our bed. She and I had slept together there the night before. I was numb . . . and shocked. I didn't feel anything. By Sunday night I was restless and disorganized. And hurt."

"And angry," Margaret added.

"I've never been so angry in my life. Do you have any idea how it feels to go to bed at night knowing your wife is in bed with another man? That she prefers someone else? We've been married for twelve . . . almost thirteen years."

"Any kids?" Doc asked.

Stacey shook his head.

"Are you using again?" Bossy appeared to already know the answer.

Stacey nodded. "Sleeping pills and . . . a little booze."

"Then you've relapsed," Bossy said, his anger surfacing. "You've let what should only be a very difficult experience devastate you. We've talked in here a thousand times about putting your health first and of being responsible for yourself. And I'm disappointed that you didn't call me. You have my phone number."

"I didn't call you." Stacey said through clenched teeth, "because I didn't want to hear any of you're fucking clichés. Like I'm hearing now. I'm dying I hurt so much. Slogans are worthless when those lights go out at night . . . I don't care about anything but getting through the night. I'll use anything to make the pain less."

"Are you only using at night?" Doc asked.

Stacey nodded.

"When I'm alone at night I see her in bed with another man. I see hands on her breasts . . ." His voice trailed off and he covered his face with his hands.

I wished I had not heard this. I felt enervated and was beginning to feel depressed. I wished I had gone when Bossy suggested I leave.

"Now do you understand," Stacey asked, his voice plaintive, "why I take those goddamn sleeping pills. I start feeling betrayed . . . and violated . . . and abandoned by the woman I've shared one third of my life with.

"When I came out of Hogarth two years ago, I thought I could live through anything. I thought that nothing could be as difficult as what I experienced here. But compared to what Linda has done to me . . . being in Hogarth was a piece of cake."

"No one in here is going to condone your taking sedatives," Bossy said. "But how can we help you? Do you want to come into the hospital?"

"You should," Margaret said to Stacey. "I'm worried about you. I've never seen you like this. I could never imagine you responding to anything in such a primitive way. Get back into Hogarth."

"Hell, no. The lights have to go out in here, too."

"Why don't you come stay with one of us?" Doc asked. "Stay with me. I live alone."

Stacey shook his head. "I appreciate the offer, Doc. But I don't think it would make a difference."

"Do you know any young women you could stay with . . . and sleep with?" Margaret asked.

"No. I wish I did."

"You can stay with me if you'd like." Katie stood and walked to Stacey. She put her arm on his shoulder and smiled at him. "I won't let you take drugs." Katie looked at Bossy. "So many people in here have helped me. Now I can do something."

I sat on the couch in the lobby and waited for Irene to get out of the physicians' spouses' group meeting. So many things had happened in the three weeks since we had sat on this couch together.

Certainly I was changed. Whether or not I was changed for the better, I was not sure. The drugs would have to be gone from my life forever. I could not compromise on that. I had allowed drugs to be the staple of my security. What a tragically poor choice.

Something would have to replace the drugs. And the only thing I could think of as a viable replacement was Irene. Thank God she still loved me. Thank God I still had her.

Or did I?

"Hi, honey."

Irene practically jumped into the seat on the couch next to me. She threw her arms around me and gave me a big wet kiss on the mouth. I wasn't prepared for her buoyancy.

"What's the matter, Pat? You look so serious."

I told Irene, without mentioning any names, of what had happened to Stacey.

"He was shattered, Babes. I felt so sorry for him."

"I could understand how something like that would happen. If you're not getting what you need at home, you'll probably look somewhere else for it."

"Irene, would you . . . you'd never do anything like that, would you?"

She pursed her lips and looked away from me. In a few seconds she looked at me.

She shook her head.

"No. I couldn't do that. I would divorce you first."

That shocked me.

"You're not thinking about . . . divorcing me . . . are you?"

"Nope." She smiled. "All my energy is going to go into reviving our marriage. I think we really had something special once. And we will again." She hugged me. "I'm not going to leave you, honey."

You've got to get things out in the open. . . . tell Irene about the vasectomy. . . . she has to know, kiddo. . . . tell her now.

I would tell Irene about the vasectomy. . . . I needed a good night's sleep. I felt tired, exhausted. Just one good night's sleep . . .

"He should wake up! He should wake up!"

I opened my eyes but saw only darkness. My heart began pounding, but I remained motionless. Maybe he would go away.

"I've brought Patrick something." There was a gentle quality to Dr. Starr's voice. "I'm trying to help him. Patrick should trust me."

There was no smell of burning incense. No yellow mist. Just his voice.

"I've brought Patrick something," he repeated in a pleasant voice. "But if he doesn't want to see . . ."

"Wait, Dr. Starr, don't go. Where are you?"

"Down here." His voice came from near the foot of my bed.

I sat up and saw some vague images of little people standing on the bed near my feet. The images were bathed in a dim, yellow light.

But even after attempting to focus, I could only determine that Dr. Starr was holding something. There were two small people, a woman and a man, off to his left.

"Patrick can come closer. I want him to see."

I pushed my blanket off and sat up. I had only shorts on, and I felt a cold draft of air hit between my shoulder blades.

I moved toward the images, and the light that was on them suddenly brightened. Dr. Starr was holding the body of a dead young child. The body had a red rash.

"Who is that?" I gasped. "What . . ."

"Does Patrick recognize this poor, dead girl?"

"Yes! It's the child, Susan Nicks, that had meningitis. But she lived. I saw her walk out. . . ."

"The child is dead," Dr. Starr shouted, "because of you!"

"Please don't say that. It's not true. Go away, Dr. Starr. Stop trying to hurt me."

"The child's mother is here." Dr. Starr, holding the dead child, looked to the woman. She was crying, her hands to her face.

"Your child lived," I said to her. "I'm sure. . . ."

"I've brought someone else," Dr. Starr said. "He wants Patrick with him."

I looked from Dr. Starr to the man. His face came into focus.

It was Logan! He was motioning for me.

"Dad . . . what are you doing here? My God!"

"Patrick's father is so disappointed in his only son," Dr. Starr said, stridency in his voice.

"Dad, I'm sorry. Please forgive me."

"There are razor blades in the bathroom," Dr. Starr said, his voice pleasant again. "And it's quiet now. Patrick will not be disturbed."

Logan began pointing toward the bathroom. So did the woman. I could still not see the details of her face.

"Patrick has failed as an adult. He has hurt himself and everyone that cared about him. He doesn't really think he will be able to stay off drugs, does he?"

I shook my head. Dr. Starr was right.

"Death by suicide is the most responsible and appropriate action for Patrick at this time." There was compassion in Dr. Starr's voice. He really did care about me.

I smiled at Logan, stood, and walked to the bathroom.

RANDOLPH'S EXPRESSION became suspicious and unfriendly when he saw me. Toni, who was sitting next to him in the Nurses' Station, gave me a perfunctory smile.

"Good morning, Patrick," Toni said.

I stopped in front of the desk.

"Good morning, Toni."

"How did you sleep?" she asked.

"Not very well."

Randolph's eyebrows raised slightly.

"Why didn't you sleep?" he asked. "Was something wrong?"

"Oh"—I took a deep breath—"it was just one of those nights. I woke up and couldn't get back to sleep."

Randolph stood up quickly and came around in front of the Nurses' Station. He walked a few steps down the hall, turned, and motioned for me.

"We haven't talked in a while," he said. "How are you feeling?"

"Pretty good. Irene's here."

"I know," he said tersely. "I talked to her yesterday."

"You seem irritated with me. Is something wrong?"

"Why didn't you tell me about the Talwin and the Equagesic you took?"

"I did. The first time we talked."

"You told me you took them 'occasionally.' "

I nodded.

"Define 'occasionally,' " he bristled.

"I took Talwin and Equagesic as needed. Sometimes every fourth day . . . every third day"—I gulped—"every other day. But sometimes I'd go a week or two without taking them. It would depend how bad my headaches got."

"You were medicating yourself into another addiction. Talwin is highly addictive."

"I wasn't addicted to Talwin."

"How the hell do you know?" His tone was severe.

"It was *my* addiction," I said angrily. "I'm an authority on it."

"No, you're not. Being an authority on ourselves requires a certain amount of insight. And that is something you sorely lack."

"That's not true."

"How much time do you spend every day doing an honest appraisal of yourself? The folks in A.A. call it a fearless moral inventory."

"I know why I've made the mistakes I've made."

"That's not enough," he said. "I've seen no evidence from you of a commitment to sobriety. That means no mood-altering chemicals, including alcohol, for the rest of your life."

"No alcohol? I didn't abuse alcohol."

"You almost destroyed yourself by abusing sedative drugs. Alcohol is a sedative drug. That's basic pharmacology. Simple logic would dictate . . . !"

I walked a few feet away and leaned against the wall. Randolph followed and stood in front of me only inches away. His breath smelled of cigarettes.

"You've spent more than enough time analyzing, intellectualizing, and feeling bad," he said. He pointed his index finger at my chest. "You need to get your ass into A.A. and do it now. That will help complete the job of saving your life."

"Are you enjoying this?" I asked weakly.

"You've got to have a support system when you get out of here. Or else you'll be out there on a high wire without a net. And eventually . . . eventually you'll fall. Goddamnit, Patrick!" He screamed. "I don't want you to die."

He stood back and with his hand trembling reached in his pocket for cigarettes.

"Can I have one of those?" I asked.

"I didn't know you smoked," he said, as he handed me a cigarette.

"Everyone should have at least one bad habit."

"Is there anything else you'd like to tell me?" He had regained his composure.

I told him about my first hallucination. About Dr. Starr and the doctors I had been in training with and about their deaths. He smiled when I told him about Henry's death from a sustained erection.

"I suppose the hallucination means that you will want to keep me."

"The fact that you've hallucinated *once* won't affect my decision." His eyes narrowed. "Is there anything else you'd like to tell me?"

I shook my head.

"Sometimes, Patrick, I think you're making good progress. But other times . . . you seem impenetrable." He moved his face close to mine. "Get your act together, man, or you'll never get out of here with my approval."

I caught up with Melanie and we walked toward the cafeteria for breakfast.

"I hallucinated again last night."

She touched my arm and we slowed our walking. "That must be so terrible."

"And Randolph did a number on me this morning. Irene must have told him some things."

"I'm sure Dr. Randolph just wants you to get better, Patrick. He's only concerned with your health."

"The man's a certifiable creep. And he enjoys seeing me grovel."

"I think you're wrong about him. It probably is an ego thing between you and him."

"Hey, goddamnit, I spend a lot of time with that jerk. I know what he's like."

Melanie shook her head. "I still think you're wrong."

I stopped.

"Melanie, get off my back! Hell, I'm too angry to eat. I'm going for a walk. See you in group."

I went out a side door and found myself in a parking lot. Several of the parking spaces had small signs with names. The *Dr. Randolph* space had a late-model green Volvo parked in it. The *Dr. O'Malley* space was empty.

I walked to the Volvo, pulled down my zipper, and urinated on the left rear tire.

"I know it didn't happen. But it was so real. They were standing on my bed. Three of them. My father was one of them. They wanted me to kill myself and . . . I agreed."

"Patty . . . you agreed . . . to commit suicide?"

Lucy handed me her cigarettes. As I lit one, I noticed Christine sit up stiffly in her chair. Her expression became cold.

I told the group about my conversation with Dr. Starr.

". . . and my own father was pointing toward the bathroom . . . where the razor blades were. And it seemed he was right.

"When I got to the bathroom, I started looking for the razor blades. I felt good. I was going to do it. But I needed to leave a note. I didn't want people to think this would be an act of desperation.

"I walked back into my room to write the note, and they were gone. At first I was angry. . . . I felt they had betrayed me. I wanted Dr. Starr and Logan to be with me when I died. I sat on my bed for a while. It took a few minutes for me to realize what had happened . . . that I had hallucinated. But it seemed so real.

"I got dressed and left my room. I spent most of the night right here in the lounge reading. Or pretending to read. It was terrible."

"Patty, I'm really upset." Hog Body was slowly running his hands from upper thighs to knees. "I think you better tell the doctors about these dreams."

"Hallucinations," Christine corrected.

"I told Randolph about my first hallucination when I talked to him this morning. He didn't seem to think it was a big deal."

"I think the one you had last night *was* a big deal," Lucy said. She looked to Melanie, who nodded in agreement.

"I agree with Hog Body," Boone said. "You better tell somebody about the one you had last night." He moved forward in his chair. "I'm very concerned, Pat."

"If I told Randolph or O'Malley, it would be one more nail in my coffin. They'd recycle me for sure."

"Boy, you sure are acting like a dumb ass," Steve said to me. "A *real* dumb ass."

"Patrick," Christine said, "you're getting some advice here from people who care about you. If you don't follow their advice, I, for one, am going to stop caring. I have to protect myself."

Christine's statement hurt me. I wanted her to be concerned, to care.

"By the end of group this morning, Patrick, you'll have to tell us if you are going to talk to one of the doctors about the hallucination you had last night." Christine took a deep breath, turned to Melanie and forced a smile.

"Melanie, have you thought any more about the feedback you got from the group yesterday?"

"Yes. I've thought a lot about it. I heard the group telling me things I didn't want to hear. That I used men the same way I abused alcohol and drugs. And Steve and Boone told me they thought I was attractive the way I am now, without alcohol or drugs in me."

"I agree with them," Hog Body interrupted. "I like you the way you are, Melanie. I wouldn't want to see you drunk or on drugs."

"It surprised me that you guys think that way," Melanie said. "I have felt so unattractive . . . so undesirable . . . since I've been here. Scooter told me when he was here that he liked me better when I was using."

"Scooter's a fucking asshole," Steve blurted.

"Scooter is probably feeling threatened by your being here," Christine said. "He's not sure he'll have you on the side when you go home."

"Scooter will not have me in *any* way when I get home. I'm finished with married men"—she looked at me—"once I get out of Hogarth.

"These last few days have been so good for me," Melanie continued. "It was a good feeling to hear that I'm attractive without using stuff. I've been to two A.A. meetings in the last two nights with Lucy and Steve. And I've gotten something out of the meetings. I talked to my mother this morning. I'm going to let her go to my apartment and clear out the alcohol and drugs. I'm starting to feel good about myself." Melanie put her hand to her forehead and started to cry. "I've never felt this good about myself. . . . I've wasted . . . so much time."

Lucy grasped Melanie lightly on the forearm.

"I'm glad we went to those meetings, Melanie. They have helped me, too." Lucy began to blink as her eyes watered.

'You had tried A.A. before, Lucy," Christine said. "And it didn't seem to work for you. What is the difference now?"

"It's the first time I've gone to A.A. when I felt I needed to." Lucy began wiping her eyes. "There is no doubt in my mind that I need A.A. if I'm going to stay sober. I've never felt this way before."

"Will someone please explain to me," I said, "what they gain by going to A.A.? I don't understand."

"I'll tell you why I go," Steve said, with excitement in his voice. "I listen to guys' stories and hear how they've fucked up their lives with alcohol and pills. I see how they're living without it. And see how much happier they are now. It makes me feel good. It makes me think I can do it, too."

"Patrick," Melanie said, "the thing I like the most is the warmth . . . the concern . . . the understanding. The people care about you. They want you to do well."

"And they told me," Hog Body added, "that if I ever feel like drinking again, I can call an A.A. member. They'll help me not to drink."

· 2 5 7 ·

"But I'm not an alcoholic, goddamnit! How can I relate to them?" I was feeling annoyed. "I've never been picked up for drunk driving. . . . I've never gone to a bar, got drunk, and got into a fight. . . . I don't need alcohol. . . . I've never had the shakes. . . . I never . . ."

"Pat," Boone interrupted, "have you ever felt lonely and desperate because of your drug habit?"

"Yes. Of course."

"What about your self-esteem?"

"It's been gone a long time. What's your point?"

"You may not be able to relate to their stories, Pat. But you can relate to their feelings."

"Yeah," Steve said. "What difference does it make how you got to the bottom, as long as you're there?"

"Patty, come to an A.A. meeting with me tonight. See for yourself."

"No, Hog. I don't think I'm ready. Maybe I'll feel different next week."

Silence. Expressionless faces. Once again my group was manipulating me with their silence. I tried, vainly, to resist feeling bad.

"All right, Hog. I'll go to a meeting with you this weekend."

"I hope that you'll be able to generate more enthusiasm than you're showing now," Christine said, disapproval in her tone.

Christine exhaled deeply and slowly made eye contact with each group member.

"Today Hog Body is on the hot seat," she said and smiled at him. "Tomorrow, Saturday, we'll have a group meeting with Karren at ten. Karren will address our concerns on sexual matters. Believe me, Karren has a way of getting people to talk about their sexuality."

Melanie turned to Hog Body and smiled. Hog Body sat up in his chair.

"One more thing," Christine said. "If any of you are to be recycled, you'll find out before group on Monday. If that happens to any of you, please come to group here so we can say good-bye. Anyone who's going to be recycled will leave us and join the new group of patients in Happy Valley."

Recycling . . . my favorite topic.

Hog Body smiled; his teeth were in place. He turned to Christine, who nodded to him.

"I'm from Cochrane," Hog Body said. "That's up North. I have a wife, Helen, that some of you have met, and only two kids, Patty and Angeline. When you live where I do, everybody expects you to have five or six kids. We spent a lot of time indoors in winter. A lot of snow up there."

Hog Body talked about his "daddy," who worked on the train going from Cochrane to Moosonee.

"It's called the Great Northern Express, and I used to ride it with him. I loved him when he wasn't drunk. He died when he was forty-five. They say his liver gave out because of drinking. He had two brothers—both boozers. Both died before they were fifty.

"I'm forty-eight now. . . ." Hog Body's expression became serious, then sad. "My mother said I'd never make it to fifty. She said I'm too much like my father . . . kind . . . gentle . . . and dumb." Hog Body had a questioning look.

"Chrissie, do you think that I might have inherited my alcoholism from my father? One of my brothers is an alcoholic, too."

"Don't quote me on this, anybody, but yes, I think alcoholism is inherited. Whether it's a biochemical thing or an inherited tendency, I don't know. And if that's true, then alcoholism is not, as someone in our group said"—she looked at me—"necessarily a 'disease of choice.' "

"It may not begin as a disease of choice," Lucy said, "but it becomes one. I knew I was an alcoholic years ago. It's only now I'm choosing to do something about it."

"I think that's too simple, Lucy," Boone said, annoyance in his voice. "Alcoholism is not just a disease, it's a life-style. Booze is not something that an alcoholic can give up like that"—he snapped his fingers—"until he's experienced a series of calamities."

"I heard one guy at an A.A. meeting last night say that alcoholics are allergic to alcohol." Steve looked at me. "He said the alcoholic's system just reacts in a bad way to booze."

I shrugged my shoulders.

"I have no idea what you're talking about," I said. "And I'm not relating to this conversation. I'm not an alcoholic, remember?"

"No, but you're still down here with us," Steve said angrily. "And you have just as far up to go as anybody in this room."

I was not sure of the accuracy of Steve's statement. But I chose not to debate it.

"I was probably an alcoholic when I was twenty," Hog Body continued. "I could drink a lot and hardly feel it. I could have fifteen, eighteen shots of rye before I got drunk. Now I get drunk on three ounces."

"That's not unusual, apparently," Lucy offered. "The same thing happened to me. And Dr. Randolph told us about that in his lecture the other day. It has something to do with the liver not working so well."

"Yeah," said Steve. "I'll bet your liver is shot to shit, Hog."

"You have such a nice, delicate way of putting things, Steve," Melanie said.

Steve glared at her.

"Why are you always jumping on my shit, Melanie?"

"It's your style, Steve. Or should I say the lack of it?"

"C'mon you two," Christine interrupted. "This is Hog Body's time."

"I've worked in a mill," Hog continued. "For over twenty-two years. I didn't miss one day of work because of drinking for the first fifteen years. That was one point I always brought up when Helen told me I drank too much.

"I never had more than eight or ten drinks on a weeknight. But, boy, when the weekends came . . . we'd start drinking right after work on Friday and stay drunk until late Sunday afternoon.

"But four or five years ago I continued my drinking on Sunday night. That made Monday mornings pretty rough. I'd have a difficult time getting to sleep on Sunday nights. And Monday mornings I had the shakes so bad . . . I'd have a couple of drinks and that seemed to calm me down.

"About five years ago I started getting really bad . . . couldn't sleep at night, so I'd get up and have a few drinks. I started missing work 'cause I felt so bad. I've missed a lot of Mondays in the last few years. The union has been getting on me about that. They figured I was drinking. They told me that missing work on Mondays is a sure sign of alcoholism.

"So four years ago I stopped drinking for a year. I didn't miss any work, but I was depressed for the whole year I was sober. It just wasn't any fun. But at least I showed Helen I could do it."

"We talked about the difference between abstinence and sobriety at the discussion A.A. meeting on Wednesday night," Boone said and moved forward in his chair. "Abstinence is just stopping drinking. Sobriety implies that there is serenity in your life . . . and some joy. Serenity is the key thing for me. That's something I've never worked on. I've got to learn to forgive . . . forgive myself"—he looked at me—"and forgive some people who have hurt me." He looked back to Hog Body. "When you quit drinking for that year, you weren't experiencing sobriety . . . no serenity, no joy."

Hog Body nodded.

"After I started drinking again, Helen left me and took the kids. She stayed away about a week. She same back when I promised I'd drink less." Hog Body smiled. "I had to drink less. I wasn't able to drink like I used to. I stayed drunk just as much, though."

"If Helen were in Al-Anon, she wouldn't have come back," Christine offered. "Spouses of alcoholics need to know that leaving and staying away is something they may have to do. It's called tough love."

"The past two years have been the worst years of my life, Chrissie. I've been in jail twice for impaired driving. I don't have a driver's license anymore. My kids won't bring their friends home because they're ashamed of me. My union has been pressuring me to come here. One of my buddies died about a year ago because of his drinking. They said the veins in his throat burst and he bled to death in seconds . . . just kept vomiting blood. Boy, that scared me. I stopped drinking for about two weeks.

"But if it hadn't been for that thing with my daughter . . . you know . . . when I undressed her and touched her . . . I'd still be out there drinking . . . and dying."

"Have you talked to Dr. O'Malley about that experience with your daughter?" Melanie asked.

Hog Body nodded.

"Why don't you share with us what you talked about?" Christine said.

"Dr. O'Malley told me to talk with Karren. So I did." Hog Body sat up. "Well, thanks for listening to my story. It's helped, talking about things."

"C'mon, Hog," Steve snapped. "What did you and Karren talk about?"

Hog Body shook his head.

"Don't you trust us?" Lucy asked.

"Sure I trust you. It's just . . . personal . . . and embarrassing. I'm so ashamed of the way I feel about my daughter. I have some strong feelings . . . sexual feelings . . . toward Angeline. Ever since she started developing . . . you know, like a woman . . . I've started looking at her . . . thinking about her . . . she's got the nicest little behind, just like her mother. I put my arm around her sometimes, and I'll let my hand fall on her breast. It's best when she's not wearing a bra." Hog Body looked at the floor. "I love to feel her nipples. They're so small. I remember her having that orgasm . . . the way she moved . . . her little cry. . . ." Hog Body's shoulders began to move as he started to cry silently. "Goddamn . . . I'm getting erect."

Hog Body's face turned red as he pulled his knees together and folded his arms on his lap.

"I'm sorry . . . please forgive me." He looked at Christine, a pitiful grimace on his face. "Can I be excused for the rest of this morning?"

"What does the group think?" Christine asked, as she looked at each of us.

"Sure," Melanie said to Hog Body. "It's all right with me if you need to leave."

"Well, it's not all right with me." Lucy was looking into her purse. She pulled out a new pack of cigarettes. "We can't help you if you're not here, Hog Body. Please stay."

"Stay with us, Hog," I said and smiled at him. "Leaving when you're feeling vulnerable is the wrong thing to do. I speak from experience."

"Hog Body, I need to identify something." Christine had an admiring smile. "I've finally realized what there is about you that I find so attractive. You can expose the most difficult, the most intimate things, without a trace of self-pity. That puts you light years ahead of most of us. Myself included. It's helped me a great deal to have you in my group."

Hog Body, with tears still running from his eyes, smiled weakly. He nodded a thank-you to Christine.

"Tell us what Karren said, Hog." There was an insistence in Boone's tone.

Hog Body spent a few seconds wiping the tears from his face and then blew his nose.

"Well, Karren said that the first step was to identify my feelings about my daughter as a problem. I've done that. The next thing I needed to do was to explain how I felt to Helen. So Helen and I met with Karren, and I explained everything to her. Helen got angry. She said I was disgusting . . . called me a pervert."

"That must have hurt," I offered.

"Well, no, not really. Karren had told me in advance Helen would probably react that way. Karren really helped us. She got us through the session. My problem is out in the open now where it should be. Helen and I can discuss it. And Karren is going to refer us to a therapist back home."

Hog Body bent forward and stared at the floor. After a few seconds he sat back. There was a smile on his face.

"You know, Chrissie, I've"—he paused and looked at each of us—"there are a lot of changes I have to make in my life. But I will make any changes I have to. I never want to feel this bad again. I will never hurt anyone in my family again. I'll die first."

"Hog Body," Christine said, an admiring look on her face, "thanks for sharing so much of yourself with us. I have such a good feeling about you." Christine smiled and looked around the room. "There's a lot of enthusiasm for recovery in this group. I love to experience that. It makes me feel good about each of you . . . and about me."

Christine turned to me.

"Well, Patrick, have you decided whether or not you're going to tell one of the doctors about your second hallucination?"

"Yes. I'll try to see O'Malley this morning. I'll tell him everything."

"And you will go to an A.A. meeting this weekend?" Christine asked, friendliness creeping into her voice.

I nodded.

"I think you should go to at least two, Pat," Boone said, authority in his voice.

"I agree with Boone," Lucy offered.

"Me, too," Steve said.

"All right. I'll go to two meetings."

Christine was looking at me, a cordialness in her expression that made me feel good.

"I want you to know, Patrick, that I'm feeling close to you again," Christine said. "And I do care about you. You're worth the risk."

O'Malley looked at his watch.

"I can give you exactly one minute," he said. "I have a patient at noon."

"You've been eating popcorn again. I can smell it."

He rested his forearms on his desk. The fingers of his right hand began tapping.

"Would you explain to me," I asked, "why you have these little spotlights in your office instead of normal lights?" I looked at his fish tank. "You have nice clean water in the tank. But you still don't have any fish."

He looked at his watch.

"Now you have thirty seconds."

"I've hallucinated twice."

He slowly reached for his phone and pushed the dial button: "Tell my next patient I'll be running late. Maybe ten minutes."

O'Malley looked at me for a few seconds, a studied calm expression on his face. He stiffly sat back and rested his elbows on the arms of his chair. His hands formed a triangle in front of his face.

"Talk to me," he said.

I told him everything about the first hallucination.

"Why didn't you tell me about this when it happened?" He closed his eyes and shook his head. "Never mind. Tell me about the second one."

I told him about Dr. Starr holding the dead child, the child's crying mother, and Logan.

"Dr. Starr was the only one that spoke. He convinced me that I should kill myself and told me to go into the bathroom and get the razor blades. My father pointed toward the bathroom, too. And so I went to the bathroom. . . . I wonder if I would have actually done it."

"You haven't had any suicidal thoughts, have you?"

"No."

"I haven't considered you to be at risk for suicide," he said. "And I still don't." He sat up and began writing. "But we better start suicide precautions with you. First, we'll get those razor blades out of your room."

"Do you think I would have done it?"

"No. Your desire for survival is much too strong. Hallucinatory suggestion can be very persuasive, but your subconscious would have resisted. And I doubt if you are capable, at this time, of such a lethal act."

"But you're still going to take away my razor blades."

"Let me review this," he said. "In your first hallucination you saw images, you heard voices, you touched the main character, and you smelled incense. Did you taste anything?"

"No."

"Last night you just saw images and heard voices."

"Yes. And I talked to Dr. Starr."

"So your second hallucination was less complex and briefer than the first. That's a good sign. Hallucinations during drug withdrawal are fortunately self-limited."

"I remember you and Randolph telling me about Presswood. How he became psychotic and actively hallucinated after he came off Valium and . . ."

"You will not become psychotic, Patrick. Nor will you go around abusing people with crude and tactless remarks like Presswood does. Your inhibitions are still intact . . . for the most part."

" 'For the most part'? Couldn't you be a little more reassuring?"

"It's your anger that concerns me, Patrick. Unless you learn how to deal with your anger, you have the potential of being just as offensive as Presswood." O'Malley sat forward and rested his forearms on the desk in front of him. "Showing anger is a new experience for you, and you are not doing it productively. And until you learn what to do with your anger, it will become an increasingly unmanageable emotion for you."

"My father was angry all the time, and his anger is what kept me from ever feeling close to him. When I was growing up, I wasn't allowed to be angry."

"Some people use their anger as an emotional battering ram. They intimidate with it . . . gives them a sense of power. That sounds like what your father did. Using anger as a weapon has some short-term gratification. But in the long run, it's personally destructive."

"My sister has already told me that she has seen glimpses of my father in me when I get angry. I don't want to become like him."

"Good. Then you've identified your inability to deal with anger as a problem. That's the first step."

"I've identified a lot of things as problems, goddamnit. I want some solutions."

The fingers of O'Malley's right hand began tapping on the desk.

"I'm going to recommend that when you get back to Cleveland, you get with a therapist. Preferably someone who has a group, so you can identify and verbalize feelings. You'll need that. This will be in addition to the A.A. meetings, of course."

"Of course."

Lorenzo was sitting behind the Nurses' Station and looking up at Toni, who was standing with her back to the hallway.

Lorenzo waved as I approached them. Toni turned her head and looked at me. A genuine smile appeared on her face.

"Hi, Patrick."

"Well, Toni, you certainly seem more pleasant than you were this morning."

"When Toni disapproves of something you've done," Lorenzo

said, "she starts acting like a head nurse. When she talks, her lips don't move, and she gets a certain tone to her voice."

"I'll get a certain tone to my right foot," she snapped at Lorenzo, "if you want to keep talking like that."

"About a year ago we had a bachelor party for a pediatrician in Cleveland. They showed a porno flick, *Hilda, Head Nurse*. That nurse did some wonderful things for her patients, Toni . . . wonderful things."

"I bet Toni could do some of those things, Patrick. And do them well."

Toni pointed her finger at Lorenzo.

"Well you, turkey, will never know."

"I shouldn't tell you this, Lorenzo, but I've seen Toni look at you a few times and start to get excited. Her feet start to move . . . her hands twitch . . . and some saliva starts running out the corner of her mouth. I think it's called drooling."

Toni glared at me. "You liar! You've never . . ."

"Hey," Lorenzo interrupted, "that happens to a lot of women when I come around them. Women find me highly desirable." He shrugged his shoulders and looked at Toni. "Some of us have it—look at me—and some of us don't—look at Patrick."

"I don't know what you think you have," Toni said, her voice rising. "It's certainly nothing that's apparent."

The phone at the Nurses' Station rang, and Toni walked over to answer it.

Lorenzo bent toward me, a broad smile on his face.

"I love to get her going," he whispered. "She takes things so seriously." He sat back. "How come you're not with your wife? Where is she?"

"I was supposed to have lunch with her, damnit, but I'm told the spouses asked for a session with Karren. That's where Irene is. Must have something to do with sex."

"Patrick," Lorenzo's voice was lowered, "have you had any problems . . . sexually?"

I nodded.

"Impotent?"

I continued to nod.

"Me too," Lorenzo said. "It's been almost a year."

"You haven't been able to get it up for a year!"

"Shhh"—he put his index finger to his lips—"not so loud. Toni might hear."

"What have you done about it? Did you see anybody?"

"Yeah. But he couldn't help. He said there was too much hostility between me and Janice. He said . . ."

Toni put down the phone and, smiling, came toward us.

Lorenzo sat back in his chair, arms folded across his chest.

"Tell us what Hilda did for her patients, Patrick. That may give Toni some ideas. Then she can practice on you and me."

"Yeah, go ahead," Toni said to me as she sat down. "Tell me about Hilda. Tell me what Hilda did to her patients, and in graphic detail. Use hand gestures, too."

My face warmed.

"C'mon, Patrick. We're waiting."

"C'mon, man. Tell us. Toni's starting to drool."

I could say nothing. I tried to smile but felt foolish.

"C'mon, man, don't let me down."

Toni turned to Lorenzo.

"The hell with Hilda," she said. "I don't need any new ideas. What would you like?"

Lorenzo's eyes widened in surprise.

"Well . . . I need some stimulation," he said, smiling.

"I can do that," Toni said, a challenging semismile on her face. "Do you want it here or in your room?"

"What I want is probably not in your job description."

"I improvise when I have to," Toni said and stood. "Let's go to your room."

Lorenzo looked to the floor, and an embarrassed smile appeared on his face.

"C'mon, Mister Macho, let's go. I don't have all day."

Lorenzo slouched in his chair. He raised his hands meekly as if surrendering.

Toni looked at me, a challenging look still on her face. "What about you?" she asked.

I raised my hands and surrendered, too.

"Well, gentlemen," Toni said, smiling pleasantly, "I've enjoyed this. But now, if you'll excuse me, I have some work to do."

Lorenzo stood and walked off, shoulders drooping. There was a sad look on Toni's face as she watched him go.

"Toni, I haven't seen Reggie in a couple of days. Will she be here tonight?"

"That was Reggie who called a minute ago. She asked if I could work her shift tonight in Happy Valley."

"Is she sick?"

"No. It's something to do with her ex-husband and her son."

"Good news, I hope. She told me how her marriage ended and about her son, Jason."

"Oh, well, I guess I can tell you the good news, then. Jim, her ex, told her she could come over and see Jason tonight. She hasn't seen him in a year."

"That's good news, Toni. I'm glad you told me."

"Reggie is one of the nicest people I've ever met," Toni said, sadness in her voice. She sat down. "There are some women who just should be a wife and a mother. Reggie's one of those."

"Maybe she'll get back with her ex-husband," I said.

"I hope it happens. Reggie desperately needs some intimacy in her life." Toni paused, a concerned expression on her face. "You need intimacy, too, Patrick." She looked down the hall. "And so does Lorenzo. God! Does he need it. It seems that every patient that I've known in my seven years here has managed to damage and sometimes completely destroy the relationship with the person they've been the closest to."

"We isolate ourselves emotionally, Toni. We became preoccupied with getting our supply of pills . . . or booze . . . or both. My drugs were more important to me than my wife. I thought I could live without Irene. I didn't think I could live without the drugs. My whole life was structured around my addiction. Intimacy hasn't been important to me for the last few years. I've had this unsatisfying, sterile relationship with those goddamn drugs. But I was trapped. And I didn't know what to do."

"You know now, Patrick. Your pattern of addiction has been interrupted, hopefully ended. It's all up to you. Now you can choose to stay clean. How does that make you feel?"

"Frightened."

"I'll give you our last table," the hostess snapped. "People make reservations when they come here. We usually never have an empty table at this time." Her eyes were slanted down and in toward her nose, and her eyebrows were sparse, the only suggestions of Oriental ancestry. She looked at us as if she were waiting for an apology. "You're just visiting Toronto, I suppose?"

"Yes," Irene said.

"I've been here about a dozen times for dinner," I lied. "I've never needed reservations before."

Her mouth opened in disbelief. Her eyes widened.

"Follow me, please," she said, her tone no longer officious.

The lights were dimmed maybe a litttle too much. All the tables had lighted candles, and everyone's complexion was unflawed, all faces appearing freshly waxed.

Irene and I were seated at a small table near a wall, and until the Chinese busboy lit the two candles at our table, I could see Irene only as a dark image.

The light from the candles softly illuminated Irene's face and hair. She looked stunning. Her auburn hair had become more red than brown in the past few years, and by candlelight, her hair became a dark mahogany.

"Denise Bossy said this place has the best sweet and sour pork in Toronto. Thanks for bringing me here, honey."

"Too bad they don't serve Moon Pies, Babes. You'd probably be speaking in tongues now."

Irene's expression brightened.

"You have a Moon Pie in your purse, don't you?"

She nodded.

"Those things are so damn sweet. I don't know why all your teeth haven't fallen out, Irene. I'd like to feed one of those Moon Pies to Hog Body. I bet they'd be too sweet even for him." I pulled out a pack of cigarettes that Lucy had given me. "And Hog Body will eat anything. Often without chewing."

Irene did not even attempt to mask her disappointment as she watched me light my cigarette.

"You haven't smoked in years, Pat. Please don't start."

"I've already started. It's too late. I'm hooked."

The waiter came to take our order for cocktails. I ordered tea. Irene asked for a ginger ale.

"It's all right if you want to order your bourbon presbyterian, Babes. It won't bother me."

"I don't need it. Besides, they told us not to drink in front of you for a while."

"I'm not an alcoholic, Irene. I have every intention of drinking again some day. I suppose I shouldn't drink for a while, though. Maybe a year."

"Pat! Do you hear what you're doing? You're prescribing for yourself. That's wrong. What does Dr. Randolph say about you drinking again?"

"Screw Randolph. He doesn't believe anything I say. Especially after you got through talking to him. Why did you tell him about the Talwin and Equagesic I take occasionally? You really hurt me by doing that."

"He asked me what else you took. I told him."

"Irene, you are rapidly becoming a serious pain in the ass."

"Pat! Don't talk to me like that. You never . . ."

The waiter was at our table with the tea and ginger ale. He sensed our discomfort with his presence and mumbled: "Come back soon for order," and walked away.

"Let's not fight, Irene. We don't have much time."

"They told us that your emotions would be raw, and that we might see you reacting to things erratically . . . and angrily. But wow! Pat. Take it easy. Please. When I stopped you from buying those aspirins before we got to the restaurant," she bent forward, "you told me to 'fuck off.' Honey, I'm not used to your anger. I don't know how to react to it. But I do know I don't like it."

"I don't know how to put a leash on my anger, yet. It will take some time."

She smiled at me.

"I wish you'd just be your old passive-manipulative self, Pat. I didn't like that, either. But at least I could handle it."

I picked up my cup of tea and held it in front of me. Irene held her glass of ginger ale up; we touched glass to cup and silently toasted each other.

Ten years before we had toasted each other for the first time. It was our wedding night, and we were both nervous. We were in a lounge somewhere near the Cleveland airport.

Irene asked me that night to write her something on the napkin on the table. And she would do the same for me.

I wrote:

> "Irene,
> "Promise never to stop loving me
> "And I'll promise never to assume I deserve it."

She wrote:

> "Honey,
> "The exhilaration I feel right now,
> "loving you,
> "Is something I thought could only be imagined."

I remember thinking about love then in clinical terms. It was a condition that could be defined only in terms of its symptoms—like a mental illness. When I was with Irene, there was nowhere else I would rather be. I cared about her welfare as much as I did my own. And I wanted, definitely wanted, to live the rest of my life with her.

Everything was so easy. So simple. Problems would be easily conquered. Sex would be often and great. I would never be lonely.

No one told us how unprepared we were for marriage. No one ever talked of the need for skills at negotiating and communication. And what did commitment really mean? And equality? And what about the art of being fair? Is it possible to disagree without arguing? Without trying to dominate? To criticize without aspersions? Without hidden agendas? Without self-serving motives? Is it possible to listen to criticism without feeling threatened? Without getting defensive? Without getting hurt?

In the ten years of our marriage, Irene had grown and expanded without me. I had chemically stunted my emotional growth. We were at different places. She was secure and strong in most areas of her life. I was a kitten rapidly and unexplainedly growing a lion's mane.

Eating dinner with Irene was enjoyable. She had ordered sweet and sour pork, and I ordered diced chicken with cashews. It was nice not having to search my food for any visceral organs. One of the cashews, however, was shaped like an adrenal gland, and I did not eat it.

I had promised myself that I would not talk about Hogarth during dinner, but there was little else I could think of. And Irene kept asking questions.

"What's your day like?"

"We have to be out of bed by seven, we have to take a shower, and then we have fifteen minutes of quiet time. Then we go to breakfast. After breakfast we see a movie on alcoholism or drug abuse. We talk for a while about our response to the film. After that we have Group Therapy. I've never had an experience quite like Group Therapy. It's . . . difficult. Then we have lunch. After that we have a relaxation class with Karren. You've met with her, haven't you?"

Irene nodded and started to say something, but stopped.

"After relaxation we have a talk. It may be on nutrition or how to deal with stress or the need for daily exercise or things we can do with our spare time . . . hobbies and stuff like that.

"Then we have an exercise class. After class we see a videotape which is a talk on how we physically, emotionally, and spiritually destroy ourselves with alcohol and drugs. Once or twice we have had people from A.A. come in and talk to us. O'Malley and Randolph have each lectured to us once."

"Sounds like you have a full day. What about the evenings?"

"We're free to do anything we want. We're supposed to go to A.A. meetings."

"Dr. Randolph told me you don't involve yourself in A.A. How come?"

"I'm not an alcoholic."

"But Dr. Randolph . . ."

"Fuck Randolph! I don't want to hear his name anymore, Irene. Please . . . But my group told me they thought I should give A.A. a try. I made a commitment to them to go to two meetings this weekend."

Irene had a quizzical look.

"You'll do what your group tells you to do, but not what your doctor suggests?"

"My group cares about me. I love them . . . and I trust them."

Near the end of dinner, Irene's face took on a fatigued expression which meant that she was preoccupied with something that was bothering her. I knew better than to ask her what was wrong. She would only get annoyed.

I had plotted with Hog Body to keep Helen out of the motel room she shared with Irene.

"Patty," Hog Body had said, "I promise I won't bring Helen back to the room until ten-thirty. So take your time."

I figured that Irene and I would get back to the motel room about eight o'clock. That would give us enough time to take a shower and then I could be alone with and make love to the woman who was as necessary to me as breathing.

After we made love and we were holding each other, I would tell her about the vasectomy.

I had felt a fullness in my groin several times during dinner. And while eating my fortune cookie, I had an erection that could have been used as a weapon. It even knocked the napkin off my lap. Being resourceful, I pulled the tablecloth so it covered my lap up to my waist. But I was sure that everyone in the restaurant knew Patrick Reilly was having a giant erection and that they were looking at me, some with repulsion, some with amazement.

"I'm not looking forward to walking out of this restaurant," I said to Irene. "Someone could lose an eye."

"Oh, yeah," Irene said, hearing me but not caring to find out what I meant.

"Tell me what's wrong, Babes."

"Can we go to church together on Sunday morning?"

"No. We have a general meeting on Sunday morning that we're all required to be at. I don't think I'd want to go anyways. God is no friend of mine."

Irene kept her fatigued expression. She started to nervously fold her napkin.

"Please tell me what's wrong, Babes."

Irene kept her eyes on the napkin.

"Pat, if they suggest you stay . . . you know, for another three weeks . . . I think you should do what they say."

"You're kidding. . . . I know you're kidding. You can't mean that."

She looked at me, but her eyes moved quickly back to the napkin, which she began to unfold.

"They've got to you. I know how persuasive they can be. I guess I've lost you. . . . you're on their side now."

"This is not a question of taking sides, Pat. You've got to understand. . . ."

"And I was looking forward to you coming here."

"Honey, I just want you to get well . . . so we can be happy again. We had something once that was so special."

"Go home, Irene. I don't want you here."

She moved forward and placed her hands on mine.

"Listen, honey, I know you're mad. I know you're disappointed. But I have to tell you how I feel. You're sick. You've got to do what they say."

"You've betrayed me, Irene. You've really let me down. And this is when I needed you most."

"Pat, I want you to get better for both of us. I want you home so badly. I need you, honey. But I need you healthy. I don't ever want to relive the last few years. And I know you don't, either."

"I suppose you think you're doing the right thing. But you're wrong. Dead wrong."

"Please don't be angry with me, honey. I really"—she was starting to cry—"miss you. You know I have to sleep on your side of the bed at night. When you left, I would stare at your side of the bed and . . . you weren't there. And sometimes when I fell asleep I'd wake up and find myself . . . reaching for you . . . trying to touch you."

I could sense Irene's pain, and I watched her cry. I felt terrible. I didn't want her to hurt so much. And she was hurting because of me. And in my anger I had been pointedly and deliberately cruel.

I didn't know what to say. I felt so deeply ashamed of myself for hurting her. A simple apology would have been so trite and an understatement of how bad I felt. But I wanted her to know.

I could feel tears in the inside corners of both my eyes. I reached for my napkin and started to bring it to my face. But I looked at Irene, who was still crying, and put the napkin back on the table. She glanced at me and saw the tears on my face. A small smile began to form on her lips.

She knew.

The shower water beating down on my back was a little warmer than what I would have liked. But I didn't care. Irene's hair was getting wet from the water bouncing off my shoulders.

I turned her around and stood to the side and let the water hit her on the back. She had brought a bar of Savon Muguet, our favorite soap, from Cleveland, and I started to soap her back.

Irene went slightly limp, as she always did when I started to lightly rub the spot on her waist at the side near the highest point of her pelvis. She had referred to that spot as her "passion point."

"Never touch me there," she had said years before, "unless you mean business."

I was fully and securely erect. And I definitely "meant business."

During Karren's meeting with Irene and the other spouses, Karren had advised that, if there were sexual problems in the relationship, a conference should be set up with the spouses with Karren before attempting a sexual encounter.

When Irene had told me that, after we got to the motel room, I took her hand and put it on my lap.

"I don't think that will be necessary," I told Irene, and I saw her face brighten. "You see, these people are not infallible."

We moved in the shower so that her back was to the water, and she took the soap from me. She began rubbing my chest and then moved in close. We kissed, and when her tongue slid out of my mouth, she started to slowly lick my lips. The soap dropped and banged loudly on the floor of the tub.

Her tongue was on my neck now . . . then my chest . . . my nipples. Her breathing was audible and labored. I grabbed her shoulders.

"Irene, let's go to bed. Now."

"In a minute," she whispered into my chest. Her hands moved to my genitals. "It's been so long . . . I want to enjoy this."

Her hands started moving slowly.

"Please . . . let's go to bed. . . . please . . . Irene . . . stop. . . ."

"Pat! No!"

I had ejaculated on her stomach.

THERE WAS a knock on my door. Since it was early Saturday morning, that could only mean one person.

"C'mon in, Ruthy. When did you start knocking?"

A balding, round head appeared as the door opened.

"Hey, Hog. What are you doing up so early?"

Hog Body came in and closed the door.

" 'Morning, Patty. Did I give you enough time alone with Irene last night?"

"More than enough time. Thanks."

"You seem pretty low. How come you're still in your suit?" He looked at my bed, which had not been slept in. "Let's go downstairs and get a coffee, Patty. Maybe we should talk."

"Yeah, I need to talk to somebody. Let's get out of here before Ruthy comes."

"Patty, do you"—Hog Body looked at his cup of coffee—"do you think you'll be ready to go home next Friday?"

"I don't know, Hog. Up until last night I thought so. But even if I'm not ready, I couldn't stay. I just couldn't. The thought of staying three extra weeks here is torturing. Would you stay if they said you should be recycled?"

"I wouldn't like it," Hog Body said, still looking at his coffee.

"But you'd stay?"

Hog Body looked up and smiled. "This hospital has been here a long time treating folks like you and me. We've got to trust some-body."

"I'll save my blind faith for God. And I'm not even too sure about that anymore. But let's not talk about that. I need some advice, Hog."

I told Hog Body about my vasectomy.

"I had it done five or six years ago, when Irene was in Mexico. She doesn't know. I told her I was sterile because of a massive exposure to X rays. God, I've lied so much to that woman. When I told her I was sterile, she wanted to adopt. But I haven't wanted to do that, either. I didn't want to take the responsibility of a child while I was a drug addict. And I never thought I'd be able to get off the stuff."

"What are you afraid of most, Patty? What's the worst thing that could happen?"

"I'm afraid Irene will leave me."

"Well, that's something you'll have to chance. You do have to tell her. And don't put it off anymore."

"I was going to tell her last night. After we made love, and when we'd be in bed holding each other."

"What happened?"

"I left my love in the shower. Hog, in the space of three weeks, I've gone from being impotent to becoming a premature ejaculator. I don't know which is more embarrassing. So I've got two issues that I have to deal with. And I'm afraid of both of them."

Hog Body moved his chair closer, put his massive forearms on the table, and folded his hands. He had surrounded his cup of coffee, as if protecting it.

"I stayed up all night, Hog, trying to decide what to do."

"Did you come up with anything . . . any decisions?"

"You said in group that you and Helen met with Karren and talked about the problem you have with your daughter. I suppose I should do the same thing with Karren and Irene."

Hog Body nodded.

"I think that's a good idea. Karren sure helped me and Helen. But I'm surprised that someone hasn't suggested that you do this before. Haven't you talked to Dr. O'Malley or Karren about this?"

I looked Hog Body in the eyes and didn't answer. I did not have to.

"Patty, when are you going to start listening to people? Every-body here . . ."

"Don't lecture me," I snapped and slammed my fist on the table. "I don't need that."

"You wouldn't listen anyway."

"Fuck off, Hog."

I started to get out of my chair, when Hog Body slapped me across the mouth. I was pushed back into the chair.

In a few seconds a stinging, burning sensation came to my face. And I could taste blood in my mouth.

"Damnit, Hog, that hurt."

"Good," he said, and a broad, toothless smile appeared on his face. "Think about me hitting you the next time you go to curse somebody."

"I guess I deserved that," I said, as I gingerly rubbed my face.

Hog Body handed me a napkin and pointed to the left corner of his mouth. "Blood," he whispered. "I'm going to get another coffee. Want one?"

I handed him my cup. I felt my lip beginning to swell. I also felt deflated.

"You O.K.?" Hog Body asked, when he returned to the table. He put my coffee in front of me.

I nodded.

"Hog, I need to tell Irene about the vasectomy. But what's the best way? Should I tell her when we meet with Karren?"

Hog Body grimaced and shook his head.

"No, I wouldn't use Karren for that."

A pensive, almost worried expression came to his face. He drank some coffee, and I lit a cigarette. It was awkward and painful trying to smoke with my lip swollen.

"I think you should have another person there when you tell her, Patty. You know who I'd want with me? Chrissie! I'd want Chrissie to be with me."

"Yeah. I like that idea. I'll ask her after our session today. Thanks for the advice, Hog. Let's get some breakfast."

I started to get out of my chair, but Hog reached over and grasped my forearm.

"Patty . . . your lip . . . it doesn't hurt too much, does it?"

"Morning, Babes, did I wake you up?"

"No. Helen and I just got back from breakfast. How are you feeling, Pat?"

"A lot better than I felt last night. I really blew it again."

"You didn't look so good when you left here. I was worried about you, honey."

"What happened last night may have been the jolt I needed. I stayed up all night thinking about how I've been screwing up."

"I'm not sure what you mean, Pat."

"I've been something less than the ideal patient. I've been refusing to do a lot of things they've suggested. I've got to change my attitude."

"I'm so glad to hear you say that. You sound sincere."

"Babes, there are a couple of difficult things I have to do yet. And I need you for both of them."

"Is one of them the problem we're having . . . you know . . . making love?"

"Irene! Is Helen in the room with you listening to this?"

"No," she laughed. "Helen's in the shower."

"Well, yeah, that's one problem we're going to need some help with. Let's try to meet with Karren."

"All right, Pat. But I don't know when it will be. I'm leaving tomorrow morning. I can't come back until next Friday."

"Well, I guess we'll meet with her then. That's the day you'll be taking me home."

"What's the other problem, Pat?"

"I can't tell you over the phone, Babes. It's a big one, though. When I tell you about it, I want Christine to be with us."

"I don't understand, Pat. Why can't you tell me when we're alone?"

"Because I'm afraid of what your reaction will be. And I'll need some support. It's really going to be difficult."

"Pat is it . . . another woman. Is that why you haven't touched me in six months? I hope . . ."

"No, Babes. It's not another woman. It's . . . worse."

"A man? Are you involved with a man?"

"No . . . God, no. We'll talk about it this afternoon. Please don't ask me any more questions, Irene."

"Helen's out of the shower now, Pat. I'll be at the hospital about two. We're going to Eaton Center now, and then we're meeting Denise Bossy for lunch. See you later, Pat. I love you."

"I love you, Babes. Remember that."

Karren and Christine were standing near the door of the lounge talking. Our group sat waiting, drinking coffee and smoking cigarettes.

"What happened to your lip, Patrick? It's swollen." Melanie touched my jaw just below the swelling. "It looks like it hurts."

"Behavior modification—Hog Body-style."

Melanie's eyes widened in surprise, and she looked from me to Hog Body, who was sitting a few feet to my left. Hog Body saw her looking at him, winked at her, and nodded.

"Well, Patrick, you must have deserved it," Melanie said and reached for her cigarettes.

Melanie had on a white T-shirt with the words California Soccer Club in bright red letters on the front. She was wearing brief cutoff jeans. Her legs were smooth, and some tiny blond hairs on her upper thighs were glistening, caught by the sun coming in the room. She had a pair of high-top black canvas tennis shoes that appeared old and battered enough to have been through the Korean conflict. Her breasts bounced slightly as she brought her feet up and sat cross-legged on the chair.

"How did you and Irene do last night?" Melanie asked, a trace of resentment in her voice.

I shook my head and a pleased expression came to Melanie's face.

"Melanie," Boone called out, "sit just like that and don't move." He was smiling and staring at her crotch.

"Perversion reigns supreme!" she exclaimed, as if quoting a line from a play. She untangled her legs and sat up. She glared at Boone. "Will you be able to keep it in your pants now?"

"Hey, Melanie," Steve yelled, "nice tennis shoes."

"Hey, Steve," Melanie called back, "bingo." And flashed him her middle finger.

I put my hand on Melanie's forearm and moved close to her.

"You seem pissed off this morning," I said to her. "What's wrong?"

"I'm going out today for the first time," she said. "I'm nervous."

"You going alone?"

"No, my mom's picking me up after lunch. We're going to my apartment and I'm going to let her take all my booze and pills."

"You told us that yesterday, and you were smiling about it."

"That was yesterday," she snapped. "It's just that . . . well, I have some well-entrenched resentments toward my parents. Especially my mother."

"It sounds as if you don't want to let her act like a mother, Melanie. Give her a chance."

"She's had twenty-six years, Patrick. It may be too late."

The door of the lounge closed with surprising loudness. I tensed. Lucy abruptly pulled her hand off Steve's knee. We remained silent as Karren and Christine came toward us. Karren was carrying some sheets of paper in one hand and a handful of pens in the other.

Karren was several inches taller than Christine, and her short red hair was wet and brushed behind her ears. Karren was athletically trim and walked with her shoulders held back. She had a strong, confident stride.

Christine was trim, too, probably from dieting. Her light blond hair was parted in the middle and fell over her ears to her shoulders. She had an erect posture and a casual manner which gave her an unassuming grace. Intimacy would come easily to her.

Karren sat in the empty seat to my right and placed the paper and pencils on the table. Christine sat on the couch next to Hog Body. I was uncomfortable sitting next to Karren, but I nodded to her and smiled. She looked at me with an unreadable expression and neither smiled nor nodded.

I noticed Hog Body, his teeth in place, smile at Karren and give her a thumb-up sign with his right hand. It was a private message which seemed inappropriate in the group setting.

"Does anyone have anything to say before we begin?" Christine asked after she had made eye contact with each of us.

Silence.

"Well, then . . ."

"Excuse me," Karren interrupted, "but if I'm going to stay in here with all this cigarette smoke, I'm going to have to open a window." She got up and passed in front of me going toward the windows. "I hope no one minds."

Karren had an extraordinarily good figure. But I didn't respond to her with any prurience.

"I guess we all know why we're here," Christine said as Karren returned to her chair. "We've set aside this time to address concerns any of us have over sexual matters. Problems are never solved unless they're identified and discussed. I've asked Karren to join us as a resource person. She'll also be our facilitator."

Christine nodded to Karren, who was slouching in her chair. Karren slowly moved into an upright position, placed her elbows on the arms of her chair, and bent slightly forward.

"First, some ground rules," Karren said as she looked at each of us. "I'll discuss anything you want to talk about as long as it's of genuine concern. I like things to be as specific as possible. But no one will be required to say anything. I'm not here to embarrass anyone or make any of you feel uncomfortable."

Karren began smoothing down the wet hair near the back of her neck. She then looked toward the open window, and I became conscious of the cold air that was coming in the room.

"We are all sexual beings," she continued. "And that is as it should be. Most of the patients who came here are dissatisfied with their sex lives. For many the dissatisfaction stems from the lack of sexual activity with a partner. For others, it's because they're sexually dysfunctional. I'm sure the problems that you folks have will be fairly representative of all the patients who have ever been in Hogarth."

Karren reached for the stack of paper, which was in individual sheets, and the pencils and passed them around.

"I want each of you to write on the sheet of paper any sexual problems you may be having. Something that is keeping your sex life from being as good as it could be. Don't sign your name. In a few minutes, I'll ask you to turn the papers in to me and we'll discuss your problems anonymously."

Karren got up and walked to the open window, folded her arms across her chest, leaned against the wall, and looked out the window.

I folded my sheet of paper several times and placed it in the palm of my left hand. I moved my shoulders forward so that Melanie couldn't see what I was writing.

"Wait a minute," Melanie called out and placed the paper and pencil on the table in front of her. "Do we really need to do this? We've been together for three weks. We've shared plenty of things about ourselves openly. Why can't we do that now?"

I felt like gagging Melanie.

Steve put his paper and pencil on the table.

"I'll go along with Melanie," he said. "But I don't have any problems, anyway."

Boone and Lucy put their papers and pencils on the table at the same time. Christine was next. Hog Body and I stared at each other.

Hog Body slowly put his pencil and paper on the table. I did the same and turned and gave Melanie a dirty look.

Karren stood in front of her chair with a surprised, delighted look.

"This doesn't surprise me," Christine said to Karren.

Karren sat and looked at Melanie.

"Well, Melanie, why don't you start?"

Melanie reached for her cigarettes, took one from the pack and lit it. She blew the smoke out slowly and then smiled.

"The dramatic pause," she said and then looked to Karren. "It takes me a long time to become aroused. A man needs to be patient with me. But so few men are. They want to get it on and get off as quickly as possible. I wish I could become aroused more easily and enjoy sex more than I do.

"I've been with a lot of men," Melanie said slowly. "With each new man I'd think it was going to be good. But . . . rarely. It was pretty good with a couple of them. Sex seemed to be best with men I had the lousiest relationship with. It's been good with Scooter. . . . He's terrific. But I'm dropping him." Melanie shrugged. "Back to jilling off, I guess."

"I bet I could satisfy you easily," Steve said.

"Well, I promise you," Melanie snapped at Steve, "that neither you nor I will ever know."

"Do you ever use your inability to easily achieve orgasm as a controlling device," Karren asked, "to make your partner feel inadequate?"

"No! I try to make every man feel he's a superb lover."

"Unless you tell a man what you need," Boone interrrupted, "how do you expect to be satisfied?"

"They hardly ever ask," Melanie snapped. "Most men have gotten in me even before I'm wet enough to enjoy it. Sometimes it hurts."

"Boone's got a point," Karren said. "During a sexual experience you need to openly communicate to your partner what pleases you. You need to tell him what you want, what you need. You have to start doing that. Give the man a chance to please you. And if he won't give you what you want, then you need to examine that relationship."

"Melanie," Christine said and moved forward in her chair, "I really believe that you've been using sex as a shortcut to intimacy. And that may be why you're not responding as you would like. I don't think you should be jumping into bed with every man who smiles at you. Sex should be used to cement a relationship after two people have gotten to know and care about each other."

"Wait a minute, Christine," Karren said, annoyance in her voice. "What you're talking about is what is right for you. That doesn't necessarily mean it's right for everybody. You and I have talked about this before."

"What I'm saying," Christine said angrily, glaring at Karren, "is that sex has got to be more than just screwing. Sex is warm feelings. Sex is caring and closeness and touching and sharing."

"For many people, that's ideal," Karren answered calmly.

"What this girl's been doing"—Christine was pointing to Melanie but looking at Karren—"has been *fucking*. She hasn't been loving."

"Melanie, how do you feel about what Christine is saying?" Karren asked.

Melanie put her cigarette to her lips but took it away before taking a puff. She looked at Christine and smiled.

"I think I'm going to try it your way," she said. "My way hasn't been working."

Christine gave Melanie a warm friendly smile.

"I can relate to you in some ways," Christine said. "I was unable to achieve orgasm with a partner until four years ago. I used to bring a lot of garbage to bed with me. I'd think about my uncle molesting me, and I'd get tense, anxious, and resentful when I was with a man. I had the opportunity to attend a conference on human sexuality several years ago. I met a wonderful man there, a sex therapist. We talked about relationships, about trust and caring and allowing yourself to become vulnerable. We talked about intimacy and sensuality and sexuality. And about the place for each of those things in a relationship." Christine looked at Karren. "I'd like to share one thing with the group that made a big difference for me."

"Please do," Karren said and sat back.

"It's nice to be sensual with someone you care about without always the need to have intercourse. I mean, you can hold and caress and fondle each other and say nice, warm things, without always having to screw. Being sensual can be an end in itself. And when I make love now, it's often just an extension of the sensual experience. And I don't feel the need to *always* have an orgasm. And sometimes my orgasms are more emotional than physical. I want my man to be satisfied, but I don't worry so much about performance as I do about feelings. This has given me a freedom and an enjoyment that I never had before."

"Sounds boring to me," Steve offered. Lucy gave him a disappointed look.

"Christine, it would take me a long time to get where you are," Melanie said.

"As time goes by," Christine said to Melanie, "and the longer you're away from being actively addicted to alcohol and drugs, the more your self-esteem will be restored. I think you will find that intimacy will come easier to you and you'll be thinking more in terms of feelings."

"Would any of you men care to comment? Steve?"

"It sounds to me that Christine's sex life isn't so good." He turned to Christine. "I think you have some problems. I think your sex life is probably lousy, and what you're doing is making it sound good with a lot of flowery talk about feelings." Steve shrugged his shoulders. "Hell, if you can't have orgasms, why have sex?"

"Steve," Karren said, the beginnings of a smile on her lips, "I hope no one has ever accused you of being evasive."

"I don't have any sex problems," Steve said boastfully. "And when I'm drinking or taking drugs, I'm still good. Maybe better. I've never had any problems gettin' it up or keepin' it up. Any woman I've ever made love to has been satisfied. Like I say, I don't have sex problems. I really don't."

"What you're saying, Steve," Karren offered, "is that you don't have any problems with sexual performance."

"Isn't that what it's all about?" Steve said defensively.

"For some people, yes," Karren answered. "And if that's good for you and your partner, fine."

"Steve," Melanie said, "didn't your wife leave you for another man?"

Steve glared at Melanie.

"You fucking bitch," he said through clenched teeth.

Lucy grasped Steve's forearm.

"Melanie's point, Steve, I think, was that your wife was probably satisfied sexually, but maybe not emotionally. Maybe she was more like Christine, and feelings were important to her, too. Feeling needed, loved, and wanted is critical for a woman."

"Hey, those are important feelings for a man, too," Boone charged.

Christine gave Boone an approving smile.

Steve sat back in his chair, arms folded, his chest visibly heaving. He was glaring at Melanie again.

"Steve, I didn't mean to be accusing you of anything," Melanie said, her voice soft and apologetic. "You may be the greatest lover in the history of the world. I don't know. We're just trying to take a look at ourselves as sexual people. I know—God do I know—that I have to improve in that area. Maybe you don't."

"In terms of your sex lives"—Karren was speaking to the group —"remember one thing—you don't have to be sick to get better. Different people need different things. Often a married person will come to me and say his or her sex life is no longer exciting. Sex has become dull, routine, and lacking in spontaneity. And the spouse may be oblivious to the fact that sex has become boring. When I get them both together, and after we get past the initial anger and defensiveness, I encourage sexual experimenting. Things can be done differently. Sex can be exciting again.

"What I do," Karren continued, "is encourage people to touch each other in different places in different ways. People need to communicate about what they like. I love to help people revitalize their sex lives."

"Walter and I could have used someone like you about twenty years ago," Lucy said, a sad smile on her face. "Sex was fair for the first few years, but after that"—she slowly shook her head—"no fantasy . . . no excitement . . . no surprises. And this was before I was a drunk.

"After I had my two kids, he seemed to lose interest. All the excuses he gave me . . . he was too tired . . . too busy. . . . my vagina was too big . . . no friction."

"That's awful!" Melanie exclaimed. "He actually said that?"

"Walter is about as interesting sexually as he is personally," Lucy said, an angry inflection to her voice. "He's your basic sap. He's like one of those husbands on the TV commercials. I mean, he's more interested in the type of soap I buy than he is in sex." Lucy put out her cigarette and a hurt look came to her face. "He's been having an affair, so he says, for the past six months. But any woman who finds that little shit exciting probably deserves him."

"You should leave him," Steve said and reached for Lucy's hand. "You deserve to be treated better."

"Leave him for what?" Lucy snapped. "I'm a forty-nine-year-old drunk with a cavernous vagina. If I lose him, I have nothing."

"Lucy," Karren said, "what I've heard you say is that Walter seemed to lose interest in you sexually after you had children and before you became an alcoholic."

Lucy nodded.

"That suggests that you and Walter have different needs sexually. That's not terribly uncommon. People can work through this in a variety of ways if, and this is a big *if*, there is a desire to work through it. Lucy, I'd be glad to talk with you and Walter if you'd like."

"Yes," Lucy said and forced a smile. "I'd like to do that. I might have to drag him in with me, though."

Karren turned to Boone, who was slouching in his chair.

"You said something before about the need to feel loved and wanted," she said to him. "I like to hear a man say that."

"This discussion is really opening up a can of worms for me," Boone said, as he sat up in his chair.

· 2 8 5 ·

Boone looked toward the open window. He started to say something but stopped. His eyes squeezed closed, and he bent his head.

"Do you need some time?" Karren asked him.

"No," he said, as he raised his head. He looked at Karren. His eyelashes were wet. He stared at her for a few seconds, and then turned to Christine.

"Some of the things you've said about intimacy have really gotten to me." Boone's voice was barely audible. "I've lived for a long time without it. It's been a lotta years since a woman has held me because she *wanted* to be close to me. I can start feeling very sorry for myself when I think about this." He took out his handkerchief and blew his nose. "I can relate to what you've been doing, Melanie. Except I've been buying sex. All that is is temporary excitement. Screwing prostitutes is not ever a poor substitute for intimacy. It's also dangerous. I've had the clap four times."

"Boone," Christine said, "I feel good about you and the progress you've made. But I'm still worried about you over this issue with your wife. It appears that in your relationship you're giving everything but receiving nothing. That's a perfect setup for harboring resentments and self-pity. And that kind of thinking is terribly dangerous for alcoholics. But I think you know that."

"I'm not going to leave her. I can't. But you're right. When I'm feeling sorry for myself, that's when my stinkin' thinkin' starts. Then it's all downhill. But at least now I know when I'm vulnerable. I know what I have to watch out for."

"I'm still worried about you, Boone," Lucy said. "You'll be walking right back into a relationship that got you here, for a second time. I really don't think you're doing the wise thing by going back to your wife. I wish you'd reconsider that."

"I hear what you're saying, Lucy." Boone smiled at her. "And I appreciate your concern. I've thought a lot about my priorities. I think they're in order now. My first priority is staying away from alcohol and doing that one day at a time. To do that, I'm going to be actively involved in A.A. Then I want to reestablish a good relationship with my daughter, Vicki. That's very important to me."

"It sounds to me," Melanie said to Boone, "that you really need somebody to care about you."

Boone smiled and nodded.

"Do you have any specific concerns on sexual matters, Boone?" Karren asked, a clinical tone to her voice.

"Well . . . yeah. In the past few years I've had some trouble. It seems that . . . well, how can I say this? I don't . . . I don't ejaculate very often." Boone smiled. "I can get my gun out. I just can't shoot it." Boone looked at Melanie. "I fake orgasms, too. The woman thinks I'm a great lover . . . that I have great staying power. And then I'm ready to get it on again a few minutes after she thinks I've had an orgasm."

"This happens when you're with prostitutes," Karren asked, "and not when you masturbate?"

Boone nodded.

"Well, we can talk more about this later, if you'd like. But I could suggest several reasons." Karren paused and looked at the floor. The heels of her feet began moving up and down alternately and rapidly for a few seconds. She looked at Boone; her feet stopped moving. "O.K., maybe I can explain it this way. Think of your ejaculation as a response, and your inability to ejaculate as something wrong with your response to that sexual encounter. This could mean that you're having strongly ambivalent feelings about the experience, and that's inhibiting your normal response. Or maybe it's because you've contracted gonorrhea from prostitutes. I suspect that could inhibit you. You might try wearing a rubber. . . ."

"Wait a minute," Christine interrupted. "It sounds to me, Karren, that you're giving tacit approval to his being with prostitutes. I don't like that."

"It's not my place to disapprove," Karren said, authority in her voice. Her expression became stern, challenging. They stared at each other for a few moments until Christine looked away.

Karren looked at me and then glanced at Hog Body.

"Well," she said, "there are two people here who haven't disclosed anything. But . . ."

"Three people," Steve interrupted. He stared at Karren. "You haven't told us anything about yourself. We're sitting here spilling our guts, and we don't know anything about you. I don't think that's fair."

"Would you like to put that in the form of a question, Steve?" Karren asked. Her back seemed to stiffen slightly.

"What's your sex life like?"

"Totally enjoyable."

"Are you married or what?" Steve persisted.

"I was married for six years. That was a life-style I wasn't comfortable with, so . . . I got divorced. That was four years ago. I've been single since then. I have a lover whom I live with."

"Well, what's so good about it?" Steve challenged. "What makes him so good?"

"Did I say *him?*" Karren had an apprehensive smile.

Silence.

Karren looked at each of us.

"Any more questions?" she asked.

Steve was making a clear statement with a mocking expression but said nothing.

"I've never been with a woman," Melanie said. "But I've thought about it. . . ."

"Well," Karren said, looking at Melanie, "all I can tell you is that my sexual preference was not a choice for me. And yours is not a choice for you. I'm neither ashamed nor proud of what I am. I was diminishing myself while I was married because it was a lie. Right now I can tell you honestly that I am comfortable with what I am. Life is enjoyable for me. I hope each of you can soon say the same."

Steve shook his head, a disgusted expression still on his face.

Karren sighed as she looked at Steve.

"I've never been one to walk around fisting air and shouting slogans," she said. "I look only to myself for approval. If you're uncomfortable being around me, Steve, that's your problem."

Karren looked expectantly at each of us, waiting for comments. There were none. Karren and Christine exchanged knowing smiles.

"It wasn't so bad this time," Karren said. "I like this group."

Karren turned her head slowly toward me.

"Is there anything you'd like to discuss?" she asked me.

"Well . . . yeah. My problem"—I took a deep breath—"my *current* problem is just the opposite of Boone's. I . . . last night when I was with my wife . . . I had . . . ah . . . I had what may have been the only spontaneous orgasm in recorded history."

Karren closed her eyes and slowly shook her head.

I turned to the group.

"Karren's disgusted with me because I was having a problem with impotence when I came here. She wanted me to see her with Irene and talk about it before I tried anything. I didn't, of course."

"Well," Melanie said, "that's in character for you, Patrick. Don't be angry with him, Karren. Patrick has to make his own mistakes."

"Are you ready to come see me?" Karren asked.

"Yes. On my knees, if I have to."

"And bring Irene?"

I nodded.

"I think this calls for a verse or two of the 'Hallelujah Chorus,'" Lucy said. "Patrick sounds almost submissive."

"Patrick, your problem with impotence was fairly simple," Karren continued. "But now your behavior has made things more complex than they should be."

"Patrick will never dazzle anyone"—Melanie paused while lighting her cigarette—"with any great display of common sense."

"Hey, Melanie"—I started to tell her to *fuck off* but I remembered my swollen lip—"get off my back."

"Patrick," Christine leaned forward, "I want you to make a commitment to the group that you will not attempt any sexual activity with Irene until after you've seen Karren."

I nodded.

"I think he should put that commitment in writing," Boone said, "and we'll all sign it."

Heads began nodding.

"What's the matter with you guys? You don't trust me?"

Heads started shaking.

I wanted to tell them all to *fuck off* but I slowly took the paper and pencil from the table. I started writing:

I will not try to have sex with Irene until after she and I have seen Karren.

I read the note aloud.

"That's good," Christine said. "Now sign your name and pass it around so we can all sign it. And I'll keep it."

"Hog Body, is there anything you'd like to discuss this morning?"

Hog Body nodded to Karren and started to speak, but he stopped and looked around the room. A timorous expression came to his face.

"I can't believe I'm doing this," he said. He took a deep breath. "Oh, well . . . You know, Karren, when you and I and Helen were talking the other day, I wanted to say a couple more things . . . but I just couldn't."

"Such as?"

"Well . . . when I'm with Helen . . . I mean, making love . . . I sometimes pretend that . . . it's not Helen. . . ." There was a plaintive expression on Hog Body's face as he looked at Karren.

"You fantasize about your daughter when you're making love to Helen," Karren said, a matter-of-fact tone in her voice.

Hog Body nodded.

"Jesus Christ, Hog!" Steve said, disgustedly.

"Normally, I encourage fantasies during sex." Karren sat back and crossed her legs. "That's one fantasy that you'll have to stop."

Hog Body still had a plaintive expression.

"Did you ever," he said, "try *not* to think of an elephant?"

"A fantasy usually comes unsolicited," Karren said. "But that doesn't mean you have to go with it. Do you have other fantasies?"

"Yeah. But . . . they're not . . . as exciting for me."

"Do they include Helen?"

"One does."

"Let me suggest this," Karren said, as she unfolded her legs, bent forward, and put her elbows on the arm of the chair. "During the sensual time when you're just beginning lovemaking but before actual intercourse, choose a fantasy that doesn't include your daughter. Concentrate on it. Hold on to it."

Hog Body was nodding his head, but he didn't appear convinced.

"It will take some time, Hog Body," Karren said. "But as long as you're motivated to change, you'll be able to do it."

There was a pained expression on Hog Body's face.

"You know what part of my problem is?" he said. "It's . . . well . . . there are some things I'd like to do with Helen. You know . . . while we're making love." He shrugged his shoulders. "Really, our sex life is pretty boring. So there's another lady I see sometimes. . . . I pay for her."

"Have you told Helen there are things you want to try?" Melanie asked. "I'm probably the wrong one to be asking that question."

"I suggested something different about ten years ago. She said no. I'm not going to ask her to do something she doesn't want to do."

"Hog Body, I want to meet with you and Helen again. I'm sensing a real void in your sex life that you need to fill. If you do, it may help with the problem you're having with your daughter. Will the two of you meet with me again?"

"I'll do anything I have to, Karren . . . whatever it takes."

Karren looked at each of us.

"Are there any questions or comments before we end this?"

"Yes," Melanie said and bent forward in her chair. "You know, my sex life has really been crummy . . . with some rare exceptions. But, then, nothing else in my life has been too good either. This has been good for me. This discussion we've just had. Finally . . . finally I'm beginning to learn something. I just want to thank you," she said to Karren and then nodded to Christine, "and you, too."

"Melanie is talking for all of us," Hog Body added.

"Well, I've enjoyed it, too," Karren said. "I appreciate the openness and honesty I've heard this morning. This has been a good session. Some of you will be coming to see me individually, I hope." Karren looked at me. "You have a commitment to come see me with your wife." She smiled and looked at Christine. "That's not happened before . . . where a group has made one of its members put a commitment in writing to come and see me."

"Karren," Boone said, "you need to understand something. Pat's an intelligent guy who makes dumb mistakes. It's easy to get impatient with him."

"I think Patty's starting to come around."

"Slowly," Lucy said. "Very slowly."

"I think he's finally started to realize that being a doctor," Steve looked at me, "doesn't mean shit. You're one of us, man, no better . . . no worse."

"That streak of resistance you have, Patrick," Melanie said and reached for my hand, "has been a real challenge for the group. It's been a battle."

"The group's winning," Christine said and smiled warmly at me.

"Patrick," Karren had a questioning look. "Do you realize that these people love you?"

I nodded and felt Melanie squeeze my hand. Tears were beginning, and so I took several deep breaths. I didn't want to cry.

"Can I have a minute of the group's time before we break?" I asked Christine. "There's something I need to talk about."

"Well," Christine said, "it's up to them."

"Sure, Pat, go ahead." Boone spoke with authority in his voice. Melanie offered me a cigarette. I took one and she lit it for me.

"There's an issue I haven't dealt with in group. I need some feedback on it now. I can't put it off anymore."

I told them about my vasectomy.

"Irene always wanted children. That was so important to her. I've denied her what she wanted most. And I lied about it. I told her I was sterile because of massive X ray exposure. I've got to tell Irene today. She's going home tomorrow. I talked to Hog Body this morning, and he suggested that I tell her, but that I have Christine with me."

"How does the group feel about that?" Christine asked.

"Sounds good to me," Steve offered.

"Yes," Lucy said. "I agree you should have a third person. I think Christine would be the best person to have with you."

"Yeah," Boone said. "Good luck."

"Patrick, I agree you need to tell her," Melanie said, a worried look on her face. "But I'm worried how Irene might react. She could . . . Are you prepared for the worst?"

"No," I said. "I'm not."

"I want you to know, Patrick, that I may not be able to help you." Christine was sitting at my desk chair, which she had turned around facing me. I was sitting on my bed.

"Just you being here is helping. I really appreciate this. I know you don't have to be here on Saturdays."

Irene appeared at the doorway.

"Can I come in?" she asked, smiling. "Or are you two talking business?"

"Hello, Irene, come in."

"C'mon in, Babes." I met Irene as she walked in and kissed her gingerly. My lip was still hurting.

I ushered her over to the bed and we sat down side by side.

I explained to Irene about my lip, and then she and Christine made some small talk about Eaton Center. Whenever Irene got nervous, her mouth would get dry, and her tongue did not glide smoothly when it touched the roof of her mouth. I noticed that "sticky" quality to some of her words as she talked to Christine. After several minutes, Irene turned to me.

"What's going on, Pat? Why are we here?"

I reached for Irene's hand and held it.

"Babes, remember when I saw that psychiatrist after Logan died?"

"Yeah. You never really told me why you went to see him."

"That was my first cry for help for my drug problem. All he did was put me on more drugs. Some antidepressants."

"That's awful," Irene said. "I didn't know that."

"I thought I was hopeless. I thought I'd never be able to get off the drugs. I didn't know there were places like this. Anyway, I felt I'd never be a responsible adult. I was barely an adequate husband. No way could I have even considered being a parent."

Irene had a quizzical expression.

"Well," she said, "that X ray exposure . . ."

I squeezed her hand and slowly shook my head.

"When you went to Mexico that summer,"—I looked to Christine, who nodded her head once—"I . . . had a vasectomy."

Irene's eyes widened. Her mouth fell open. She pulled her hand away from mine.

"You . . . lied . . . Pat. You lied to me! All my life I've wanted kids. God! How could you do that to me?" She stood and looked at Christine. "I feel like I've been betrayed." She looked to me. "Damn you! Damn you!"

"Babes . . ."

"Don't talk to me. Don't say a word. I don't want to hear your voice." Tears were coming down her cheeks. "I don't want to see you!" she screamed. "If you loved me at all, you would have never done that. I would have helped you through anything. I would have supported you. You bastard! You bastard!"

Irene sat down near the end of the bed as far from me as she could get. She put her hands to her face and began sobbing.

After several seconds Christine reached into the front pocket of her jeans and took a handful of Kleenex. She separated a few sheets, handed them to me, and nodded toward Irene. I tapped Irene's forearm. She pulled away.

"Don't ever touch me again, Pat," she yelled, as she took the Kleenex. She wiped the tears from her face. "Am I supposed to understand this?" she asked Christine. "Am I expected to forgive him?" She shook her head. "No! Not this time."

Irene put her face in her hands again. And her hands were trembling. This was the most visibly upset I had even seen her. I felt frightened, desperate. I didn't know what to say. And I was sad because I knew I had hurt her so much.

I looked to Christine with an expression that I hoped she understood. I was pleading for help.

Christine only glanced at me and looked back to Irene. She wanted to say something to Irene. But she was waiting.

After a few moments, Irene's sobbing was becoming less intense.

"Here, Irene," Christine said and handed her more Kleenex.

Irene wiped her eyes and blew her nose. She looked at Christine.

"I guess . . . I have to decide . . . what I'm going to do about this." She stood. "I want to go now."

"Don't leave, Irene. We have to talk," Christine said.

"There's nothing to be said," Irene snapped. "I don't want to be in the same room with him." She didn't even look at me.

"Please sit down," Christine persisted. "I know you're hurt. . . . I know you're angry. You have a right to be. But nothing will be solved if you walk out the door."

Irene sat down slowly and stared at the floor. She shook her head several times but remained silent.

"Irene, I want you to repeat to me what Patrick told you about why he had the vasectomy. I want to know what you heard."

"He said he went to a psychiatrist for help. The guy couldn't help him, so Patrick gave up and had a vasectomy." Irene glanced at me. "*Gave up*," she repeated. Tears were falling down her cheeks again. "I never thought . . . I could hurt . . . this much."

I wanted to hold Irene and tell her I was desperately sorry that I had hurt her. Tears were beginning to burn my eyes.

"Patrick, tell Irene again why you had the vasectomy."

I lit a cigarette, wanting some time to regain my composure. It tasted awful, and after the second puff I put it out.

"Irene, when I saw that psychiatrist, I was miserable. God! I was so unhappy . . . I was scared. . . . I was lonely . . . depressed . . . embarrassed. . . . I couldn't admit to anyone that I had a drug problem . . . not even you. I didn't know what to do"—tears were running freely down my cheeks—"I didn't have control of myself. . . . I couldn't allow myself to be a parent so . . . I had the . . . I had it done. I was desperate. . . . I was sick. Please, Irene . . . please forgive me. I'll get the vasectomy reversed. I promise."

I put my hand on the bed and moved it slowly toward her.

"Irene, I want you to repeat what Patrick just said."

Irene stared at me. She seemed not to hear Christine. A compassionate look came to her face.

"You were sick. I think . . . maybe . . . I finally understand. You really were sick." She grasped my hand. "You'll get the vasectomy reversed? We can have kids?"

"Yes, Irene. We can have children."

Irene picked up my hand and kissed the back of it. She pressed my hand to her face.

"I have a lot to make up for, Irene. I've disappointed you. . . . I've hurt you. Ride this one out with me and I promise . . . I promise you won't be hurt like this again."

A hurt smile appeared on her face, and she nodded. She kissed the palm of my hand, and then rolled my hand into a first and squeezed my fist tightly. It had been years since she had done that.

"I love you, Babes."

Irene's eyes closed tightly, and with the smile still on her face, she wept.

There was a big guy at the door shaking everyone's hand as he or she walked into the Auditorium.

"Hello, Patrick," he said, as he looked me in the eyes and crushed my hand. "Welcome to A.A. My name is Bill."

How did he know my name? I didn't have my name tag on.

"Hello." I said and started to walk past him. But he didn't let go of my hand.

"Patrick, I want you to meet Leonard."

Leonard was standing next to and was dwarfed by Bill. Leonard was a thin, small black man probably in his mid-sixties. He had on a shiny black suit and seemed overdressed for the occasion. His expression was sober, almost suspicious, as we shook hands. His small hand gave a good, firm handshake.

"Hello, Leonard."

"Hello, son," he said, as his eyes examined my face. "I understand."

Understand what?

A warm smile appeared on his face, and he gave my hand an extra squeeze.

I headed for the back row, but Hog Body grabbed my arm.

"Up front, Patty."

"I want to stay in the back, Hog. I'm not a participant, you know. Only an observer."

"All patients are supposed to sit up front."

As Hog Body directed me to the front of the room, at least a dozen people smiled at me and shook my hand.

"Why are these people smiling?" I asked as we sat in the second row.

"Because they enjoy being alive."

Sitting off to our right were Lorenzo and Toni. I smiled and waved to them.

"Why's Toni here, Hog?"

"She's one of us, Patty. She's an alcoholic."

Melanie and Lucy sat in the two seats to my left. Melanie was next to me.

"How did it go with Irene?" she asked.

"Good. Better than I hoped for. How was your afternoon with your mother?"

"It was all right." Melanie had no enthusiasm in her voice. "I accomplished what I needed to do. My apartment is now drug-free, alcohol-free, and man-free. I gave my mother Scooter's clothes to return." She moved close to me. "I'm as horny as I've ever been in my entire life," she said softly.

I felt a warm rush of excitement and I placed my hand on her knee. A surprised expression appeared on her face.

"I'll tell Presswood you want to see him," I whispered.

"Patrick," Melanie said, as she pulled my hand off her knee, "you're a creep."

Bill, with a large, syrupy smile, was at the podium. Leonard was sitting facing the audience in a chair off to the right of the podium. Bill looked around the auditorium and waited for quiet. He then read. "Alcoholics Anonymous is a fellowship of men and women who share their experience, strength, and hope with each other, that they may solve their common problem and help others to recover from alcoholism. . . ."

A lot of familiar faces here . . . people who were patients when I got here . . . I'll be gone in a week . . . never set foot in here again. . . . wonder why they're here. . . . they must need this. . . .

"Most of you know Leonard," Bill continued. "He was the janitor here for twenty years before he retired six months ago. He's returned tonight to be our speaker for this evening."

Bill stood away from the podium, and Leonard moved slowly to the microphone.

"My name's Leonard," he said in a strong, clear voice, "and I'm a grateful, recoverin' alcoholic. Hi, everybody."

"Hi, Leonard," the audience shouted in unison.

"Will you please join me in the Serenity Prayer?"

As we said the Serenity Prayer, I glanced back at Toni. It was hard to imagine her as an alcoholic. I was disappointed in her.

"I know most of you folks," Leonard said and smiled as he looked around the audience. "I remember when some of you were patients here, when you were sick and scared. I'm so happy to see you smilin' now. And you new people, I'm glad to see you keepin' with the Hogarth tradition and sittin' up front.

"I started that tradition eighteen years ago," he said boastfully. "One thing I want to tell you new people. Don't think when you're at these meetin's, just listen. Listen hard!"

Leonard paused and looked around the audience. He took a deep breath.

"I grew up in Talladega, Alabama. I was the youngest of seven children. I remember havin' my first drink when I was seventeen. . . ."

God, Irene looked so hurt when I told her about the vasectomy. . . .

I'll never hurt her again. . . . how can I make up for all the pain I caused her. . . . I'll get my vasectomy reversed. . . . they're reversing vasectomies at the Cleveland Clinic. . . . a long operation, includes microsurgery . . . that means I'll have to be put to sleep. . . . my hands are perspiring. . . . can't wait to see Irene pregnant. . . . she'll be even more beautiful. . . . I can see her just after delivery holding the baby. . . . let's see . . . two kids . . . first a daughter . . . Katherine Erin . . . an Irish flavor to that name . . . Logan would like that. . . . my son will be Daniel Logan. . . . I like Daniel. . . . you can go either way. . . . Daniel Webster . . . tall, intelligent, stentorian voice, persuasive . . . O Danny Boy . . . the maudlin sentimentality gets to me every time. . . . Katie Erin will be an artist like her mother. . . . better get a husband with a good job. . . . Daniel Logan Reilly . . . good name for a poet . . . better have a wife with a good job. . . . hope Danny will play third base. . . . wonder what Logan would want Daniel to be. . . .

"We moved to Detroit in the late 1940s. My wife and I had two kids by that time, a son and a daughter. That's when my drinkin' took control of me. I had a good job, was makin' good money. I bought a bar, not so I could make more money, but because I could be important. I'd bring my friends over every day after work. And they never had to pay one penny. Everybody looked up to me. Or at least I thought they did. Some of these so-called friends I had included women. . . . Leonard paused and his hands began to fidget nervously on the podium. "My wife left me in 1951 and took the kids. . . ."

I wish I were going home with Irene tomorrow . . . can't wait to sleep with her . . . I want to hold her all night . . . won't have to worry about wetting the bed . . . that was so embarrassing . . . be able to take my own night calls now . . . no more paying residents . . . haven't had a migraine headache in three weeks . . . those fucking drugs were doing that, too . . . going home next Friday . . . Irene and I will see Karren before I go. . . . I guess we need help with our sex life, too . . . those fucking drugs. . . . God, I love Irene. . . . I need her so much. . . . I know how Lorenzo feels. . . . he's been a changed person since he and his wife started talking. . . . he's leaving early tomorrow morning for the Georgia program . . . at least four months . . . they can keep you up to a year. . . . I'm glad I don't need that. . . . I'll miss Lorenzo. . . . this is his last night here. . . .

". . . my wife and I lived apart, but we never did get a divorce. In 1953 my wife and son were killed in a car accident. God, how I loved that woman and that boy, but . . . they were gone. And all of a sudden I had my sixteen-year-old daughter livin' with me. As much as I hated myself when my wife and son were killed, I wasn't about to change.

"I let my daughter drink. I'd let her come to parties with me. I let her work at the bar. I . . . I encouraged her to be like me. And she did become like me . . . an alcoholic. . . ." He shook his head.

I can't relate to this . . . wasting my time . . . Hog Body's not missing a word . . . sitting there smiling and nodding his head. . . . Melanie's looking interested, too. . . . what the hell can she be learning from . . . oops . . . she just saw me looking at her. . . . what a smile she has. . . . I bet she has no idea how much I want her . . .

". . . by 1960 I had lost everythin' I owned. My daughter and I moved to Toronto. We lived with relatives. The only job I could get was a janitor here. In Detroit I had been a big shot. I had a good job, a big car, owned my own bar. And here I was a janitor. But workin' here saved my life. There were A.A. people all over. And they were smilin'. They were happy. Six months after I started here, I asked the doctor if I could be a patient for a while. He let me, and I joined the program of Alcoholics Anonymous. Several years later my daughter joined the program. I'm so proud of that woman. She's made so much of herself.

"I want to tell you people how I work my program. I'm not very smart so I have to keep it simple. I go to meetin's and I work the Twelve Steps. When I get up in the mornin', I get on my knees and thank my Higher Power, who I choose to call God, for keepin' me sober the day before. And I ask Him to keep me sober that day." He looked at me. "See how simple sobriety is."

. . . Higher Power . . . God . . . I wish it were that simple for me . . . Sarah's words . . . Never, Patrick, never for a moment doubt the existence of God. . . . I do doubt, Sarah. . . . I wish I didn't, but I do. . . . It's so easy for Irene, too. . . .

"You new people may not understand what were doin' here. It does take some time. My message to you is to keep comin' back. Alcoholics Anonymous is the answer. But don't try to gulp it. Take it in small sips. Peel one potato at a time. This is a simple program, but not an easy one. But if you keep comin' back, it'll get better. I promise you that. So . . . keep comin' back."

Leonard left the podium to a thunderous applause. Bill stepped to the microphone.

"Thank you, Leonard," he said. "Now I'd like to open the meeting for comments."

Irene's Al-Anon meeting should be over soon. . . . I want to see her. . . . these people giving testimonials to Leonard have to be exaggerating . . . or did I miss something. . . . maybe I should have listened. . . .

"Well, of course I've heard your story before." Toni was standing and talking to Leonard. "I learn something new every time I hear it. I realize just how beautiful a person you are because of the help and inspiration you've been to so many people. Especially me. If it weren't for you and for this program, there is no doubt in my mind that I'd be dead now. Thanks for always being there when I need you. I love you, Pop."

Pop! Is that pop as in dad . . . Christ! . . . the circle tightens. . . .

We ended the meeting with everyone holding hands and saying the Lord's Prayer. I stood between Hog Body and Melanie.

> . . . for thine is the kingdom, and the
> power, and the glory, for ever.   Amen.

Hog Body and Melanie both gave my hands a gentle squeeze.

"Thanks for bringing me, Hog. It's been interesting. I gotta go now."

"Patty, new people in A.A. are supposed to come to meetings early and stay late. Don't run off."

I grimaced, and Hog Body let out a loud sigh. He looked nervously at the small group of people surrounding Leonard.

"Patty, you can't leave until you tell Leonard you enjoyed his talk. Go tell him. And look interested, damnit!"

Two of the men in their second week were talking to Leonard as I approached him. I reached around one of them and offered my hand to Leonard.

"I really enjoyed your talk," I said to him as we shook hands. "Thanks a lot."

"I'm glad you came, Patrick. You're in your first week?"

"End of my third week."

"Third week! I haven't seen you at a meetin' before this."

"An easy explanation for that, Leonard. This is my first meeting."

Leonard turned to the two men he had been talking to.

"Will you gentlemen please excuse me? I need to talk to Patrick for a minute."

Leonard took me by the arm and ushered me toward the back corner of the room. We passed Toni on the way, and she and Leonard exchanged what looked like a conspiratorial glance.

Leonard and I sat near the back of the room. I pulled out a pack of Players cigarettes and offered one to Leonard. He shook his head.

"I don't want to die from those things, either," he said. "But you go ahead."

I felt a little guilty as I lit up.

"You've heard my story, Patrick. Tell me yours."

Leonard never blinked as I told him about my fourteen years of drug use.

". . . so you see, Leonard, I'm not an alcoholic. I had a problem with drugs . . . sedative drugs. They call it sedativism. I don't think I belong in A.A." A sympathetic smile came to Leonard's face. Maybe, finally, someone understood.

"Thanks for tellin' me your story, Patrick. I see why you don't think of yourself as an alcoholic. Sedativism!" He laughed and slapped his knee. "That's one of those *special* diseases. That sure doesn't sound as bad as"—a feigned serious look came to his face; he pointed both hands at me and started wiggling his fingers—"alcoholism."

I sat back and readied myself for a barrage of clichés.

"Tell me somethin', Patrick." His tone became genuinely serious, and he placed his hand on my knee. "Do you want to save your life?"

I nodded, hoping to indulge him.

"I'll tell you how to do it. It's very simple. Think of yourself as an alcoholic."

"No. That's not accurate. I can't do that."

"Oh, me," he sighed. "Some people have to work awfully hard to make things simple. You know, Patrick, I'm not very smart. Fifth-grade education is all. But nobody's too stupid for A.A. But some people are too smart for this program. And those are the people that die."

"I won't die from drugs, Leonard. I'll never take them again. I know. I won't. My sense of outrage alone will maintain me."

"You'll be bettin' your life on that. And that's not smart. Don't be just a well-educated fool. Join A.A. Go with a winner. You're not any different from me, Patrick. I was addicted to alcohol. Alcohol is a drug. A wet drug. You were addicted to pills. Those are dry drugs. You got drunk in your way. I got drunk in my way. Would you agree with that?"

I slowly nodded my head, and his grip on my knee tightened.

"With awareness comes responsibility, Patrick."

I was taking deep, heavy breaths and I was perspiring freely. I wanted to get away from Leonard. There was nothing stopping me from getting up and walking away. But I couldn't move.

"I know I'm just an old simple janitor. And you . . . you're a bright young doctor. But I wouldn't change places with you. Because I have peace and . . . well . . . I'm happy. Are you happy, Patrick?"

I shook my head.

"If you come into this program and work at it, I promise you happiness. The first step for you is to say 'I'm an alcoholic and I need help.' When you can say that . . ."

I couldn't look at him anymore. I put out my cigarette and kept looking at the ashtray.

"All I ask for you to do is to come to an A.A. meeting every night for as long as you're in this hospital. At the end of that time, if you don't see a difference, well, you can have all your misery back.

"Patrick, come into A.A. and let me be your sponsor."

I slowly looked up at him and nodded my head.

Irene and I sat on the couch in the lobby where we first sat the day I was admitted. We held hands, but Irene was distant, preoccupied with something.

"Pat, you know if you hadn't had this drug problem, we'd have kids now. Seven years old . . . and maybe another five years old. I've been thinking about that all day. I did most of the talking at the Al-Anon meeting tonight. They could see I was angry."

"You still angry, Irene? I can't keep apologizing, you know."

"I know, Pat. I know. I don't want you to keep feeling guilty. It's just that, well . . . you've really hurt me. I have resentments now that I didn't have before. And I know that I have to make a choice. I can either let those resentments grow and fester, or I can put them behind me."

"Well, Irene, if you want to save our marriage, the choice you need to make is fairly obvious."

"Obvious," she said softly, "but not easy." She stood. "I'm going back to my room now, honey. This is going to be a long night."

She kissed me on the cheek and walked off.

I walked back to my room. I was afraid . . . unhappy . . . tired. It had been a long time since I had slept. The possibility of losing Irene was, once again, very real. But I couldn't think about that. I needed sleep.

As I went to go into my room, I could see a light under Lorenzo's door.

As I approached his room, I could hear his stereo playing soft music. I needed to say good-bye to him. I knocked on his door. After several seconds his door opened. He was smiling. I tried to smile but couldn't. I would never see him again. The smile left his face as we stared at each other.

I wanted to say something to him, but sadness was overwhelming me. I put my arms around him. His arms squeezed around my back.

We stood and held each other. And cried.

THINK of yourself as an alcoholic. . . . do you want to save your life. . . . some people are too smart for this program. . . . those are the ones that die. . . . do you want to save your life. . . . alcohol's a wet drug. . . . pills are dry drugs. . . . you got drink in your own way . . . well-educated fool. . . . with awareness comes responsibility. . . . are you happy, Patrick. . . . if A.A. doesn't work, we'll give you all your misery back. . . . do you want to save your life. . . .

How could I let that little son of a bitch talk to me like that? A fucking janitor, for Christ's sake. A fifth-grade education. Acts like he's a fount of wisdom. Probably thinks he's important. I'll show him how important he is. I'll ignore him.

"Good morning, *doctor*. Here." Ruthy handed me a container for urine.

"You know, Ruthy, the way you snarl is part of your special charm."

"I want you to put some urine in that cup. Fill it up now, *doctor*."

"Ruthy, I'm going to miss these pleasant and informal chats," I said, walking toward the bathroom. "Your style and wit have added so much to my weekends. Gosh, I'll miss you."

Ruthy followed me into the bathroom.

"I'm going to watch you fill up that cup," she said with a sneer. "No more tricks."

"I can't pee with someone watching me. At least turn your back."

She folded her arms across her chest and stared at me. She was in command here.

"We're going to be in this bathroom a long time, Ruthy, if you insist on watching me."

She reached over and turned on the faucet in the sink.

"That will get you going," she snapped. "Stop stalling."

"That's not going to do anything. I'll tell you what might help, though," I said and lowered my voice. "Let me put a couple of my fingers in your mouth."

A look of disgust came over her face. "I'll just listen," she said and slowly backed out of the bathroom.

I turned off the faucet and tried to urinate in the cup, but my stream wouldn't start. I put the container on the sink, sat on the toilet, folded my arms, and put my feet on the tub.

"Hey, Ruthy, will you miss me?"

"You don't really think you're going home next Friday, do you, *doctor*?" She laughed. "They'll ask for my opinion, you know. They listen to me. They like my observations."

"What'll you tell them, Ruthy?"

"It's confidential. Hey, I don't hear anything. Are you trying?"

I grunted. "Doing my best, Ruthy. You think I have a lousy attitude."

"Correct."

"And you don't trust me."

"Correct. They should have sent you home weeks ago. I suggested it. I suggested that they put you in a hospital somewhere with *your own kind*. I'll just bet they're saying now: 'Ruthy was right. We should have listened to her.'"

"You don't think I've made any progress?"

"None! It's possible you're one of those people who just can't be helped."

"Thanks, Ruthy. That's the kind of encouragement I like to hear."

"It will really take some wind out of your sails when they tell you to stay. Yeah, it sure will. You won't be such a smart aleck. You'll give me some respect then, *doctor*. You'll do what I say. I'm going to enjoy that," she laughed. "Boy, if it were up to me, I'd have you washing floors. That would take you down a peg or two. And that's what you need. You're no better than anybody else." I could hear her chuckling. "Washing floors . . . yeah . . . I like that. I'll suggest it. Hey, I don't hear anything in there. What are you doing?"

"I'm close. Real close. I know you're enjoying yourself, Ruthy, and I hate to spoil your fun, but this is our last day together. I'll be going home next Friday."

"And what if they suggest you stay, *doctor?*" There was anticipation in her voice. "What will you do tomorrow morning when they tell you you have to stay?"

"I'll refuse. I'll tell 'em *so long it's been good to know ya, so long it's been good to know ya . . .*" Ruthy appeared in the doorway. There was excitement on her face. "C'mon, Ruthy, join me. . . . *so loooong it's been good to know ya, what a long time since I've been hoooome, and I gotta be driftin' along.*"

Ruthy's expression manifested pure delight. She now knew what only I had known. That I would refuse to stay. She could tell the staff. Ruthy could be important now. She heaved to the left and headed for the door. I followed her out into the hall.

"Hey, Ruthy, you forgot something." I had the empty urine container in my hand.

She didn't even turn around. Like a giant, panicked lemming heading for the sea, Ruthy moved her quivering hulk toward the Nurses' Station.

She had no idea she had been used.

" 'Morning, Babes. Did I wake you?"

"No. I've been . . . we've been up all night. I just got out of the shower."

"You and Helen been up all night?"

"Me and Helen and Denise Bossy. There were three others. Let's see . . . Walter was here, too. I think his wife is in your group."

"Yeah . . . Lucy."

"Well, we had kind of an all-night Al-Anon meeting. It wasn't planned, really. It just happened."

"What did you guys talk about?"

"A lot of things. A couple of us are really having some problems. It was good for me. How are you feeling this morning, Honey?"

"Pretty good. I got a couple of hours sleep last night. And we just had a great breakfast. I even recognized everything they served. Waffles and sausage. I had a double serving."

"I'm glad, Honey. I hope they fatten you up a little before I take you home."

"Irene . . . you sound better this morning than you did last night. You had me worried when you left."

"I felt awful, Pat. I was so depressed. When Helen saw me last night, she called Denise Bossy, and Denise came over. We ended up talking all night. Denise told me I was overdosing on self-pity and that I needed to learn the Serenity Prayer. She told me there was nothing I could change, that whatever is in the past is gone forever and that resentments are terribly destructive. God, I wish that woman lived in Cleveland. I could really use her. She just won't let me feel sorry for myself. I hear her husband is a pretty nice guy, too."

"*Nice* is not exactly the word I would use, Irene. He's . . ."

"A few more people came to our room and it seemed like all of us had similar problems . . . resentments . . . hurt . . . anger. It kind of helps when you know other people are going through the same thing. Helen has had some rough times, too. Maybe worse that what I've had. By the way, do you know Walter?"

"I only know *of* him . . . only what Lucy's told us. I've only . . ."

"Walter takes complete responsibility for his wife being an alcoholic. He feels terrible. He said that Lucy wanted more than he could ever give her. I feel sorry for Lucy, though. She's in for some bad news, Pat. Take care of her."

"All right, Babes, I'm glad you told me. I'll make sure . . ."

"All of us had to promise Denise that we'd join Al-Anon. She said we could be at Al-Anon meetings when you were at A.A. meetings. I'm going to do what she says. I think I'm going to need a support system, just as you will."

"Good idea. I think . . ."

"Wait a minute, Pat—See you downstairs in a minute, Helen— all right, Pat. Sorry. Helen and I are going to church now. After that I'm going to come back here and try to sleep a little before I drive back. Honey . . . do you think we can be alone here . . . in my motel room . . . for a little while before I go back? I want . . . you."

"I can't, Babes. I've made a commitment to my group that I won't try to make love to you again until you and I have talked to Karren."

"Wait a minute, Pat! Are you saying you've told your group about what happened between you and me? You've talked about our sex life?"

"Yes. There aren't any secrets in my group, Irene. None. We discuss everything that's a problem. And you'll have to agree we've had some problems."

"Yeah . . . nuts! I've been thinking about being alone with you all morning. I should've made my shower a cold one. Well, when I get back to Cleveland, I'll pick up Gabe and drive around and see what we can pick up."

"I know you're joking, Irene. Aren't you?"

"Hmmm . . . maybe some young college guys . . . well . . . I gotta go to Mass. I'll stop at the hospital and see you before I go back. See you later, Pat. Love ya."

Ruthy was unusually excited as she talked on the telephone. When she saw me coming toward the Nurses' Station, she stopped talking. A suspicious look came to her face.

"Just a minute, *doctor*," she twerped at me as I tried to scurry past the Nurses' Station. "You have a visitor." She nodded her head toward the lounge.

There were several patients sitting in the lounge reading the Sunday newspaper. Lucy was the only one there from my group. But sitting in a chair in the far left corner was Leonard. He wore a shiny green suit. He sat unmoving, staring at his hands, which were on his lap. He had some pamphlets in his hands.

"Ruthy, I thought we weren't allowed visitors this early," I said, as I turned back to her.

Ruthy clapped her hand over the receiver and stood slowly. Her eyes widened.

"You have to see all visitors," she said, making up a new rule.

"I don't want to see him."

Ruthy's shoulders arched slightly, and her neck stiffened, bringing her head into a fixed position. Her authority was affirmed.

"All right . . . all right. I'll see him."

Lucy looked up and smiled at me as I entered the lounge. 'Take care of her, Pat. She's in for some bad news.' There was no hurt in her smile. No bad news yet.

"'Morning, Lucy," I said and bent over and kissed her on the cheek. "You look nice this morning. I mean *especially* nice."

"Hmmmm." She had a curious smile. "We'll have to meet like this more often, Patrick. Have a seat."

"Can't right now. I've got a visitor." I closed my eyes and slowly shook my head. "Hopefully, this will be brief. Another exercise in attempting to solve complex problems with simple slogans."

"Patrick." Lucy grasped my hand. "Those aren't slogans. These are truisms."

I nodded, but she knew I was patronizing her. I walked over to Leonard.

Leonard was still sitting with his head bowed. His eyes were closed. I stood in front of him, waiting for him to wake up. He didn't move.

I put my hand on his shoulder and gently shook him.

"I'm sorry to wake you, Leonard, but they told me you wanted to see me."

He looked at me, smiled, and stood up. He grabbed my hand with enthusiasm.

"Good mornin', Patrick. How are you feelin'?"

"I feel fine, Leonard. Listen, if you want to rest, we can talk later."

"I wasn't sleepin', Patrick. I was spendin' some quiet time with my Higher Power. I was thankin' Him for helpin' me to stay sober yesterday. And I was askin' Him to help me not to take a drink today. You know, Patrick"—Leonard sat down and motioned for me to sit next to him—"every day I stay sober is a miracle. The whole A.A. program is a miracle."

"Don't confuse miracles with self-discipline," I said, as I sat next to him. I wanted a cigarette, but I knew Leonard disapproved.

"You have a lot to learn, son."

"Leonard, why are you here?"

"I'm your A.A. sponsor, Patrick." His manner and inflection became earnest, almost solemn. "We need to talk. Did you think about what I said to you last night?"

"A little."

"And how do you feel about our conversation?"

"I'm angry, Leonard. And annoyed. And I'm furious at you for being here now. I said you could be my sponsor. Just how much liberty does that give you?"

Compassion began to show on Leonard's face. That was not what I wanted.

"I wish you'd leave me alone, Leonard. Go bother somebody else. I don't need A.A. And I sure as hell don't need you."

"Why were you at the A.A. meetin' last night, Patrick?"

"Because other people think I need A.A. And I agreed to go to some meetings."

"Tell me, Patrick, do you want to stop usin' drugs? Do you want to stop drinkin'?"

"I want to stop using drugs."

Leonard paused and looked at the pamphlets on his lap. After a few seconds he looked at me.

"All right," he said. "The only requirement for you at this time for membership in A.A. is the desire to stop usin' drugs. Do you understand that? Is that simple enough for you?"

I nodded.

"Tell me, Patrick, what is your major hang-up about A.A.? What's keepin' you away from us?"

I knew, but I didn't want to answer.

"You think you're too smart for this program, don't you?"

"Yes."

Leonard started chuckling, and he nodded his head.

"I thought I was too smart, too," he said.

"You thought you were too smart?"

"Yeah. Me. An old colored janitor thought he was too intelligent. Can you believe that?"

"Well . . ."

"You will find, Patrick, that there is more sound wisdom in A.A. for the people who need it than in a bottle of alcohol. Or a pill bottle."

"Leonard, I'm sorry I got so angry before. But . . . well . . . you people just don't seem to understand. I can look you in the face right now and tell you that I will never take drugs again."

"We don't use the word *never* in A.A. You see, Patrick, the future happens one day at a time. I don't worry about takin' a drink tomorrow. Or next week. Or next year. I just think about today. I ask my Higher Power to help me not to take a drink today. And tomorrow I'll worry about tomorrow."

"Leonard . . . why are you here right now? Why are you doing this?"

"Because somebody did it for me. And that person gave me a gift more precious than gold. Sobriety. And sobriety is like love. It only works when you share it. Let me love you, Patrick, until you love yourself."

I sat back in my chair and took a deep breath.

"Leonard, you exhaust me."

He smiled.

"Damnit!" I said. "Why can't I walk away from you?"

His smile broadened.

I had intended to go to the Sunday morning general meeting, but when I saw Bossy standing at the lectern, I walked out.

It was cold outside, and there was an unusually sweet smell in the air. It was a smell that belonged inside, in a room full of beautiful women. The trees and the grass appeared a more brilliant green than

I had noticed. And the tulips. God! I was proud of those little guys. There they stood. Staunch. Resilient. Plucky. Beautiful.

When we were younger, much younger, Gabe and Sarah and I would spend rainy afternoons feasting on Lewis Carroll. *Alice's Adventures in Wonderland . . . Through the Looking Glass.*

"Read with feeling, Gabriel. Read with feeling, Patrick," Sarah would admonish us.

Gabe would make her voice high and squeaky when she spoke for the oysters.

> "But wait a bit," the Oysters cried,
>   "Before we have our chat;
> For some of us are out of breath,
>   And all of us are fat!"

When I talked for the Walrus, I would make my prepubescent voice as deep as possible.

> "The time has come," the Walrus said,
>   "To talk of many things:
> Of shoes—and ships—and sealing wax—
>   Of cabbages—and kings—
> And why the sea is boiling hot—
>   And whether pigs have wings."

The idea of walruses, oysters, rabbits, lobsters, and inanimate objects answering my questions and making pithy comments had always held a certain fascination for me.

I learned early that if you are going to converse with a nonperson, especially when you talk for it, you had best do this when you are alone.

Although I still had an occasional chat with my dog and kindred spirit, Lucifer, my cadaver in medical school was the last inanimate object I spoke with. It was late one night, and I was alone with it. We called it Virginia. I don't remember why. Except that it was female. Probably age sixty at time of death.

I was studying the female external sex organs, and I was amazed to find an intact hymen. Virginia was a virgin!

"Virginia," I said to her, "I'm sorry for you. You've missed a lot."

"Maybe," she answered in a deadpan voice. "But I'm sure much of what I missed was painful."

Another med student had been working on his cadaver three tables over. I hadn't seen him.

"Reilly!" He called out. "Are you a fucking loon?"

"Maybe he is," Virginia answered him. "But there are worse things to be."

Canadian tulips late on a Sunday morning in April would speak with a young, airy, determined voice. Gender unspecified.

"I've been admiring you guys for weeks from my window," I said and smiled at them.

"We know."

"I would've helped you if I could. I didn't know what to do. But just think. You've survived! It's all downhill now. All you have to do is stand around and receive approval, have people tell you how beautiful you are, and want to take you home. That sounds like a pretty good life to me."

"We've been admiring you, Patrick."

"Me! Why?"

"You can choose not to die in a couple of months. We can't."

"Wait a minute. You guys have been talking to Leonard. I don't want to hear any more of his postcard slogans. I'm leaving if you try any of that stuff. I just came to say hello. Stop trying to do a number on me."

"Patrick, how many more mistakes do you have to make before you learn? How many more people do you have to hurt? When are you going to start listening to people who care about you?"

"You guys sound like a chorus in a Greek play. Almost as bad as my group. Nobody thinks I can do this on my own. Everybody wants me to go to A.A. meetings and sit around drinking coffee in church basements listening to a bunch of yokels giving drunkalogues. All right, damnit! I'll give it a shot. I'll go to thirty A.A. meetings in thirty days. After that . . . well . . . we'll see what happens."

I started walking away from them. After walking a few yards, I stopped and looked back. I pointed at them.

"I'm going home next Friday. That's nonnegotiable. I won't even discuss it."

I waved to them and walked back toward the front door. In a window of the fourth floor lounge was a massive, shapeless, white object. As I got closer, I could see a malicious smile on Ruthy's face.

Where is a harpoon when you really need one?

Leonard and I walked into the A.A. meeting together but we were soon separated. It seemed that everybody in the room wanted time alone with him. People would smile and shake hands with

Leonard and then move off alone with him where they would talk in hushed tones.

I had taken a seat near the back of the room. When Leonard finally noticed me, he walked quickly to me.

"Sit up in the front row," he commanded. "And save me a seat next to you." He looked at me, sternness in his expression. "I want you always to sit in the front row. You smart people let your minds wander if you stay in the back."

Grudgingly, I stood.

"And one more thing, Patrick. After you save us seats, get off your butt and introduce yourself to people and shake some hands. These people want to love you. That's part of the reason they're here."

Most of the patients in Hogarth were in the first three rows. I was able to save two seats in the second row, and then I walked around introducing myself and shaking hands. After several introductions, I began to feel comfortable. The genuine smiles and sincere, warm expressions began to make me feel welcome, as if . . . as if I belonged.

I almost didn't recognize Reggie. She was actually wearing a dress. A white, summery dress. And she was wearing lipstick and blush on her cheeks. She came toward me with a spring in her step and a cheerful smile.

Her lips were parted slightly as she kissed me on the mouth. I held the kiss for an extra couple of seconds.

As we moved apart I gave her an exaggerated looking over.

"Girl," I said, "you sure don't look like one of them drug addicts."

"You don't either, man," she said as she looked up and down. "At least not no more. You could pass for one of them alcoholics, though."

That was an arrow well placed, and I had no response. So I hugged her. I was happy for her because she looked so cheerful. I avoided kissing her again, though. I couldn't make an emergency trip to Karren's mole hole. I didn't have the key.

"Patrick, after this meeting I'm going to see my son for the second time. Do I look all right? Do I look like a mother? I haven't over-done it, have I?"

"You look great, Reggie. Any child would be proud to say you were his mother. Believe me."

She smiled a thank you.

"Is it going well with your ex-husband?"

"Pretty well, Patrick. Jim still sees me as a woman who was im-moral . . . who was bad and is trying to get better. He doesn't understand that I was a sick person who is still trying to get well. I'm not sure if I'll ever be able to change his attitude. He refuses Al-Anon. All I can do is keep saying the Serenity Prayer and lead my life the best way I can. And hope . . . Oops! I'm starting to feel sorry for myself. I've got to let go of that.

"So tell me, Patrick, what's been going on? By the way, have you met Leonard, Toni's father?"

"Yeah. I've met him. He's really important. It looks like everybody here wants a piece of him."

"He's got a lot of years of quality sobriety under his belt, Patrick. And he works a good program. He 's one of those people that if you know him, you love him. He was a janitor here for a long time. Well, part-time janitor, part-time therapist. Whenever they had a particularly tough nut to crack, they'd slip Leonard the word, and he would start talking to the guy. They still do that." Reggie smiled in admiration. "Leonard has a way of cutting through bullshit faster than anybody I know. And some people have to work through a lotta bullshit."

"Hi, Reggie," Leonard said as he approached us. He and Reggie kissed. "I guess you know Patrick. He's let me be his first sponsor in A.A." Reggie slapped her hand over her open mouth. "C'mon," Leonard said to me and took my arm. "Let's go to our seats."

I looked back at Reggie as Leonard and I walked away. She remained frozen, her hand still over her mouth. I smiled at her and winked.

Irene was waiting for me in the lobby when the A.A. meeting was over. I introduced her to Leonard.

"Pat, you look shell-shocked," she said. "What's the matter?"

"The man who was the speaker in the meeting was a Catholic priest."

"Alcoholism is a very democratic disease, Patrick," Leonard offered. "It respects no one."

"It was painful to listen to him, Leonard. The way he graphically described his feelings of isolation and loneliness and despair . . . I could relate to those feelings."

"But you see how well he's doing now? See, Patrick, A.A. works. Take his story home with you and think about it."

"I don't want to think about it. It'll hurt too much."

Leonard moved close to me. I could feel his chest moving against my abdomen. He glared at me.

"How are you ever going to learn unless you think about things? No pain, no gain."

I nodded, hoping that would get him off me.

"You and I still need to do a lot of talkin'," Leonard said and stepped back. He reached into his pocket, pulled out a card, and handed it to me. It was his name and phone number.

"I want you to call me every day, Patrick, some time in the afternoon. And I'll be takin' you out to an A.A. meetin' every night." He turned to Irene, and they shook hands. "It was so nice meetin' you, Irene. You'll be going to Al-Anon meetin's back in Cleveland?"

Irene nodded and Leonard smiled approvingly.

He turned to me and we shook hands.

"I think you've gotten a good start, Patrick. I'm happy with you so far. But still I think you need to think of yourself as an alcoholic. That will speed up your progress. You have to join us, but you won't until you think you're one of us. That will take some blind faith on your part. And it's probably hard for you to give blind faith to an old colored janitor. But . . . it's up to you."

Leonard put one hand on Irene's shoulder and his other hand on my shoulder.

"Kids," he said, "this experience will make your marriage more solid than ever before if you use the people in A.A. and Al-Anon wisely. Just keep it simple. And go slow. I love you both."

"He sounds as if he's speaking *ex cathedra*, Pat," Irene said as we walked toward the door. "Is he as wise as he seems?"

"The people in A.A. approach him on their knees," I said. "I think I'm going to listen to him. For a while. That business about thinking of myself as an alcoholic is totally absurd."

We walked down the steps holding hands. At the bottom, Irene turned to me.

"Pat, why don't you try it his way? I mean, an addict is an addict. What difference does it make if it's alcohol or drugs? Don't they destroy you equally? Go ahead and think of yourself as an alcoholic."

"Irene! You are not an instant authority on addiction. Don't try to sound like one. Give me a break, will you? Everybody wants to preach to me. I'm really . . ."

Irene put her hand over my mouth.

"Don't say any more, Pat. I'm leaving now. Let's not say good-bye when we're angry. Please."

Once again, I felt stupid.

I put my arm around Irene's shoulder, and we walked to our Citation without talking. By the time we got to the car, I had squeezed her as close to me as possible.

We faced each other. Irene's eyes were wet, but there were no tears.

"I have hope for us now, Pat. I know we can make it. Coming here has made a big difference to me. I think I understand what you were going through." She put her hands on either side of my face. "I love you so much, Honey. I'll always love you and be whatever support for you that I need to be. I want you healthy and back home with me. You're a beautiful, kind man, Patrick Reilly."

"I'm sorry, Babes . . . for everything. You'll have our children . . . soon . . . I love you."

"Hello, Gabe."

"Pat! How ya doin', kiddo?"

"Oooh . . . all right, I guess. Kinda sad, really. Irene just left. Going back to Cleveland."

"You sound pretty low. How did you two do?"

"Well, our relationship has changed. That's for sure. I think it's going to be O.K., though. We still love each other. But there are a lot of things we have to work out."

"I'll do anything I can to help, Pat. I hope you know that."

"Thanks, Gabe."

"Did you tell Irene about your vasectomy?"

"Yeah. She knows now. She handled it pretty well."

"Good. I knew she would. . . . So when will you be coming home, Pat?"

"Well, tomorrow they make the decision about who will be asked to stay three extra weeks. I'm pretty sure they'll let me come home. And I'll probably be in Cleveland next Friday. Correct that. I'll definitely be coming home next Friday. I couldn't possibly stay an extra three weeks. I don't need to."

"Sarah will be in town next weekend, Pat. It will be nice for the three of us to be together again. It's been a long time. And, well, if for some reason you're still in the hospital next weekend, Sarah and I will drive up to see you."

"I'm looking forward to seeing her, Gabe. We never were around her when she was happy. And she really seems to be content down there in North Carolina with Vic. I'm really happy for her.

"How's my main man, Number Eighty-two?"

"Adrian is no longer Number Eighty-two. He's now 'Grover.' "

"Who or what is a grover?"

"Adrian's father took him to see the Cleveland Indians on opening day. Adrian got this guy's signature on a baseball before the game. And then this Grover hit a run in or something during the game. I think Adrian's father said Grover plays on a base."

"Yeah. Mike Hargrove. Plays first base. He's a good ballplayer."

"Wonderful! I don't like Grover any better than I liked Ozzie. And I won't call my son by a number anymore. And this guy Grover is apparently left-handed, because Adrian now wants to be left-handed. He's eating with his left hand, writing with his left hand, combing his hair with his left hand. And he stands in front of the mirror for hours practicing a left-handed batting position. He goes through all sorts of funny motions."

"The kid sure likes to be like his heroes. I used to pretend I was Rocky Colavito."

"Well, I decided two could play this game. Yesterday I told Adrian I wouldn't answer to 'Mom' anymore. I told him I wanted to be called Willa Cather. He didn't like it. And next fall I'll be Edna St. Vincent Millay. I'll wear the kid down, Pat, until he's ready to strike a deal."

"Tell me how you're feeling, Gabe."

"Well, things could be worse . . . I suppose. I'm about to turn forty, and I'm not at a very secure place. About to be divorced for the second time . . . this isn't where I wanted to be. Thank God for Adrian. He seems to know when I'm hurting, and he always says the right thing. He reminds me a lot of you when you were a kid . . . loves sports, and he's got his heart right out there on his sleeve. He gets hurt so easily. I don't know what I'd do without that kid."

"You're still seeing Scott, I hope."

"Sure am. I'm learning some things. Like how insecure I am. And he said because of the partners I've chosen, I must have a pretty low opinion of myself. He was appalled when I told him how Martin treated me. He wants me to join a group. I guess they meet once a week for therapy sessions."

"You going to do it?"

"Yes. You told me to do what he says. And besides, Scott will be there." Gabe paused and took a deep breath. "Pat, I'm going to get it together. Eventually . . . I'm going to work things out. I owe it to my son."

"That's true, Gabe. But first you owe it to yourself. You got to do it for you. And then the rest of us will benefit from that."

"Thanks," she said, her voice softening.

"Tell Grover that I'll be taking him to see some Indians games this summer. And tell him I love him. And, Gabe, I love you, too."

"Gosh, Pat, you sound so much better than you did last week. Hurry up and get back here, will ya? I miss my brother. . . . I love you, kiddo."

"Whatcha reading, Melanie?"

"Hi, Patrick. C'mon in." She held up the book. *Twelve Steps and Twelve Traditions*. Melanie was lying on her bed. She had on a pink and white striped T-shirt and white shorts. Her feet were bare. She patted the bed in front of her for me to sit down.

"Is your wife gone?"

I nodded.

As I approached her, I could see those tiny blond hairs on her upper thighs shine in the sunlight. A warm rush of enthusiasm went directly to my groin as I sat on her bed.

"I've been struggling a bit with Step Two," she said. "The concept of a Higher Power is a tough one for me. I talked to my sponsor about it this morning. But I'm just not getting it. Have you worked on that yet?"

"I don't know anything about the steps, Melanie. But I'm going to start reading about the first one this afternoon."

She started laughing.

"They talk about being restored to sanity in the second step. God! I've done some insane things. A little over a year ago I was doing Blanche in *Streetcar*. Blanche has a line in the last scene, 'I've always depended on the kindness of strangers.' It's a perfect line for that character at that moment in the play. Two nights before our opening I decided that line could be improved. Me! Improve on Tennessee Williams! Can you believe that?

"I thought the line should read: 'I've always depended on the kindness of *other people*.' I had been doing cocaine that night, and I was really buzzing. Well, I decided to call Tennessee Williams and tell him how to improve the play. I had heard he lived in Key West. I spent most of one night trying to call Tennessee Williams in Florida. I called information and got the telephone number of every Williams in Key West. I called them all. I never got a hold of him. So I made plans to fly there the next day to get his permission to change the line. Fortunately, I couldn't afford the plane fare." Melanie turned over on her back and stared at the ceiling. "That was insanity, Patrick . . . insanity."

I reached for her hand.

"That's all over now, Melanie. You don't do that crazy stuff again."

"Patrick," she said, still staring at the ceiling, "right now, at this moment, is the horniest I have ever been in my entire life. I thought it was bad last night. I always get horny when I'm ovulating, but . . . wow."

"Do you want me to leave you alone?" I asked and pulled my hand slowly away from her.

She looked at me, an intense expression on her face.

"That's the last thing I want."

I stood. My breathing was becoming labored.

"Melanie, I better go. I was just with my wife. I told her I loved her. She trusts me now. I won't violate that trust again. I can't. . . . I just can't."

I started walking toward the door but stopped and turned back to her.

"I'd love to be alone with you," I said, "and hold you . . . and touch you . . . and feel you close to me. Do you think we can do that and not make love?"

She sprang out of the bed.

"Sure! Let's do it, Patrick."

"But we can't do that here. There aren't any locks on our doors."

An excited smile appeared on her face, and she walked over to her desk. She picked up a key that was attached by a chain to a slice of pineapple.

"Know what this is?" she asked.

"I sure do." I walked to her and took her hand. "Let's go."

"This bed seems much smaller with two people on it, Melanie."

"Yes. It does. And it's more uncomfortable than I remember. That's probably because I have my clothes on. Karren's got some pretty interesting pictures under the bed. Did you see them?"

"See them! Hell, I've memorized half of them."

"Patrick, if you'll tell me your favorite sexual fantasy, I'll tell you mine. You go first."

"Well, let's see. I've thought a lot about making love outside on a warm spring day. Preferably in the woods. But not secluded. I want other people to be in the woods, so there'd be the possibility of getting caught. I think that would be exciting."

"Sounds pretty tame, Patrick. Are you sure that's your favorite?"

"Well . . . I have another one. I fantasize about making love to two women on a large circular bed. One woman is submissive. . . . the other is aggressive. . . . and there are mirrors . . . no whips or anything . . . just me and them. . . . Melanie, I've never told anyone these things."

"You haven't told me much. What about some details?"

"No," I said and shook my head. "Now it's your turn."

"I see myself making love to three men. All perfect strangers. We're on a bed . . . on a stage. . . . there are a hundred people watching. There's a spotlight on us. And the audience is cheering for me to get all three of these guys to come at the same time. I do one of them with my mouth while the other two are doing me"—I could feel Melanie trembling—"I have to make sure I'm moving just right. The audience is going wild. I'm sweating like mad, and so are the three men, and . . ." an embarrassed smile appeared on her face, and she snuggled her face into my chest.

"Melanie, you really get into your fantasies."

I could feel her head nod against my chest. I kissed her on the head.

"Patrick," she said softly, her face speaking into my chest, "you would be angry with me later if we made love, wouldn't you?"

"Yes. And I'd be angry at myself, too."

"Then it won't happen." She turned her head up and looked at me. "All right?"

I nodded.

"Patrick . . . let's take our clothes off. Trust me. Please."

Melanie was out of her clothes smoothly in seconds, and I was still unbuttoning my shirt.

"Let me help you with that, Patrick. Take your hands off. Lean back."

I leaned back and stared at the ceiling.

"I can't believe," I said with as much nonchalance as I could muster, "that a beautiful, naked, blond woman is unbuttoning my shirt and now unzipping my fly and . . ."

She stood in front of me and pushed my shirt back off my arms. Her breasts touched my face. She stood back. Her pubic hair was a light brown, much darker than her eyebrows and the hair on her head.

· 318 ·

"Yes, Patrick," she said, touching the hair near her temple. "This is my real hair color. Every man asks me that."

"*Every man*, Melanie?"

"Ooops," she said and laughed.

Melanie bent down and untied my shoes and took them off. She pulled off my shorts and pants together.

She pushed me back on the bed and fell on top of me. Her hands were folded on my chest. She rested her chin on her hands and smiled at me.

"How many affairs have you had, Patrick?"

"None. No reason to. Came close once, though."

"Do you mean that there are actually men like you still around? That makes you even more challenging . . . and desirable. You're getting erect, by the way. Am I tempting? Would you have had an affair with me? Do you fantasize about me?"

"The answer to all your questions, Melanie, is yes."

"Do you think you could ever love me, Patrick? Could you ever marry someone like me?"

"I do love you, Melanie. I don't know you well enough to be *in love* with you. Marriage. I don't know. We're two sick people."

Melanie rolled off of me and lay on her back. She placed her left arm inside my arm and her hand held my wrist.

"Do I have nice breasts?"

"Nice? Hmmm . . . No. Magnificent. Yes!"

"How about my butt? Do I have a good one?"

"Extraordinary. But I believe your buddy, Presswood, has already commented on it."

"I'm not going to ask you about my legs. Every time I lose weight, my upper thighs get real thin. I wonder why that is. Anyway, when I'm like this, I can't wear a one-piece bathing suit. It looks terrible. I think I look O.K. in a bikini, though."

"I'm sure you do, Melanie."

"You have a pretty good figure, Patrick. Good shoulders . . . nice chest. But . . . well. One area where you need improvement." She turned and faced me and raised up on one elbow. "Want to know where?"

"No."

"Your butt's too small. I like a man that's got a full butt. One that looks powerful . . . muscular. You know . . . an ass like a racehorse." She trembled slightly and fell on her back. "Boy, does that get my fantasies going."

I rolled toward Melanie and placed my arm across her chest, my hand resting on her far shoulder. My fully erect penis rested on her thigh. My mouth was close to her ear.

"Patrick, if you blow in my ear, it'll be every man for himself."

"I think you're more nervous than I am," I whispered.

"Pretty transparent, eh? I'm sorry. I've never done this before. I mean, agree not to make love."

She turned her face toward me, and I kissed her forehead. She closed her eyes and I kissed each eyelid. Then I kissed her mouth. Her lips parted, and her tongue was touching my lips. Her tongue then came into my mouth and moved slowly, touching the roof of my mouth, then the inside of my cheeks. Her tongue then went between my upper lip and gums and started moving furiously back and forth.

Her hand grasped my penis.

I moved up, my head above hers, my tongue in her mouth.

She sighed deeply when my hand touched her between her legs. I moved down and began kissing her neck.

"My breasts," she whispered. "Do my breasts."

I kissed her breast and felt her nipple become erect against my tongue.

She began a soft, stuttering cry. Her hand moved softly on the back of my neck.

"Hold my other breast. . . . suck harder. . . . bite my nipple . . . yes . . . yes . . . like that. . . . God, that feels so good. . . . Patrick . . . I love you. . . ."

I could feel a small fullness happening amidst her moist pubic hair. I touched it with my middle finger. Her pelvis began to slowly move.

"Stroke up, Patrick. . . . stroke up . . . a little slower. . . . press harder . . . yes . . . yes . . . that's so good. . . . Patrick, look at me. . . . I want to see your face. . . ."

Our faces were inches apart. Melanie was smiling. Her eyes partially closed, and she sucked in her breath.

"I'm very close," she whispered. "I want you to come with me."

"You're beautiful, Melanie. . . . I love you."

She brought her left hand to her face, and wet her fingers with her tongue. She then grasped my penis and began stroking.

"Tell me what you want, Patrick. Is this good?"

"Yes . . . a little slower . . . yes . . ."

I kissed her breasts again. Then I licked the skin of her abdomen as I moved down toward her pelvis, which was thrusting against my hand.

"No, Patrick, not yet."

Her hand directed my head up toward her breasts.

She bent her knees, and her legs went further apart, opening herself.

"Touch me all over," she whispered and lifted her hips ". . . all over."

Suddenly she tensed. Her knees closed. Her legs fell to the bed.

"No . . . we've got to stop," she said. With both hands she pulled my head up. We were face-to-face. "We can't do this. . . . I promised you. . . . You trusted me."

"Melanie . . . I can't stop now . . . please . . ."

She began shaking her head. Tears were streaming down her face.

"I've got to stop . . . for both of us . . . and for your wife. . . . I've got to stop sometime. . . . you're married. . . . it's wrong. . . . I'm using you, Patrick. . . . please forgive me. . . ."

I rolled over on my back and we lay silently on the bed.

"Are you angry?" She asked timorously.

"You were using me? Is that all?"

She turned on her side facing me and put her hand on my chest.

"I love you, Patrick, very much. I care about you. But Christine was right. I use men like I use alcohol and drugs. Just so I can feel better. I have no business making love to you. You're married. . . . you're in love with another woman. I've got to stop doing this . . . being with married men. God, I'm sorry that I've hurt you. Please forgive me. It was so difficult to stop. I find you so desirable."

"Even though I don't have an ass like a racehorse?"

"You're still breathing a little heavy," she said with concern. "Are you going to be O.K.?"

"And what if I said no?"

"C'mon, Patrick." She slapped me on the shoulder. "Don't do that." Melanie rolled over on her back. "I'm really proud of myself . . . that I was able to stop like that. Normally I'd be consuming you right now."

"This doesn't seem totally fair, Melanie. I'm lying here with a pair of rock-hard testicles and a growling penis, and you're lying there full of self-satisfaction. I wish you had a throbbing penis to contend with."

"I'm throbbing, Patrick. Believe me, I'm throbbing. I wish you could appreciate that." She looked at me. "Stop feeling sorry for yourself. Someday you'll thank me for this."

"Thank you? Thank you?"

I started laughing explosively. I turned on my side toward the wall. "Melanie . . . that's a great line."

After a few seconds, I could feel Melanie's mouth next to my ear.

"Patrick," she whispered. "You had a good erection, kept it, and you didn't come right away. What does that tell you?"

"Well . . . maybe I'll thank you next month."

She pulled me back and rolled on top of me. She put her hands on my chest and rested her chin on her hand.

"Melanie, if we're not going to make love, maybe we should put our clothes on."

"Maybe later. You know," she said, "I'm finally starting to feel good about myself. Three weeks and I haven't used any drugs or alcohol . . . or men. If I had used you like I wanted to—and I wanted to—I would have been back to square one. I'm feeling myself getting stronger, Patrick. That's exciting for me. I know now that I don't have to use things to make me feel good. If staying away from drugs and alcohol can make me feel this good about myself, then this is the way I want to lead my life."

"What about men, Melanie? You going to give us up, too?"

"Absolutely not! Intimacy with a man, you know, intimacy on all levels, is something that I want. I've never had a good relationship with a man. And I always blamed men for that. But that was wrong. Nine times out of ten I was the one who screwed up. I usually chose the wrong type of man to begin with. I like what we've talked about in group about relationships. About getting to know someone first before getting sexually involved, then learning to trust and then allowing yourself to become vulnerable. But I've got a lot of things to learn about myself. And I've got a lot of growing up to do."

Melanie turned her head and lay the side of her face on my chest. She put her hands on my shoulders.

"How do you feel about yourself, Patrick? You're looking better."

"I'm still very angry at myself. And I still have some strong guilt feelings. But the more I say the Serenity Prayer, the more sense it makes. I don't know if A.A. is the answer for me, but I've made a commitment to the tulips to go to thirty meetings in thirty days. Someone told me that if I didn't get A.A. by then, it would get me. And the meeting I went to this morning, well . . . I started to feel as if I belonged there. And that was a shock. I don't feel quite so smug."

"The tulips? You talked to the tulips? Well . . . whatever works for you." Melanie slid off me and snuggled against my side, her head lying on my shoulder. I put my arm around her. "Patrick, I think your biggest problem is reaching out and asking for help. You're too used to giving and curing. Now it's time for you to take. Maybe it's because you're a doctor. I don't know. You think of yourself as being so self-sufficient that it's difficult for you to express need. Your ego is a big stumbling block for you."

I squeezed Melanie closer to me, and we lay silently. I could feel her soften in my arm as she snuggled up against me. I was relaxing, too, but because of her touch, her smell, and her closeness, I felt warm and content and exhilarated. This was an experience I wanted to go on forever, but because it wouldn't, I wanted it fixed indelibly in that part of my mind where there would be instant and total recall. And this was a memory that, like all future memories, would never— ever—be blotted out with drugs.

It was dinner time and the fourth floor lounge was usually empty, but our group was in there, and Lucy was the center of attention. Steve and Boone sat on each side of her. Steve was holding her hand. Hog Body was standing in front of her, looking down at her.

Boone was the first to see Melanie and me enter the lounge, and he stood as we approached and motioned for Melanie to take his seat.

"Walter asked me for a divorce," Lucy said to Melanie as she sat next to her. Lucy lit a cigarette. The ashtray in front of her was filled with cigarette butts, some only half-smoked. "That little shit! I can't believe he's doing this. I suppose . . . our marriage wasn't salvageable. But, damnit, I sure don't like his timing. At least he could've waited six months." An angry expression came to her face. "Another woman. He's leaving me for another woman. Younger . . . prettier . . . she's not a drunk. But what in the hell could she see in him? What am I missing?"

Lucy put out her cigarette and sat back.

"I'm angry. . . . I'm hurt. . . . I'm feeling sorry for myself . . . and, God, do I want a drink. If I weren't loaded up with Antabuse . . . damnit! I thought I was on firmer ground than this. It shouldn't be upsetting me this much. I shouldn't be letting it threaten my sobriety. I'm so . . . disappointed in myself."

I felt myself weakening as I watched Lucy. I hurt for her. How would I feel if Irene left me for another man? Devastated, probably. Would I be able to stay off drugs? No way.

"Lucy, what can we do?" Boone asked.

Lucy stared at the ground and shook her head slowly.

"I don't know. I don't want to be alone, though. Not tonight."

"Maybe we could stay with you in shifts," Boone suggested. "We could . . ."

"I'll stay with her," Steve interrupted and moved close to Lucy. In a protective manner, he put his arm around her. "I'll take care of her."

"Lucy, if we can do anything for you," Hog Body said, "will you ask us? We'll do anything we can for you."

"Thanks, Hog Body," Lucy said and stood. "You folks better hurry, or you'll miss dinner."

I walked up to Lucy, hugged her, and kissed her on the cheek.

"Thanks, Patrick," she said.

Melanie took the key to the mole hole out of her pocket, pressed it into Lucy's hand and whispered in her ear. A small smile came to Lucy's face, and she looked slyly at Steve.

"C'mon, Patty, let's go to dinner. By the way, where were you when all the excitement happened today?"

"What excitement? What happened?"

"Presswood. Gosh, he went nuts. Him and some new patient got in an argument over which TV program to watch. Presswood started screaming and went after the guy. It took me and Boone to hold him down. The nurse gave him a shot and called Dr. Randolph. They transferred Presswood to some nut ward downtown. What is Presswood? Alcoholic . . . or drugs . . . or what?"

"Valium. That was my drug of choice, too." I could feel my palms perspiring. "Hog, you go on to dinner. I need to make a phone call."

"Patty, what's the matter? You don't look so good."

"Well, I was feeling bad for Lucy . . . and now Presswood. I'm feeling kind of nervous. And tomorrow they make the decision about recycling us."

I went to the phone, took the card out of my pocket, and dialed the number.

Finally, a man's voice.

"Hello."

"Hi. It's me, Patrick Reilly at Hogarth. I called because I've had a couple of jolts, and I'm feeling shaky. I wonder if you could spend some time with me tonight."

"Sure, Patrick. I'll be over in a little while."

"Thanks, Leonard."

27

"'MORNING, PATRICK. I'll get your vitamin pill for you." Toni was wearing an attractive blue suit.

"Hi, Toni." I walked into the Nurses' Station, took the pill and a small glass of water from her. "Thanks. What's the occasion?" I asked her as I sat in one of the nurses' chairs. "You're all dressed up."

Toni sat next to me and pulled out my chart.

"Today's a special day for me," she said, a boastful smile on her face. "I've been in A.A. for ten years. Today's my anniversary day." She held out her hand. "You can be the first."

"Congratulations," I said and shook her hand. "Toni, were you ever a patient here?"

She shook her head.

"No. My father wanted me to come in as a patient. But I have this streak of defiance that usually gets me in trouble. I wanted to show him I could do it without being hospitalized. And I did. If I had it to do over, though, I'd come in. It would have speeded up my recovery by about six months. I also had two kids, and I was their sole support." Toni sat back in her chair and folded her arms. "These last ten years have been the best time of my life. I've seen my two boys grow into men. I went back to school and got my degree in nursing. Then they offered me a position here. They like to have recovering alcoholics on the staff. As they say, Patrick, you can't bullshit a bullshitter. And when I was drinking, I was a champion liar."

"How old are your kids?"

"I have two sons. My oldest boy is twenty-two, and he's in the program. His wife is supposed to deliver in June, and you know what that will make me. My other boy is nineteen, and he's a freshman in college. You're supposed to look surprised when I tell you how old my kids are, Patrick. I'm forty-three. Look surprised, darn it!"

"You're not married?"

"Been married twice. Lost both husbands because I was a drunk. I shot my first husband one night when I was drinking. Almost killed him. I went to jail for twenty-three months. I'm the speaker at the A.A. meeting here tonight. Come hear the rest of my story."

"Toni, I can't imagine you with a gun in your hand."

"I was insane then. Alcoholism is one of the few reversible causes of insanity. Didn't you do any crazy things while you were doing drugs, Patrick?"

"Yeah. I had a fourteen-year-old girl in the hospital with pneumonia about three months ago. I put her on Valium. She didn't need it. I just wanted a supply in the Nurses' Station so I could steal it. But I had boxes of the stuff at home. Wouldn't that qualify as insane behavior, Toni?"

"It sure would, Patrick. See, you're one of us."

"Yes. Your father reminds me of that often. But I don't understand why Leonard wants me to think of myself as an alcoholic."

"Well, that's between you and him. He's probably trying to help you keep things simple. Trust him, Patrick. Do what he says. Helping people like you is his whole life."

"All right, Toni. I guess I can listen to him for one more week. By the way, how does a forty-three year old, single, attractive, sober woman, mother of two adult children, who is about to be a grandmother celebrate ten years of sobriety?"

"Let's see. Dr. Randolph is taking me out to lunch. Tonight I'm having dinner with Dr. O'Malley and his wife at their home. Then I'll come to the A.A. meeting here with some friends, and after that we'll be going to a nightclub." Toni touched my arm. "I'm hell on a dance floor, Patrick."

"A nightclub?"

"Sure," she said indignantly. "We do what everybody else does. We just don't drink."

"Do O'Malley and Randolph drink, Toni?"

"Yes. They both do. No reason why they shouldn't. They don't have our disease, Patrick."

Coming toward the Nurses' Station walking faster than usual and chewing gum was Dr. Randolph.

"Oh, Lord," Toni whispered. "He's trying to give up cigarettes again." She forced a smile and said "Good morning, Dr. Randolph."

He came into the Nurses' Station and shook Toni's hand, congratulated her, and, stiffly, kissed her on the cheek.

"I'm proud of you," he said, smiling, and stepped back from her. "You look radiant."

She thanked him, and he then looked down at me. His smile disappeared.

"Good morning, Patrick. How are you feeling?"

"Well, I'm kind of nervous since this is decision day. I only slept for about an hour. Other than that, I'm feeling pretty good. I really am."

Randolph pulled over the chair Toni had been sitting in and sat down, uncomfortably close to me. He reached into his pocket, pulled out a pack of gum, and offered me a piece.

"No, thanks," I said. "I'd rather have a cigarette." I pulled out my Players and offered him one.

"I don't smoke anymore," he said nervously. "I gave those up."

He furiously unwrapped a piece of gum as I lit my cigarette. I blew the smoke close to his face.

"You don't mind if I smoke, do you?"

"Of course not," he said unconvincingly. "Now tell me why you're feeling good."

"Well, I guess it was somewhat of a pivotal weekend. It's as if everything came together for me. Irene and I have established a new relationship. I feel positive about it. And I spent time with some A.A. people, and I've made a commitment to A.A. I'm not convinced I need it. But I'm going to give it a try."

He stared at me as I puffed on my cigarette.

"Keep talking," he said, an attentive look on his face.

"A lot of things have happened in the past three weeks," I said. "Some of it has been pretty rough. The depression . . . the seizure . . . hallucinating"—I looked at Toni, who was smiling at me—"but the biggest thing is that I haven't taken a drug. I can't tell you how good that makes me feel. I think I now have the freedom to choose not to take drugs. I don't want to lose that freedom." I put out my cigarette. "When I woke up this morning, I knelt down and said the Serenity Prayer. When I stood up and looked out the window, I could appreciate the fact that there were birds out there."

Randolph stood slowly, eyeing me suspiciously.

"I like what I'm hearing," he said. "I hope you mean it."

"He means it," Toni said, assurance in her voice.

A faint smile appeared on Randolph's face for a brief moment. Then he turned to Toni.

"We'll be meeting at eight-thirty this morning instead of nine," he said to her. "Will you be able to make it?"

She nodded.

"I'm going to meet with Presswood's family at eleven-thirty," Randolph said. "I'm afraid he won't be coming back here. He's strictly a psychiatric problem now. Any problems on the floor, Toni?"

"Yes. A couple."

"I'll go now," I said, and I walked up to Toni and kissed her warmly on the cheek. "Congratulations again."

"Patrick," she said. "Stay with A.A. and you'll have a lot of happiness ahead of you."

Melanie had her hand on my knee as we sat in the dining room drinking coffee.

"I went back to check on Lucy three times during the night," Melanie said. "She wasn't in the room."

"Don't go professing any ignorance, Melanie. I saw you give her the pineapple. I'm glad you did. Ol' Steve probably techniqued her to exhaustion."

"I hope so," Melanie said.

"You're not going to eat any breakfast, Melanie? I thought I was the only one who was nervous."

"Hey," she said, "they could recommend that I stay, too."

"Would you, if they suggested it?"

She pressed her lips together in an expression of firm resolve and nodded her head.

Steve and Lucy were coming to our table carrying only cups of coffee.

"Nobody's eating breakfast this morning," Melanie said. "I guess we're all worried about the same thing."

"Well, Lucy," I said as she and Steve sat down, "how was your evening?"

"Marvelous," she said. "Simply marvelous."

Steve had an admiring expression as he looked at Lucy.

"This is a hell of a woman," he said. "Wow!"

"Did you have any doubts about that?" Melanie asked Steve.

"Would you guys stay if they decided to recycle you?" I asked.

"I expect them to ask me to stay," Lucy said. "They know Walter wants a divorce. They probably think I'll be at a very vulnerable point. Sure, I'd stay. But I wouldn't want to. God! I want to go home and be with my kids."

"I figure since I had the seizure, they'll probably want me to stay," Steve said, acceptance in his tone. "I don't think I need three extra weeks of this, though. I'd stay, I suppose. These people probably know what's best for us."

Boone and Hog Body walked past us and sat at the next table. Boone had only coffee. Hog Body had a tray full of food.

"Why the serious faces over there?" Hog Body called to us.

"We're talking about being recycled and whether we'll stay or not," Steve called back. "How 'bout you guys?"

"I'm expecting to stay," Hog Body said and placed a whole piece of toast in his mouth and swallowed it. "No sense worrying about it."

Boone, a somber look on his face, nodded and took a drink of coffee.

"I'm going to see O'Malley for a minute," I said and stood. "I think you guys are wrong. There has to come a time when we're responsible for ourselves. This protected environment is not reality. I need to go out there now and prove to myself I can do it. If they want me to stay . . . I won't do it. I'll walk."

O'Malley was sneaking into his office carrying a stuffed large brown paper bag with grease marks, when he saw me.

"Is that your breakfast?" I asked as I approached him.

"Can I help you, Patrick? I'm in a hurry."

"I'd like to see you for a few minutes. It's not an emergency or anything like that."

"I don't have time for nonemergencies on Monday morning," he said briskly. "See me after lunch."

He went into his office and the door closed.

I opened the door and walked in. He turned, a surprised look on his face.

"Give me a minute," I pleaded. "I need to see you now."

He inhaled deeply, gave me a long-suffering expression, and nodded toward the chair in front of his desk.

He sat in his chair, bent down, and disappeared behind his desk. He was securing his bag of popcorn. In a few seconds he sat up, put three fingers on the knot of his tie to make sure it was straight, then bent forward and put his forearms on the desk.

"Yes," he said, and the fingers of his right hand began tapping.

"I know the staff meets this morning to discuss if any of my group is going to be recycled. I want to tell you a few things."

I told him, basically, the same things I had told Randolph.

". . . and I feel I've come to a new awareness of what I did to myself. I'm allowing a lot of the guilt I felt to slip away. I realize now that I'm sick, that I have a disease. And I want to get well and stay well. I've made a commitment to the . . . I've promised that I'll go to thirty A.A. meetings in thirty days. I'll give A.A. my best shot. I don't want to hurt myself again."

O'Malley, mercifully, stopped tapping his fingers. His clinically passive expression changed slightly as he furrowed his brow.

"Why are you telling me this, Patrick?"

"Because I don't want to be recycled, and I think I don't need to repeat this program. I wanted you to know that I've made some changes. . . . I felt I should tell you before you met with the staff to decide my future here. I've already talked to Randolph."

"Did he believe you?"

"I don't know. He's such an untrusting, suspicious son of a bitch. Do you believe me?"

O'Malley sat back in his chair, formed a triangle with his hands in front of his face, and stared at me. My palms began to sweat. My breathing became more rapid.

He got out of his chair and walked slowly to his fish tank. His back was to me, and the spotlight was directly on the back of his head. He mumbled something.

"I didn't hear you," I said excitedly. "What did you say?"

"I said"—he turned slowly toward me, and his face came into the spotlight—"that one of these days I'm going to put some fish in this tank again. The last two fish I've had died." He began walking back to his chair. "I don't know what I do wrong. But it just kills me when I make a mistake and things die."

He sat down slowly and rested his arms on the desk. He looked fatigued.

"I believe you, Patrick."

"Well, it's nine forty-five, fifteen more minutes," Lucy said. She was sitting on the coffee table in front of Steve. Both of them were smoking. "Maybe we've all made it. Wouldn't it be great if none of us is recycled?"

"I have nine forty-seven," Boone corrected. He was leaning against the wall near the doorway.

"Nine forty-seven," Hog Body agreed. "Thirteen minutes." Hog Body was sitting at a card table. He had been playing solitaire but now sat with his hands slowly running from thighs to knee. His watch was on the table facing him.

Melanie and I stood close to each other near an open window. We were both smoking, but my cigarette tasted awful.

"Well, if Christine comes in and starts group," Melanie said, optimism in her voice, "we know we've all made it."

I was putting out my cigarette as Christine appeared at the doorway. She looked nervously around the room. When she saw me, a reluctant smile appeared on her face.

"Patrick, they need to see you." There was a forced buoyancy in her tone. "They're down in the conference room."

"Why?" I asked weakly.

"They need to see you right away. Do you know where the conference room is?"

I nodded.

Melanie squeezed my hand. A worried expression came to her face when she looked at me.

I walked slowly to the door.

"Why do they want to see me?" I asked Christine, when I was next to her.

"You go on down, Patrick. I'll be there in a minute. I need to speak to the group."

I walked out into the hall, and Christine pulled the door closed.

I was alone.

There was an uncomfortable familiarity about the conference room. It was where the physicians' support group met.

Randolph, chewing gum, sat at the head of the table where Bossy sat during the physicians' meeting. I was at the other end of the table where Stacey had agonizingly told about his relapse when he found his wife was pregnant by another man. I didn't like this seat.

O'Malley sat to Randolph's left. In the next seats were Reggie and Edith. Toni was on Randolph's right. Next to her was Karren. Sitting in a chair against the wall and behind O'Malley was Bossy.

There was a knock on the door, and Christine breezed in and sat next to Karren. All heads were turned toward me.

"No," I said. "I don't want a blindfold."

Their sober expressions remained unchanged.

"Coffee, Patrick?" Toni asked.

I shook my head and lit up a Players.

"Patrick, we've been discussing you for a long time." Randolph spoke as he looked at some notes in a folder. "We even asked Dr. Bossy to help us." Bossy was glaring at me as only he could. "We've had several opinions about what your disposition should be. The consensus is now that you should stay with us an extra three weeks."

"That means," I said, "that some people think I'm ready to go home Friday."

"Oh, no!" Randolph said, an incredulous smile on his face. "An opinion was stated that you should be asked to go to the doctors' program in Georgia. You're going home on Friday wasn't discussed."

"I don't understand this. I talked to you this morning"—I looked to O'Malley—"and you. I've told you what my thinking is now. What more do I have to do? How much farther along do I have to be?"

"Patrick," O'Malley said and sat forward, "we're happy with the way you're thinking now. We feel that, finally, you're teachable. But it took you a long time to get where you are now. We want you to experience this program now that you're ready for it so you can get its full impact. You've missed a lot."

"I think you're wrong," I said. "I haven't missed a thing. I've been to every lecture, every relaxation and exercise class, every Group Therapy session. You people have wanted me on my knees since day one. Maybe I did resist a little bit. I'm sorry you've felt so threatened by someone who asks questions."

"I gave a talk to your group two weeks ago," O'Malley said, and he looked at his hands. "Do you remember what the topic was?"

"Let's see . . . something on alcoholism . . . or was it on addiction? I don't remember exactly. This is a small point. You're just groping now."

O'Malley exchanged a glance with Randolph and then he sat back in his chair.

"Does anyone else have any comments?" Randolph asked.

There were a few moments of silence.

"Somebody better say something," I said. "Because I'm sure not convinced I have to stay."

"Patrick," Reggie said, a compassionate look on her face. "What's three weeks compared to the rest of your life? And that three weeks can be critical. It will be twenty-one more days when there will be little or no temptation to take a drug. You'll be that much stronger when you leave. I was recycled twice when I was a patient here. And I had just as many doubts as you do. But they were right. I needed that extra time."

"Damnit, Reggie! How can you get stronger if you're not tempted? Isn't that what this is all about? I'm ready for the outside now. I really am. You people . . ."

"Patrick," Toni interrupted. "Trust us. Trust that we know what we're doing. You can't be objective about this. We can. We're not trying to hurt you."

"I need to understand, Toni. I want to go home to my wife. I want to see my patients and start acting like a doctor again."

"You're not ready for that," Bossy said as if speaking from a throne. "You'd be asking for a relapse if you started seeing patients a week from today."

"How can you be so goddamn sure of that?" I challenged. "How much do you know about me, anyway?"

"Well, you know what our decision is." Randolph sat back in his chair. "You can either accept it or . . ." he shrugged his shoulders.

"You"—I stood slowly and glared at Randolph—"you mother-fucker! You just want to be a hero. You want to make sure you have good statistics. I'm not going to let you do this to me. I'm not going to give you three more weeks of my life."

"He's still sick," Bossy announced and looked at Randolph.

"Fuck off, Bossy. You're not infallible. How many times have you relapsed?"

Randolph stood.

"You're not intimidating anyone," he said. "And this display of emotional violence has only served to cement our opinion. If we let you go Friday with our stamp of approval, it could invalidate our entire program." He slammed the table. "And I won't let that happen."

He closed the folder in front of him and picked it up. "You have until noon to let us know if you're staying. And if you do stay, it's on our terms."

Randolph turned and walked toward the door. "We're adjourned," he said as he opened the door and walked out.

They all stood and walked slowly out of the room. Except Christine. She walked over to me and sat down in the chair next to me.

"I'm sorry for that outburst, Christine. But I just know you people are wrong. I guess I better pack my stuff and call Irene. I'll tell her I'm coming home."

"Patrick, before you start packing, come back to group with me. Let's talk about this some more."

The members of my group had their chairs arranged in something approximating a circle as Christine and I entered. It was as if group had been going on as usual.

Christine walked to one of the empty seats. I stopped and looked at my group. I wasn't one of them anymore.

"I guess you guys know," I said. "They want to keep me. I just . . ."

"Patrick is having some trouble understanding the staff's decision," Christine interrupted. "We thought we'd talk about it. Is that all right?"

"Sure," Boone said.

"Patrick," Melanie called. "Come here." She stood and motioned for me to sit in her chair.

I took Melanie's chair, and she sat on the floor by my feet and leaned against the side of my leg.

"Christine, how do they know I'm not ready? How do they know if I go out on Friday I'll use again?"

Christine moved forward in her seat, elbows on her knees.

"Patrick, no one said either of those things. We don't know what will happen to any of you when you're discharged. We make mistakes. But we have a pretty good track record. Almost eighty percent of the people who come through this program cooperatively and get actively involved in A.A. are sober two years after discharge. Seventy percent are still sober after five years." Christine sat back in her chair, inhaled deeply, and crossed her legs. Her eyes never left me. Her expression was intense. "Patrick, I want to tell you and the rest of the group what my feelings are and some of the things I said in the staff meeting." Christine looked around the group. "Would any of you rather not hear this?"

"Go ahead, Chrissie."

Christine smiled at Hog Body and she bent forward again.

"I believe that all of you, with the exception of Patrick, will be as prepared for discharge on Friday as you will ever be. Keeping some of you longer than this week could even be counterproductive. When each of you came into this hospital, it was an admission on your part that your life had become unmanageable and that you were powerless over alcohol and drugs. All of you now are aware that you have a terminal illness. For the past three weeks that illness has been arrested. Not cured. Arrested. When you're discharged from Hogarth, you will be responsible for yourselves. If you drink or use again, that terminal illness will start up again as if it were never arrested. And you will have blown it. And eventually that illness will kill you, insidiously destroying you in the process. Patrick, I believe that you are the only person in the group not ready to take responsibility for yourself."

"Christine, I think I've made some fairly dramatic changes over the weekend that you may not be aware of."

"Until Dr. Randolph and Dr. O'Malley told the staff about your conversations with them this morning, I felt you should be sent to the Georgia program. By the way—I suppose I shouldn't tell you this—Dr. O'Malley and Dr. Randolph were your advocates in the meeting."

"They were? My God!"

"I was glad," Christine continued, "when they repeated their conversations they had with you early this morning. It made me feel good about you. I feel that you're just beginning to learn how to ask for help. You must accept completely the fact that you will not be able to stay clean without the help of other people. I think you're close. But you're not there yet."

"I want to go home, Christine. I want to be with my wife. I want to be a doctor again. I really feel like I'm as ready as anybody in this room to leave at the end of the week."

"I don't think you are, Pat," Boone said. "You didn't really believe that you were as sick as the rest of us until the last few days. And I'm still not sure you're as willing as the rest of us to ask for help to stay sober." Boone had a caring smile as he looked at me. "I wouldn't have felt good about it if they had let you go home on Friday. Do what they tell you to do, Pat."

"I don't know if you're ready to go home or not," Lucy said, a nervous smile on her face. "I didn't think I was ready. I just thank God that I've got Antabuse to take every day. And A.A. I was secretly hoping they'd keep me. That would have given me three more weeks to level off a little more. But they're telling me that I'm ready to be on my own. They're telling me that they've helped me as much as they can. That scares me. I feel very weak." She lit a cigarette, looked at me and smiled. "Stay, Patrick, if they tell you to. It's probably the best thing for you and Irene. You have a lovely wife. Don't jeopardize your marriage. . . . you may be doing that if you leave too soon." She set back in her chair and closed her eyes, vainly attempting not to cry.

"Thanks, Lucy," I said. "I'm sorry that you've been hurt."

"Patty." Hog Body had a serious expression. "You're going to stay. Don't talk about leaving around me, because I'll get mad. A toothless smile appeared on his face. "You know I'm twelve years older than you, Patty. That's twelve years of being in control of your life that you'll have that I lost. Do you realize how lucky you are?"

My eyes began to water, and I reached for the box of Kleenex.

"Hog, I think I'm just starting to realize . . . how lucky I am . . . to have known you."

"I'm really surprised they didn't tell me to stay," Steve said, turning from Lucy to me. "I think I need it as much as you do. But I'll be taking Temposil and going to A.A. meetings with Lucy. It's my thinking that will get me in trouble. That's what I'm afraid of. And I think you have the same problem, Pat. They tell you in A.A. to surrender to the program and do what they tell you to do. I'll try to do everything they tell me. I won't question anything. Could you do that now, Pat?"

"Probably . . . not."

Melanie was looking up at me.

"I don't know what's right," she said. "I have no idea if it's best for you to stay . . . or go home. The staff has suggested that you stay. They've got to know more than we do. I love you, Patrick, and I want the best for you. I think you should do what they say." She reached up and took my hand. "I want you to stay."

"If you leave now, Pat," Boone added, "you'll be disappointing us."

I stood slowly and walked to the window. The tulips . . . courageous little guys . . . the boy in the wheelchair . . . tough kid . . . beautiful kid . . . wonder if he's still practicing his swings . . . Charlie . . . my kid dying of cystic fibrosis . . . gave me the peace sign . . .

I walked back to my chair and sat down. I looked at each member of my group.

"I've worked with you guys for the past three weeks," I said. "I've finally got you to the point where you're almost ready to go home. I guess I'll stick around here for a few more weeks and see if I can help a new group." I smiled at Christine. "They should put me on the payroll here."

"Patrick"—Melanie took my hand—"I'm proud of you."

"We're all proud of you," Boone said.

"You've made the right decision," Christine said and smiled proudly. "I knew you wouldn't let me down."

"Can I stay in this group the rest of the week, Christine?"

"No. That wouldn't be a good idea. The group will be spending the next five days talking in detail about how they will resume their lives and strategies for recovery. And we'll be having evening meetings every night. These sessions wouldn't be appropriate for you now, Patrick. Since you're going to be recycled, you need to move all your things back into a room in Happy Valley. You should start from day one with your new group."

"Happy Valley! I have to go back there? That's barbaric. I won't do that. I'll stay . . ."

Christine was smiling at me and shaking her head.

"All right," I said. "I don't want to make it too easy on you. I'll move my stuff down there today."

"It's time," Christine said, "to say good-bye to Patrick."

An uneasy, sad silence came over the room. After a few seconds, Christine stood and walked toward me. I stood.

"Patrick," she said and grasped my hand. "I won't be the facilitator of your new group. But I know who is and she's good." Christine smiled. "She can handle herself pretty well. But I'll still warn her about this tall, arrogant guy from Cleveland with the smart mouth. I'll also tell her that"—she hugged me—"I love him."

Christine walked away. Tears were forming in the corners of my eyes.

Lucy came up to me.

"Take care of yourself, Patrick," she said and hugged me. "I love you."

"I love you, too," I said. "Be kind to yourself, Lucy,"

Steve stood in front of me, and I held out my hand to shake. He brushed my hand away, and he put his arms around me.

"Good luck," he said as we hugged. "I love you."

"Good-bye, Steve. Be good to Lucy. I love you."

Boone was next.

"You're a good man, Patrick."

"I love you," I said to him as we hugged.

Large tears were streaming down Hog Body's cheeks as he stood in front of me. But that wonderful, toothless smile slowly appeared and he put his huge arms around me.

" 'Bye, Patty," he said and kissed me on the mouth. Then he walked away.

Melanie put a folded piece of paper in my hand and we hugged. I didn't want to let her go. In a few seconds she pulled away and walked over to a window.

I walked to the door, paused for a moment, and then left them. In the hall I unfolded the sheet of paper.

Patrick,

Very soon you will be only a beautiful memory for me.
At least in that way I'll always have you.

Mel

"Honey, are you saying you were going to leave to come home, but your group talked you into staying? You won't do what your doctors recommend, but you'll do what your group wants you to do. I don't understand that."

"Irene, finally I understand what they do at Hogarth. It's brilliant. They take us addicts and alcoholics who want to get well and put us together so we can help each other. No doctor would have ever helped me get off drugs. But I'll listen to another person who has a problem like mine, because she or he *understands* me.

"Randolph and O'Malley are very smart men. They recognize just how little they have to be involved."

"I'm still not sure I understand, Pat. I can't imagine . . ."

"It's simple. The people in my group have been where I've been, and they want what I want. I learned to trust them . . . love them . . . care for them. I'd do anything they tell me to do, because I know they want what's best for me. And not one of them has an M.D. after his name."

"Well, Pat, whatever your reason for staying is, I'm glad you're following their advice. Because if you had come home now, I wouldn't have been here. I would have moved in with Gabe."

"Are you kidding, Irene? No . . . no, I know you're not. Well, fortunately that's a problem we won't have to deal with. Will you still be coming here next Friday so we can see Karren together?"

"Yes, Pat, I'll be there. I want to have a good sexual relationship with you again. I'll do whatever I have to. But we have a lot of things to work on. I'm a little afraid, Honey. I still have some anger and resentments to work through."

"I don't want to lose you, Irene."

"And I don't want to lose you, Pat. I think that gives us a good start."

"That makes me feel good, Babes. I love you."

"See you Friday. Pat, I love you . . . so much."

"Are you going to search me this time, Edith?" I asked as I un-packed my clothes.

"No, Patrick, we trust you."

"How was I so *lucky* to get the same room I had three weeks ago?"

"I wouldn't let any members of the new group take it. I knew you'd be back with us."

"Is that a compliment, Edith? Never mind. Don't answer that. By the way"—I turned and faced her—"I want to apologize for the way I acted this morning."

"That's all right," she said, brushing the air with her hand. "We know you're still sick. We make allowances for that. If we got defensive every time a patient got angry and abusive with us, we'd be in the wrong business. Patrick, have you talked to Irene yet?"

"Yes," I said and sat on the bed. "Irene said that if I had come home before they wanted me to, she wouldn't have been there. That woman's getting stronger, Edith."

"Good," Edith said. "I'm glad she's stronger. That will act as another safeguard against relapse. You know now that you could lose her."

"Irene won't be policing me all the time, will she?"

"Irene won't have to. If you start using, she'll be the first to know. We'll also be suggesting to you that you submit twice-weekly urine samples for drug screening to a laboratory in Cleveland that we'll designate. We'll recommend you do that for the next two years. We'll also try to find a place where we can get Antabuse blood levels on you to make sure you're taking the Antabuse."

"I won't do that!" I said and stood.

"Oh," Edith smiled, "we'll have to work on that. Irene, of course, will know what our suggestions are."

"That's not fair, Edith."

"We'll use anything we can to help you help yourself. And in your case, Patrick, we're helping protect your patients, too. If drugs are found in your urine, you'll be asked to come back. If you don't, your state medical society will be notified. That's an agreement we'll have to get from you before you're discharged. Our obligation to you doesn't end when you walk out the door. Sometimes it may seem like we're holding a gun to your head . . . but we'll do whatever we have to. . . . this is not an easy disease to treat"—she smiled—"but I guess you know that now."

"I guess I do."

"Will Irene be coming back to see you?"

"Yes. She'll be here next Friday. She and I have to see Karren. And Saturday my sister, my nephew, and my mother will be coming. So I have more than just Ruthy to look forward to next weekend."

"I'll see you later, Patrick. As soon as you're finished unpacking, go into the Happy Valley lounge and meet your new group. Some interesting patients—there's a doctor, a lawyer, and of all things, a nurse."

"Edith, I wish I could say it's nice being back in Happy Valley. But it's not nice. It's awful."

"I know," she said.

The first person I saw when I walked into the lounge was Leonard. It was comforting to see him. I walked over and sat next to him.

"Hello, Patrick," he said, as we shook hands. "How are you feelin'?"

"Depressed . . . angry . . . resentful . . ."

"What have you done about it? Have you said the Serenity Prayer? Did you try to call me?"

I shook my head.

"Haven't you learned anythin', Patrick? Haven't you been listenin'? When you're feelin' bad, get off your butt and do somethin' about it. Don't just sit around mopin' and feelin' sorry for yourself."

"I'm sorry, Leonard."

"Are you doin' any prayin', Patrick?"

"Yes."

"Can you think of yourself as an alcoholic yet?"

I shook my head.

"I have a lot of work to do with you," he said.

"What are you doing here, anyway?"

"Toni called. Said she thought you were goin' to leave. I wouldn't have let that happen. But I'm glad you decided to stay, Patrick. Really glad."

We stood and shook hands.

"I'll pick you up here at seven-thirty, Patrick, and you can come to the meetin' with me."

"Good-bye, Leonard."

I turned and looked at my new group. There were four of them, one man and three women, sitting huddled in the far corner of the lounge.

"Hi," I said, and I approached them. "I'm Patrick. I'm going to be in your group."

The young woman I sat next to held out her hand. "I'm Marty," she said.

Marty could have stepped out of a Modigliani painting. She had reddish brown hair that was tied in a bun. A few wisps of hair fell by design in front of her ears. She had light gray eyes that had no sparkle, a small mouth, and a long, straight nose. Her neck was long, thin, and curved slightly forward. Marty's skin was white, almost translucent, giving her a delicate appearance.

"You're the doctor?" the man asked as we stretched to shake hands.

"Yes."

His name tag read Howard. He was about my age and had alert, observant eyes that seemed to judge as well as see. He had a suspicious, almost cynical expression. Howard sat forward in his chair, waiting to challenge.

"You're a lawyer, Howard?" I asked innocently.

"Yes! How did you know?"

"Hi," said the lady next to Howard. "They call me Gams." Gams was close to seventy, petite, and had beautiful white hair. She had a kind face and a detached, amused smile. "I don't belong here," she assured me.

"Gams, if you say that one more time, I'm gonna puke," said the young girl next to Gams. "Hi," she said to me. "I'm Kathy." Kathy had a Rod Stewart haircut and her hair was dyed orange.

"What kinda shit were you into, Doc?"

"Tranquilizers. Sleeping pills. A little booze. What about you, Kathy?"

"Strictly booze," she said and put her foot up on the coffee table. "Why fuck up a good drunk with drugs?"

"Oh, my!" Gams said and laughed uncomfortably.

"I've been drinking since I was thirteen," Kathy boasted and lit a cigarette. "Almost six years. I've been drinkin' longer than Gams. She started mellowing out on sherry only three years ago."

"I only started drinking a little sherry during the day after my husband died," Gams corrected her. "I don't belong . . ." Gams stopped as Kathy started to put a finger down her throat. Gams bent forward and looked at Marty. "I don't understand why she does that to her hair, Marty. Do you?"

"It's a statement, Gams," Marty said.

"Yeah," Kathy laughed gleefully. "I'm sayin' 'blow it out your ass, world.' "

"Oh, my!"

"Don't let her bother you, Gams," Howard said. "She's just trying to shock you." He looked at me. "How did you know I was a lawyer?"

"Because you're so fucking unpleasant, Howard," Kathy answered.

"I'm a nurse," Marty said to me. "I've been doing Demerol for almost four years."

"Did you get caught?" I asked.

She nodded.

"Three months ago I transferred into Surgical Intensive Care. There's always a supply of Demerol there. I stole some of it. But I got caught using it at work. I'd inject the patients with sterile water and shoot up with what was ordered for them."

Marty looked at Howard.

"I drink," Howard said to me, "all the time. I've lost everything."

"Here comes 'Fishhead,'" Kathy said, looking toward the door. "He's still not wearing his name tag."

A tall man wearing an expensive three-piece suit walked toward us. He had a narrow face and a long prominent nose. His face was frozen into a serious, secretive expression. He sat in the chair next to Kathy.

"You sure smell good," Kathy said to him. "How much did those shoes cost you?"

He looked at her with complete disdain.

"If I knew there was going to be riffraff in here," he said, "I wouldn't have come." He looked at me. "Are you the doctor that's going to be in our group?"

"Yes," I said.

"Are you a medical doctor?" he asked, suspiciously.

"Yes."

"What is your practice?" he continued.

"Pediatrics."

"Oh," he said with disappointment. "Well, where did you train?"

"Memphis and Cleveland."

He nodded approvingly.

"I'm a neurosurgeon," he said and straightened up in his chair. "From Chicago."

"I'm Patrick Reilly."

"I'm Dr. Sherwood Fish."

"What do you want us to call you?" I asked him.

"Dr. Fish. Well . . . I suppose you can call me Sherwood."

"I like Fishhead," Kathy said and smiled at him.

"You insolent little . . ." He then looked at me. "Can you and I go and talk somewhere?"

"Why don't we just stay here, Sherwood. Let's not have any secrets."

"I don't like this place," he said. "They searched me when I came in. And that musician who's in our group, he started having a seizure about an hour ago. I offered to help, and the nurse just told me to go away. I don't appreciate being talked to like that."

"You're here to get well, Sherwood," I said. "Forget the fact that you're a doctor."

"That may be easy for you," he challenged, "being just a pediatrician."

"A fucking alcoholic brain surgeon," Kathy exclaimed to the group. "You know, that's creepy. Have you killed anybody, Fishhead?"

Sherwood looked at her with contempt.

"When was the last time you bathed?" he asked her.

"I see a problem developing here," Howard said. "It has to do with equality. Sherwood, if you think you're better than the rest of us, I, for one, wish you would leave."

"We're all going to die eventually," Gams said, looking at Sherwood. "Doesn't that make us all equal?" Gams looked at Marty for approval.

"I'm not kissing anybody's ass," Kathy stated.

"This is no place for an ego trip, Sherwood," Marty said and lit a cigarette.

Sherwood stood.

"Well," he said. "I'll just have to think about this." He started walking toward the door.

"Hey," Kathy called to him. "If you take off that suit, get in some jeans, and wear your name tag, I won't call you Fishhead anymore. I promise."

Sherwood nodded and walked out the door.

"I think we've won that round," Howard said. "And that was good Kathy. Maybe we can negotiate with him."

"Well," I said and stood. "If you people will excuse me, I'm going outside for a while. I want to enjoy the birds, and there are some flowers I want to talk . . . ah . . . look at."

"Can I go with you?" Marty asked me.

"Next time, Marty, O.K.? I'd like to do this alone."

"All right," she said, smiling. "Next time. I'll consider that a promise."

As I walked out of the lounge, I heard Howard.

"How did he know I was a lawyer?"

Before going outside, there was something I needed to do. I walked to the end of the hall and knocked on the door that read:

Dr. Michael Randolph
Medical Director

"Come in."

He looked surprised when he saw me.

"Sit down, Patrick."

"Dr. Randolph," I said as I sat down. "I want to apologize for the way I talked to you this morning. I was out of line."

"Thanks for the apology," he said. "I accept it."

"I just met my new group," I said.

"I have yet to meet them. I was just going to start interviewing them."

"Well, you got an uptight lawyer and an arrogant neurosurgeon in the same group. Should be interesting."

"Oh, no," Randolph groaned and put his head on his desk. "God spare me any more lawyers or doctors. And not in the same group. That's not supposed to happen."

I stood and put my hand on his shoulder.

"Well," I said. "We'll just have to work harder, won't we?"

His head raised slowly and he looked at me. He was smiling.

"Yes, Patrick. *We* will."

As I walked toward the flowers, I looked up at the window of the fourth floor lounge. Hog Body. Melanie. Boone. Lucy. Steve. Christine. They were up there. Talking about going home. I missed them. I wondered if they would remember me. Tears were starting again as a passionate loneliness began to overwhelm me.

"Hey, Reilly." Sherwood was walking toward me. He was wearing blue jeans. He was also wearing his name tag. "Listen, don't tell anybody," he said in a whisper when he was next to me, "but I have to stay. My hospital won't let me do surgery there until I complete the entire program here."

"I won't tell anyone. But you will."

"What's it like here? I bet they feed us a lot of A.A. bullshit."

"Yes. They really promote A.A."

·3 4 4·

"Damnit! I wish there were more doctors here as patients, more professional people like us. You know what I mean . . . people on our level . . . people I can relate to."

"Sherwood, the fact that I'm a doctor was a major reason for me becoming a drug addict. And until I could forget that I'm a doctor and get honest with myself, I was just wasting everybody's time."

"You mean to tell me," he said, his voice getting louder, "that I'm supposed to learn something from a teenage punk rocker with orange hair, a doddering old woman whose mental poise is somewhere near the level of a tortoise, a speed-freak musician who's clanking away in there right now. . . ."

"Yes," I interrupted, "that's exactly what I'm telling you. I'm just a run-of-the-mill drug addict, and Sherwood, you're just a drunk. We have to use the same tools everybody else does to get sober and stay sober."

"Let me correct you," he said slowly. "I am not a drunk. I just drink too much because I'm under a lot of stress. I operate in people's heads, for Christ's sake. You don't know what I'm talking about. What would a pediatrician know about stress? Anyway, drunks are people who lay in alleys and suck on wine bottles. I'm not that bad."

"Not yet."

His eyes widened and an uncertain smile came to his lips.

"Sherwood Fish will never end up in the gutter, my friend. That's absurd."

"We all have our own personal bottoms, Sherwood. I reached mine before I came in here. And hopefully, you reached yours. We can always go back out there and hurt ourselves some more . . . and maybe kill some of our patients in the process."

He looked to the ground. His shoulders slumped.

"I deluded myself for the first few weeks that I was in here," I said. "I felt sorry for myself, didn't think I belonged here, resisted everything the doctors and nurses told me. But there were some people—members of my group—who cared about me. They really helped me see what I am. And I'm going to help you."

His eyes moved slowly to my face. He pulled his shoulders back.

"I'm here, so I have to make the best of it. But don't ever talk to me like this in front of those people," he said, nodding toward the building. "And don't assume that I'm simple enough to be brain-washed as easy as you've been."

"Sherwood," I said as I put my arm around him. "Let's walk over here by the flowers and talk some more. I know exactly how you're feeling. It gets better. You just need to hang in there."

As he and I walked toward the flowers, I looked over my shoulder and glanced at the window of the fourth floor lounge.

"Thanks," I said silently.

Sherwood looked at me. There was a quizzical look on his face. He didn't understand why I was smiling.